THE ✦ TIMES HISTORY OF EUROPE

THE TIMES
HISTORY
OF
EUROPE

TIMES BOOKS

First published in 2001 by
TIMES BOOKS
HarperCollins*Publishers*
77-85 Fulham Palace Road
London W6 8JB

First published in 1994 as
The Times Atlas of European History
Second edition published 1998
Paperback edition published 2001,
reprinted 2003, new edition 2006

© Times Books 1994, 1998, 2001,
2002, 2006

The HarperCollins website address is
www.**fire**and**water**.com

Editorial Direction:
Thomas Cussans
Philip Parker
Barry Winkleman
Cicely Oliver
Jane Cheverton

Maps prepared by:
Bartholomew, Edinburgh

Cartographic Direction:
Gavin James
Alistair Calder
Janet Mykura
Jackie Galloway
Martin Brown

Place-name consultant, index:
Pat Geelan

Design:
Ivan Dodd
Lesley Branscombe

Updates to 2006 edition:
Kate Epstein

Printed in Hong Kong

British Library Cataloguing in
Publication Data
A catalogue record for this book is
available from the British Library

ISBN-10 0-00-723239-X

ISBN-13 978-0-00-723239-0

Front cover photographs
(from left to right):
Ruins at the Ancient Forum Rome
Italy, © image100 / Alamy
Aachen Treasure, The Charlemagne
Reliquary (detail), © Photo12.com -
Oasis
Napoleon Bonaparte, © Nigel Reed /
Alamy
The Fall of the Berlin Wall, © Tom
Stoddart Archive/Getty

CONTRIBUTORS

Mark Almond
*Fellow of Oriel College, University of Oxford, and of the Institute for
European Defence and Strategic Studies*

Jeremy Black
Professor of History, University of Exeter

Felipe Fernández-Armesto
Faculty of Modern History, University of Oxford

Rosamond McKitterick
*Professor of Early Medieval European History and
Vice-Principal of Newnham College, University of Cambridge*

Geoffrey Parker
Andreas Dorpalen Professor of History, The Ohio State University

Chris Scarre
McDonald Institute, University of Cambridge

Richard Vinen
Department of History, King's College London

Maps conceived and compiled by
András Bereznay

CONTENTS

INTRODUCTION

HISTORY today has come increasingly to be written in terms of societies rather than states, communities rather than dynasties, cultures rather than countries, and economies or even ecologies rather than politics. This atlas puts the politics back in. Unashamedly, it is a work of political history, narrowly defined.

The atlas concentrates on mapping the frontiers of Europe's states at key dates over the last 3,000 years. At each date, frontiers are drawn on identical base maps of the whole continent, allowing the evolution of its nations, states and empires – their appearance and growth, their contraction and disappearance – to become immediately clear. After every principal map, two pages of subsidiary maps at larger scales highlight the major processes which led to the condition of Europe as it appears on the main maps and focus on details too small to be shown on them. The accompanying text provides background and draws attention to the principal changes to borders.

Some redress in favour of a neglected traditional discipline may well be salutary. But the reason for adopting this resolutely state-based approach goes to the heart of the European historical experience. The complex state-system, in which a large number of competing, sovereign, territorial states have been crammed together, pushing and tugging at each other's frontiers, wresting and re-educating each other's populations, is an almost unique feature of European history, one which sets the continent apart from most of the rest of the world. Only Southeast Asia has had a long experience of anything similar. For other continents, it represents a model of what to avoid, or a reservoir of lessons for the future. Like other European vices and virtues, the state system was exported as empire builders extended the reach of Europe to other parts of the world.

The withering of the traditional European state has been widely predicted in one form or another. Marx thought it would disappear in favour of proletarian internationalism. More recent visionaries have hoped it would blend into a united Europe or fragment into a "Europe of regions" or a "Europe of the peoples". At the moment, the existing framework continues to appear unconquerably robust. Even if one of these predictions came true, it would probably mean only that the state-system continued in a new guise. As a glance through this atlas shows, the state is always with us, however much borders – and names – may change. Without knowledge of it, no one can hope to understand Europe today.

Because European history has taken place within a framework of states, the reach of cultural, social, intellectual and economic change has been directed or deflected, influenced or ordained by powerful state institutions. But in concentrating on political borders, *The Times History of Europe* is not meant to belittle non-political history or those kinds of political history – movements and mentalities, party-strife and popular revolutions – which cannot be represented on maps of this kind. On the contrary, the purpose of this work is to provide a view of the network of frontiers inside which the rest of European history has been trapped. It is a starting-point, not a substitute, for the study of these and other themes.

TIMES BOOKS
June 2001

900 BC

The First States

The story of European societies in the centuries before 900 BC is largely dependent on the evidence of archaeology. The first European written records are the Linear A tablets, bureaucratic documents produced by the Minoan palace administration on Crete during the first half of the 2nd millennium BC. These are in an unknown language which has not yet been translated, but judging from their general appearance they are inventories of palace storerooms, lists of rations, and the like. The same is true of the Linear B tablets which succeeded them in the 15th century BC. These are written in an early form of Greek for the Mycenaean rulers who took control of Crete at this time. Linear B in turn went out of use with the demise of the Mycenaean palaces on both Crete and the Greek mainland during the 12th century BC. The Greek world then entered a "Dark Age" which lasted until the 8th century BC, when the Greeks adopted and adapted the use of the alphabet from their eastern trade rivals, the Phoenicians. From the Greeks the alphabet was passed to the Etruscans and Romans early in the 7th century BC, and thence to the Celts and Scandinavians.

What we know of European societies around 900 BC therefore comes almost entirely from the evidence of archaeology. This reveals a varied pattern consisting largely of small-scale farming societies, known as Urnfield societies from their custom of burying the ashes of their dead in pottery vessels (or "urns") grouped in cemeteries. Warfare was a conspicuous component of these Urnfield societies. They built hilltop fortresses – perhaps more as refuges than settlements – and leading members of society armed themselves with bronze breastplates and helmets, and wielded long bronze swords. The Mycenaean rulers of 2nd millennium Greece were in a sense merely one of these Bronze Age warrior societies, with a more sophisticated material culture than most. The demise of the Mycenaean aristocracies was not echoed in other parts of Europe, however, where the Urnfield societies continued to develop until the 1st millennium BC.

But Europe on the threshold of the 1st millennium BC was beginning to change in a number of important respects. By 900 BC, communities on the Greek mainland had re-established their trading links with the Near East. In Greece, as in northern Italy, the foundations were being laid of the city-states which were to arise during the 8th century BC. Political developments in the Near East were also shortly to have important repercussions on the West Mediterranean, for the spectacular growth of Assyrian power in the 9th century encouraged the Phoenicians to seek new markets overseas. By the 8th century BC Greeks and Phoenicians were fierce commercial rivals, and Greek and Phoenician colonies were already established around the shores of the central and western Mediterranean. Thus around 900 BC Mediterranean societies in Italy and the Aegean were already embarking on that dynamic of development which was to lead to the rise of city-states and the establishment of a fully literate civilisation. Under the Romans this was ultimately to permeate the greater part of the continent.

At the beginning of the 1st millennium BC, however, northern Europe was set on its own separate trajectory of development, its warrior societies the direct ancestors of the later Celts, Germans and Thracians. Meanwhile, on the steppelands north of the Black Sea, were the Cimmerians, one the many horse-riding nomadic peoples who were to terrorise and control the settled farmers of Eastern Europe until the defeat of the Mongols in the 16th century.

Teutonic Peoples

BALTIC SEA

Baltic peoples

Slavs

Finno-Ugrians

Volga

Don

Volga

Dnieper

Dniester

Cimmerians

Caucasian peoples

Illyrians

Thracians

Danube

Danube

BLACK SEA

URARTU

Oder

Vistula

Elbe

Etruscans

Italic peoples

Illyrians

Sicily

Malta

SEA

GREEK
Thebes
Corinth   Megara
Argos   Athens
Sparta
CITY
Crete   STATES
Gortyn

Phocaea

Ephesus

Halicarnassus

Gordium ○ PHRYGIA

NEO-HITTITE
CITY-STATES

Nineveh
ASSYRIA
Ashur

Tigris

Euphrates

Aradus
Cyprus   PHOENICIA
Berytus   Byblos
ISRAEL

Aramaeans

9

THE NEAR EAST IN THE 2ND MILLENNIUM BC `1`

- Hittite heartland
- Maximum extent of Hittite Empire
- Egyptian heartland
- Maximum extent of Egyptian Empire
- Mitannian heartland
- Maximum extent of Mitannian Empire

HITTITE EMPIRE
Boğazköy
Miletus
Carchemish
MITANNIAN EMPIRE
Washshukanni
Ugarit
Ashur
MEDITERRANEAN SEA
Byblos
Kadesh
Euphrates
Tigris
Babylon
EGYPTIAN EMPIRE
Memphis
Arabia
Thebes
RED SEA
Buhen
Nile

THE ASSYRIAN EMPIRE `3`

- Assyria under Ashur-dan II, 934-912 BC
- Added under Shalmaneser III, 858-824 BC
- Added under Sargon II, 721-705 BC
- Added under Ashurbanipal, 668-627 BC

BLACK SEA
Anatolia
Carchemish
ASSYRIA
MEDITERRANEAN SEA
Tyre
Israel
Samaria
Memphis
Arabia
EGYPT
(held c.667-660 BC)
Thebes
Nile

THE AEGEAN WORLD, c.1500-1300 BC `2`

- Maximum extent of Mycenaean control, c. 1300 BC
- Minoan civilization, c. 1500 BC

Troy
Dardanelles
Iolchus
AEGEAN SEA
Ithaca
Orchomenus
Gla
Thebes
Athens
Andros
Argos
Mycenae
Tiryns
Miletus
Pylos
Naxos
Milos
Rodhos
HITTITE EMPIRE
Khania
Knossos
Mallia
Palaiokastro
Crete
Phaistos
Gournia
Zakro
Cyprus →

DIALECTS OF POST-MYCENAEAN GREECE `4`

- Northwest Greeks
- Aeolians
- Ionians
- Dorians

Thessaly
Acarnania
Aetolia
Doris
Delphi
Boeotia
Thebes
Achaea
Corinth
Elis
Arcadia
Olympia
Argos
Argolis
IONIAN SEA
Messenia
Sparta
Laconia

The Near East in the 2nd Millennium BC

1 By the middle of the 2nd millennium BC, urban societies had existed in the Near East for some 2,000 years. The first cities had arisen in Sumer, in southern Mesopotamia, around 3500 BC. These were self-governing polities known as city-states, and were often at war with each other. Within a few centuries, cities had developed in the lands to the north and west, in northen Syria, Mesopotamia and the Levant. These, too, became involved in the power politics of the 3rd millennium, when the Akkadian rulers of southern Mesopotamia sought to extend their power as far as the Mediterranean.

By 3000 BC or a little later, a major new kingdom had formed in the Nile valley, that of ancient Egypt, and during the 2nd millennium the Egyptians cast their eyes northwards to the cities of the Levant and Syria. In the 15th century BC Egyptian armies of the New Kingdom period (1550-1070 BC) advanced as far as the River Euphrates. This brought them into conflict with the kingdom of Mitanni in Upper Mesopotamia and with the Hittites of central Anatolia. For a while, a careful three-hand game of war and diplomacy was played, until in the 14th century BC the Hittites destroyed Mitanni and took control of its territories west of the Euphrates. The division between Hittite and Egyptian zones was drawn by mutual agreement after the Battle of Kadesh (1286 BC). Within a century or so, both Hittites and Egyptians had been crippled by foreign attack and internal unrest. The Hittite kingdom collapsed, while the Egyptians retreated to the Nile valley.

The Aegean World, c.1500-1300 BC

2 The first European civilisation arose on the island of Crete early in the 2nd millennium BC. It takes its name, "Minoan", from the legendary King Minos, who annually fed Athenian youths and maidens to the savage Minotaur. Crete may have been divided into a number of separate states, governed from impressive palaces such as those at Phaistos, Mallia and Knossos. The rulers kept records of their administration in the form of clay tablets inscribed with a still-undeciphered script known as Linear A. The development of the Cretan states was brought to a sudden end during the 15th century BC, when the palaces were destroyed. Only one, at Knossos, was rebuilt after this destruction, and when the dust clears we find that Mycenaean Greeks rather than indigenous Minoan rulers are in control.

Mycenaean Greece was a land of small independent kingdoms centred on palaces or small fortresses. These tiny states arose during the 16th century BC by a process of internal development, as local war-leaders became increasingly powerful, agriculture improved and foreign trade fed new wealth into the economy. The most famous of the palace-fortresses is that of Mycenae in the north-western Peloponnese, from which site the whole civilisation of Mycenaean Greece takes its name.

In the 15th century the Mycenaeans took control of Crete, and by the 14th century they were the dominant power in the Aegean region, raiding the coasts of Asia Minor and perhaps (if legend is to be believed) attacking the strategic city of Troy at the mouth of the Dardanelles. Soon afterwards, the Mycenaean rulers were in crisis, and by the end of the 12th century their palaces had been abandoned.

The Assyrian Empire

3 Assyria – the land around the city of Ashur on the River Tigris – had been an important state throughout most of the 2nd millennium BC. In the 14th century the destruction of Mitanni gave the Assyrian kings their first great opportunity for territorial expansion, and during the 13th century BC they extended their frontiers as far west as the Ephrates. However, by the 10th century Assyrian control had declined and was once again limited to the core area around Ashur and Nineveh.

Assyrian kings began a new campaign of expansion in the 9th century BC. Two powerful rulers, Ashurnasirpal II and Shalmaneser III, campaigned as far west as the Mediterranean coastlands and struck deep into southern Mesopotamia. The Euphrates again became the Assyrian border, and the proceeds of conquest went to build elaborate palaces at Nimrud, the new capital city of Assyria. Then, after the accession of King Tigath-pileser III in 744 BC, the Assyrians seized control of more extensive territories than ever before, from Israel in the west to the Persian Gulf. It was the greatest empire the Near East had seen, but it survived for little more than a century. Ashurbanipal, the last great Assyrian ruler, invaded Egypt and conquered Elam, but his power was weakened by civil war. Within a mere two years of the Medes' invasion from Iran in 612 BC, the once mighty empire was destroyed.

Dialects of Post-Mycenaean Greece

4 With the abandonment of the Mycenaean centres between 1200 and 1100 BC Greece entered a "Dark Age". Tradition held that during this period of some 300 years, before the rise of the city-states in the 8th century, southern Greece was conquered and colonised by newcomers from the north known as the Dorians. For many years it was thought that the Dorians had introduced the Greek language. The decipherment of Mycenaean texts in Linear B has shown, however, that the Mycenaeans themselves spoke a form of Greek, and many people now argue that there were no Dorian invasions.

When literacy returned to Greece in the 8th century BC, a patchwork of dialects had emerged, with Doric dominant in the old heartlands of the Mycenaean kingdoms in the Peloponnese, Ionic in Attica, the Aegean islands and the colonies of western Asia Minor, while to the north and west Aeolic and other local dialects were spoken. There is no reason to believe that any of these dialects, or the people who spoke them, were recent arrivals from beyond Greece.

900 BC

The Rise of Greece

By the 6th century BC, the Mediterranean and Black Sea European coasts were dominated by a series of city-states. They were founded by three separate peoples: the Greeks (successors of the Bronze Age Mycenaeans); Phoenicians (founders of Carthage, from modern Lebanon and Syria); and Etruscans (from northern Italy). Meanwhile, north of the Alps, a new order of Celtic leaders had established themselves in eastern France and southern Germany, linked by trade in luxury goods with the Mediterranean world.

In Greece, the 8th century witnessed a whole series of crucial innovations. One of the most important was the adoption of writing using the alphabet, which was borrowed and adapted from that of the Phoenicians. Already in the 8th century writing was being used to record the first great works of Greek literature, the Iliad and Odyssey, attributed in their final form to Homer, a poet who may have lived on the island of Chios at this time. Equally if not more important was the rise of the Greek city-states, which again can be placed in the 8th century. Their development was fuelled by a growth in overseas trade, by a rise in population, and by a new ethos which banded the people of a region together as a single political entity in which all adult males had citizen rights. Democracy was not yet born, however, and government lay usually in the hands of aristocratic families, or of powerful self-made individuals referred to as "tyrants".

One highly visible result of the so-called "Greek renaissance" was the development of new artistic and architectural styles. Brightly painted pottery manufactured at Corinth and later at Athens was widely traded. A tradition of human sculpture in marble began which was to lead directly to the masterpieces of the Classical style. And great stone temples were built in several Greek cities during the 7th and 6th centuries. With the establishment of Greek colonies around the Black Sea and the west Mediterranean, from the 8th century onwards, these new styles and traditions spread also, and Greek goods were traded northward to the Celts and the Scythians. From the 9th century, the Phoenicians, too, had established colonies on the fringes of the Mediterranean. The most important of these was Carthage, but they also founded settlements in western Sicily, southern Sardinia and southeastern Spain.

In northern Italy, the development of city-states in the 8th century BC was associated with a native people known as the Etruscans. These had their own language and literature (now largely lost) in an alphabetic script they borrowed from the Greeks. During the 7th and 6th centuries they expanded their power into the Po valley, and southwards to Latium – taking control of Rome – and the region of Naples (Neapolis) and Pompeii.

Both Greek and Etruscan goods turn up in richly furnished Celtic graves during the 6th century. A whole series of princely centres developed at this time in eastern France and southern Germany, based in each case in fortified hilltop settlements which were the residences of the leading families or dynasties. These leaders derived their power and prosperity from control over the agricultural resources of the surrounding territory and from their trading relations with neighbouring regions and with the Mediterranean world. It was to be several centuries, however, before the first states and cities were to arise in Europe north of the Alps.

Teutonic Peoples

Finno-

Ugrians

BALTIC
SEA

Baltic peoples

Volga

Oder

Elbe

Vistula

Slavs

50°

Danube

Scythians

Don

Volga

Dnieper

Dniester

Tanais

Olbia

Tyras

Phanagoria

Panticapaeum

Theodosia

Chersonesus

BLACK SEA

Dioscurias

Phasis

Istrus

Tomi

Callatis

Danube

Odessus

Sinope

Amisus   Trapezos

Caucasians

Mesembria

Apollonia

Heracleia

40°

ETRUSCAN
CITY-STATES

Cortona

Perusia

Rome

Illyrians

Italic peoples

Epidamnus

Apollonia

Taras

Sybaris

Neapolis

Pompeii

Methone

Abdera

Acanthus Aenus

Potidaea

Maronea Perinthus Byzantium

Cardia

Sestus   Cyzicus

Lampsacus

EMPIRE OF THE MEDES
(Persian conquest in progress)

LYDIA

CILICIA

Tigris

Croton

Ambracia

Phocaea

Pisidians

Euphrates

Nineveh

anormus   Himera

Selinus

Akragas

Sicily

Rhegium

Catana

Syracuse

GREEK CITY
STATES

Thebes

Corinth

Argos

Sparta

Athens

Ephesus

Miletus

Halicarnassus

NEW BABYLONIAN EMPIRE

Malta

SEA

Crete

Gortyn

Lycians

Salamis

Cyprus

Semites

Illyrians

Thracians

13

ITALY: ETRUSCAN EXPANSION AND RETREAT, 9TH TO 4TH CENTURIES BC 3

Controlled by the Etruscans before 600 BC
Added during the early 6th century BC
Held c.600 – 474 BC
Held c.550 – 400 BC
Limit of Etruscan control, c.530 BC
Greek city-states, mid-6th century BC
Limit of Roman control, 380 BC

ANATOLIA AND THE BLACK SEA: GREEK AND PHOENICIAN COLONIZATION, 9TH TO 6TH CENTURIES BC 2

Colonized by Phoenicians from the 9th century BC
Core area of Greek city-states at the end of the 9th century BC
Colonized by Greeks from the 8th to the 6th centuries BC
CORINTH Principal mother cities

THE MEDITERRANEAN: GREEK AND PHOENICIAN COLONIZATION, 9TH TO 6TH CENTURIES BC 1

Colonized by Phoenicians from the 9th century BC
Core areas of Greek city-states at the end of the 9th century BC
Colonized by Greeks from the 8th to the 6th centuries BC
CORINTH Principal mother cities

14

The Mediterranean: Greek and Phoenician Colonization from the 9th to the 6th Centuries BC

1 Greek and Phoenician settlers founded a number of colonies around the shores of the west Mediterranean from the 9th century BC. The Phoenicians concentrated their efforts on the North African coast and southern Spain. Their most important colony was the city of Carthage in modern Tunisia, traditionally founded in 814 BC, though the earliest archaeological evidence dates from the 8th century. The earliest Greek colony in the west was the settlement of Pithekoussai (c.750 BC), on the small island of Ischia off the coast of Italy, and Euboeans, Corinthians and Phocaeans went on to found a whole series of colonies in southern Italy, Sicily and southern France. Some of these, most notably Syracuse (733 BC) and Massilia (Marseilles, 600 BC), became major cities.

By the early 6th century, Greeks and Phoenicians had established separate spheres of interest in the west Mediterranean, but friction between them led to a number of wars, many of them focused on Sicily where the Greeks and Phoenicians occupied opposite ends of the island. In around 540 BC the balance of power was disturbed when Phocaean Greeks, who had been driven from their own city by the Persians, established a new home at Alalia on Corsica. The Carthaginians allied themselves with the Etruscans, and in a great sea battle forced the Phocaeans to abandon their settlement. Greek attempts to plant colonies in southern Spain (such as Mainake) were also suppressed by the Carthaginians as the latter strengthened their hold over the coasts and sea-lanes of the west Mediterranean basin. The Greek colony of Massilia continued to flourish, however, while southern Italy became so firmly hellenized that it was later known to the Romans as Magna Graecia, "Greater Greece".

Anatolia and the Black Sea: Greek and Phoenician Colonization from the 9th to the 6th Centuries BC

2 Greek merchants may have begun trading in the Black Sea as early as the 8th century BC, but the first permanent colonies were established only towards the end of the 7th century. The attraction of the region was the fertile cereal lands, especially those of what is now the Ukraine. The Greeks traded manufactured goods, some imported from Greece, to the native peoples in return for raw materials and foodstuffs. North of the Danube, political power over the interior was in the hands of the Scythians, a nomadic horse-riding people of the steppes, who acted as overlords to settled agriculturalists in the Crimea and in the valleys of the major rivers. Greek manufactures, including painted pottery and metalwork, were passed to Scythian leaders either as gifts or through trade, and they occur in the great Scythian burial mounds on the southern steppes. Greek craftsmen of the Black Sea colonies also produced metalwork to order, in a style designed specifically to appeal to their Scythian customers. Trade between the Black Sea and the Aegean made control of the sea-routes between them increasingly important, and a number of Greek colonies were founded on the coast there in the 7th and 6th centuries, including the key city of Byzantium (c. 660 BC). During the 5th century, Athens in particular came to rely heavily on Black Sea grain to support her large population, and it was loss of control over the straits to the Spartans that eventually brought her to defeat at the end of the Peloponnesian War (*see* page 20).

Italy: Etruscan Expansion and Retreat from the 9th to the 4th Centuries BC

3 The Etruscans became the leading power in northern and central Italy during the 6th century BC. United by a common language and culture, they were divided politically into a series of city-states. The most important of these were the members of the League of Twelve Cities, which met together for religious ceremonies and political discussions at the sanctuary of Voltumna, their principal goddess, near Volsinii.

The Etruscans soon began to extend their control into neighbouring regions of Italy. In the 7th century a line of Etruscan kings established themselves at Rome, turning the modest existing settlement of Latin farmers into a minor city. Further to the south, they won control of Greek colonies around the Bay of Naples, including Capua and Pompeii. This brought them into conflict with the Greeks, and in 535 BC the Etruscans fought a naval engagement in alliance with the Carthaginians, which resulted in the Greeks being expelled from Corsica. During the course of the 6th century, the Etruscans also cast their eyes northward, establishing colonies in the Po valley. The most important of these new cities were Spina and Adria, trading centres at the mouth of the Po which gave the Etruscans direct access to the Adriatic.

Etruscan power reached its peak in around 530 BC. The tide began to turn six years later, when they tried and failed to capture the Greek city of Cumae. In 510 BC, the Latins of Rome expelled their Etruscan king and established a republic. This cut the overland communications between Etruria and Campania, a problem which was compounded in 474 BC when the Greeks defeated the Etruscans in a sea battle off Cumae. Etruscan power was already sharply in decline when, in 396 BC, the Romans captured Veii, the first of the League of Twelve Cities to fall into foreign hands. By that time, the Etruscans had lost control of the Po Valley to the invading Gauls, while the cities of Campania had fallen to local Italic peoples. During the 4th and 3rd centuries, the remaining Etruscan cities were steadily absorbed by the expansionist Roman state.

550 BC

480 BC

The Battle of Salamis

The Persian Wars of the 5th century BC were a turning point in the early history of Europe. The victories over the Persians at Salamis in 480 BC and at Plataea the following year gave the Greeks new confidence and prosperity, leading to developments in art and literature which were the hallmark of the Classical age. Athens attained a particular prominence, taking her place alongside Sparta as one of the two leading city-states. This in itself was a marked change from the previous century, when Athens had been only a secondary power, with few warships to her name. Then in 483 BC a rich new seam was discovered in the Athenian silver mines at Laurium, and the Athenians used this new-found prosperity to build a fleet of 200 warships. These proved her salvation during the Persian invasion of 480 BC, and laid the foundations of the great Athenian maritime empire which survived until the capitulation of Athens at the end of the Peloponnesian War in 404 BC (*see* page 20).

The Greek cities of Ionia remained a significant force during the 5th century, though the conquest by Persia in 546-45 BC had damaged their power and prosperity. Still hankering after their lost freedom, they led an abortive revolt against Persian rule in 499 BC (beginning in the city of Miletus) which directed the wrath of the Persians against Greece itself. Two major Persian expeditions against the Greeks in 490 BC and 480 BC failed in the face of stiff resistance from Athens and Sparta, and the Persians gave up their attempts to subdue mainland Greece. Freed at last from Persian rule after the Salamis campaign (480 BC), the Ionian Greeks found all too soon that they had merely exchanged their old masters for new; and the Delian League, founded for their mutual defence, soon transformed itself into an Athenian empire (*see* map 1, page 23).

In the central Mediterranean, Greek interests were opposed by an alliance of Carthaginians and Etruscans. In 535 BC the two sides came to blows at the battle of Alalia, which forced the Greeks to abandon Corsica. But the Carthaginian attempt to expel the Greeks from Sicily in 480 BC ended in disaster when their invading force suffered crushing defeat at Himera. Nonetheless, the Carthaginians retained a significant presence in western Sicily. Their erstwhile allies, the Etruscans, seem to have played no part in this campaign, and indeed Etruscan power in central Italy was already past its peak. In 524 BC the Etruscans had attempted to extend their power deep into southern Italy by an assault on the Greek city of Cumae, but this was repulsed with heavy loss. A few years later, in 510 BC, the city of Rome broke free from Etruscan rule, expelling the Tarquins (an Etruscan dynasty) and establishing itself as an independent republic.

Europe north of the Mediterranean and Black Sea first entered the writings of Greek historians in the 5th century BC. They divided the continent between Celts (occupying Western and Central Europe) and Scythians (in the lands north of the Black Sea). Imports of Greek and Etruscan pottery and metalwork show that both Celts and Scythians were in contact with the Mediterranean world, though both peoples also had indigenous identities and traditions, as shown in the richly furnished burials of Celtic and Scythian leaders. It was the Scythians, together with their neighbours the Thracians and the Greek cities of the northern Aegean, who first encountered the expansionist ambitions of the Persian empire under Darius the Great.

Teutonic Peoples

Finno-Ugrians

BALTIC SEA

Baltic peoples

Slavs

Scythians

Volga

Don

Dnieper

Dniester

Tanais

Olbia

Tyras

Panticapaeum   Phanagoria

Theodosia

Chersonesus

Dioscurias

Phasis

BLACK SEA

Tomi

Odessus

Sinope

Apollonia

Amisus   Trapezus

Thracians

Danube

Danube

Oder

Vistula

Elbe

Illyrians

Cortona

Perusia

ulonia

Rome

CITIES

Italic peoples

Cumae

Neapolis

Pompeii

Taras

Croton

Panormus   Himera

linus

Sicily

Catana

Akragas

Syracuse

Malta   SEA

Epidamnus

Apollonia

Ambracia

MACEDONIA

Methone   Acanthus

Potidaea

Thebes

Plataea

Corinth

Argos

Sparta

Athens

Salamis

Perinthus   Byzantium

Sestus   Cyzicus

Pergamum

Phocaea   Sardis

Ionia

Ephesus

Miletus

Halicarnassus

Salamis

Cyprus

PERSIAN EMPIRE

Tigris

Euphrates

Nineveh

Semites

Crete

Gortyn

MACEDONIA

PERSIAN

Thasos
Samothrace
Imbros
Lemnos
Sestus
Abydos
Hellespont

EMPIRE

Epirus

Thessaly

Corcyra

Ambracia

AEGEAN

Mytilene

Scyros

Acarnania
Leucas

Artemisium
Oreus
Thermopylae
Euboea

SEA

Cyme

Aetolia

Delphi

Boeotia
Thebes
Plataea
Eretria
Marathon

Ionian Islands

Erythrae

Cephallenia

Achaea
Sicyon
Megara
Attica
Salamis Athens
Corinth

Andros

Ephesus

Elis
Argolis
Argos

Tenos

Icaria

Zacynthus

Arcadia

Cyclades

Miletus

Tegea
Messenia
Sparta
Laconia

Paros
Naxos
Naxos

Dodecanes

Amorgos

Asine

Melos

Cythera

SEA OF CRETE

Carpathos

Cydonia

C   r   e   t   e

Illyrians

Thracians

Istrus
Tomi
Callatis

Odessus

Mesembria
Apollonia

Thrace

PERSIAN

MACEDONIA
Abdera Maronea
Perinthus
Byzantium

EMPIRE

Lampsacus Cyzicus
Sestus

Potidaea

Thessaly
GREEK
Boeotia
Corinth Marathon
Salamis Athens
STATES
Sparta

Sardis
Ephesus

Miletus

Halicarnassus

Gortyn

THE AEGEAN AND THE BALKANS: PERSIAN EXPANSION, 513-480 BC **1**

Secured by Persia by 540 BC

Added to Persia

in c. 518 BC

in 513 BC

by 480 BC

Persian vassal from 513 BC

Allied with Persia, 480 BC

—— Approximate Western frontier of Persian influence from 449 BC

GREECE AND THE PERSIAN WARS, 490-479 BC

The Persian Empire and vassal state, 490 BC

Conquered by Persia by 480 BC

Greek states allied with Persia by 480 BC

Greek states opposed to Persia

Neutral Greek states

PERSIAN EMPIRE

Chalcedon
Byzantium
Perinthus
Aenus
Sestus
Lampsacus
Cyzicus
Cius
Abydos

Mytilene
Cyme
Sardis
Chios
Erythrae
Ephesus
Samos
Lade Miletus
Halicarnassus
Caria
Lindos

THE IONIAN REVOLT

Persian territory, c.500 BC

Free Greek islands

Extent of the Ionian revolt, 499 BC

Maximum extent of the Ionian revolt, 494 BC

The Aegean and the Balkans: Persian Expansion 513-480 BC

1 The Persians made their first expedition into Europe during the reign of King Darius I (522-486 BC). In 513 BC Darius led a substantial Persian army across the Bosphorus to conquer Thrace and the lands south of the Danube. He then crossed the Danube and fought a wide-ranging but inconclusive campaign against the Scythians, who simply retreated before him, burning crops and blocking wells. It was only with difficulty that Darius managed to extricate his army. Despite this reverse, the Persians succeeded during the remainder of 513 BC in consolidating their hold on the northern shore of the Aegean and the Greek cities of the Hellespont. The Persians also reached the borders of the Kingdom of Macedonia in northern Greece, and accepted the submission of the Macedonian king Amyntas.

That remained the limit of Persian power until 480 BC, when Darius's son and successor Xerxes invaded Greece with an enormous army, receiving the submission of the Thessalians and Boeotians. By the end of August his forces had conquered Athens and Attica, but defeats at Salamis and Plataea forced them to withdraw, and within five years Persian possessions in Europe had been reduced to a handful of coastal cities. By 460 BC, even these had been lost, and Persian dreams of empire in Europe were over.

The Ionian Revolt

2 The Greek cities of western Asia Minor had been brought under Persian rule in 546-45 BC, during the reign of Cyrus the Great. They remained restless in their subjection, and in 499 BC broke out in open revolt against the Persians. The revolt was master-minded by Aristagoras, the ruler of Miletus, but soon spread to Caria in the southwest and northwards to the Greek cities of the Bosphorus. Aristagoras sought assistance from the free cities of mainland Greece, but Sparta refused assistance and only Athens and Eretria responded with men and ships. Mainland enthusiasm for the struggle petered out, however, after an abortive attempt to capture Sardis ended with heavy losses for the Greek side. The rebel fleet was eventually defeated by the Persians at the battle of Lade in 494 BC, and remaining resistance was soon stamped out. The Persians did not forget, however, that the Athenians had assisted the rebels, and it was to teach them a lesson that Darius in 490 BC sent an expeditionary force against Athens itself, only to encounter defeat at the battle of Marathon (*see* below).

Greece and the Persian Wars, 490-479 BC

3 In 490 BC the Persian king Darius I sent an expeditionary force by sea across the Aegean to punish Athens and Eretria for the help they had given to the rebels during the Ionian revolt. They captured Naxos and burned Eretria before moving south to Attica. They chose as their landfall the sandy bay of Marathon, on the opposite side of the peninsula to Athens. The Athenians mustered their forces and marched out against the enemy, and in a confused engagement won a resounding victory over a Persian army which was more than twice the size of their own force. The Persians lost several thousand men; the Athenians fewer than 200.

When next the Persians turned their attention to Greece their aim was to conquer the whole country. This was the famous expedition of Xerxes (486-464 BC), Darius's son and successor. The Greek historian Herodotus claims that the massive Persian invasion force numbered over five million men, and though the true figure was probably nearer 300,000, it was a truly formidable army, since even major Greek states such as Athens and Sparta could muster only 10,000 soldiers apiece .

In the spring of 480 BC Xerxes gathered his forces at the Hellespont and led them across to Europe over a bridge of boats. They marched along the northern shore of the Aegean as far as Macedonia, the Persian fleet shadowing them along the coast. Many states in northern Greece remained neutral, and Thessaly even entered an alliance with the invading Persians. North of the Peloponnese only Athens was a firm member of the anti-Persian alliance. Xerxes encountered the first serious resistance at Thermopylae, where a narrow pass barred the way to southern Greece. The Greeks had determined to defend the pass as long as possible, and for six days a force of 7,000 men, led by the Spartan king Leonidas, held the pass against the entire might of Xerxes' army. At last, on the seventh, they were surrounded and overcome by the weight of the Persians' superior numbers, Leonidas and his Spartans being killed in the fighting.

Xerxes next advanced to Attica, and captured Athens itself, though most of the Athenian citizens had already been evacuated to safety. Some of the Greeks were for staging a final stand at the Isthmus of Corinth, but the Athenians persuaded them to risk all on a sea battle in the narrow straits of Salamis. The result was a decisive Greek victory, which greatly discouraged Xerxes. The Persian king returned to Sardis in Asia Minor, leaving a reduced Persian force to continue the campaign under the command of his son-in-law Mardonius. When he too was defeated at Plataea in 479 BC and the Persian fleet was destroyed at Cape Mycale, the Persians finally gave up their hopes of conquering Greece. But they had stirred up a hornet's nest, and during the following decades the Greeks remained a thorn in their side, ejecting the Persians from Thrace and the Hellespont and chipping away at Persian territories in Asia Minor.

480 BC

Europe after Alexander

In the summer of 323 BC, on the eve of yet a further campaign, Alexander the Great died at Babylon. In a reign of only 13 years (336-323 BC) his Macedonian armies had defeated the Persian ruler Darius III and conquered the vast Persian realm. For a brief moment, the Greek and Persian worlds were united in a single mighty empire extending from the Adriatic to the River Indus.

The political power of the Greek city-states had passed its peak by the middle of 4th century BC. The defeat of the Persians in 480-479 BC had been followed by the establishment of the Delian League, under the leadership of Athens, in 478 BC. The league was soon transformed into an Athenian empire, and the growing power of Athens brought her into direct conflict with Sparta, Thebes and Corinth, which led to the outbreak of the Peloponnesian War in 431 BC. No match for Sparta on land, Athens was nonetheless secure as long as her fleet retained supremacy at sea. The turning point came with the ill-judged Athenian expedition against Syracuse in 415-413 BC. Crushingly defeated, the Athenians managed to struggle on for a further eight years, but finally lost their fleet and surrendered to the Spartans in 404 BC. The Athenian Empire was dissolved: she was forced to become an ally of Sparta; she had to give up her fleet; and her defensive walls were destroyed.

With the defeat of Athens, Sparta became the leading Greek state for over 30 years, until the Spartans in turn were defeated by the Thebans at Leuctra in 371 BC. But while the power of individual city-states rose and fell, Greece remained a divided land, and last-minute efforts to unite against Philip of Macedon were to no avail. Greece lost her political independence at the battle of Chaeronea in 338 BC and became a dependency within the empire of Philip and his son Alexander the Great. In 334 BC, Alexander crossed into Asia Minor. He defeated the armies of Darius in several engagements against overwhelming odds. By 330 BC he had conquered most of the Persian lands, and then pressed eastwards as far as the borders of India.

The story of the west Mediterranean during the 4th century BC can be summarised under two major themes: the continuing rivalry between Greeks and Carthaginians in Sicily; and the changing fortunes of Rome and the Etruscans in Italy. Rome grew as Etruscan power waned; the Etruscan city of Veii fell to the Romans in 396 BC. By 350 BC Rome controlled the whole of Latium and southern Etruria, and by 320 BC had extended her power far to the south, to the region of Capua and Naples.

The rise of Rome was not without its setbacks, however: in 390 BC the city was captured and sacked by the Senones, one of several peoples from north of the Alps known as Gauls to the Romans and Celts to the Greeks. Celtic expansion into Italy had begun in the 5th century, and though accompanied by raids on wealthy Italian cities, its main aim was to settle new territory. The Celtic heartland lay in eastern France and southern Germany, but Celtic incursions into northern Italy were so successful that the land beyond the Po became known to the Romans as Gallia Cisalpina, "Gaul this-side-of-the-Alps". It became part of Celtic Europe, a conglomeration of kingdoms and peoples known to us through their art, their princely burials, their fortified centres, and through the writings of Classical historians.

Carthaginian possessions

Greek city-states

Dependencies of Alexander's Empire

10°   20°   30°   40°   50°   60°

60°

Finno - Ugrians

Volga

BALTIC
SEA

Teutonic Peoples

Baltic peoples

Oder

Elbe

Vistula

50°

Slavs

Don

Volga

Danube

Dnieper

Scythians

Dniester

Illyrians

Thracians

Olbia

Tanais

BOSPORAN
KINGDOM

Tyras

Panticapaeum   Phanagoria

Chersonesus   Theodosia

Caucasian peoples

ium
Cortona
USCAN
CITIES
onia

Veii
Rome
ROME
Capua
Neapolis
Pompeii

Italic peoples

Taras

Tomi

Danube

Odessus

Apollonia

BLACK SEA

Dioscurias

Phasis

Sinope

Amisus   Trapezus

Epidamnus
Apollonia
Pella
Methone
Acanthus
Sestus
Perinthus   Byzantium
Cyzicus

E M P I R E

Gordium

Tigris

Croton
Ambracia
EPIRUS
Chaeronea
Thebes
Corinth   Athens
Argos
Sparta

Pergamum
Phocaea
Ephesus
Miletus
Halicarnassus

O F

Gaugamela

Arbela

Panormus   Himera
inus
Akragas
Sicily
Catana
Syracuse

A L E X A N D E R

Issus
Antioch

Euphrates

Malta

S E A

Salamis
Cyprus

Crete
Gortyn

A r a b s

21

THRACIAN KINGDOM

Epidamnus
Apollonia
MACEDONIA
Aegae
Methone
Pella
Stagirus
Olynthus
Potidaea
Eion
Maronea
Aenus
Perinthus
Byzantium
Calchedon
Cardia
Cyzicus
Sestus
Abydos
Abdera
Antandros
Assos
Larissa
Thessaly Pherae
Pagasae
Ambracia
AEGEAN
SEA
Cyme
Phocea
Teos
Ephesus
Samos
PERSIAN
EMPIRE
E. Locris
Delphi **Phocis** **Euboea**
W. Locris **Boeotia**
Achaea Thebes
Attica Carystos
Corinth Athens
Argos Aegina
Sparta
Delos
Naxos
Miletus
Halicarnassus
IONIAN
SEA
Melos
Rhodes
Thera
Crete
Carpathos

THE RISE OF MACEDONIA 3

— Approximate limit of the Thracian Kingdom to 358 BC

Core area of Macedonian control, early 4th century BC

Added to Macedonia by 359 BC

Added to or subdued by Macedonia by 336 BC

Added to or subdued by Macedonia after 336 BC

Probable extent of the Corinthian League from 337 BC

Other Greek states

Paeonia
Epidamnus
MACEDONIA
Apollonia
Pella
Aegae
Methone
Chalci
Stagir
Olynthus
Potidaea
Parauaea
EPIRUS
(MOLOSSIAN KINGDOM)
Perrhaebia
Larissa
Corcyra
Pherae
Thessaly Pagasa
Crocotus
Campus
Ambracia
Acarnania
Thermopylae
Delphi Chaeron
Phocis
Boeotia
G R E E K The
Corinth Ather
IONIAN
SEA
Peloponnese
Sparta

THE EAST AND CENTRAL MEDITERRANEAN: THE DELIAN LEAGUE AND ITS ALLIES 1

— Temporary Athenian possessions, 456–446 BC

Controlled by Athens, 431 BC

Allies of Athens, 431 BC

Other Greek states, 431 BC

Allies of Athens at earlier periods

ITALY AT THE TIME OF DIONYSIUS I OF SYRACUSE, 375 BC 2

— Held temporarily by Syracuse, 390–375 BC

Held by Syracuse, 375 BC

Controlled by Rome, c.380 BC

Free Greek cities

Adria
Celts
Arretium
Ancona
Cortona
ETRUSCAN CITIES
Issa
Pharos
Volsinii
Vulci
Italic peoples
Rome
Latium
Cora
Antium
Capua
Illyrian peoples
Cumae
Campania
Neapolis
Posidonia
Taras
Elea
Metapontum
Thurii
Croton
Panormus
Messana
CARTHAGE
Himera
Rhegium
Lilybaeum
Sicily
Naxos
Selinus
Catana
Akragas
Syracuse
IONIAN
SEA

THE EMPIRE OF ALEXANDER AND ITS DIVISION 4

— Boundary of the Macedonian Empire of Alexander at the time of his death, 323 BC (including dependencies)

Greek cities

KINGDOM OF CASSANDER
KINGDOM OF LYSIMACHUS
KINGDOM OF BOSPORUS
BITHYNIA
PAPHLAGONIA
Pella
Lysimacheia
Kassandreia
KINGDOM OF ANTIGONUS
ARMENIA
MEDIA ATROPATENE
CASPIAN SEA
Athens
Gordium
Sparta
Ephesus
Alexandria
Gaugamela
Antioch
Nicephorium
Arbela
MEDITERRANEAN SEA
KINGDOM OF S
Ecbatana
Cyrene
KINGDOM OF PTOLEMY
Alexandria
Jerusalem
NABATAEA
Memphis
Seleuceia
Babylon
Susa
Alexandria
Charax
Persepo

The East and Central Mediterranean: the Delian League and its Allies

1 The Persian invasion of Greece and its defeat had demonstrated the importance of uniting in the face of a powerful and aggressive neighbour. Individual Greek city-states could not hope to resist the might of the Persian Empire, which remained a serious threat even after the Greek victories at Salamis (480 BC) and Plataea (479 BC); *see* map 3, page 19. It was the continued need for mutual protection which led to the formation of the Delian League in 478 BC. The league had a treasury on the island of Delos, into which member-states paid an annual contribution. This revenue was used to support naval expeditions aimed at freeing the Greek cities of Thrace and Asia Minor from Persian control, and confronting Persian counter-attacks.

Leadership of the League fell to Athens, and such was the power of the Athenian fleet that by the middle of the 5th century what had begun as a voluntary defensive confederacy was transformed into an Athenian empire. In 454 BC, the treasury of the League was transferred from Delos to Athens, where some of it was used for the building of the Parthenon. A series of revolts were ruthlessly suppressed, but though many League members grew increasingly discontented, Athens steadily strengthened her position as the head of a maritime empire, covering most of the shores and islands of the Aegean. This led to direct confrontation with the cities of Peloponnesian League, led by Sparta, and the outbreak of the Peloponnesian War in 431 BC.

Italy at the Time of Dionysius I of Syracuse, 375 BC

2 The Greek victory at Himera in 480 BC had far from put an end to Carthaginian ambitions in Sicily, where Carthaginian cities continued to dominate the western end of the island. In 409 BC the Carthaginians staged a second major invasion of Greek Sicily, capturing the cities of Selinus and Akragas.

It was in this crisis that Dionysius, an able man of humble origin, seized power at Syracuse, the principal Greek city, and gradually extended his rule over the greater part of the island. In two hard-fought wars against the Carthaginians (398-397 BC, 392 BC), Dionysius drove them back again to the western end of Sicily. He then turned his attentions to the Italian mainland, and by 379 BC had conquered the southern peninsula, and made the Greek cities beyond this into dependencies of Syracuse. He even gained control of the distant Adriatic cities of Issa, Ancona and Adria.

Dionysius strengthened his hold over these territories by building up a powerful fleet, and protected himself at home by constructing a formidable ring of fortifications around Syracuse, which remained the capital of his empire. His reign ended in setback, however, for in 379 BC the Carthaginians once again won the upper hand in western Sicily, and Dionysius was still trying to recover his losses when he died 12 years later.

The Rise of Macedonia

3 The kingdom of Macedonia lay outside the core area of Classical Greece, and first rose to prominence only in the 4th century BC. The architect of Macedonia's greatness was Philip II, who came to power at a time when the kingdom was threatened by foreign enemies and internal unrest. He quickly established his authority, and by remodelling the Macedonian army created a fighting force which he then used to expand Macedonian power far beyond the frontiers he had inherited. By 352 BC he had conquered Thessaly and the Greek cities of the northern Aegean. By 341 BC he had added most of Thrace to his territories.

To counteract the growing power of Macedon the city-states of southern Greece formed an alliance led by Thebes and Athens, but their army was decisively defeated by the Macedonians at the battle of Chaeronea in 338 BC. The following year, Philip organised the Greek cities into the Corinthian League under Macedonian control. Each member of the League was to provide ships or men for a great expedition against the Persian Empire. It was on the eve of his departure for this campaign, in the summer of 336 BC, that Philip was assassinated, and his son Alexander came to power.

The Empire of Alexander and its Division

4 The conquest of the Persian Empire by Alexander the Great is one of the great hero-stories of ancient history. His army not only subjugated the vast Persian realm but also crossed the River Indus and fought against the rulers of the Punjab. Greek colonies were founded at strategic places, and Alexander endeavoured to bind his heterogeneous territories together by a policy of harmony and co-operation between Persians and Macedonians. His plans were cut short by his illness and death at Babylon in June 323 BC.

Though loyal generals attempted to hold Alexander's empire in trust for his infant son and heir, others were driven by personal ambitions and rivalry and division soon set in. By 300 BC the empire had broken into several independent kingdoms, the largest being those ruled by Seleucus, Ptolemy and Antigonus. Further fragmentation followed, as these generals devoted their energies to fighting each other in Greece and the Near East rather than to countering the secessionist tendencies of local rulers. The most significant losses were in the east, where Seleucus ceded the frontier provinces of his kingdom to the Indian ruler Chandragupta Maurya, founder of the Mauryan empire which dominated the subcontinent throughout the following century.

323 BC

The Rise of Rome

The struggle for supremacy between the generals of Alexander the Great continued during the first decades of the 3rd century BC. Egypt and many of the Aegean coasts and islands were ruled by the Ptolemies with their powerful fleet, though several smaller maritime states, such as the important island of Rhodes, managed to maintain their independence. The city-states of southern Greece, too, tried to regain their independence, playing off the larger powers against each other, and forming separate confederacies: the Achaean League in the north of the Peloponnese, and the Aetolian League on the opposite side of the Gulf of Corinth. But the Greeks were as often fighting each other as uniting against a common enemy, and periods of true independence were transitory and brief.

Greece was still overshadowed by the power of the kingdom of Macedon to the north which, after years of civil war and disputed succession following the death of Alexander, entered a new period of relatively stable rule under Antigonus Gonatas (276-239 BC). Eastwards again lay the enormous Seleucid Empire, comprising most of the Asiatic territories of Alexander's empire. Already by 270 BC, however, powerful centripetal forces were in motion, and independent kingdoms had formed in Asia Minor and Bactria. Particularly important in later years was the kingdom of Pergamum, in western Asia Minor, which declared its independence from the Seleucids in 263 BC.

In the central Mediterranean, the major powers of the early 3rd century BC were Rome and Carthage. For Rome, this was a period of conquest and consolidation, from which she emerged as ruler of virtually all peninsular Italy. Carthage, meanwhile, was still preoccupied with the threat posed by the Greek city-states of Sicily. In 310 BC, the Carthaginians had attempted to conquer the whole of the island, and came near to achieving their aim until Agathocles, ruler of Syracuse, turned the tables on them by invading the Carthaginian homeland in North Africa. Agathocles was eventually defeated in 307 BC, and the peace treaty which followed restored the previous balance of power between the Greeks and Carthaginians, with no significant gains for either side. The campaign launched against the Carthaginians by Pyrrhus in 278 BC likewise achieved no significant changes. The western Mediterranean remained largely a Carthaginian sphere until their defeat in the Punic Wars (*see* map 1, page 31), though the Greek colony of Massilia and its western outposts retained a hold on trade along the coasts of southern France and the Spanish Levant.

To the north of these lands lay the territories of the Celts, Scythians and Celtiberians. The Celts had already invaded the Mediterranean lands in the 4th century, and did so again during the 3rd. In 281 BC they defeated Ceraunus, king of Macedonia, and two years later mounted a major invasion of Greece, lured by the wealth of the cities and sanctuaries there. They were turned back at Delphi, and decisively defeated by the Macedonians at Lysimacheia in Thrace in 277 BC. But meanwhile another Celtic army had crossed the Hellespont into Asia Minor, where they established the kingdom of Galatia, and spread alarm and dismay among their neighbours by their raids and warfare. Eventually brought to heel by King Attalus of Pergamum in 240 BC, Galatia nonetheless survived as a separate kingdom until it was absorbed into the Roman Empire in 25 BC.

Carthaginian possessions

Small Greek states

Teutonic Peoples

Finno-Ugrians

BALTIC SEA

Baltic peoples

Slavs

Scythians

Volga
Don
Volga
Dnieper
Dniester

Oder
Vistula
Elbe

Danube

Illyrians

Thracians

Danube

Tanais

Olbia

BOSPORAN KINGDOM

Tyras

Panticapaeum   Phanagoria
Theodosia

Chersonesus

BLACK SEA

Caucasian peoples

Dioscurias
Phasis

Istrus
Tomi
Callatis
Odessus
Mesembria
Apollonia

TYLISIAN KINGDOM

Sinope
Amisus   Trapezus

PONTUS

ARMENIA

Arretium
Perusia
ulonia
ROMAN-LED
Rome
ITALIAN
Capua
Neapolis   ALLIANCE
Pompeii
Tarentum

Epidamnus

Apollonia

EPIRUS

Ambracia

MACEDON

Pella
Methone
Potidaea

Abdera   Maronea
Acanthus   Aenus
Sestus
Lampsacus

Perinthus   Byzantium
Cardia
Cyzicus

BITHYNIA   PAPHLAGONIA

GALATIA

CAPPADOCIA

MEDIA ATROPATENE

Tigris

Euphrates

SELEUCID EMPIRE

Croton

AETOLIAN LEAGUE

Delphi   Chalcis
Thebes
ACHAEAN LEAGUE   Athens
Corinth
Argos
Sparta

PERGAMUM
Pergamum

Phocaea
Sardes
Ephesus
Miletus

Halicarnassus

Antioch

anormus   Himera
nus
Sicily
Rhegium
Akragas   Catana
Syracuse

Malta

SEA

PTOLEMAIC EMPIRE

RHODES

Crete   Gortyn

Salamis
Cyprus

Arabs

The Successors of Alexander's Empire, 301 BC

1 The death of Alexander the Great at Babylon in June 323 BC was followed almost immediately by warfare between his generals over the division of the empire. The attempt to install Alexander's half-wit half-brother and infant son as joint kings of Macedon and overlords of the whole empire was soon overwhelmed by the forces of *realpolitik*. The political map shifted continuously as alliances were forged and broken and battles won and lost.

By 310 BC there were five main players left in the game: Ptolemy in Egypt and Palestine; Cassander in Macedon; Seleucus in Mesopotamia and most of the old Persian territories; Lysimachus in Thrace; and Antigonus in Asia Minor. The death of Antigonus at the battle of Ipsus in 301 BC reduced the main rivals to four; 20 years later Lysimachus was killed in battle at Magnesia.

The three major protagonists who survived – the Ptolemies, Seleucids and Macedonians – were to maintain an uneasy balance of power for the next 100 years. Native kingdoms reasserted their independence on the fringes of the vast Seleucid Empire, and smaller kingdoms broke away, most notably Pergamum, which came to dominate western Asia Minor in the mid-3rd century BC, and the remarkable kingdom of the Bactrian Greeks, which broke away from Seleucid control in the east. But the first real disturbance to this fragile political map came only when Roman armies began to interfere in the affairs of the region in the aftermath of the Second Punic War (218-201 BC).

Italy: the Roman Conquest, 350-270 BC

2 By the middle of the 4th century BC, the Romans had established their ascendancy over the Etruscan city-states and switched their attention to the peoples of southern Italy, notably the Samnites of the interior and the Greeks of the coast. The First Samnite War (343-341 BC), which the Romans fought in alliance with the Greek cities of Campania (around Neapolis), ended with no conclusive outcome, but paved the way for further Roman intervention in the region.

The Second War (328-304 BC) was an altogether more serious affair, and saw Roman armies operating for the first time on the Adriatic coast of Italy. By the end of the war Rome had extended its direct control from Latium south into Campania (the area round Capua), and had built the first and most famous of its all-weather roads, the Via Appia (312 BC), to speed the movement of its armies into southern Italy. Colonies of Latin citizens were established at strategic points (Luceria, Interamna, Tarracina, Saticula, Suessa Aurunca) to strengthen the Roman hold over the newly acquired territories.

The Samnites were not conquered, however, but merely forced to accept terms. Peace was soon broken by the Third Samnite War (298-290 BC). The Romans fought a crucial battle against the Samnites and their Gaulish allies at Sentinum north of Rome, and after hard fighting they carried the day. The Samnites were reduced to the status of allies, and Rome was free to expand her power into the southernmost corners of peninsular Italy. Faced with resistance from some of the Greek cities, most notably Tarentum, the Romans still succeeded in defeating the forces of Pyrrhus, king of Epirus (*see* map 3, below), who came to their aid (280-275 BC).

With Pyrrhus's withdrawal from the scene, the Greek cities hastened to make alliance with the new regional superpower. To consolidate Roman gains, Latin colonies were established at Venusia (291 BC), Beneventum (268 BC) and Aesernia (263 BC) in the south, at Cosa (273 BC) in Etruria, and at Ariminum (268 BC) and Firmum (264 BC) on the Adriatic coast. The Roman conquest of peninsular Italy was, by the mid-3rd century, secure.

Pyrrhus's Central Mediterranean Empire

3 Pyrrhus, King of Epirus, is one of the more romantic figures of ancient history, a man in the mould of Alexander the Great, of huge ambitions and enormous energy, but without Alexander's military genius or good fortune. His greatest legacy, indeed, is the concept of the Pyrrhic victory, a technical win but at such enormous cost as to constitute a defeat.

Pyrrhus came to the throne of Epirus as a boy in 307 BC, but in the disturbed conditions of the time was twice exiled before securing his hold on that mountain kingdom in 297 BC. After attempts – only partially successful – to extend his power east into Macedonia, he switched his attention west to the Greek cities of Sicily and southern Italy. In May 280 BC Pyrrhus crossed into southern Italy with a substantial army, including elephants, to assist the Greek city of Tarentum against Roman encroachments in the Adriatic. With the help of his elephants he defeated the Romans at Heraclea in 280 BC, and again the following year at Ausculum to the north.

But the Romans refused to accept his terms, and in 278 BC he was lured to Sicily at the invitation of the Greek cities there to lead a campaign against the Carthaginians in the west of the island. Within 18 months he had reduced Carthaginian possessions in Sicily to the single fortress of Lilybaeum in the extreme west, but once again he could not bring himself to agree to terms, and after falling out with his Greek allies he returned to southern Italy in 276 BC. There he was decisively defeated by the Romans at the battle of Beneventum the following year and returned to Epirus. Tarentum fell to the Romans in 272 BC, and in the same year Pyrrhus was killed at Argos in Greece.

270 BC

ITALY: THE ROMAN CONQUEST 350-270 BC

2

- Roman territory and colonies, 300 BC
- Allies of Rome, 300 BC
- Additional allies of Rome by 270 BC
- Added to Roman territory and colonies by 264 BC
- —— Frontiers, 270 BC

THE SUCCESSORS OF ALEXANDER'S EMPIRE, 301 BC

1

- The kingdom of Seleucus and dependencies
- The kingdom of Ptolemy and dependencies
- The kingdom of Cassander and dependencies
- The kingdom of Lysimachus and dependencies
- Independent Greek cities

Roman Expansion in the Mediterranean

Between 270 BC and 121 BC the map of southern Europe was transformed by the steady expansion of Roman power. The first stage came in the conflict between Rome and her North African rival Carthage. Founded as a Phoenician colony on the north coast of Africa in the 9th or 8th century BC, by the early 3rd century BC Carthage had grown to become one of the greatest centres of the Mediterranean world, and under her leadership the Phoenicians had succeeded in retaining their hold on the west Mediterranean sea-lanes despite fierce competition from the Greek cities of Sicily and southern Italy. It was a dispute over control of the Sicilian city of Messana in 264 BC which first drew the Carthaginians and Romans into direct conflict.

The First Punic War, as it was called ("Punic" from the Latin word for Phoenician), was fought mainly in and around Sicily, by both land and sea, and rapidly developed into a large-scale war of attrition. It ended in 241 BC, when Carthage was finally obliged to come to terms. The peace that was reached lasted little over 20 years, however, and was broken by the outbreak of the Second Punic War in 218 BC. From southern Spain, the Carthaginian general, Hannibal, launched an invasion of Italy across the Alps, inflicting crushing defeats on Roman armies at the River Trebia in 218 BC, at Lake Trasimene in 217 BC, and finally at Cannae in 216 BC. He was unable to capture Rome itself, however, and was eventually forced to return to Africa, where he faced final defeat at the battle of Zama (202 BC). Carthage lost her Spanish possessions, and many of her North African territories were given to Rome's Numidian allies.

Further conquests in Spain occupied the Romans for another 70 years, but at the same time they became increasingly involved in Greece and the Balkans. The ambitions of the Macedonian king Philip V and the Seleucid ruler Antiochus III drew the Romans into wars with both in turn, but Roman victories over Philip at Cynoscephalae (197 BC) and over Antiochus at Magnesia (190 BC) were not immediately followed by any attempt to extend Roman territory in the Balkans. That development came later in the century, when repeated "provocations" led the Romans to make first Macedonia, and then Greece, into Roman provinces.

By 133 BC the Romans possessed an empire extending from the Atlantic to Asia Minor. This now included the former kingdom of Pergamum as well as North African territories annexed during the Third Punic War (149-146 BC) when Carthage itself was finally destroyed. But important developments were also taking place in northern Europe. By the 2nd century BC, powerful Celtic groups had emerged in some regions, and fortified Celtic towns were to be found across a broad band of territory from France in the west to Bohemia in the east. Rome had already subjugated the Celtic peoples of northern Italy; in the 120s the Celtic peoples of southern France were also drawn forcibly into the Roman sphere. The Mediterranean world was poised to extend its power yet further into northern Europe: Celts and Romans were destined to become still closer acquaintances in the century which followed.

Independent Greek states

Finns

BALTIC SEA

Teutonic peoples

Baltic peoples

Ugrians

Slavs

Iranian peoples

Oder
Elbe
Vistula

Danube

Dnieper
Dniester

Volga

Volga

Don

Caucasian peoples

Olbia

Tyras

BOSPORAN
KINGDOM

Panticapaeum

Chersonesus

Dacians

Tomi

Danube

Thracians

Odessus

Mesembia

Apollonia

GREEK
CITIES

BLACK SEA

Amisus   Trapezus

ARMENIA

anum

Aquileia

Verona

isae

Ariminum

etium

Salonae

Narona

Illyrians

Rome

Corfinium

Cannae

Neapolis

Dyrrachium

Stobi

Byzantium

Perinthus

Prusa

BITHYNIA

PONTUS

Ancyra

Dorylaeum

Mazaca

CAPPADOCIA

PARTHIAN
EMPIRE

Tigris

Tarentum

Brundisium

Thessalonica

Cynoscephalae

Nicopolis

Alexandria
Troas

Demetrias

Pergamum

Antiochia

COMMAGENE

Iconium

PISIDIA

SELEUCID EMPIRE

E P U B L I C

Panormus

Messana

Sicily

Catana

Syracuse

Malta

SEA

Magnesia

Patrae

Corinth

Athens

Ephesus

Aphrodisias

Halicarnassus

Sparta

CIBYRA

Rhodus

RHODES

LYCIA

Side

Tarsus

Antioch

Cyprus   Salamis

PTOLEMAIC
EMPIRE

Arabs

Crete

Gortyn

29

Numantia

(121)

Narbo

MASSILIA

Pisae

Massilia

Corsica
(238) Aleria

Rome   Italy   Cannae

(222/191)

(177)

(168)

(229/219)

(229/219)

Apollonia

Mace

Tarraco

Hispania

Tarentum

Capua

(154/139)

Saguntum

(181)

(216/123)

Sardinia
(238)

Croton

Lusitania

Baecula

Citerior

Ac

Ilipa

Lilybaeum   Sicily
(241)

Messana

Gades   Ulterior   (206/197)   Carthago Nova

MEDITERRANEAN   Syracuse

Cartenna

NUMIDIA

Carthage
Tunis
(146)
Zama   Hadrumetum

SEA

MAURETANIA

Theveste

Leptis Magna

THE BALKANS: ROMAN EXPANSION, 270-31 BC

2

Controlled by Rome by c. 270 BC

by c.100 BC (with dates)

Areas retaining partial autonomy
for varying periods following
Roman conquest

Added to Rome:

by c.200 BC (with dates)

by c.50 BC (with dates)

Roman frontier, 31 BC

by c.150 BC (with dates)

by c.31 BC

ROMAN
REPUBLIC

MACEDO

Apollonia

Pella

(229/
191)

(177)

Celts

DACIA

Larissa

THESSALY   De

Epirus

(33)

Dalmatia   Illyria

Leucas

Cynoscephalae

Ambracia

(168)

Salonae

AETOLIAN
LEAGUE

Falerio   (229/219)   Narona

Acarnania   BOEC

Pharus

Cephallenia

Doclea

**GREECE AND THE AEGEAN:
THE EVE OF THE SECOND
MACEDONIAN WAR, 202 BC**

3

Corfinium

Macedonian dependencies

Corinth

Thracians

Beneventum   Dyrrachium   Stobi   Byzantium

Allies of Macedon

ELIS   ACHAEAN
LEAGUE

Zacynthus

Macedon
(148)

Neapolis   Brundisium   Beroea   Thessalonica   Perinthus

Aetolian League

Argos

Tarentum   (229/219)   Pydna   Prusa

Allies of the Aetolian League

Messene
MESSENIA   Sparta

Buthrotum   (74)

Achaean League

LACONIA

Cynoscephalae   Demetrias

Pylos

Nicopolis   **Asia**
(133/129)   Sardis

Rhodes

Patrae   Thermopylae   Smyrna
Magnesia
Ephesus

(241)
Sicily
Catana   **Achaea**
(146)   Athens   Corinth   Aphrodisias

Other Greek states/areas

Syracuse   Sparta   Halicarnassus

Frontiers, c.202 BC

Crete (67)   Rhodus
RHODES

The Western Mediterranean: Roman Expansion, 264-121 BC

`1` The 118 years between the outbreak of the First Punic War in 264 BC and the destruction of Carthage in 146 BC saw Rome grow from ruler of Italy to mistress of the Mediterranean. The peace terms which ended the First Punic War in 241 BC gave the Romans the island of Sicily. Three years later they were able to demand Corsica and Sardinia as well. The next expansionist move was the conquest of northern Italy, and the defeat of the Celtic peoples who had inhabited it since the 6th century. This was achieved in three major campaigns from 224 to 222 BC, and consolidated in 191 BC after a series of rebellions. Victory over the Carthaginians in Spain in 206 BC, during the Second Punic War, handed the coastal regions of the south and east to Roman rule, and in 197 BC the conquered territories were divided into two separate provinces (Hispania Ulterior and Hispania Citerior). That same year, however, the peoples of Spain mounted a general uprising against Roman rule, which was not finally suppressed until 181 BC.

This was far from being the end of the story, for in 154 BC the Lusitanians of western Spain invaded the conquered territories. Lusitania was annexed in 139 BC, but war dragged on until the fall of Numantia, the last independent stronghold, in 133 BC. Even then, Roman control did not extend to northernmost Spain. By that time, however, Rome had achieved final victory over Carthage in the Third Punic War, and the core Carthaginian territory had become the Roman province of Africa (146 BC). Rome completed her domination of the west Mediterranean by seizing the Balearic islands in 123 BC, and by campaigns against the Gauls in southern France in 125-121 BC, ostensibly in defence of her ally Massilia. These south French territories were ultimately to become the Roman province of Gallia Narbonensis.

The Balkans: Roman Expansion, 270-31 BC

`2` Roman expansion east of the Adriatic began in 229 BC, when an army and a fleet were sent to suppress Illyrian pirates and a Roman protectorate was established over the Greek cities of the Adriatic coast. The piracy of Demetrius of Pharus in 219 BC was stamped out in a similar way. Soon afterwards, the Romans came into conflict with Philip V, King of Macedon. Their victory at Cynoscephalae in 197 BC forced him to pull back within his own frontiers, but they did not attempt to capitalize on this victory in territorial terms. Nor did they try to do so after their victories over Antiochus III at Thermopylae in Greece in 191 BC and at Magnesia in Asia Minor the following year.

Roman policy changed only after the Third Macedonian War (171-167 BC). Aemilius Paullus defeated Philip's son and successor Perseus at the battle of Pydna in 168 BC, and brought the kingdom of Macedon to an end. Macedonia was divided into four republics, and coastal Illyria into three, but 20 years more were to pass before further fighting at last forced Rome to reduce Macedonia to the status of a province. Greece itself was absorbed into the same province two years later. Roman control was finally extended to Asia Minor in 133 BC when the last king of Pergamum, Attalus III, bequeathed them his kingdom, which then became the Roman province of Asia.

Greece and the Aegean: the Eve of the Second Macedonian War, 202 BC

`3` As the 3rd century BC drew to a close, two great monarchs dominated the Aegean region: Antiochus III, "the Great", ruler of the Seleucid Empire (223-187 BC), and Philip V, King of Macedon (221-179 BC). Both were men of boundless ambition. Antiochus dreamed of reconquering all the territories held by his predecessor Seleucus I a century before. His most spectacular undertaking was the reconquest of the eastern provinces in a seven-year campaign (212-205 BC) which took him as far as the borders of India. It was followed in 202 BC by a campaign in which Antiochus defeated the Ptolemaic army and seized control of the whole of the southern Levant up to the borders of Egypt.

Philip's eyes, meanwhile, were focused on Greece and the west. His attempts to subjugate Illyria and a foolish alliance with Hannibal and the Carthaginians led to the First Macedonian War with Rome (214-205 BC). The Romans allied themselves with Philip's enemies in Greece, the Aetolian League, but though the sporadic fighting continued for several years (marked by Aetolian atrocities), neither side made any significant gains and the peace which followed simply restored the status quo from before the war. Philip then turned his attention to the Aegean, attacking Rhodes and Pergamum (both friendly to Rome) and entering into a secret understanding with Antiochus.

The threat of an alliance between the two rulers was too much for the Romans. During the Second Macedonian War (200-196 BC), a Roman expeditionary force under the consul Flaminius defeated the Macedonian forces at the battle of Cynoscephalae (197 BC). Philip was forbidden to interfere any further in the affairs of Greece, and even Thessaly – which had long been his ally – was broken up into a series of independent leagues. Flaminius declared the Greek cities liberated from foreign control, and the Roman forces withdrew to Italy in 194 BC. Events were soon to show, however, that their involvement in Greece had only just begun.

121 BC

31 BC

Roman Expansion Beyond the Mediterranean

The 90 years between 121 BC and 31 BC were marked by a dramatic further extension of Roman control, both around the shores of the Mediterranean and, for the first time, across large areas of Atlantic Europe. Rome grew steadily stronger and more prosperous as successive Roman commanders used military campaigns as a route to wealth and power at home. The political history of Rome during the 1st century BC is largely one of confrontation between leading generals, the factions who supported them, and the senate, which remained in principle the governing body of the state, but was often powerless in the face of military force.

The first of these over-mighty commanders, Gaius Marius, made his name in the war against the Numidian ruler Jugurtha in 111-104 BC. He gained still further renown in 102-101 BC when he defeated the Cimbri and Teutones, Germanic war-bands who had invaded southern France and crossed into northern Italy. After Marius, the position of leading general at Rome passed to Lucius Cornelius Sulla, an officer who had played a key role in suppressing the Italian rebellion of 90-88 BC and was then entrusted with the command of the war against Mithradates of Pontus. On his return to Rome in 82 BC he became absolute ruler until his abdication in 79 BC. With his demise the following year, Gnaeus Pompeius (Pompey) became the leading general, clearing the Mediterranean of pirates in 67 BC, finally crushing Mithradates in 66 BC, and later joining with Marcus Crassus and Julius Caesar in a power-sharing arrangement (known as the First Triumvirate) which completely overshadowed the traditional authority of the senate.

Crassus died fighting the Parthians at Carrhae in 53 BC and rivalry between Pompey and Caesar broke into open hostility in 49 BC. The civil war which followed lasted until March 45 BC, but the outcome was not in doubt after Caesar's victory at Pharsalus in 48 BC and Pompey's subsequent murder. Caesar became undisputed ruler of the Roman state, but his attempt to establish a lifelong dictatorship ended with his assassination on the Ides of March in 44 BC. There followed 13 more years of uncertainty and civil strife, during which Mark Antony and Caesar's adoptive son and heir Octavian first defeated Caesar's assassins at Philippi (42 BC), then became increasingly estranged from each other as Antony allied himself with the Egyptian queen, Cleopatra. The sea battle at Actium in 31 BC gave final victory to Octavian. Four years later, in a special arrangement with the senate, Octavian formally established the Roman Empire, taking the name Augustus and with it imperial powers over the government, the armies and the frontier provinces.

Beyond the Roman frontiers lay the Celtic peoples of Britain and the Alpine region, the Germans across the Rhine, and the Dacians and Thracians in the northern Balkans. A large part of Celtic Europe now lay within the empire, in northern Italy and the territories conquered by Julius Caesar in Gaul. Even before their conquest by the Romans, the Gauls were far from being disorganised barbarians, and had their own coins and kings, towns and trade, and sophisticated craftsmanship in bronze and gold. It was the less centralised Germanic peoples, however, which were to be the greatest threat to Rome's European provinces during the centuries which followed.

Roman dependencies

Independent Greek cities

Finno-Ugrians

BALTIC
SEA

Teutonic peoples

Baltic peoples

Slavs

Iranian peoples

Oder

Vistula

Elbe

Danube

Dnieper

Dniester

Don

Volga

Volga

Celtic peoples

DACIA

Danube

Thracians

GREEK
CITIES

Olbia

Tyras

BOSPORAN
KINGDOM

Panticapaeum

Heraclea

Caucasian peoples

BLACK SEA

Amisus Trapezus

PONTUS

ARMENIA

Siscia

N

Aquileia

Verona

anum

Ariminum

isae

etium

Rome

Corfinium

Neapolis

Tarentum

Salonae

Narona

Doclea

Dyrrachium

Brundisium

Beroea

Stobi

Philippi

Thessalonica

Perinthus

Byzantium

Prusa

Dorylaeum

Ancyra

GALATIA

SOPHENE

CORDUENE

CAPPADOCIA

COMMAGENE

OSRHOENE

Tigris

Euphrates

PARTHIAN
EMPIRE

E

M

P

I

R

E

Alexandria

Troas

Pergamum

Antiochia

Carrhae Iconium

Tarsus

Antioch

Nicopolis

Actium

Demetrias

Pharsalus

Patrae

Corinth

Athens

Sparta

Ephesus

Side

Panormus

Sicily

Catana

Syracuse

Halicarnassus

Rhodus

RHODES

LYCIA

Cyprus Salamis

Palmyra

Arabs

Malta

SEA

Crete

Gortyn

10° 20° 30° 40° 50° 60°

60°

50°

40°

20° 30° 40°

33

**THE DACIAN KINGDOM OF BUREBISTA,
c.80–44 BC** [1]

Approximate extent of Burebista's territory, c. 80 BC

Conquered by Burebista by c.45 BC

Greek cities taken over by Burebista

Approximate extent of the main Dacian kingdom after Burebista's death, 44 BC

Roman frontier, c. 50 BC

**GAUL : THE ROMAN CONQUEST,
c.58–53 BC** [2]

Roman Republic, 58 BC

Conquered by Rome:

in 58 BC

in 57 BC

in 56 BC

in 54 BC

Frontiers, 53 BC

**THE EMPIRE OF PONTUS UNDER
MITHRADATES EUPATOR, 120–110 BC** [4]

Frontiers, 121 BC

to Pontus temporarily, 129 BC – 120 BC

Added to Pontus in 110 BC

Other areas added to Pontus under Mithradates VI

Olbia
Bastarnae
Tyras
D A C I A
Sarmizegethusa
Celtic peoples
Getae
Istrus
Tomi
Callatis
Illyrians
Odessus
Mesembria
Apollonia
Thracians
BLACK SEA

BOSPORAN KINGDOM
Panticapaeum
Heraclea
Chersonesus
GREEK CITIES
BLACK SEA
Sinope
Trapezus
Colchis
GREEK CITIES
BITHYNIA
PONTUS
Amaseia
Zela
ARMENIA
ROMAN EMPIRE
Galatia
Phrygia
CAPPADOCIA
PARTHIAN EMPIRE
KIBYRA
PISIDIA
COMMAGENE
RHODES
LYCIA
SELEUCID EMPIRE

Gaul
(*Roman conquest in progress*)
Vienna
Mediolanum
Gallia Ulterior
Aquileia
DACIA
(*in expansion*)
Tolosa
Gallia Ulterior
MASSILIA
Gallia Citerior
Verona
Genua
Salamantica
Hispania Ulterior
Salduba
Toletum
Tarraco
Dertosa
Hispania Citerior
Valentia
Palma
Ariminum
Salonae
Narona
Pisae
Falerio
Rome
Dyrrachium
Stobi
Thessalonica
Felicitas Julia
Corduba
Hispalis
Carteia
Carthago Nova
Caralis
Beneventum
Puteoli
Neapolis
Tarentum
Brundisium
Buthrotum
Alexandria Tr
Demetrias
Nicopolis
Patrae
Corinth
Athens
Sparta
Panormus
Catana
Syracuse
Carthage
MAURETANIA
N U M I D I A
MEDITERRANEAN SEA
Illyricum

ROME : THE FIRST TRIUMVIRATE, 55 BC 3

— Frontiers, 55 BC

Assigned to:

Caesar

Pompey

Crassus

Other Roman territory

The Dacian Kingdom of Burebista, c. 80-44 BC

1 The Dacian kingdom founded by the great war-leader Burebista lay north of the lower Danube in modern Romania. The peoples of this region had come under considerable pressure from the Celts during the 4th century BC, but by the beginning of the 1st century BC the Dacians, together with their eastern relatives the Getes, had re-established themselves as the major power in this region.

Unification came only with the rise to power of Burebista around 80 BC. He forged the Getes and Dacians into a single kingdom, with a new civil and religious capital at Sarmizegethusa in Transylvania, and embarked on a series of expansionist wars, beginning with the Celtic Scordisci. The defeated Scordisci then became allies of Burebista in his westward drive against other Celtic peoples. Dacian forces struck deep into central Europe, and in 60 BC they defeated the Boii, a Celtic people who gave their name to modern Bohemia.

Burebista also conquered the Greek cities of the Black Sea coast, but was careful to avoid confrontation with the Romans. Nonetheless, Julius Caesar viewed the Dacian kingdom as a danger, and made plans to attack it. It was saved by his assassination in 44 BC, and the death of Burebista in the same year. With the loss of its founder, the kingdom of Dacia disintegrated once again into warring tribes and factions.

Gaul: The Roman Conquest, c. 58-53 BC

2 Julius Caesar was a rising star of the Roman political world when he was appointed provincial governor of northern Italy and southern France in 59 BC. Not content to remain within the boundaries of his province, he immediately embarked on an ambitious campaign of conquest. At first, he posed as an ally of various Gallic peoples, aiding them in their struggles against their neighbours or against foreign aggressors, but he soon decided to conquer the whole country. He even made two celebrated forays across the Channel to Britain. The kingdoms of central Gaul were fairly easily defeated, but the warlike Belgae of the northeast put up a fierce struggle, and on more than one occasion came close to inflicting a serious defeat on the Roman legions. Six years of dogged campaigning yielded results, however, and by the winter of 53 BC Gaul was at last in Roman hands. Gallic resistance ended the following year with the siege of Alesia and the defeat of the war-leader Vercingetorix.

Rome: the First Triumvirate, 55 BC

3 The First Triumvirate was an accord reached between the three leading men at Rome, who effectively stripped the senate of its power and divided the most important Roman provinces between them. The cause was growing tension and confrontation between the senators and a series of powerful military commanders. Pompey had suppressed Mediterranean piracy, finished off the war against Mithradates of Pontus, and imposed a general political settlement on the Near East, but could not get the senate to grant land to his legionaries nor ratify his eastern settlement. Julius Caesar was standing for consul, only to find the senate changing the rules and refusing the provincial governorship which always followed. Crassus, the wealthiest man at Rome, desired a prestigious military command for himself.

By bribery. and force, these three men overruled the senate to achieve their aims. In 60 BC Caesar was appointed governor of the two Gauls and Illyricum, while Pompey received the land-grant and treaty ratification he required. In 55 BC Crassus became governor of Syria, Pompey became governor of the two Spanish provinces, and Caesar's command was extended for a further five years. Crassus was captured and killed by the Parthians at Carrhae in 53 BC, but the accord between Pompey and Caesar lasted a further two years, and was only ended definitively when Caesar led his legions across the Rubicon and embarked on a civil war against Pompey and the senate in 49 BC.

The Empire of Pontus under Mithradates Eupator, 120-110 BC

4 Mithrades VI "Eupator", king of Pontus, was the last great independent monarch to oppose Roman ambitions in Asia Minor. His kingdom consisted of hill country and fertile plains on the southern shore of the Black Sea, with the former Greek colony of Sinope as its capital. Mithradates was only 12 years old when his father was murdered in 120 BC, and it was not until 112 BC that he was able to seize control in a palace coup. He soon expanded his power to the eastern end of the Black Sea, and in 110-107 BC he came to the rescue of the Greek cities of the Crimea, who were being threatened by Scythians and Sarmatians: so effectively, indeed, that he ended up controlling this region also. Mithradates' next move was to the east, conquering territory which included Colchis. He attempted to take the territory the Romans had granted to his father in 129 BC, but taken back to themselves on Mithradates' accession. He then installed his son as king of Cappadocia and married his daughter to the king of Armenia. During his campaigns he invaded much of Asia Minor and even Greece.

The Romans sought more than once to contain Mithradates' ambitions by threats and diplomacy, but it took three hard-fought wars (88-85 BC, 83-82 BC and 74-66 BC) to bring him finally to heel. Mithradates himself committed suicide in 66 BC, a sad ending to a spectacular career.

31 BC

The Triumph of Rome

The famous statue, which until recently stood on the summit of the Capitol in Rome, shows the Emperor Marcus Aurelius, who died in AD 180, victoriously horsed, baton in hand. No image of command has ever been so influential or so often copied for portraits of other rulers. It expresses the triumphant serenity of the Roman Empire at its height, spreading its peace through strength over an unprecedented swathe of the Western world. Yet the reign of Marcus Aurelius (AD 161-80) has also been traditionally regarded as the high point of Roman achievement, after which decline set in, punctuated only by lower peaks of recoveries.

Even after a long period of rarely interrupted success for Roman arms and Roman methods of control of subject-peoples, the empire bequeathed by Marcus Aurelius was not much bigger than that founded by the first emperor, Augustus, in 27 BC. True, Britain had been invaded by Claudius in AD 43 and by 160 was under Roman control as far as the Forth-Solway isthmus, and Dacia had been conquered by Trajan between 101 and 106. But many of the gains since Augustus's death had the nature of frontier adjustments: between the Rhine and the Danube; in North Africa (where Mauretania was annexed in AD 42) and on the eastern frontier. Augustus had established not only boundaries of surprising sustainability but also a remarkably enduring system of government. He founded an hereditary monarchy without offending the republican traditions of the Roman elite, using republican rhetoric to justify his personal power. Even so, the idea of an autocratic magistracy became compromised by associations with monarchical traditions. The power of the traditional republican institutions – the senate and the elective magistracies – was progressively weakened or by-passed. The imperial system had some advantages: unified command, strong leadership and popular appeal. But it carried with it a potentially fatal disadvantage: there was no enforceable method of ordaining the succession, and the army effectively usurped a constitutional role in making and unmaking emperors. No means was ever devised of forestalling the consequent dangers of fragmentation and civil war.

By the time of Marcus Aurelius two further dangers could be discerned. First, Christianity was making new converts and penetrating ever higher levels of society. From the perspective of most of the traditional elite, this was a development incompatible with the survival of the state, since – to the pious – Rome's greatness was at the disposal of the gods, while – to the practical – Roman political unity depended on adherence to the state religion and worship of the divine Emperor. Second, the subject peoples within the Empire and the barbarians on its borders were growing increasingly covetous of the status of Roman citizenship and the wealth of the Roman world. Already in AD 167, Marcus Aurelius had had to fight a three-year campaign to restore the Danubian frontier after a German horde invaded the Empire and besieged Aquileia.

Marcus Aurelius himself anticipated two ways in which the empire was to cope with these pressures. First, he embraced stoicism as his personal philosophy. He was a patron and practitioner of the culture, based on stoicism, in which Christians and pagans became reconciled and which made it possible in the long run for Christianity to replace the old religion at an official level. Second, he sensed the need to divide the unwieldy responsibilities of governing the vast empire, admitting his adoptive brother, Lucius Verus, to the rank of co-emperor in what was to be a recurrent formula for saving the state from crisis.

Roman dependencies

10°   20°   30°   40°   50°   60°

60°

50°

F i n n o - U g r i a n s

BALTIC
SEA

Baltic peoples

Volga

Oder
Elbe
Vistula

S l a v s

50°

Dnieper

Don

Volga

Dniester

I r a n i a n   p e o p l e s

Castra Regina
Augusta
Vindelicum   *Danube*   Vindobona
Lauriacum   Carnuntum
Aquincum
Teurnia   Virunum   Savaria
Aquileia
atavium
Verona   Siscia
Sirmium
Ariminum
Arretium   **A   N**
Salonae
Narona
Rome   Corfinium
Doclea
Dyrrachium   Stobi
Neapolis   Brundisium
Tarentum   Thessalonica
Beroea
E   **M**   Perinthus   Byzantium
Demetrias   Prusa
Nicopolis   Alexandria Troas
Pergamum   **P**
Patrae   Sardis
Panormus   Smyrna
Sicily   Corinth   Athens
Catana   Sparta
Syracuse   Halicarnassus
Malta   Rhodus
SEA
Crete   Gortyn

Porolissum
Potaissa
Dacia
Sarmizegethusa

Oescus   Durostorum   Tomi
Danube
Naissus
Serdica
Trimontium

BOSPORAN
KINGDOM
Panticapaeum

Chersonesus

Caucasian peoples

BLACK SEA

Sinope
Amisus   Trapezus
Heraclea Pontica
Amaseia
Nicopolis

ARMENIA

Ancyra
Dorylaeum
Caesarea
Melitene

Antiochia   **R**   Iconium
E

Tarsus
Attaleia   Side   Antioch
Apamea
Cyprus   Salamis   Palmyra
Tigris
Euphrates

PARTHIAN
EMPIRE

A r a b s

40°

37

The Expansion of the Roman Empire, 31 BC - AD 180

1 Too many battles have been called "decisive" but Octavian's victory at Actium (see page 32) certainly helped to re-shape the Roman Empire. The "imperial" provinces, which he governed directly, included eastern territories such as Egypt and Galatia (annexed in 25 BC); but his commitment to expansion on the northern frontier helped to make the empire more "western" than would have been the case had Antony triumphed, with his power-base and ambitions in the east.

Augustus – as Octavian was known after he became Emperor – added Cantabria (17 BC), Noricum and Raetia (15 BC), Illyricum and Pannonia (AD 10) to the Empire, planned the conquest of Britain and initiated those of Bohemia and Germany as far as the Elbe (9 BC). The need for military cuts and the demands of internal security forced the most ambitious of these plans to be aborted, and the conquests beyond the Elbe were abandoned. By the end of his reign, the empire had, on most fronts, attained its manageable limits. Apart from the conquest of Britain (see map 2, below), the acquisition of Mauretania in AD 42 and the annexation of Thrace in AD 45, the most important adjustment during the 1st century AD was made in the critical space between the upper Rhine and the sources of the Danube where the awkwardly shaped frontier could be shortened only by the laborious incor-poration of heavily forested uplands. It was an arduous undertaking, not completed until the campaign of Domitian in AD 83.

The start of the new century, coinciding with an era of unprecedented prosperity and the accession of the aggressive and ambitious Emperor Trajan, initiated a brief period of further conquests. Victory over the Dacians in AD 107 stimulated Trajan's appetite and liberated resources for an assault on what was perceived as the great-est security problem of the time: the power of Parthia in the east. A new province of Arabia was created on the fringes of the Syrian desert, and in AD 114 Trajan's armies invaded Armenia and Meso-potamia, advancing as far south as the Persian Gulf. These gains could not be held, however, and Mesopotamia was already lost when Trajan died in 117.

Britain: The Roman Conquest, AD 43-185

2 The conquest of Britain, though hard to justify on grounds of military secu-rity or economic interest, became a dynastic obligation for Caesar's heirs. Repeatedly announced and deferred by Augustus, it was at last undertaken in AD 43 by Claudius (AD 41-54), who saw a chance of easy laurels. The rapid submission of the southeast was decep-tive – procured by co-operation with local elites who already had close relations with Gaul, and who saw opportunities to profit as clients of Rome. Beyond the Humber native resistance proved much more stubborn. In the last quarter of the century, however, a new Roman governor, Agricola, inaugurated a decisive policy. He believed that to secure existing conquests, the whole island had to be subjugated regardless of cost, together with the offshore bastion of Anglesey and, if necessary, Ireland as well.

The effects of this policy were short-lived in the north of Britain. In AD 80, Agricola was recalled, the conquest of Scotland was halted and his remoter con-quests were gradually abandoned, perhaps in the belief that the far north of Britain was too thinly populated to pose a serious threat to imperial security. If so, these expectations were misleading. Hadrian drew a frontier line from Tyne to Solway in 122 with the building of a wall, but by 142 the Romans had once again advanced to the Clyde and a second defence, the Antonine Wall, was built. This heavily fortified zone absorbed a garrison of at least 10,000 men. The history of the Roman frontier in Britain illustrates a problem of the Empire as a whole: there was no rational limit to expansion and frontier security was expensive.

The Roman Empire: Administrative Divisions, AD 180

3 The expansion of Roman rule under Augustus and his successors had made necessary administrative arrange-ments for the new provinces. In the far west, Hispania, the first conquest outside Italy, had been divided by Augustus into three provinces whose configurations reflected the heavy Roman colonisation of the southwestern regions of the peninsula in his day. The division of Gaul into six provinces was also the work of Augustus, but here he seems to have been guided more by geography and the boundaries of the pre-Roman native states.

Despite its remoteness and its active military frontier, Britain remained a single province from the start of the conquest, per-haps reflecting its relatively superficial Romanisation. Italy had been re-modelled as early as the time of Caesar, who extend-ed Roman citizenship to the inhabitants of the former "Cisalpine Gaul" between the Rubicon and the Alps. On its western edge, the mountainous terrain favoured the retention of small units, which became provinces in AD 64-5. Caesar wanted to incorporate Sicily into Italy, but it was left a separate province by his heirs. Sardinia and Corsica were constituted as a province under senatorial rule by Nero (AD 54-68), then retrieved for the direct rule of the emperor under Vespasian (AD 79-81).

Raetia, conquered in AD 39, always retained a marchland character, contrasting with neighbouring Noricum which was very accessible to Romanisation. Both these, together with Pannonia, Dalmatia and Moesia Superior, were carved out of the vast province of Illyricum after Augustus's death. Broadly speaking, the border of Noricum and Pannonia represented an eth-nic frontier between Celtic peoples to the west and a predominantly Illyrian popula-tion to the east. Beyond Illyricum again lay the anomalous Dacian province – a kingdom on the north bank of the Danube annexed by Trajan – and the provinces of "Greek Europe", where, except in Moesia, Greek and Thracian peoples predominated and where Roman rule and colonisation did not displace Greek language and culture.

AD 180

BRITAIN: THE ROMAN CONQUEST, AD 43-185 **2**

- Conquered by Rome by AD 43
- Conquered by Rome by AD 80
- Temporary Roman conquest by AD 80
- Reconquered by Rome by AD 142
- —— Northern frontier of the Roman Empire by AD 185

THE EXPANSION OF THE ROMAN EMPIRE, 31 BC - AD 180 **1**

- The Roman Empire, 31 BC

Added to Rome:
- by AD 14 (with dates)
- by AD 98 (with dates)
- by AD 117 (with dates)
- by AD 180 (with dates)
- Temporary conquests (with dates)
- —— Frontiers, 180

395

The Decline of Rome

The empire bequeathed by Marcus Aurelius in AD 180 was recognisably the same state as that created by Augustus some two centuries before. After the lapse of two more centuries it had been transformed into "the triumph of barbarism and Christianity". The key changes had been the extension of Roman citizenship to all inhabitants of the Empire in 212 and the entry of Christians into the highest ranks of the ruling class – including, after the conversion of the Emperor Constantine, traditionally dated to 312, the Imperial throne itself. The rise of the Church from persecution to predominance was completed in 395, when the Emperor Theodosius proclaimed Christianity the official religion of the empire and reduced pagan traditions to the underprivileged status formerly imposed on Christians. The imperial elite was becoming more diversified: Christian bishops became servants of the state; the old ruling class was displaced by a new meritocracy; barbarian technicians were increasingly appointed to military commands; and the senatorial aristocracy began, especially in Italy, Gaul and Asia Minor, to withdraw from civic life and political responsibility and retire to the management of their estates.

On the borders of the empire – especially those with Germanic peoples – the pressure from barbarians for admittance to the empire, not just as mercenaries but as permanent settlers, grew ever more intense. The vast length of the frontiers could not be policed effectively and the trickle of immigrant communities could not be completely staunched. Raids *en masse* were almost as hard to cope with for the over-stretched imperial authorities. Those of the mid-3rd century, which devastated much of Gaul and penetrated Italy, coincided with internal political crisis (*see* map 1, page 43) and almost dissolved the empire.

Not until the late 4th century, however, did the struggle to exclude mass migrations of barbarians become hopeless. The Visigoths were the first people to be admitted *en bloc*. In about 275, when the Romans abandoned trans-Danubian Dacia, the Visigoths were settled in the vacated territory. After border trouble in the 320s they were granted federate (allied) status but by the late 360s relations had greatly deteriorated. Even so, long experience of life as the Romans' neighbours had profoundly influenced Visigothic culture: they had been converted to Christianity, although to Arianism, a heretical form. In 376 a Hun invasion obliged them to beg the Romans for refuge, and a reputed 200,000 were allowed over the Danube. But they were then left to starve, provoking a terrible revenge which culminated in the Visigoths' victory over the Romans at Adrianople in 378 and destroyed the Roman reputation for invincibility.

Henceforth, the empire could not guarantee to manage the barbarian war-bands whom it was forced to admit in increasing numbers. In Roman relations with other barbarian groups too, there were periods of tense collaboration; but from 395 to 418 the Visigoths undertook a destructive migration across the empire, terrorising the areas they traversed. Yet the Visigoths and other Germanic peoples did not come simply to destroy: they wished to share in the wealth and security of Rome. As the Roman armies came increasingly to depend on Germanic recruits and commanders, the difference between Roman and non-Roman diminished, especially in the west. After Theodosius' death in 395, when land was divided between his sons Honorius (west) and Arcadius (east), the Roman territories were never again ruled by a single emperor. In the decades which followed, the western provinces fell progressively under German control.

F i n n o - U g r i a n s

T e u t o n i c

BALTIC
SEA

Baltic peoples

Volga

Elbe
Oder
Vistula

p e o p l e s

S l a v s

Dnieper

Dniester

Volga

H u n s

A l a n s

Don

Panticapaeum

Caucasian
peoples

tra Regina
Augusta
Vindelicum
Lauriacum
Danube
Vindobona
Carnuntum
Teurnia
Virunum
Savaria
Aquincum
Aquileia
atavium
Siscia
Verona
Sirmium

D a c i a

Chersonesus

B L A C K   S E A

Pisae
retium
Ariminum
Salonae
Narona
Doclea
Naissus
Serdica
Oescus
Durostorum
Tomi
Danube

Sinope
Amisus
Trapezus

Rome
Corfinium
M P I R E
Philippopolis
Adrianople
Perinthus
Constantinople
Heraclea Pontica
Amaseia
Nicopolis

E A S T E R N   R O M A N

Amancyra

Dyrrachium
Stobi
Thessalonica
Prusa

Neapolis
Brundisium
Beroea
Alexandria Troas
Dorylaeum

Tarentum

Caesarea
Melitene

Demetrias
Pergamum
Antiochia
Iconium

PERSIA

Nicopolis
Smyrna
Sardis

(SASANIAN

Panormus
Patrae
Corinth
Athens
Halicarnassus
Attaleia
Side
Tarsus
Antioch
EMPIRE)

Sicily
Catana
Sparta
Rhodus
Apamea
Palmyra

Syracuse

Malta
S E A
Crete
Gortyn
Cyprus
Salamis

GHASSANIDS
LAKHMIDS

THE REORGANISATION OF THE ROMAN EMPIRE BY DIOCLETIAN, 284-305 2

- - - - - Borders of Dioceses

———— Frontiers, 305

Towns shown were seats of co-emperors

Map 2 (upper):

Barbarians

Britanniae

ATLANTIC OCEAN

Barbarians

Treveri

Galliae

Illyricum
Pannoniae

Mediolanum

Sirmium

BLACK SEA

ROMAN

Hispaniae

Italia

Thraciae

Nicomedia

ARMENIA

Pontus

Thessalonica

Moesiae

E M P I R E

Asiana

MEDITERRANEAN SEA

Africa

Oriens

Barbarians

Barbarians

Inset map 3 (right):

Celtic pe

ATLANTIC OCEAN

Lucus Augusti

Scallabis

R

Gades

THE ROMAN EMPIRE UNDER CONSTANTINE, 324-37 3

Praefectura Gallia

Praefectura Italia

Praefectura Illyricum

Praefectura Oriens

- - - - - Borders of Dioceses

———— Frontiers, 337

Towns shown were seats of Praefecti Praetorio

Map 3 (lower):

Barbarians

Britanniae

ATLANTIC OCEAN

Treveri

Galliae

Barbarians

Septem Provinciae

Italia
Annonaria

Illyricum
(Pannoniae)

ROMAN

Mediolanum

Sirmium

BLACK SEA

Hispaniae

Italia
(Suburbicaria)

Dacia

Byzantium
(Constantinople)

ARMENIA

Thraciae

A N

Macedonia

E M

Pontus

PERSIA
(SASANIAN
EMPIRE)

MEDITERRANEAN SEA

Asiana

P I R E

Oriens

Africa

Aegyptus

Barbarians

Barbarians

Postumus's Secessionist Empire in the West, 259-74

1 In the mid-3rd century the Roman Empire endured its worst crisis yet. In 251 the Emperor Decius was slain by the Goths. In 260 Valerian was captured and humiliated by the Persians. His son, Gallienus, was confronted by a near-fatal combination: mutinous armies and invading barbarians. "Thirty tyrants" – in reality, 18 contenders for the purple – competed to usurp his throne. Empire-wide authority was effectively unenforceable and the state seemed about to dissolve into defensible regional networks of self-help.

The most promising of these was the "Gallic empire" which lasted for nearly 20 years after the election of the general Postumus on the Rhine frontier in 259 in a typical proclamation of the time, following a dispute over booty. He defeated Frankish and Alemannic raiders in Gaul and called himself "the saviour of the provinces". He was killed in a mutiny in 268, and his territories were reconquered from his successors by Aurelian in the 270s. Yet his experiment seemed to offer a glimpse of a workable future: the adherence of neighbouring provinces briefly pre-figured future administrative divisions; and his capital at Augusta Treverorum (Trier) became one of the centres of autonomous government under a the devolved system established by Diocletian (*see* below).

The Reorganisation of the Roman Empire by Diocletian, 284-305

2 The anarchy and invasions of the third quarter of the 3rd century were checked by the energy and generalship of Aurelian (270-5), but the next six emperors all ruled briefly and died violently. Diocletian, proclaimed emperor at Nicomedia in 284, was able to exploit reactions against instability. During the first 10 years of his reign he devised a new system for governing the Empire as a union of four effectively autonomous imperial territories.

In theory, the four Emperors formed a college under Diocletian's presidency but in practice each ruled his own area. In the west, Maximian's title of Augustus gave him direct rule over Italy and Spain; his subordinate "Caesar", Constantius, ruled Britain and Gaul. Diocletian was pre-eminent in the rest of the Empire, and his "Caesar", Galerius, shunted between marchland-areas of special responsibility in Illyricum and on the Persian front. Their capitals were close to theatres of frontier warfare but consciously rivalled Rome: Lactantius complained of Diocletian's "mania" for making his residence at Nicomedia the equal of Rome. By the force of Diocletian's personality and of their common interest in preventing rebellion, the four emperors remained loyal colleagues. In 305, Diocletian and Maximian were able to take the unprecedented step of "retiring" from imperial office, though the outcome was not entirely peaceful.

Diocletian continued and accelerated the tradition of "slicing" provinces into ever-smaller units: there were perhaps about 50 at the start of his reign and he seems roughly to have doubled their number. This made taxation, administration and jurisdiction more thorough but multiplied bureaucracy – especially when a layer of supervision was added to the provincial structure in the form of 13 "dioceses", groups of governorships overseen by imperial "vicars". Perhaps the most far-reaching aspect of his reforms was in personnel: the traditional senatorial elite was passed over in favour of a new "aristocracy of service", intended to be directly dependent on imperial patronage.

The Roman Empire under Constantine, 324-37

3 Constantine formalised the division of the Empire into eastern and western halves by founding a "second Rome" at Constantinople, where he resided, and devolving western government to his sons. In effect, by the 330s, his system resembled the system devised by Diocletian, with one "Caesar" ruling the "Prefecture" of Gaul, another Italy and two others commanding on the eastern fronts. He also continued the diocesan structure, splitting Moesia into two: Dacia (formerly the name of a province on the north bank of the Danube); and Macedonia. From his time onward, not only was the seat of the emperor transferred to the east, the centre of gravity of the empire as a whole shifted in the same direction. The last great imperial monument of Rome – the basilica of Maximian in the Forum – dates from just before his time; the Arch of Constantine, though impressive, is a second-rate construction, employing a lot of recycled reliefs. Constantine was the first Christian emperor and though Christianity was not definitively established as the official religion of the state until 395 AD, his patronage ensured its irreversible ascent.

The Black Sea: the Ostrogothic Empire in the 4th Century

3 The origin of the peoples collectively known in antiquity as the Goths has often been conjectured but never demonstrated. They were reputed to have crossed the Baltic from a Scandinavian homeland during the 1st century AD, in the time of Tacitus and Pliny. The Visigoths separated from the rest, perhaps because they baulked at crossing the Pripet marshes. The division known as the Ostrogoths pressed on to the Black Sea by the end of the 2nd century AD and founded an "empire" bounded by the Sea of Azov, the Black Sea and the lower Don. Though war bands split off and invaded the Roman world, the Ostrogothic state remained intact until it was destroyed by Hunnic invaders from the east on its vulnerable steppeland flank in 376, in the reign of King Ermanarich. After a series of bloody defeats, the Ostrogothic army was forced over the Dniester into the territory of the Visigoths who, unable to oppose the Huns, were forced to seek refuge in the Roman empire. The Ostrogoths remained in this area until their conquest of Italy in the 6th century (*see* map 2, page 51)

POSTUMUS'S SECESSIONIST EMPIRE IN THE WEST, 259-74 **1**

Empire of Postumus, 261

Recovered by the Roman Empire, 268-70

Retaken from Postumus's successors by the Roman Empire, 274

Frontiers, 274

THE BLACK SEA: THE OSTROGOTHIC EMPIRE IN THE 4TH CENTURY **4**

Approximate extent of the Ostrogothic Empire under Ermanarich, c.370

Frontiers, 370

395

The Barbarian Settlements

Between 370 and 470, there was a steady build-up of Hunnic power on the fringes of Roman territory. Despite its brevity, this had profound consequences for the subsequent development of western Europe. Notwithstanding their ferocity in battle and their reputation for enduring cold, hunger and thirst "from the cradle", as the Roman historian Ammianus Marcellinus said, the Huns could not pose a serious threat to the Roman Empire nor construct a large state of their own while their primitive, pastoral economy rendered political integration impossible and united military action impracticable.

By the early 5th century, however, infusions of booty and fiscal exactions from subject-peoples were transforming the economic base of Hunnic society. The conquest of the Ostrogoths in 376 presupposed an unprecedented concentration of force. The Goths were permitted to cross the Danube and settle in Thrace. In 378 they inflicted a resounding defeat on the Emperor Valens, on the plains outside Adrianople. The Huns' advances forced other barbarian groups deeper into Roman territory, most notably in the winters of 395 and 405-6, when the Vandals, Sueves and Alans crossed the Rhine. These advances led indirectly to the creation of the barbarian kingdoms in Gaul, Italy, Spain and North Africa.

By about 420 a Hunnic confederacy was in being, which was further enriched in tribute, booty and land by supplying mercenaries to Rome and extorting "protection money". Under the rule of Attila, from the mid-430s, this system came under intolerable strain as the Huns' ambitions were fed by success and by the revenues of an empire which stretched from the Baltic to the Black Sea and the Caspian. In 445 Attila murdered his elder brother and co-ruler, Bleda. In 447, needing a continuous intake of plunder to sustain his warriors, he attacked the Eastern Roman Empire, at a time when an unusual combination of natural disasters – plague, famine and earthquakes – sapped resistance. In 451 he launched a similar attack on the Western Empire, on the unconvincing pretext that he intended to discipline the Visigoths on the Empire's behalf. Though severely beaten in Gaul on the Catalaunian Plains, by the united resistance of Romans and barbarians, he turned on Italy in 452. He seems to have fancied himself as the puppet-master of the whole Roman world, but the Empire was spared by his sudden death before the start of the campaign season of 453. Divided among his sons, the Hunnic state lasted only a dozen more years before being torn apart by internecine strife and swept aside by other Asiatic nomad-hordes.

Meanwhile, with the foundation of barbarian kingdoms within the territory of the Western Roman Empire, Europe was beginning to take on the configurations it was to display in medieval and modern times. The barbarians were often given the notional status of "federates" or allied peoples, but in practice came to rule over the areas in which they settled. Thus the Visigoths dominated southwestern France and the Sueves controlled the western half of the Iberian peninsula before being marginalized by the Visigoths in the early 6th century. North Africa, save for its westernmost reaches, was overrun by the Vandals early in the 5th century. In the late 5th century, the Ostrogoths settled in Italy. Gradually a series of effectively sovereign kingdoms took shape. The various elements of the cultural heritage of Europe were assembled when the Germanic traditions of these groups were fused with the Graeco-Roman and Judaeo-Christian legacies which formed the civilisation of 4th-century Rome.

10°   20°   30°   40°   50°   60°

F i n n o - U g r i a n s

onic peoples

Volga

BALTIC
SEA

60°

50°

Oder

Elbe

Vistula

Don

grippina

Volga

Dnieper

Dniester

H u n n i c   p e o p l e s

a Regina

Augusta
Vindelicum

Danube

Vindobona
Carnuntum

Lauriacum

Aquincum

Teurnia   Virunum   Savaria

Aquileia

tavium

Verona

Siscia

Sirmium

Panticapaeum

Chersonesus

BLACK   SEA

Lazi

isae   Ariminum

Durostorum

Oescus

Tomi

AN EMPIRE   Salonae

Danube

Narona

Naissus

Sinope

Rome   Corfinium

Doclea

Serdica

Amisus   Trapezus

Philippopolis

Heraclea Pontica

Dyrrachium

Adrianople

Perinthus

Amaseia

Stobi

Byzantium

Nicopolis

Neapolis

Brundisium

Beroea

Thessalonica

E A S T E R N   R O M A N   E M P I R E

Ancyra

PERSIA

Tarentum

Prusa

Dorylaeum

Caesarea

Melitene

Alexandria Troas

Demetrias

Pergamum

Antiochia

Iconium

(SASANIAN

Nicopolis

Smyrna   Sardis

Tarsus

Panormus

Patrae

Athens

Antioch

EMPIRE)

Sicily   Catana

Corinth

Halicarnassus

Attaleia   Side

Apamea

Syracuse

Sparta

Rhodus

Cyprus   Salamis

Palmyra

Malta   SEA

Crete

Gortyn

GHASSANIDS

LAKHMIDS

45

BRITAIN: ANGLO-SAXON SETTLEMENT, 350-450

2

- Supposed Anglo-Saxon homelands
- Approximate extent of Anglo-Saxon settlement by 450
- Roman territory, c.350
- Frontiers, 395

THE WESTERN ROMAN EMPIRE: BARBARIAN PENETRATION, 395-476

3

- Frontiers, 395
- Official Roman withdrawal, 410
- Kingdoms established by Teutonic federates and the Vandals in the Western Roman Empire by 431
- Regions settled by other federates in the Western Roman Empire, 450
- Given up by the Romans to the Huns by 446
- Other Western Roman territories occupied by Teutonic peoples by 476
- Western Roman Empire, 476

THE ROMAN EMPIRE: LOSSES, 180-450

- Given up in c.185
- Given up in the 3rd century (with dates)
- Loosely held area abandoned by 3rd century
- Held temporarily in the 3rd century (with dates)
- Official Roman withdrawal, 410
- Lost to the Empire of the Huns by 446
- Frontiers, 450

Map labels:

Map 2 (Britain Anglo-Saxon): NORTH SEA, Celtic peoples, Eburacum, Lindum, Viroconium, Angles, Glevum, Londinium, Saxons, Jutes, Isca, Domnoniorum, Jutes, Teutonic peoples, Novomagus, Colonia Agrippina, WESTERN ROMAN EMPIRE

Map 3 (large map): NORTH SEA, Eburacum, Celtic peoples, Glevum, Londinium, Anglo-Saxons, Franks, Colonia Ag, Rotomagus, (Soissons), Augusta Treverorum, (We, Lutetia, Civitas Aurelianorum, Aventicu, Portus Namnetum, Lugdunum, Kingdom of the Visigoths, Burdigala, Burgundians, Medio, Augu, Taur, Tolosa (Toulouse), Massilia, Lucas Augusti, Kingdom of the Sueves, Pompaelo, Toletum, Tarraco, WESTERN ROMA, Felicitas Julia, Valentia, Palma, Cara, Corduba, MEDITE, Carthago Nova, Gades, Caesarea, Tingis, Kingdo of the Vanda, Berbers

Map (bottom left): Celts, NORTH SEA, Eburacum, Britain, Teutonic peoples, Glevum, Londinium, Colonia Agrippina, Augusta Treverorum, Agri Decumates, (260), ATLANTIC OCEAN, Lutetia, Hunnic peoples, (271) Dacia (c.215-271), Pannonia, Burdigala, Verona, WESTERN, Genua, Salonae, Byzantium, Tolosa, ROMAN EMPIRE, EASTERN, Rome, ROMAN EMPIRE, Ceasaraugusta, Neapolis, Toletum, Brundisium, Valentia, Corduba, Athens, Carthago Nova, MEDITERRANEAN SEA, Syracuse

The Roman Empire: Losses, 180-450

1 The Western Roman Empire survived by adapting in the course of the 3rd, 4th and 5th centuries. The most striking examples are the extension of citizenship to former subject peoples in 212 and the domestication of Christianity– a potentially subversive religion which was converted to the service of the state. The leadership of the government itself was taken over by the barbarians, though much of Roman life and administration was only slowly transformed.

The defence of the vast frontier, employing limited resources in the face of ever-greater barbarian pressure, proved an impossible task. In 271 the exposed province of Dacia across the Danube was abandoned, and by the early 5th century Britain had, in effect, been left to defend itself. Barbarian pressure on the frontier increased in the late 4th century, when Gothic war-bands forced their way into the empire and proved difficult to control. Many Germanic groups, moreover, were established as "federates" with the function of military protection. A process of adaptation and assimilation got underway with a consequent gradual transformation of the Roman world. The Huns' own intrusion in imperial territory was short-lived, albeit proverbially destructive, although the loss to them of Pannonia in 446 proved permanent. Also, the effects of the many less spectacular invasions they helped to cause were long-enduring and included the fragmentation of the unity of the Roman Empire among numerous "sub-Roman" states and barbarian kingdoms within the frontiers.

Britain: Anglo-Saxon Settlement, 350-450

2 Writing *The History of the English Church and People* in the early 8th century, Bede divided the Germanic invaders of Britain into Angles, Saxons and Jutes. But though institutional peculiarities in medieval Kent have been ascribed to Jutish origins, the differences between these groups are conjectural and the validity of Bede's classifications are open to doubt. Evidence of localised Germanic communities scattered over a wide area by the mid-4th century suggests that the first settlements were of mercenaries imported with imperial connivance. Frankish mercenaries were employed in Gaul as early as 350, and the process of troops becoming settlers was probably similar in Britain.

In the early 5th century, the Emperor Honorius withdrew the last legions from Britain. The numbers of barbarian newcomers increased and their relations with the native authorities, who bore both Roman and Celtic names, is a matter for conjecture, though the outcome was the assertion of Anglo-Saxon dominance in eastern parts of Britain. The traditional date of the "Adventus Saxonum" ("arrival of the Saxons") is 449: this can perhaps be taken as the approximate starting-point for their establishment of kingdoms of their own in Britain, in which the fate of the British is unclear, though the assimilation process appears to have been thorough.

The Western Roman Empire: Barbarian Penetration, 395-476

3 With hindsight, the Roman empire in the west can be seen to have come to an end with the foundation of Germanic kingdoms inside the Roman frontier in the 5th century. At the time, this appeared by no means clear. Most of the Germanic kingdoms were founded by relatively small war bands, accommodated within the empire as uneasy allies, entrusted with tasks of imperial defence, quartered in rural garrisons at the expense of their host-communities and only gradually taking over the cities and usurping or accepting authority over the non-Germanic populations. The Empire had successfully absorbed non-Roman peoples at intervals in the past, and the Germanic settlers were all, in varying degrees, susceptible to Romanisation and their kings, in most cases, were prepared to show some measure of deference to imperial institutions.

Yet increasing territorial loss sapped Roman revenues, manpower resources and the will to resist. In 413 the Emperor Honorius had to reduce the taxation levels for southern Italy to one-fifth of their former level. As part of this movement, the Sueves (and Alans) invaded Spain and were only confined to the western part of the peninsula by the Roman employment of Visigothic troops. The Visigoths afterwards settled in Aquitaine and founded the Kingdom of Toulouse there in 418. Under Euric (466-84), the Visigoths greatly extended their kingdom to cover a large area of southern France. Their regime co-operated with the Gallo-Roman population, both in the administration of the region and in their participation in imperial politics by supporting candidates from southern France for the imperial throne.

The Vandals, who had followed the Sueves into Spain, crossed into Africa in 429, and in 439 captured Carthage. In 442 the imperial government recognised their possession of the richest provinces in Africa, leaving the Roman inhabitants under Vandal rule, which the Catholics among them, at least, deeply resented.

The Burgundians founded a kingdom around the city of Worms in about 410, but were settled in Savoy by the Roman Commander Aetius after Worms had been destroyed by the Huns in 437. On the whole they were allied to the Romans, but in the 460s they extended their territory by seizing Lugdunum (Lyons), which became their capital.

In northern Gaul, imperial authority was eroded by the gradual expansion of the Franks from their bases in the old Roman province of Belgica. Around 462 the general Aegidius withdrew recognition from the Emperor and he and his successors Paul and Syagrius governed an independent Roman enclave around Soissons. The Franks under Childeric seem to have co-operated with the Roman leaders there, although this stance was to be reversed under Childeric's son Clovis (*see* map 4, page 51), who eventually assumed control of the whole of northern Gaul.

450

The Barbarian West

Although the period from 450 to 526 saw the formal dissolution of the Western Roman Empire into various successor kingdoms under Germanic kings, in fact much of the fabric and structure of Roman life and provincial organisation remained and was even deliberately maintained and adapted by the Germanic rulers. From the mid-5th century there had been a succession of puppet emperors in the West, with real power in the hands of the *magister militum*, the leader of the Roman army, often, as in the case of Stilicho, Ricimer or Odoacer, a barbarian. After 476, when Odoacer overthrew the Emperor Romulus Augustulus, the Roman Senate sent a message to the Eastern Emperor Zeno informing him that there was no further need for a separate ruler in the West, though an eastern candidate, Julius Nepos, retreated to Dalmatia and held the title until 480.

The other provinces of the Western Roman Empire – Gaul, Spain and North Africa – had become gradually dissociated from the central government in Italy during the 5th century and military governors played an increasingly dominant role. Thus for much of the century the principal authority in Gaul had been the Roman military commander Aetius, and after 461 administrative links between Gaul and Italy no longer existed. The local populations reached their own *modus vivendi* with the barbarian groups who had originally been settled among them as military federates. In many cases, although the barbarian leaders emerged as the rulers, they were staunchly assisted by the Roman administrative classes, both civilian and ecclesiastical.

The Germanic kingdoms of Western Europe which emerged during the late 5th and the 6th centuries were the heirs of Rome in every sense. The evidence points to integration and adaptation in varying degrees, with much that was Roman – in government, law, administration, social organisation, religion and intellectual culture – maintained and even promoted under barbarian rule. Huneric (477-484), King of the Vandals, married the sister of the Roman Emperor Valentinian. Theodoric, the Ostrogothic king, had his daughter Amalsuintha taught both Greek and Latin. Carthage continued to expand under the Vandals, with King Thrasamund in particular initiating a number of new buildings on Roman models. Yet as the concerns of the barbarian successor kingdoms became increasingly regional and the Eastern Roman Empire became preoccupied with defending its eastern borders against the Sasanian rulers of Persia, trading and diplomatic links diminished.

The Christian church became a factor to be reckoned with in the political formation of Western Europe in the 5th century, not only in such missionary endeavours as St Patrick's in Ireland, but in collaboration between the church and the new Germanic rulers in Gaul and Spain. In Italy by the 540s, the bishops increasingly became powerful political leaders. The Papacy, too, began to emerge as a power, at least in Rome itself.

Of the development of much of the rest of Europe in the period, especially that of Scandinavia and the Slav regions, little is known. Britain was gradually being settled by groups of Angles, Saxons and possibly Jutes from northern Europe, though their penetration was limited and knowledge of their relations with the Romano-British population, as well as the nature of their social and political organisation, remains elusive. It is possible, too, that Frankish links with the southeast of England may have been quite strong.

F i n n o -

U g r i a n s

Volga

Northmen

(Scandinavians)

BALTIC
SEA

Baltic peoples

S l a v s

Dnieper

Dniester

T u r k i c   p e o p l e s

Volga

Don

Oder

Vistula

Elbe

Thuringians
Thuringians

KINGDOM

Lombards

KINGDOM

OF THE GEPIDS

Danube

Danube

Chersonesus

Alans

LAZICA

B L A C K   S E A

anum
Verona

Bononia

tia

Iadera

OF THE

Dalmatia

Spalatum

Naissus

Odessus

Trapezus

Perusia

Serdica

Philippopolis

Rome

OSTROGOTHS

Adrianople

Constantinople

E A S T E R N   R O M A N   E M P I R E

PERSIA

Tigris

Naples

Barium

Salonica

Tarentum

(SASANIAN

Smyrna

EMPIRE)

Euphrates

anormus

Sicily

Messana

Patras

Athens

Malta

S E A

Cyprus

Crete

GHASSANIDS

LAKHMIDS

3

Celts

Anglo-Saxons

London
KENT

SALIAN
FRANKISH
KDM.

Cologne

RIPUARIAN
FRANKISH
KDM.

Trier

Teutonic peoples

Rugians

KINGDOM OF THE GEPIDS

Celts
(Bretons)

LAND OF
SYAGRIUS

Paris

Nantes

Tours

Orléans

Savaria

ATLANTIC

OCEAN

Limoges

Bordeaux

KINGDOM
OF
BURGUNDY

KINGDOM
OF
ODOACER

Virunum

Aquileia

Emona

Mediolanum

Verona

Sirmium

Ostrogoths

LAND OF EMPEROR NEPOS

Brittan
(497)

Ravenna

Dalmatia

Salonae

KINGDOM OF THE VISIGOTHS

Toulouse

Narbo

Provence

Nice

Marseille

Cantabrians
Basques

EAST ROMAN
EMPIRE

Cantabrians
B

KINGDOM

OF THE

SUEVES

Caesaraugusta

Salamantica

Barcino

Rome

Tarentum

Tarraco

Toletum

Valentia

Emerita
Augusta

Cordoba

KINGDOM

Lilybaeum

MEDITERRANEAN
OF THE

Sicily

SEA

Hispalis

Gades

Carthago Nova

Caesarea

Hippo Regius

Carthage

VANDALS

Berbers

1

THE WESTERN MEDITERRANEAN: THE VISIGOTH AND VANDAL KINGDOMS, 419-555

The Visigoths

- Approximate extent of the Visigothic Kingdom from 418
- Added by 475
- Held temporarily 477-500
- Lost in 507
- The Visigothic Kingdom from 555

The Vandals

- Secured by the Vandals by 431
- Added in 439
- Added by c.460
- ——— Frontiers, 526
- Dates indicate Visigothic losses

2

ITALY AND THE ADRIATIC: THE OSTROGOTHIC KINGDOM, 453-526

- ——— The Ostrogothic Kingdom, 453-74
- Approximate extent of the Ostrogothic kingdom, 474-88
- The Ostrogothic kingdom from 493
- Areas under loose Ostrogothic control
- Added, 494
- Added, 508
- ——— Frontiers, 526

KINGDOM
OF
BURGUNDY

Vouillé

Limoges

FRANKISH KINGDOM

Kingdom
of
Toulouse

Bordeaux

(531)

Toulouse

Septimania

Provence

Nice

Narbo

Marseille

KINGDOM

OF THE

OSTROGOTHS

Cantabrians Basques

KINGDOM
OF THE
SUEVES

Caesaraugusta

Barcino

Tarraco

Rome

KINGDOM OF THE
VISIGOTHS

Toletum

Valentia

KINGDOM

Caralis

Hispalis

Cordoba

(554)

Carthago Nova

OF THE

Lilybaeum

Caesarea

Hippo Regius

Carthage

VANDALS

Berbers

FRANKISH KINGDOM

Ba

KINGDOM
OF
BURGUNDY

Viru

Aquilei

Mediolanum

Verona

Augusta
Taurinorum

KIN

Provincia

Ravenna

OF T

Marseille

Nice

Florentia

OSTRO

Rome

KINGDOM

Na

OF THE

OSTRO

VANDALS

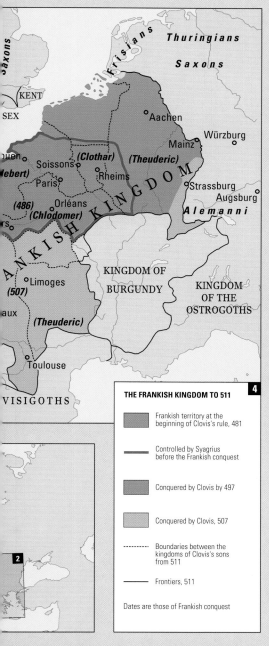

THE FRANKISH KINGDOM TO 511

4

- Frankish territory at the beginning of Clovis's rule, 481
- Controlled by Syagrius before the Frankish conquest
- Conquered by Clovis by 497
- Conquered by Clovis, 507
- Boundaries between the kingdoms of Clovis's sons from 511
- Frontiers, 511

Dates are those of Frankish conquest

The Western Mediterranean: the Visigoth and Vandal Kingdoms 419-555

1 After their employment by the Romans to defeat the Sueves in Spain (*see* map 3, below), the barbarian Visigoths were settled in Aquitaine as a Roman allied army from 418. Gradually they came to rule over a defined area, the Kingdom of Toulouse. A pattern of Roman provincial administration was retained, with many senatorial aristocrats playing a major role in establishing the kingdom and working for the Visigothic rulers in running their government.

The Visigoths invaded Spain in 454, driving the Sueves, who had dominated the Iberian peninsula since 430, into the northwest. The Visigothic conquest of Spain was consolidated under Euric (466-84). In France, they expanded their control to the Mediterranean between 462-3, the Auvergne was ceded to them in 475 (by the Eastern Emperor) and Provence in 476 (by the barbarian ruler of Italy, Odoacer). In 507, however, the Visigoths suffered a crushing defeat by the Franks at Vouillé. The Franks then pushed the Visigoths out of most of Gaul except Septimania.

In 429 the Vandals crossed from Spain, to North Africa. They gained Mauretania and Numidia by treaty in 431, and took Carthage in 439. Although the Romans for a time retained a hold on the western regions, the Vandals by 442 occupied all the richest areas of North Africa and maintained their kingdom there until 534. The Vandal rulers, who, like the Visigoths, subscribed to Arianism, a heretical form of Christianity, conducted an allegedly vicious campaign of persecution against the Catholic church, but left Roman provincial life otherwise mostly undisturbed.

Italy and the Adriatic: the Ostrogothic Kingdom, 453-526

2 In 489, Theodoric the Ostrogoth and his people entered Italy. His initial arrival in 489 appears to have been a consequence of the Eastern Emperor again trying to intervene in western affairs by sending a ruler to replace Odoacer (*see* map 3). After four years of warfare, Odoacer was treacherously murdered at Ravenna. Theodoric then ruled Italy peacefully until 526. His precise constitutional position in Italy remained uncertain, however, though he styled himself "King of the Goths and Romans". In 497 the Emperor Anastasius conceded Theodoric's status as ruler of Italy. Like Odoacer before him, Theodoric appears to have worked from within the Roman system. He had high ideals of government, insisting on the rule of law, with Gothic law prevailing for Goths and Roman law for Romans. He was assisted in his administration by many aristocratic Romans, notably the scholar Boethius, and elevated many new men, such as Cassiodorus, to high office. Although himself an Arian Christian, Theodoric appears to have been tolerant of the Catholic church. Under Theodoric, many magnificent buildings were erected, especially in Ravenna. He established marriage ties with the Germanic rulers of Aquitaine, northern Gaul, Burgundy and North Africa. He was the effective ruler in Septimania and Provence from 508 to 521.

Southwest Europe at the Overthrow of the Last Western Emperor, 476

3 To view 476 as the "collapse" of the Empire in the west is a retrospective view. At the time, and in the context of the rapid succession of no fewer than 19 emperors in the west between 394 and 476, many of whom were the candidates of rival factions who held the throne for a very short time, the deposition of the teenage Emperor Romulus Augustulus by Odoacer would have seemed like yet another coup and temporary vacancy. Romulus was proclaimed emperor by his father Orestes in October 475 and thus "ruled" for only 10 months. The empire, moreover, had already suffered a series of reverses and territorial losses, so that by 476 the whole of the Iberian peninsula was ruled by the Sueves and Visigoths, and in Gaul the largest Roman-controlled area, that governed by Syagrius, did not acknowledge the authority of the Emperor.

Odoacer in fact maintained peace and stability in Italy between 476 and 493. He ruled from Ravenna, retained Roman administrative structures and personnel and rewarded many of the Roman senatorial families for their support. Although the 6th-century Greek historian Procopius says Odoacer "ceded his right" to Provence to Euric, ruler of the Visigoths, and a North African chronicler recorded the cession of Sicily to Gaiseric, king of the Vandals, Odoacer also made some attempts to expand his territory, conquering Dalmatia after the murder of the imperial claimant Julius Nepos in 480 and possibly conducting a campaign against the Rugians.

The Frankish Kingdom to 511

4 Clovis had ruled as king of the Franks from 481, gradually expanding the territories over which he ruled. In a contest for power in northern Gaul he had defeated the Roman Syagrius in 486. He ruthlessly eliminated his Frankish rivals, pushed the Visigoths out of southern Gaul in 507 and achieved a victory in battle against another barbarian group, the Alemans, between 486 and 508. Clovis's baptism as a Catholic has added a religious flavour to these campaigns for some historians. On the death of Clovis in 511, his hard-won kingdom was divided among his four surviving sons – Theuderic I, Chlodomer, Childebert I and Chlothar I. Each brother was given a portion providing equal revenues and in accord with current political circumstances. Each brother based himself in one of the old Roman centres within his territory: Childebert I at Paris, Chlodomer at Orléans, Chlothar I at Soissons and Theuderic I at Rheims. Control of the former Visigothic kingdom of Aquitaine, which was conquered after the battle of Vouillé in 507 (*see* map 1, above), was insecure and it is not clear how the area was divided among the brothers. The kingdom of Burgundy, meanwhile, retained its independence until 534.

526

The Frankish Kingdom

The first half of the 6th century saw the emergence of a strong Frankish kingdom in Gaul, ruled over by the Merovingian dynasty, and a Visigothic kingdom in Spain. In both of these much of the old Roman way of life survived. The roads, buildings, centres of population, and social institutions remained little altered at first, though in Gaul at least urban life appears to have been little favoured by the Franks. Latin remained the prevailing language throughout the former Western Empire, at least for religion, learning and the law. Its strength can be measured by the fact that with the exception of Britain, the tongues of the countries that were once within the Western Roman Empire are "Romance" languages descended from Latin. The incoming Franks, Visigoths, Ostrogoths, Sueves, and Burgundians adopted the language and mores, the institutions and culture of the peoples among whom they settled while the Roman Empire still flourished. They continued to use Latin as their principal language for communication, centuries after the Empire became simply a memory and an ideal. Latin was given new life after the introduction of Christianity to the Germanic and Slavic areas.

Although as a result of the reconquests of the Byzantine Emperor Justinian (*see* map 2, page 55), the Eastern Roman Empire's dominion was ostensibly restored across the whole of the Mediterranean, in practice each region was left to its own devices. The new political leaders, notably in Gaul and Spain, drew on what remained, or on what they wanted and seemed appropriate, from their Roman heritage and forged new political entities. In this they were undoubtedly assisted by many members of the Roman upper class families in these regions, who thereby maintained their social position, and no doubt their wealth. A notable feature of the period was the degree to which the Christian clergy, and especially the bishops, assumed positions of social and political responsibility.

These developments were not so marked in the eastern Mediterranean, where the Byzantine emperor was in any case pre-occupied with the attacks of the Persians. This was one reason, indeed, why Justinian failed to consolidate the western conquest with the resources and manpower needed for lasting success. Nevertheless, Persian success was limited to an area around the Black Sea. Internally, many reforms were instituted in the Eastern Empire. There were severe internal tensions which culminated in the Nika riots of 532 and which were exacerbated by the plague which wiped out a large portion of the population of Constantinople in 542. But Justinian was an administrative genius. His tax reforms and the wholesale reorganization of existing Roman law (Code and Digest of Justinian) as well as his own legislation (Novels) were a lasting legacy to Europe, though in the west the principal sources of Roman law until the 11th century remained the earlier Code of Theodosius and the Breviary of Alaric. The establishment of a silk monopoly in Constantinople boosted the economy.

Events in far off Mongolia and Asia among the Turks also impinged on Europe for they drove groups of steppe peoples, later to be known as the Avars, towards the west; they ferociously attacked the areas now known as the Ukraine and Bessarabia and established themselves on the lower Danube. In the far west, groups of Irishmen or Scoti established the kingdom of Dal Riada in what later became known as Scotland. The Scoti and the Picts clashed with the people of North Britain and the incoming Anglo-Saxons, as they pressed farther into Britain.

Finnic peoples

Northmen

(Scandinavians)

BALTIC
SEA

Baltic peoples

Slavs

Volga

Hungarians

Ugrians

Don

Dnieper

Volga

Turkic peoples

ingians

Elbe

Oder

Vistula

ast
nks

avarians

Danube

Dniester

KINGDOM
OF THE
LOMBARDS

KINGDOM
OF THE GEPIDS

Alans

Verona

Bononia

Iadera

Spalatum

Perusia

Rome

Naissus

Serdica

Danube

Odessus

Chersonesus

BLACK SEA

Trapezus

PERSIA

Philippopolis

Naples

Barium

Tarentum

Salonica

Adrianople

Constantinople

NTINE EMPIRE

ERN ROMAN EMPIRE)

(SASANIAN

EMPIRE)

Tigris

normus

Sicily

Messana

Patras

Athens

Smyrna

Euphrates

SEA

Malta

Crete

Cyprus

GHASSANIDS

LAKHMIDS

JUSTINIAN'S RECONQUESTS, 527-65 2

- The Byzantine Empire, 527
- Added 533-5
- Added by 554
- Ruled by the Gepids, 539-51
- Frontiers, 565

BRITAIN: THE ORIGINS OF THE ANGLO-SAXON KINGDOMS 3

- Approximate extent of Anglo-Saxon states established by c.530
- Other Anglo Saxon states created by the end of the 6th century

FRANKISH EXPANSION TO 561 1

- Frankish territory, 511
- Added 531/2
- Added by 534
- Added by 537
- Frontiers, 561

THE PARTITION OF THE FRANKISH KINGDOM, 561

4

Area inherited by:

Chilperich

Charibert

Guntram

Sigibert

——— Frontiers, 565

Frankish Expansion to 561

1 With the death of Clovis in 511, his sons embarked on a ferocious expansion of Frankish territory. The Burgundian kingdom under Gundobad and Sigismund had been perhaps the strongest political presence in Gaul at the end of the 5th and in the early 6th century. In 523, however, Sigismund was murdered by the Frankish King Chlodomer (he later became the object of a saint's cult) and in 534 the Franks conquered the Burgundian kingdom. They gained Provence from the beleaguered Ostrogoths in 537, and consolidated their control of Gascony and the Auvergne.

The Franks, under the Merovingian dynasty, exercised influence over Brittany rather than direct rule. To the east they exercised at least nominal control over Alemannia (present day German- and French-speaking Switzerland) and to the north of Gaul as far as Utrecht, though in practice day-to-day administration may well have been left largely to the local inhabitants. For the time being, Bavaria retained its independence from the Merovingian rulers under the Agilolfing dukes, themselves, however, generally believed to be of Frankish origin.

In the Frankish areas, Roman administrative structures and institutions remain in evidence, most obviously in the organization of the church whose bishops were closely involved with secular government and whose dioceses were based on the old Roman *civitates*.

Justinian's Reconquests, 527-565

2 The Eastern Emperor Justinian embarked on a campaign of reconquest of the former Western Roman Empire in the second quarter of the 6th century, skillfully supported by propaganda from Constantinople which stressed the need to rescue the West from the barbarians and identified 476 as a crucial turning point.

Justinian seized on the excuse of internal political disputes in the west to intervene. In the short term the campaigns were a brilliant success. His military commander, Belisarius, conquered the Vandal kingdom of North Africa in 533. In Italy, Belisarius's initial campaign of 534 was followed up by a grim war of attrition under the general Narses until the last garrison of the Goths under their king Totila had fallen in 552. The Byzantines also occupied Cartagena and the southeast coast of Spain in 551.

Yet the irony of the reconquests was that much of the old Roman system in the areas "reconquered" appears to have been swept away in the course of the wars. It is from this period that archaeological evidence yields layers of destruction rather than from the earlier period of the so-called "barbarian invasions". Nor did the Byzantine reconquests last long. After fierce campaigns the Visigoths drove out the Byzantines in 624, while in Italy the arrival of the Lombards after 568 reduced Byzantine territory in Italy to the northeast portion around Ravenna and the southern tip of Italy. Similarly, North Africa was lost to the Arabs by 700.

Britain: the Origins of the Anglo-Saxon Kingdoms

3 The tentative consolidation of various Anglian and Saxon tribal units to form territorial kingdoms was underway in the course of the 6th century, though political balances remained indeterminate and boundaries exceedingly ill-defined. Our information about the origins of Anglo-Saxon kingdoms largely stems from Bede, an early 8th-century source, who was writing at a time when there were indeed coherent kingdoms and when it may have been difficult to imagine a time when this was not the case. Still later, political writers and historians constructed genealogies of their kings in an effort to impose political structure onto a distant past.

Similarly, the later 7th-century kingdoms of the Northumbrians, the West Saxons, the men of Kent, the south Saxons, the east Saxons and the Mercians, the Hwicce, the Magonsaete, the east Angles, the middle Angles and others were reduced to seven (Wessex, Sussex, Essex, Kent, Mercia, East Anglia and Northumbria) in the 12th century and in the 16th century misleadingly entitled the "Heptarchy", thus distorting our understanding of the essential fluidity and diversity of the many early English kingdoms and implying a level of political coherence which did not exist at this early stage.

The institution of kingship itself, as well as the kingdoms, can only really be clearly discerned in the 7th century and, indeed, may not have been a form of social organization that the Angles and Saxons brought with them from north Germany and Denmark. Whatever the case, in the 7th century royal power began to be exercised over territories on which kings imposed fiscal and military obligations. In the 6th century, however, only the faintest glimmer of what were to become in due course the English kingdoms described by Bede can be made out.

The Partition of the Frankish Kingdom, 561

4 In 561 the grandsons of Clovis took over the kingdoms created in 511 (*see* map 4, page 51). Charibert I ruled from Paris, Guntram from Orléans, Chilperic from Soissons and Sigibert I from Rheims. Aquitaine and Burgundy were included in the partition, however, and in due course, especially after the further partitions of 567, the deaths of brothers without heirs meant the emergence of the three main political territories north and east of the Loire. These were to remain the principal focus of Frankish political activity for the next two centuries: Neustria in the west, Austrasia to the east, and Burgundy.

565

732

The Arab Advance

At the end of the 6th century, the Emperor Maurice of Byzantium assisted the Persian ruler Chosroes II to regain his throne, in return for which Byzantium was ceded Armenia and territory east of the Black Sea. But the days of Persian and Byzantine dominance of the eastern Mediterranean and Middle East were numbered. In 622 Mohammed fled from Mecca to Medina where he proclaimed the true religion devoted to one God, Allah, and Islam, submission to Allah's will. By Mohammed's death in 632 his teaching was widely accepted in Arabia and the Arabs then set out to spread the true religion. From 634 the Arabs embarked on a spectacularly successful and aggressive war of conquest, overrunning the Holy Land (Palestine) in 636, Mesopotamia in 637, Syria and Egypt in 640 and as far as the River Oxus in Central Asia by 651. The extent of the Byzantine Empire was thus drastically diminished while the Persian Empire was almost totally extinguished. However, though the Arabs went on to break the power of the Khazars, conquer Tashkent and push as far east as the province of Sind (modern Pakistan), they failed to conquer Constantinople itself or the Byzantine territories of Asia Minor.

Meanwhile, Byzantium's links with the western Mediterranean were significantly reduced, notably in Italy, with ties of respect and dependence increasingly weakened. The Imperial troops in Ravenna, Byzantium's foothold in northern Italy, rallied to the support of Pope Sergius (687-701) in his conflict with the Byzantine emperor, while Gregory III (731-41) was the last Pope to obtain the Byzantine mandate before his consecration as Pope.

The Arabs also moved westwards, capturing Carthage in 698 and converting the Berbers of the interior to Islam. Muslim troops had reached Tangier by 708 and, reinforced by Berbers, they crossed over to Spain in 711 under the leadership of Tariq ibn Ziyad, a Berber chief. The Visigoths fought bravely under their king Roderick, after a frantic march from the north of the kingdom to meet the invader, but Roderick was killed. Tariq took Cordova and Toledo. Mérida fell to Musa ibn Nusayr, Tariq's superior, in 713. By 716 virtually the whole peninsula, except for the Pyrenees and the northern region of the Asturias was under Muslim rule. Now known as El Andalus, the peninsula was ruled from Cordova by governors appointed by the governor of Qayrawan or his superior, the emir of Egypt. Raids into the Frankish Kingdom were conducted under the leadership of Abd al'Rahman but were definitively repelled by Charles Martel at the Battle of Poitiers in 732.

Since 567 the Franks had gone from strength to strength, consolidating their power under such rulers as Chlothar II, who reunited the realm in 613, and Dagobert I, while various Merovingian queens, such as Brunhild and Balthild, also played a conspicuously influential rule as adept politicians. They enjoyed a military strength which was admired and feared by their neighbours. But by the end of the 7th century control of the kingdom was slipping into the hands of the leading court officials, the "mayors of the palace" and other aristocrats in Neustria and Austrasia. Control of cross-Channel trade and the economy was also largely in the hands of the Frisians. The civil wars of the early 8th century, however, enabled the Carolingian mayor of the palace, Charles Martel, to seize power and start the steady process of winning back the areas that had once been under Merovingian control.

Finnic   peoples

Northmen   Bulgarians

(Scandinavians)   Hungarians

BALTIC
SEA

Baltic peoples

Volga

Oder   KHAZAR KINGDOM

Elbe   Vistula   Volga

S   l   a   v   s

Don

Dnieper   Sarkel

Ratisbon   Dnlester

Danube

BAVARIA

Salzburg   AVAR KINGDOM

Verona Venice   Chersonesus   BLACK SEA   LAZICA   Tiflis

Ravenna   S   Trapezus

Bologna   Iadera   l   BULGARIA

Spalatum   a   Danube   Pliska

Nish   v   Varna

rusia   Serdika   s   Philippopolis

Rome   Vlachs   Adrianople   Constantinople

Naples   Barium

Tarentum   Salonica   Tigris

Z   Mosul

A   B Y Z A N T I N E   E M P I R E

normus   Smyrna   Euphrates

N   Sicily Messana   Patrae   Athens

T   Malta   SEA   UMAYYAD

Cyprus   CALIPHATE

Crete   Damascus

57

THE AVARS, 590-791

- Northern frontier of the Byzantine Empire to 567
- Avar possessions secured by c.590
- Lost by Avars by 598
- Approximate extent of Samo's Slav state, 623-58
- Lost by Avars, 630
- Lost by Avars, 680
- Approximate extent of Avar territories, 680-791
- Frontiers, 732

ITALY IN THE AGE OF THE LOMBARDS, 590-732

- Early kingdom of the Lombards, evacuated 568
- Secured from Byzantine Empire by Lombards by 590
- Byzantine territory conquered by Lombards and ceded to the Franks, 575
- Byzantine territory conquered by Lombards by 605
- Other 7th-century Lombard conquests from the Byzantines (with dates)
- 8th-century Lombard conquests from the Byzantines (with dates)
- Bavarian territory conquered by Lombards (with date)
- Byzantine Empire, 732
- Frontiers, 732

ENGLAND IN 600

- Anglo-Saxon kingdoms
- Celtic states
- Frontiers, 600

SPAIN: THE VISIGOTHIC KINGDOM AND THE MUSLIM CONQUEST, 565-732

- Kingdom of the Visigoths, 565
- Added in the 6th century (with dates)
- Added in the 7th century (with dates)
- Western limit of the Byzantine Empire, 565
- Byzantine possessions, 732
- Northern limit of Muslim conquest, 732
- Frontiers, 565

Spain: The Visigothic Kingdom and the Muslim Conquest, 565-732

1 In 589 the formal conversion of King Reccared and all the Visigoths from Arianism to Catholicism made the Catholic Hispano-Roman bishops their allies. Thereafter the Christian kings of Spain, whose authority was said to be bestowed by God, worked closely with the church to form a coherent and powerful ideology of kingship. This was reinforced by the firm basis which Reccared's predecessor Leovigild (569-86) had established for Visigothic royal power. In a series of campaigns, he subdued Cantabria, and in 586 conquered the Suevic kingdom and deposed the last king, Audeca. He also recaptured Corduba, which had been in revolt against the Visigothic kings since around 550. Leovigild, too, issued a law code, and introduced new regal styles and new coinage.

Under Sisebut (d. 621) campaigns were mounted against the Basques, and against the Byzantines, who had occupied a strip of southeastern Spain since the Emperor Justinian's expedition of 551 (*see* map 2, page 55), and who were finally expelled in 624. In the 7th century much anti-Jewish legislation was promulgated as well as the *Forum Iudicum*, a territorial law code which marked the thorough integration of Goths and Romans in the peninsula. Spain was nevertheless characterized by strong regional loyalties; internal dissension may well have contributed to the success of the Arab conquest in 711.

In that year Tariq ibn Ziyad crossed from Africa and routed and killed Roderick the Visigothic king. The Arab forces soon took Corduba, Toledo and Merida, and by 716 they had taken virtually the entire peninsula. They then destroyed the vestigial Visigothic kingdom which was based on Narbonne, and began raids into the territories of the Franks. A Visigothic remnant clung on in the northeast and began to forge the Christian kingdoms of Asturias, Leon, Pamplona and the County of Aragon, which in due course were to form the bases for the launching of the long centuries of the Reconquista, the Christian reconquest of Spain.

The Avars, 590-791

2 Almost nothing precise is known of the Avars in this period, save that they were a confederation of steppe peoples from inner Asia, whose base was situated near present-day Belgrade. There is, however, archaeological evidence of weapons in graves, suggesting that the Avars remained formidable well into the 8th century. Occasional references in written sources indicate a vast territory under their control, aggressive expansion and enormous wealth. Among their military triumphs were the eviction of the Gepids and Lombards from the Danube region in the 6th century and a major assault upon Constantinople in 626. Their rule came to an end in 791, when the Franks destroyed their massive military fortifications, the "Avar Ring".

Italy in the Age of the Lombards, 590-732

3 The Lombards settled in Pannonia (modern-day Hungary) in the early 6th century and first entered Italy as mercenaries in the pay of the Emperor Justinian's general Narses. In the aftermath of the Gothic wars (*see* map 2, page 55), Alboin and his armies re-entered the Po valley in 568-69, leaving dukes to govern from the major cities. Pavia was captured in 572 and by 571 the Lombards were forming duchies along the Italian peninsula in Spoleto and Benevento. Their kingship was essentially elective. King Rothari issued a law code in 643. Other kings, notably Liutprand (d. 742) directed their energies to expanding Lombard territory, presenting an aggressive front to the Byzantine exarchate of Ravenna and to Rome and the popes. The exarchate, although a local and to some degree isolated political entity comprising a local landed aristocracy of military officers, remained within the Byzantine orbit until its conquest by the Lombards in the mid-8th century. As well as consolidating their own secular power within the "Republic of St Peter" (*see* map 2, page 63), the popes had to contend with jurisdictional disputes with Byzantium over southern Italy and Illyricum as well as Lombard aggression. The Frankish kingdoms and the new missionary areas of England and Germany represented a further sphere in which they could begin to exert a spiritual influence.

England in 600

4 By 600 some of the English kingdoms, notably Kent, East Anglia, Mercia and Northumbria (made up of Deira and Bernicia), became a little better defined. In 597 Augustine, sent by Pope Gregory I from Rome, arrived in Kent and converted King Aethelbert (d. 616) and his people to Christianity. Aethelbert was married to a Christian Frankish princess who had been permitted to have her own chaplain. The marriage may be one indication of Merovingian Frankish hegemony in southeast England in this early period.

More is known of the other kingdoms from the early 7th century, especially about their reactions to Christianity. Raedwald (d. *c.*625) of the East Angles, who may be the king buried in the spectacular ship-burial at Sutton Hoo and was also almost certainly in contact with the Merovingian Franks, maintained both a Christian and a pagan altar. His son Sigibert (a Frankish name) fled into political exile in Francia and was there converted to Christianity. Aethelfrith of Bernicia (d.616 or 617) was a mighty warrior who defeated the Scots of Dal Riata at Degestan and the men of Powys at Chester, but it was his successor Edwin (d. 633 or 634) who was converted to Christianity.

732

The Death of Charlemagne

On his death in 814 the Frankish ruler Charlemagne left a vast territory, comprising most of Europe west of the Elbe and north of the Pyrenees. Many peoples had been brought under Frankish rule during his reign, and with law and religion as his principal tools and weapons, Charlemagne had forged a strong polity, with methods of government and principles of rulership, as well as many common elements of culture, which were to endure throughout the Middle Ages.

Charlemagne was fortunate in the pioneering work of his father, for it was Pippin III, king from 751 to 768, who had begun to forge a distinctive relationship with the Frankish church, and who had given the clergy a key place in the administration of the kingdom. He had also begun to develop effective instruments of government, including control of the coinage. The acquisition of the title of Emperor in 800 did little to affect Charlemagne's style of rulership or his actual power. For the most part he was an itinerant ruler, travelling the length and breadth of his empire to reinforce his authority with his presence, though towards the end of his reign he based himself principally at his new palace at Aachen. An immensely cultured man, Charlemagne promoted education and rewarded scholars throughout his realm, with the view of creating both a strong Church and an efficient network of administration based on the rule of law and written records. His surviving legislation is replete with his instructions on all matters, secular and ecclesiastical, within his kingdom. He was in touch with rulers as far afield as Cordova, Constantinople and Baghdad. Yet there were movements elsewhere in Europe which indicated new development ahead. Trade in the North Sea region was well established, with ports established on both sides of the English Channel at Hamwic, Ipswich, Quentovic and Dorestad, as well as in the Baltic at such places as Birka.

The late 8th century saw the beginnings of Viking raids in Europe. The Vikings were Scandinavian-based seafarers who had reached the Shetlands in about 790; subsequently, their first raid on England was the sack of the island monastery of Lindisfarne in 793. Charlemagne himself began to organise coastal defences against them.

In the Arab world, while the Umayyad emir Abd al'Rahman and his descendants ruled in Spain from 756, at the other end of the Mediterranean the Abbasids held sway in the Middle East well into the 9th century, though a diminution of their power was becoming evident, while the Arabs were active as a maritime power for the first time throughout the Mediterranean. The northern Christian kingdoms of Spain began their first efforts to push back the Arabs, with a gradual coalescence of the political divisions of the north into the kingdoms of the Asturias (León from the 10th century), Pamplona and the County of Barcelona, all of which fostered links with the Franks in different degrees. As a result of campaigns in the Septimanian region, the Franks secured the county formed by Vich, Cardona and Caseras and between 800 and 813 captured Barcelona, Tortosa and Pamplona. This marcher region was incorporated into the Frankish Kingdom.

Byzantium also began to acquire new territory, mounting successful campaigns in Thrace at the end of the 8th century, and subsequently in the early 9th century, in the Greek peninsular under Nicephorus I against the Slavs, who had overrun it since the 6th century, but meeting too formidable an enemy in the Bulgars led by Khan Krum (802-14).

Kaupang

DENMARK

BALTIC
SEA

...en
...edeby
...nburg
Bremen

...furt

Scandinavians

Finnic peoples

Baltic peoples

Slavs

Oder

Vistula

Elbe

Danube

Salzburg

Volga

Bulgar

VOLGA BULGARIA

Hungarians

KHAZAR KINGDOM

Don

Volga

Sarkel

Dnieper

Dniester

50°

...PIRE

Venice
...n Verona
Bologna
...ce
Iadera
Spalatum
Perugia
Rome

PAPAL STATE

PRINCIPALITY OF BENEVENTO

Naples
Barium
Tarentum

...ANTINE

...Panormus

Messana

Malta

SEA

Slavs

Vlachs

BULGARIA

Danube

Nish

Sredets

Philippopolis

Adrianople

Salonica

Patrae

Athens

Pliska
Varna

Cherson

CONSTANTINOPLE

Smyrna

Crete

Cyprus

Nicosia

BLACK SEA

LAZICA

Tiflis

Trapezus

EMPIRE

Tigris

Mosul

Euphrates

Damascus

ABBASIDS

Ugrians

60°

50°

40°

ITALY: THE DEVELOPMENT OF THE PAPAL STATE FROM 756

2

Patrimonium Petri to 756

Acquired in 756

Acquired in theory by 757

Acquired in theory by 774

Acquired in theory by 781

Acquired in theory by 787

Acquired in theory by 789

—— Frontiers, 814

DENMARK

BALTIC SEA

IRISH KDMS

NORTHUMBRIA

WELSH STATES

MERCIA

WEST WALES

WESSEX

NORTH SEA

F r i s i a (734)

Saxony (772/98)

(789)

S l a v s

(lost 695, reconquered 722/804)

Aachen

Mainz

Würzburg

Rouen

Soissons

Rheims

Metz

A l e m a n n i a

Strassburg

Ratisbon

(direct rule from 744)

B a v a r i a
(lost late 7th century, reconquered 728; direct rule from 788)

Salzburg

(805/6)

Brittany
(lost c.630 reconquered 786/99)

Nantes

Tours

Loire

Seine

Paris

Orléans

Dijon

Danube

Steinamanger

Pannonia (796)

Mosapurc

BULGARIA

F R A N K I S H   E M P I R E

Geneva

Carinthia (788)

(799)

BAY OF BISCAY

Limoges

Clermont

Bordeaux

Lyons

(575)

Milan

Verona

Turin

Lombardy (774)

Genoa

S l a v s

D a l m a t i a

B Y Z A N T I N E   E M P I R E

Aquitaine
(lost c.670 reconquered 768)

Toulouse

Rhône

(575)

Nice

Bologna

Florence

PAPAL

ASTURIAS

Roncesvalles

S p a n i s h   M a r c h

Septimania (759)

Marseille

GULF OF LIONS

Corsica

Perugia

STATE

Spoleto

(774)

(795)

(812)

Barcelona

Rome

DUCHY OF BENEVENTO (787/9)

Barium

Tarentum

EMIRATE OF CORDOVA

Sardinia

B Y Z A N T I N E   E M P I R E

Balearics

1

THE GROWTH OF THE FRANKISH EMPIRE TO THE DEATH OF CHARLEMAGNE, 814

Frankish territory, 565

Added before the accession of Charlemagne in 768 (with dates)

Temporary Frankish possession (754-98)

Added by Charlemagne (with dates)

Brought into dependency by Charlemagne (with dates)

—— Frontiers, 814

3

ENGLAND: THE SUPREMACY OF MERCIA, 625-796

Mercia in c. 625

Mercian dependency from 777

Added by the end of Offa's rule, 796

—— Frontiers, 796

The Growth of the Frankish Empire to the Death of Charlemagne, 814

1 When Charles Martel died in 741, he divided the Merovingian kingdom between his sons Carloman and Pippin III. Although he still only occupied the position of "mayor of the palace", he had ruled without a king for the last four years of his life. Carloman and Pippin had to deal with revolts against Carolingian attempts to enforce their authority in Aquitaine, Alemannia, Alsace, Bavaria and Saxony.

Carloman's abdication in 745 to become a monk left the field free for Pippin, who deposed the last Merovingian king Childeric III in 751 and had himself crowned king, with the Frankish clergy adding a new element to the king-making ritual, namely, anointing. Pippin conquered Aquitaine between 759 and 768; he quelled the attempts of the Etichonid dukes of Alsace to assert their independence, and led campaigns against Brittany (in 753) and Burgundy (in 761) as well as a successful foray into the Lombard kingdom to protect the pope's interests.

Pippin III divided the kingdom in his turn between his sons Carloman and Charlemagne. A great military leader, the latter, left as sole ruler after 771, waged war energetically for the next 30 years, greatly expanding the borders of his realm. He confirmed the acquisition of Aquitaine and handed it on to his son Louis as a subkingdom in 781. He conquered the Lombard kingdom of Italy in 774. Charlemagne then led an expedition into Spain, which was defeated on the way home at Roncesvalles in 778, an episode immortalised in the *Song of Roland*. Bavaria was annexed in 788, and the power of the Avars destroyed between 791 and 793. Charlemagne waged war against the Lombard Duchy of Benevento in 787-9, and clashed with Byzantium for control of Venetia and Dalmatia. The Saxons, too, were hammered into submission after a long and very bloody series of campaigns between 772 and 798. Systematic evangelization, forced conversions and the establishment of new sees accompanied the military conquests of these new territories.

Italy: the Development of the Papal State from 756

2 In 754 the popes had taken the first crucial step towards realigning their sympathies away from Byzantium in favour of the Franks, for Pope Stephen II (or III) journeyed to France in order to re-anoint Pippin III, the Frankish ruler and his wife and sons as the legitimate line of rulers of the Franks and made Pippin the protector of the Roman church. The Frankish ruler's aid was thereafter invoked against the Lombards, whose attacks on the papal territories were particularly fierce under Aistulf (749-56) and Desiderius (757-774), culminating in the Frankish conquest of the Lombard kingdom in 774 by Charlemagne. Leo III strengthened the ties still further by crowning Charlemagne emperor and governor of the Romans on Christmas Day 800 in St Peter's, Rome. With Frankish protection and support, the popes consolidated their secular and independent rule of the Papal State, though Frankish protection was to become somewhat heavy-handed at times. The popes played an increasingly articulate role in the re-organization of the church in Western Europe, and in Rome itself the popes, especially Hadrian I (772-795) and Leo III (795-816) who erected and refurbished many magnificent churches and other buildings, extended the system of social welfare within the Papal State and streamlined the papal administration.

England: the Supremacy of Mercia, 625-796

3 The three strongest kingdoms in England at the end of the 7th century were Northumbria under Egfrith (670-85), Wessex under Caedwalla (695-8) and Mercia under Aethelbald (716-57). Egfrith waged successful campaigns against the Picts. Caedwalla tried to expand eastwards into Sussex and even Kent, but retired to Rome after only two years. Aethelbald appears to have attacked the Welsh, the Northumbrians and the East Saxons. Kentish charters suggest that he was in control of London and appears to have done much to establish the strength of Mercian rule in his 41-year reign from which his successors were to benefit.

Aethelbald was assassinated in 757 and buried at Repton; his successor Beornred held the kingdom for only a short time before Offa, with a tenuous family claim to the kingship, took power. Offa, firmly based in the Midlands, with a palace at Tamworth, set about expanding his territory in the Middle Saxon area and London, and by 770 London emerged as an important Mercian mint. The southern kingdoms were relatively stable in the earlier years of Offa's reign but later he was able to intervene successfully in Kentish affairs. In 764-5 Kent re-asserted its independence under King Egberht, only to lose it again on Egberht's death and with the subsequent decisive intervention of Offa in Kentish affairs. The local dynasties of Kent, Sussex, the Hwicce and East Anglia seem to have become subordinated to Mercia and Offa's daughters married the kings of Wessex and Northumbria.

Offa raided Wales and had the massive fortification known as Offa's Dyke erected on the Welsh border (possibly as a defence against further Welsh penetration), of which 80 miles of imposing earthwork are extant. Offa's power within England was no doubt considerable. He even went so far as to try and create a new ecclesiastical province based on Lichfield, independent of York and Canterbury. His relations with external rulers, however, seem to have been confined to a trade agreement with Charlemagne and arrangements for the protection of English pilgrims travelling through Francia. Offa died in 796 and was succeeded by his son Ecgfrith who survived his father by only five months. Mercia was unable to retain its dominant position and in due course it was Wessex that emerged as, and remained, the strongest kingdom of England.

814

The Viking Conquests

The start of the 10th century saw a marked increase in contacts between the Scandinavian and Slavic peoples to the north and east of Europe and the older established kingdoms of Western Europe, in both economic and political spheres. The Vikings were adventurers, originating in Scandinavia, who ranged far and wide across the North and Baltic seas, travelling vast distances in their sailing ships and using oars for short journeys, sea-fights and voyages through narrow waters. They moved down through Russia to Byzantium; across the Atlantic Ocean to establish farming communities in Iceland, Greenland and, for a short time, Vinland on the coast of Newfoundland; and colonized many territories in Britain, the Orkneys, Shetlands, Hebrides, Isle of Man, and on the western tips of Europe.

Despite their reputation as ferocious raiders, the Vikings in fact became closely involved in local politics and contributed constructively to the political development of every region they settled. The trading links they maintained in particular, and the enterprise of their explorations, opened up the North Sea and contributed substantially to the later mercantile and commercial development of northern Europe. The Danes in particular, who in the 9th century settled in England and in France, where they became known as Normans, ventured still further into southern Europe and the Mediterranean, and continued to make their mark on the map of medieval Europe well into the 12th century. Nonetheless, the Viking kingdoms of York and Dublin were reconquered in the 10th century by native rulers, though the Scandinavian presence remained strong in Scotland and the islands well into the 12th century.

The Frankish conquest of the Saxons at the end of the 8th century made them neighbours of the Danes. This led to clashes of interest with the Franks, particularly over the lands of Obodrites and other Slavs in northern Germany. The Franks therefore tried to influence Danish politics. One means was by intervening in the political succession within Denmark. Another was to send Christian missionaries: Ebbo had mixed success with the Danes; Anskar, in the mid-9th century, sent first to Denmark and later to Sweden, made some headway in establishing Christianity. This was later reinforced by missionaries from Germany and England in the 10th and 11th centuries.

West Frankish energies in the second half of the 9th century were directed both at maintaining the stability of the kingdom and defending its towns and monasteries from Viking raids. In the East Frankish Kingdom, in contrast, there was still room for expansion into the Slav regions, particularly under Louis the German (d.876) and his sons. The marches, or special stretches of territory in the frontier regions under military organization, constituted an important means of regulating relations with Slavic peoples on the Franks' northern borders, including the Obodrites, Linones, Sorbs and Daleminzi. In the south, the four peoples of importance were the Moravians, Bohemians, Bulgars and Slovenes. Relations involved tribute, supporting contenders for leadership in the regions and, again, infiltrating missionaries. The Moravians, particularly under Moimir I, Rastislav and Svatopluk (Zwentibald), proved formidable neighbours.

Western Europe, apart from Italy, had little contact with the Byzantine Empire at this time. Only Louis II in Italy asserted his rulership and imperial title, at a safe distance and in writing, against the claims of the Byzantine Emperor Basil I with any vigour, but for the most part he administered Italy efficiently as part of the Frankish realm.

NORWAY

Lade

Kaupang

SWEDEN

DENMARK
Aarhus
Roskilde   Lund
deby
burg
Bremen
urt

FRANKISH
(OM
NY)

Salzburg

Venice
Verona
Bologna
Perugia
ce
PAPAL
STATE
ITALY
Rome

Naples
DR OF
BENEVENTO
Barium
Tarentum
anormus
Messana
Sicily
Malta   SEA

Finnic peoples

BALTIC
SEA

Baltic peoples

S   l   a   v   s

Oder
Elbe
Vistula
Danube

HUNGARY

CROATIA
Iadera
Spalatum
SERBIA

BULGARIA
Nish
Sredets
Scupi   Philippopolis

Janina

Salonica

Patrae   Athens

Crete

Novgorod

K
I
E
V
A
N

R
U
S

Slavs

Kiev

Dnieper

Dniester

P e c h e n e g s

Danube   Preslav
Varna

Adrianople
Constantinople

Smyrna

VOLGA BULGARIA
Bulgar
Volga

KHAZAR   KINGDOM

Don

Sarkel
Volga

Cherson

BLACK   SEA

LAZICA
Tiflis
Trapezus

BYZANTINE   EMPIRE

ABBASIDS
Tigris
Euphrates

Cyprus
Damascus

Ugrians

BYZANTINE

Viking Kingdoms and Conquests, c. 800-1200

1 Viking raids on France and the British Isles increased in intensity throughout the 9th century, with the Vikings establishing settlements there which later developed into polities. In 911 Charles the Simple, King of the West Franks, ceded Rouen and the lower Seine valley to a Viking group led by Rollo, who extended their authority to the west and took over the entire area now known as Normandy; they were later known as Normans. In 878, meanwhile, a frontier was agreed between the English king Alfred and the Danish leader Guthrum. This established much of the territory which became known as the Danelaw. The Vikings also settled extensively in East Anglia and set up a kingdom in Ireland based on Dublin.

By the 11th century, four independent kingdoms, in Denmark, Sweden, Norway and the Republic of Iceland had emerged. Danish power seems to have weakened in relation to Norway towards the end of the 9th century, and with it the limited influence over the Viking armies abroad which the sources suggest. Denmark recovered, however, under the Jelling dynasty of Kings Gorm and Harald in the 10th century; Harald established himself as overlord of Norway. The fortunes of Norway, Denmark and Sweden remained closely intertwined throughout the 10th and 11th centuries.

In the 12th century the Normans expanded farther from Normandy. Led by the brigand Robert Guiscard, they conquered Sicily from the Arabs and Apulia and Calabria from the Greeks, becoming a power of great importance under his successors Roger I (Count of Sicily 1072-1101) and Roger II (1105-54), the latter being accorded the title of king by the pope. The Normans also secured some short-term settlements on the North African coast.

Evidence of Scandinavian activity east of the Baltic in the 9th and 10th centuries is ambiguous. The large numbers of coins from north Russia found in Scandinavia may indicate trade, plunder, tribute or the payment of mercenaries. Islamic texts refer to the "Rus" as traders who were settled in Kiev as early as the middle of the 9th century. They also held bases at Novgorod and Staraya Ladoga. Links with Byzantium led to their conversion to Christianity.

Moravia and Other Early Slav States in the 9th century

2 The emergence of Moravia is connected with the collapse of Avar hegemony in the middle Danube region. In the 9th century, the Moravians expanded into the Nitrava region. Moravia's prince, Moimir, was, however, deposed by the Franks and Prince Ratislav imposed on the Moravians the Frankish king, Louis the German, in 846. But Ratislav's power grew so great as to cause the Franks unease. However, when he attempted to establish Christianity independent of the Franks, the pope refused to send a bishop. An appeal to the Byzantine Emperor then resulted in the short-lived but effective mission of Constantine and Methodius, who translated many church texts into Slavonic.

Frankish suzerainty in the area, over Pannonia and Croatia, dated from about 795, and over Dalmatia from about 803. Liudevit, a ruler of one of the Slav groups in the region, however, reneged on his oath of loyalty to the Franks and sought refuge with another Slavic group south of his territory, where he was murdered in 823. The western part of his territory remained within the Frankish sphere of influence, but the eastern area attracted the interest of the Bulgars, under whose "protection" it passed in 827.

Based at Pliska, the Bulgars under Omurtag allied with the Byzantine Emperor Michael II in 822-23. Later, Khan Boris (852-89 and 893) concluded a peace treaty with Byzantium. There were, however, serious tensions in Bulgar relations with Byzantium.

The Partition of the Frankish Empire, 843

3 Louis the Pious (814-840) inherited his father Charlemagne's entire empire in 814. With the *Ordinatio imperii* of 817, he tried to preserve both the idea of Empire and the Imperial title by dividing the lands between his three sons – Lothar, Louis (the German) and Pippin I (of Aquitaine) – and by making his eldest son Lothar co-emperor with him. By Louis's death in 840, however, the situation had been complicated by the death of Pippin I (though his son tried in vain to claim his father's portion) and by the birth of a further son, Charles (the Bald) to Louis the Pious and his second wife Judith in 823. Thus the fate of the Empire was bitterly contested between Lothar, Louis the German and Charles the Bald, and resolved after a fashion at the Treaty of Verdun in 843. The west and east portions created by this partition developed into France and Germany respectively. The Middle Kingdom, whose northern part became known as Lotharingia, remained a bone of contention between France and Germany, not finally resolved until the 20th century.

The Partition of the Frankish Empire, 870 and 880

4 The Emperor Lothar's portion, created in 843 (*see* above, map 3) had been divided between his sons Lothar II and Louis II on his death in 855. On Lothar II's death with no legitimate heirs, his uncles hastened to claim his kingdom. At the Colloquy of Meersen in 870, Charles the Bald divided Lotharingia with his brother Louis the German according to the number of counties, bishoprics and abbeys rather than natural boundaries or language. In this way Aachen, Charlemagne's great centre, became part of the East Frankish kingdom.

A further, short-lived partition was agreed in 880 in the West Frankish kingdom by the Frankish nobles between two of Charles the Bald's grandsons, Louis III and Carloman. An aristocrat called Boso, who had married a Carolingian, claimed a kingdom, while the east was ruled by Louis the German's youngest son, Charles the Fat, who took the title of Emperor. As kingdoms and territories were parcelled out, the position of Emperor outside Italy was becoming little more than an honorific title.

VIKING KINGDOMS AND CONQUESTS, c.800-1200

Viking core areas, c.1000

States created by conquests from core area in 9th and 10th centuries (with dates)

States created by conquests from Normandy in 10th and 11th centuries (with dates)

Conquests made from England by 1200

Held notionally from England

Conquests made from Sicily in the 12th century (with dates)

910

The First Russian State

After 888, many "petty kings" – Berengar in Italy, Rudolf in upper Burgundy, Guy and Louis in Gaul and Provence, Odo, son of Robert the Strong in Neustria and Ramnulf in Aquitaine – acted "as if they were kings". For a time it looked as if the fragmentation of Charlemagne's empire was complete and all semblance of unity lost. Yet many ties bonded the whole together, and the legend of Charlemagne himself, as well as surviving members of his family, proved resilient.

In the West Frankish kingdom, Carolingian rulers regained the throne and reigned throughout the 10th century, though the character of the monarchy was gradually changing in the face of developments towards greater autonomy of the territorial principalities which forged new bonds of loyalty to their royal overlord. The last Carolingian king, Louis V, died in 987 and in his place Hugh Capet was elected. Hugh inaugurated a new ruling dynasty in France, which was to last more than 800 years. Whatever the power of the nobles, the monarchy continued to exist as a political institution of significance. It rested firmly on its Carolingian foundations.

In the East Frankish kingdom, the last Carolingian ruler, Louis the Child, died in 911. In his place Count Conrad of Franconia was elected king. In 919, he was succeeded in turn by the Liudolfing Henry I, "the Fowler", the first of the Saxon or Ottonian dynasty, whose son Otto I, and grandson and great-grandson forged an empire in emulation of Charlemagne, which stretched from the Baltic to the Mediterranean. Otto I, who came to the throne in 936, made himself king of Italy in 951 and was crowned Emperor by Pope John XVI in 961. He established strong institutions of government and made clever use of ecclesiastical personnel and resources, both bishoprics and monasteries, within his system of administration. The royal women – mothers, wives, aunts and sisters of the reigning king – played a particularly conspicuous role in politics in this period, especially during the minority of Otto III when Queen Adelaide and Queen Theophanu acted as regents.

Otto I's son, Otto II, was greatly concerned with military consolidation in Italy, notably against the Byzantines, and died on campaign in 983. Otto II had, however, married a Byzantine princess, Theophanu, and asserted his title of Emperor in apparent competition to that of the Byzantine Emperor. Similarly their son Otto III developed imperial ideology still further before his premature death in 1002. It was left to his cousin Henry II to consolidate the practical government of the kingdom, especially in Germany itself and to forge a strong polity for his successors. Good relations were maintained with the West Frankish kingdom as well as the Kingdom of Burgundy and elsewhere which had broken away under their own rulers. It is striking how marriage alliances throughout the 10th century created links of varying strength between such kingdoms as England, France, Burgundy, Germany, Bohemia, Russia, Bulgaria and Byzantium, and how international many of the royal courts of Western Europe were at this time, welcoming scholars and ambassadors from many countries.

The 10th century was marked, too, by the emergence of political organizations in northern and eastern Europe. The marauders of the previous century (the Vikings in the north, the Magyars in the east) formed settled kingdoms; in England the successors of Alfred the Great conquered the Danelaw; in Poland the Piasts extended their rule to Cracow in the south, and east and west. Significant expansion by the Kievan Rus and their conversion to Christianity in 987 meant that their interests were increasingly pursued in the west and south towards the end of the 10th century.

10°   20°   30°   40°   50°   60°

60°

N O R W A Y
(under Danish rule)

F i n n i c   p e o p l e s

Ugrians

Ladoga

Uppsala
Birka

Novgorod

SWEDEN

Pskov

Suzdal

Bulgar   VOLGA
BULGARIA

Vladimir

Volga

50°

Aarhus

Roskilde   Lund

DENMARK

BALTIC
SEA

Baltic peoples

Polotsk

Smolensk

K I E V A N   R U S

Vitebsk

Hamburg

Bremen

Slavs

Minsk

Oder

Gniezno

Vistula

Don

NGDOM

Elbe

POLAND

Wrocław

K I E V A N   R U S

OF

Kiev

Sarkel   (to Kiev)

rt

Meissen

Prague

Cracow

Volga

uttgart

Dnieper

MANY

Munich   Danube

Vienna   Pozsony

Esztergom

Salzburg

Fehérvár

T u r k i c   p e o p l e s

Dniester

(to Kiev)

Alans

Venice   Verona

VENETIAN
REPUBLIC

HUNGARY

Kalocsa

Pécs

Ajtony

Tmutarakan

Kaffa

Bologna   isa

CROATIA

Florence   Zara

Perugia   Spaleto

Belgrade

B U L G A R I A

Cherson

Nissa

Danube

Varna

BLACK SEA

GEORGIAN
STATES

SMALL
STATES

Rome

PAPAL
STATE

PRINCIPALITY
OF BENEVENTO

Serdica

Preslav

Philippopolis

Scupi

Adrianople

Trebizond

A R M E N I A

COUNTY
OF CAPUA   Naples

Barium

Tarentum

Salonica

Constantinople

PRINCIPALITY
OF SALERNO

B Y Z A N

Janina

anormus   Messana

Catana

Malta   SEA

Athens

T I N E   E M P I R E

Smyrna

BUWAYHIDS

HAMDANIDS

Euphrates

Tigris

Nicosia

Crete

Beirut   FATIMIDS   Damascus   KARMATIANS

69

THE DEVELOPMENT OF THE KIEVAN RUS, 800-1031 — 1

- Approximate western frontier of the Khazar Empire, c.800
- Approximate extent of the Kievan Rus, c.900
- Added to the Kievan Rus by 1000
- Frontier of the Khazar Empire in the 10th century (to 967)
- to Poland until 981 and 1018-31
- Frontiers, 1003

THE BALKANS, 931-1018 — 4

- The Serbian state of Chaslav, 931-950
- Lost by Bulgaria to the Byzantine Empire, 971
- Lost by Bulgaria to the Byzantine Empire, 971; regained, 976
- To Bulgaria from the Byzantine Empire, 986
- Frontiers, c.990
- The Byzantine Empire from 1018

EAST-CENTRAL EUROPE, 928-1000 — 2

- Germany in 928
- Added to Germany by c.1000
- Added temporarily to Germany (with dates)
- Polish at times during the second half of the 10th century
- Eastern frontier of Poland to 981
- The Kievan Rus in 970
- Added to the Kievan Rus by c.1000
- Bohemian from c.950, Polish by c.1000
- Czech lands
- Western limit of Hungarian control from c.910
- Western limit of Hungarian control, 973-995
- Eastern frontier of the Holy Roman Empire, 1000
- Frontiers, 1000

ENGLAND AFTER ALFRED THE GREAT, 899-1018 — 3

- Wessex and dependencies, 899
- Welsh principalities, vassals of Wessex
- Added to Wessex by 924
- Added to Wessex by 939
- Northern and western limits of England in 1018
- Extent of Danelaw, 886
- Frontiers, 899

Pechenegs

Drstar

(971-976)

Tirnovo   Preslav   Varna

A   R   I   A

Philippopolis

Thrace

Adrianople

Constantinople

alonica

E   M   P   I   R   E

AEGEAN

SEA

Smyrna

Athens

os

Edinburgh

NORTH
SEA

Durham

KINGDOM
OF YORK
York

Chester

DANISH
MERCIA

Nottingham

(FIVE

WEST
MERCIA   BOROUGHS)

EAST
Thetford

Ely

RHWNG GWY
A HAFREN

ANGLIA
Cambridge

Worcester

Gloucester

GWENT

ORGANNWG

ESSEX

London   Kent
Canterbury

Winchester

ENGLISH   CHANNEL   FRANCE

(COTS)

The Development of the Kievan Rus, 800-1031

1 Rapid expansion on the part of the Kievan Rus (see map 1, page 67) in the 10th century, notably under Igor in the 940s, enlarged the territories over which they had control at the expense of their Polish and Khazar neighbours. Later expeditions by Sviatoslav against the Khazars (965), Volga Bulgars (966) and the Bulgars on the lower Danube (967), however, resulted in mainly temporary gains.

Trade, too, played an important part in the growing importance of the Rus. From the coin evidence it is clear that the Samanid rulers of Transoxania had become very rich at the end of the 9th century as a result of the discovery of silver in Afghanistan. They minted vast quantities of coinage and their merchants began to trade with the Volga Bulgars, Rus, Ves, Lapps and Finns, though the Samanids themselves succumbed to the Turks in 998. Bulgar on the Volga developed rapidly as a trading centre. The Volga Bulgars were supplied in turn by the Rus. The Rus also traded actively with Constantinople and the Islamic regions.

Wealth had much to do with the political expansion of Kievan Rus, but the cultural links formed in the wake of mercantile connections were also crucial for political developments as Rus interests increasingly focused to the west and south towards the end of the 10th century. The formal conversion of Vladimir and the Rus to Greek Orthodox Christianity after 987, in the wake of the personal conversion of the regent Olga (d. 969, Igor's widow) and the marriage of Vladimir to the Byzantine princess Anna, provided an essential connection with Byzantium of great importance for Russia's future development.

East-Central Europe, 928-1000

2 The expansion eastwards of the German kings proceeded apace in the course of the 10th century. The establishment of the Christian church in newly created dioceses such as Magdeburg (968) and Bamberg (1007) was a fundamental component of political consolidation. Political relations with the princes of Poland, Bohemia, Moravia and Hungary were played out in the context of the conversion of the ruler and his people to Christianity. In the late 10th century, for example, a bishopric of Prague was created whose second bishop was Adalbert Vojtech, educated at Magdeburg and canonized in 990. In his position as national saint, he was soon joined by King Wenceslas.

By the second half of the 10th century, the Piast rulers of Poland, such as Mieszko (c. 963-992), had extended their rule to the east and south with Cracow occupying a vital strategic position.

England After Alfred the Great, 899-1018

3 By his death in 899, Alfred, who styled himself King of the English, had successfully consolidated the kingdom of Wessex; was in effect the overlord of the ruler of Mercia; reached a modus vivendi with the Danes in the Danelaw;

and in 886 occupied London. Alfred's methods of government, stressing the rule of law and encouraging learning, established a new style of kingship which became a model for future kings of England.

Alfred's sons and grandsons, Edward the Elder (899-924), Aethelstan (924-39), Edmund (939-46) and Eadred (946-55), extended the English kingdom. Edward established his rule over the entire area south of the Humber, and east of the Welsh and secured Mercia, thus effectively creating the kingdom of England consolidated by Aethelstan. He and his successors moved against the Vikings in the Danelaw and Northumbria; the last Viking ruler of the north, Eric Bloodaxe, fell in battle in 954 and the Viking kingdom of York was once more incorporated into the English kingdom. In 945, however, Cumbria was ceded to the Scots and Northumbria itself can never said to have been fully integrated with the south, as became clear in the years around the Norman conquest of the mid-11th century (see map 2, page 79).

The Balkans, 931-1018

4 In the 10th century, Bulgaria remained the principal rival to Byzantium in the Balkans. Symeon of Bulgaria (d. 927) brought particularly effective rule to Bulgaria. Moreover, by the treaty of 904, Byzantium recognized Bulgaria's possession of the greater part of Thrace and Macedonia. Between 913 and 927, Symeon asserted his status as an emperor equal in status and importance to the Byzantine ruler. He attacked Constantinople itself and was crowned as emperor in a ceremony whose significance has been much disputed.

The Serbs, too, had expanded their territory, especially under Vlastimir in the mid-9th century, but under Peter (d. 917) an alliance with Bulgaria was reached which lasted from 897 to 917. Thereafter Serbia attempted many times to break free of Bulgarian dominance, finally succeeding under Chaslav (d. c.960) after Symeon of Bulgaria's death. The Serbs, however, acknowledged Byzantine overlordship until about 976.

Symeon's successor Peter of Bulgaria (d. 969) confirmed peace with Byzantium by marrying Maria Lecapena and the borders were restored to those of 897 and 904. After his reign, however, Bulgaria was attacked by both Russia and Byzantium. Samuel (986-1014) fought back manfully and by 997 had secured a greatly enlarged territory. Not till 1000 or 1001 did the Byzantine counter-offensive of Emperor Basil II begin. Bulgaria was annexed to Byzantium in 1018.

Croatia, meanwhile, under Tomislav (d. 928), an ally of Byzantium, was a dangerous neighbour for the Bulgars and continued to pose a threat into the late 10th century under Stjepan Drzislav (d. 997) when it came under the overlordship of Venice with the doge ostensibly acting as the representative of the Byzantine emperor.

1003

Feudal Europe

Feudalism was the dominant system of political control and social organisation over much of 11th-century Western Europe. Its essential characteristic was a personal relationship between lord and vassal, cemented in an act of homage. The state in the modern sense – an agreed territory with sovereign powers and with a precise relationship with its citizens – did not exist. Instead, there was a series of individual rulers each effectively sovereign within his own lands, though each in turn nominally owing allegiance to a king or other ruler. As a consequence, the map of feudal Europe is complex. Given the disparate and many-sided relationships between lord and vassal, the political map of much of Europe was dominated by principalities, duchies and counties, so that countries such as France, while united in theory, were in practice far from being so. This fragmented authority nonetheless provided the political context for a marked rise in Europe's population, prosperity and culture. The Church, too, had an important impact on the map of Europe since many monasteries and bishops were landowners on a grand scale, often with correspondingly great political powers.

Even outside the lands of the former Carolingian Empire, where feudalism was at its strongest, "states" were dependent on successful military-political leadership. The death of a strong leader could easily lead to political collapse. This danger was amply demonstrated in the early decades of the 11th century by the fortunes of Kievan Rus and the Umayyad Caliphate of Cordova. The Kievan state dissolved after the death of Vladimir I of Rus (c.978-1015), who was succeeded by sons who ruled separate principalities based on Novgorod, Polotsk and Chernigov. Similarly, the death in 1002 of al-Mansur, who had effectively ruled Cordova since 981 and achieved many successes at the expense of the Christians, was followed by the fragmentation of Islamic Spain. A strong leader, by contrast, could rapidly restore the fortunes of a state. The Byzantine Emperor Basil II (976-1025), for example, destroyed the West Bulgarian Empire (1018), a bitter rival to Byzantium, and reduced the Serbs to vassalage. He gained his surname "Bulgar-slayer" from the battle of the Belasica mountains (1014) after which thousands of prisoners were blinded and sent home in groups of 100 each led by a one-eyed man. Shortly before his death in 1025 he even contemplated the re-conquest of Italy.

Because the existence of "states" often depended on the personal authority of a strong leader, large areas could be joined together in a single life-time. Thus in 1013, King Swein of Denmark conquered England, while the English king, Aethelred "the Unready" fled to Normandy. He returned when Swein died in 1014, but Swein's son Cnut continued the struggle, while divisions among the English handicapped the resistance. After Aethelred's death, England was divided between Cnut and Edmund, Aethelred's son, by the Peace of Alney (1016), with Cnut receiving Mercia and Northumbria. Edmund, however, died the same year and Cnut became King of all England (1016-35). On the death of his older brother, Harold, King of Denmark (1019), England became part of a Scandinavian empire, which further expanded with the conquest of Norway in the 1020s. In 1031 Cnut advanced to the Tay and received the submission of Malcolm II of Scotland.

The essentially personal and transient nature of authority was, however, demonstrated by Cnut's empire: he did not create any administrative structure to weld it together. Cnut was the king of a number of kingdoms, not a monarch seeking to enlarge one of them. After his death in 1035, his empire dissolved.

NORWAY
(To Denmark)

Trondhjem

SWEDEN

Uppsala

Aarhus
Roskilde

DENMARK

BALTIC
SEA

Finnic peoples

Baltic peoples

Novgorod

Pskov

Polotsk

Vitebsk
Smolensk

Minsk

Vladimir
Suzdal

Bulgar
VOLGA
BULGARIA

Finnic peoples

KIEVAN RUS

Slavs

Bremen

GDOM

OF

Poznań

POLAND

Prague
BOHEMIA

Wrocław

Cracow

Chernigov

Kiev

Oder

Vistula

Elbe

Don

Volga

Galich

Dnieper

Sarkel
(to Kiev)

Turkic peoples

MANY

Danube

Vienna
Salzburg

Pozsony

Esztergom

Fehérvár

HUNGARY

Pécs

Zágráb

Dniester

Dnieper

(to Kiev)

Tmutarakan

Alans

Verona

Venice

VENETIAN
REPUBLIC

Bologna

Zara

Spalato

CROATIA

Belgrade

Kaffa

Cherson

BLACK SEA

GEORGIAN
STATES

SMALL
STATES

ARMENIA

sa

Florence

Perugia

Danube

Naissus

Serdica

Odessus

Trapezus

Rome

PAPAL
STATE

NCIPALITY
OF CAPUA

PRINCIPALITY
OF BENEVENTO

COUNTY
OF APULIA

Naples

Barium

Philippopolis

Scupi

Ochrid

Adrianople

Constantinople

Ancyra

BUWAYHIDS

COUNTY
F AVERSA

PRINCIPALITY
OF SALERNO

Tarentum

BYZANTINE EMPIRE

Salonica

Janina

Local

Tigris

Mosul

Palermo

Messana

Sicily

Catana

Smyrna

Athens

dynasties

Euphrates

SEA

Nicosia

Crete

FATIMIDS

Beirut

Damascus

KARMATIANS

ENGLAND
(to Denmark)

ENGLISH CH

DUCHY
NORMA

COUNT
MAIN
Rennes
COUNTY OF BRITTANY
COUNTY
OF
ANJOU
Angers
Nantes

COUNTY
OF POITO

BAY OF
BISCAY

Po

A
Q

COUNTY OF
SAINTONGE

COU
ANGO

Bordeaux

DUC
O
GASC
Bayonne

NAVARRE

CALIPH
OF
CORD

G W Y N E D D

P O W Y S

MERCIA

RHWNG GWY
A HAFREN

BUELLT

S E I S Y L L W G

BRYCHEINIOG

GWENT

D Y F E D

MORGANNWG

WESSEX

**THE EXPANSION OF POLAND UNDER BOLESŁAW THE BRAVE,
992-1025** 4

Poland at the beginning of Bolesław's rule, 992

Added by Bolesław (with dates)

Added temporarily by Bolesław (with dates)

Lost by Bolesław

Frontier of the Holy Roman Empire from 1031

Frontiers at the death of Bolesław, 1025

THE UNIFICATION OF WALES, 800-1057 2

Frontiers, c.800

Possessions of Rhodri Mawr, 872

Limit of area held by Hywel Dda, 942-950

Possessions of Maredudd ab Owain, 999

Possessions of Gruffyd ap Llywelyn, c. 1057

**FRANCE:
FEUDAL FRAGMENTATION, 987-1030** 3

French Royal Domain, 987

Added temporarily before 1032

Added by 1032

Church lands

Other fiefs of the Crown

Fiefs of the Duchy of Aquitaine

Notional boundary of the
Kingdom of France

Frontiers, 1030

NORTHERN SPAIN: CHRISTIAN STATES, 718-1030 1

Northern boundary of the Islamic Empire until c.740

Asturias from 718

Frontiers of the Frankish Empire and of Asturias in 814

Catalan counties (nominally part of France)

Frontiers, 1030

Kołobrzeg

P r u s s i a n s

Szczecin

S l a v s

Gniezno
Płock
Poznań **Great Poland**

Brześć
(1018-22)

**Lusatia
(1018)**
Meissen
Budziszyn

P O L A N D

Oder

KINGDOM OF GERMANY

Wrocław

Silesia

Vistula

**KIEVAN
RUS**

Czerwień

**Little Poland
(999)**

(1018)

Prague
**BOHEMIA
(1003-4)**

Cracow
Przemyśl

Olomouc
**Moravia
(1003)**

(1017-18)

Trencsén
Nyitra

H U N G A R Y

Oviedo
Santand

Santiago
León

N A V

Burgos

**LEON
(to Navarre, 1034-35)**

CASTILE

Braga

Salamanca
Segovia
Ávila

C A L I P H A T E O F
(in s

Northern Spain: Christian States, 718-1030

1 When Muslim Arab invaders swept through Spain in the decade after 711, the inhospitable lands of the north successfully resisted absorption into Islamic Spain. A nucleus of resistance formed in Asturias, following the victory of its first ruler, Pelayo, over the Muslims at Covadonga in about 722. Asturias expanded southwards in the 9th century and became, under Garcia I (911-14), the Kingdom of León. Alternative centres of Christian power developed further east in the Basque country, notably the Kingdom of Navarre, centred on Pamplona, under King Sancho I (905-26), and, from the mid-10th century, the County of Castile. Catalonia was a French fief, the "Spanish Marches", created by Charlemagne following his conquest of the territory from the Muslims around 801. Catalonia consisted of numerous small counties, the most important of which proved to be Barcelona, which steadily expanded at the expense of the others.

The southward expansion of the Christian states suffered a setback in the 10th century, as strong rulers of the Caliphate of Cordova resumed incursions into northern Spain. Under al-Mansur (976-1002) almost every Christian capital was sacked, but after his death the Caliphate of Cordova disintegrated into a series of independent lordships, ill-placed to resist the Christians' raids and forced to pay heavy tribute to them.

The Unification of Wales, 800-1057

2 Early-medieval Wales was divided into a number of small kingdoms. As in England, the tendency from the 6th century was for a decline in their number as the less successful kingdoms were absorbed by their more powerful neighbours, such as Dyfed and Gwynedd. They were based on fertile lowland, but also benefited from a degree of immunity from English attack. In contrast, Powys suffered from Mercian incursions.

Welsh inheritance customs – the division of property among sons – made it more difficult to translate territorial gains into more cohesive statehood. Rulers such as Rhodri Mawr of Gwynedd, who accumulated several kingships in the 9th century, allocated them to different sons. His grandson, Hywel Dda, however, came to rule most of Wales. He was the first Welsh king who definitely issued his own coinage. Hywel's death was followed by internecine conflict in which the English, with their growing pretension to overlordship in Britain, intervened ever more frequently.

The rise of Gwynedd under Llywelyn ap Seisyll (d. c. 1023) and his son Gruffyd ap Llywelyn (d. 1063) was the most critical development in Wales in the period preceding the Norman conquest of England. Both men had to fight to gain control of Gwynedd and both campaigned in south Wales, most of which was conquered between 1039 and 1055. The length of the process reflected the difficulty in obtaining a decisive "political" settlement short of slaying rivals, as Gruffyd twice did. The power of the rulers of Gwynedd rested on military success. Unlike their Anglo-Saxon counterparts in England – and like the Scottish kings – they did not build up any sophisticated administrative structures.

France: Feudal Fragmentation, 987-1030

3 Under the early members of the Capetian dynasty, which gained the French throne in 987, the effective power of the king was greatly limited by powerful feudal lords, and indeed by the end of the 10th century the king's writ was essentially confined to the Ile de France, the area around Paris. Elsewhere, the counties and their courts ceased to be public institutions and local official posts were absorbed into the patronage systems of the greater nobles. Counts wielded governmental powers: they minted coins, raised troops and built castles, the last a powerful expression of autonomy. The counts did not seek to replace the king: they scarcely needed to do so. Some, such as the Count of Toulouse and the Count of Champagne, were themselves as powerful as the king. Furthermore, Gascony and Toulouse, both south of the Loire, were sufficiently distant from Paris to be little concerned about its Capetian rulers. North of the Loire, however, rivalry between the powerful local feudatories and the crown was more important. As rulers of Blois and Champagne, the Counts of Champagne were powerful both to the east and west of the Ile de France. The Dukes of Normandy, meanwhile, competed with the Capetians for control of the Vexin to the northwest of Paris. The idea of a powerful monarchy was kept alive by the Church, but there was little basis to it in the 11th century.

The Expansion of Poland under Boleslaw the Brave, 992-1025

4 Boleslaw I Chrobry ("the Brave", 992-1025) of Poland built on the foundations laid by his father, Prince Mieszko I, who had converted to Christianity in 965. Boleslaw strengthened the centre by creating an administrative system based on counts, and used this as a base to expand Polish territory to the east, south and west, taking Cracow (formerly a Bohemian territory) in 999. Many of Boleslaw's conquests were temporary and involved long, debilitating wars on all frontiers. The conquest of Little Poland, which included Cracow, was permanent, however, and Casimir I (1038-58) transferred his residence there.

At first a dependent ally of the Holy Roman Emperor Otto III (who crowned Boleslaw king of Poland in 1000), Boleslaw broke with the Empire after Otto's death in 1002. He seized the imperial lands of Moravia (1003), Lusatia (1018) and Bohemia, though he controlled the latter for only two years (1003-4). Boleslaw further increased Polish influence in the east, when he placed his son-in-law, Svyatopolk, on the throne of Kiev in 1018. Boleslaw was again crowned king of Poland in 1024, this time by an Archbishop with the assent of the Pope, so symbolising his independence from imperial control.

1030

The Age of the Normans

In the late 11th century the conflict with the Muslim forces which had pressed at Europe's borders since the 7th century intensified once more. In Spain the Christians made gains, taking advantage of the dissolution of the Caliphate of Cordova into a variety of successor-states. Byzantium, however, proved unable to defend the frontiers won over the previous century by emperors such as Basil II. The Byzantine military machine found itself starved of funds, and a much-weakened Byzantine army was smashed by Seljuk Turks at Manzikert in 1071. The defeat was followed by the loss of almost all of Anatolia. The Byzantine Empire managed to retain its grip on most of the Balkans. Outside the Byzantine sphere of influence, however, there was instability as the Kingdom of Hungary gained Croatia in 1091.

At the other end of Europe, the Kingdom of England experienced particular turmoil during the 11th century. Cnut's empire (*see* page 72) fell apart in the 1030s: Norway rebelled successfully under Magnus the Good (1033-47), while Cnut's sons by different unions, Harthacnut and Harold Harefoot, competed to control England. Harthacnut succeeded to Denmark in 1035, and in 1040 gained the English throne when Harold died. On Harthacnut's death in 1042, he was succeeded by Aethelred's son, Edward "the Confessor" (1042-66).

In 1066 William Duke of Normandy conquered England with a small force, bringing to an end the Anglo-Saxon state and ushering in a new era in which England's fortunes would be tied to France and the south. Scandinavian involvement with England was not quite over, however: Harald Hardrada of Norway invaded England (unsuccessfully) in 1066, the Danes in 1069-70. But the Viking period of English history, which had begun when Norse ships were first recorded off the English coast in 789, was then over. For the Normans, by contrast, the conquest of England was just one of a series of successful military adventures, which brought them large territories in southern Italy and Sicily.

A divided succession characterized Kievan Rus as well as Cnut's empire. The Kievan principalities had been united under Iaroslav the Wise (1019-54) of Novgorod, who, after the death of his brother, the Prince of Chernigov, ruled them all save Polotsk. It was a period of particular Kievan political and cultural influence. However, on Iaroslav's death he left each of his sons an autonomous principality. The Great Principality of Kiev took precedence but it exercised little control over the others. Raids by Polovtsy nomads, who sacked Kiev in 1093, weakened the Great Principality, moving the centre of Rus activity farther north to the forest belt, away from the exposed steppes.

At the same time, in Italy and Germany a bitter power-struggle between the Holy Roman Empire and the Papacy raged: the Investiture Contest. At its height, Pope Gregory VII (1073-85), excommunicated and deposed Emperor Henry IV (1056-1106). Gregory condemned the practice of investiture by which newly appointed bishops and abbots were invested with symbols of spiritual office by the emperor, rather than by the Pope. At Canossa in 1077 Henry stood three days barefoot in the snow in the dress of a penitent to win the lifting of his excommunication, a powerful display of papal authority. Gregory helped to unite Henry's opponents and thus to weaken Imperial authority both in Germany and Italy. Meanwhile, Henry I (1031-60) and Philip I (1060-1108) sought to increase royal power in France, a goal challenged by the power of their vassals, especially the Dukes of Normandy, who were strengthened after 1066 by the Norman conquest of England.

NORWAY

Nidaros

gvin

Oslo

Uppsala

SWEDEN

Finnic peoples

NOVGOROD

Novgorod

ROSTOV-
SUZDAL

Bulgar

VOLGA
BULGARIA

Suzdal

Vladimir

Finno-Ugrians

Pskov

Aarhus

Roskilde

BALTIC
SEA

Baltic peoples

Polotsk

SMOLENSK

Volga

DENMARK

Slavs

Vitebsk

Smolensk

urg

Bremen

POMERANIA

Poznań

POLOTSK

Minsk

CHERNIGOV

Don

Oder

Vistula

Brest

NGDOM

Elbe

POLAND

Wrocław

KIEV

OF

Prague

Cracow

PEREYASLAVL

Kiev

Turkic peoples

Volga

Sarkel
(to Chernigov)

Nuremberg

BOHEMIA

Dnieper

ttgart

GALICH-
VOLHYNIA

Galich

MANY

Danube

Vienna

Pozsony

Esztergom

Dniester

Salzburg

Innsbruck

HUNGARY

(to Chernigov)

Alans

M Venica

Veron

Trieste

VENETIAN
REPUBLIC

Pécs

Szeged

Gyulafehérvár

Kaffa

Zágráb

Temesvár

Y

CROATIA

Cherson

GEORGIA

Bologna

isa

Florence

Zara

Spalato

ZETA
(SERBIA)

Belgrade

BLACK SEA

Tiflis

Perugia

Nissa

Danube

Odessus

Rome
PAPAL
STATE

BYZANTINE

Serdica

Trapezus

Scupi

Philippopolis

o Byzantine
Empire)

Naples

Bari

EMPIRE

Adrianople

Constantinople

Angora

SELJÜK

Manzikert

EMPIRE

Taranto

Salonica

DANISHMENDS

NORMAN PRINCIPALITIES

Janina

RUM
(ICONIUM)

Armenian
rulers

Mosul

Palermo

Messina

Smyrna

Tigris

Catania

Athens

Euphrates

SEA

Malta

Nicosia

Bedouins

Crete

Beirut

Damascus

EARLDOM OF ORKNEY

LEON — CASTILE

ATLANTIC OCEAN

Coria

Toledo

KINGDOM OF BADAJOZ

Badajoz ○ Zallaca

Lisbon

Mérida

KINGDOM OF SEVIL

SCOTLAND

○ Inverness

○ Aberdeen

Cordova

Perth ○

KING
Granac
OF GRA

Seville

Dumbarton ○

Málaga

Edinburgh ○

EMPIRE OF THE

○ Newcastle

Carlisle ○ ○ Durham

TUSCANY

Cumbria

ULSTER

KGDM.
OF MAN
(from 1075)

NORTH
SEA

PENTAPOLIS

PAPAL S

Armagh ○

CONNAUGHT

York ○

Ouse

Rome ○

Tuam ○

MEATH ○ Tara

Chester ○

GWYNEDD

Derby ○

Dublin ○

LEINSTER

POWYS

Shrewsbury ○

Leicester ○

○ Norwich

Kilkenny ○

MUNSTER

Hereford ○

ENGLAND

Ely ○

DEHEUBARTH

Cork ○

MORGANNWG GWENT

Oxford ○

Bristol ○

Thames

London ○

○ Canterbury

ST GEORGE'S
CHANNEL

Bath ○

Winchester ○

Salisbury ○

Hastings

○ Exeter

ENGLISH CHANNEL

Rouen ○

Bayeux ○ ○ Caen

N o r m a n d y

KINGDOM
OF
FRANCE

B r i t t a n y

M a i n e

NORMANDY AND THE BRITISH ISLES, 1062-92

Possessions of Gruffyd ap LLywelyn, 1062

Possessions of William the Conqueror, 1066

Added, 1092

Norwegian possessions

Added by 1070

Limit of Norman-held
areas in Wales, 1086

Frontiers, 1062

IBERIA: SUCCESSOR STATES OF THE CALIPHATE OF CORDOVA, 1086 | **3**

— The Caliphate of Cordova, 1010

— The Kingdom of Toledo, 1031-85

▨ Muslim-held areas in 1030, lost to Christian states by 1085

— Frontiers, late 1085

ADRIATIC SEA

TYRRHENIAN SEA

IONIAN SEA

Malta

NORMANS AND BYZANTINES IN SOUTHERN ITALY, 1030-1156 | **1**

— Frontiers, c.1030	— Limit of Norman conquests by 1090
— Southern frontier of the Holy Roman Empire, 1030	▨ Counties secured by the Normans by 1042
▨ Byzantine possessions, 1030	▨ Temporary Byzantine expansion, 1155-56
▨ Temporary Byzantine expansion, 1036-43	▨ Further 12th-century Norman conquests (with dates)

The Normans and Byzantines in Southern Italy, 1030-1156

1 The Norman conquest of England (see below, map 2) was paralleled by other Norman conquests: of Sicily from the Arabs in 1090 and of Apulia and Calabria in southern Italy from the Byzantine Empire and from local principalities. These conquests all demonstrated the Norman genius for adaptability. Small groups of invaders, essentially adventurers, at first became important as professional soldiers, serving in the incessant conflicts in southern Italy. They then seized power. Richard of Aversa succeeded in becoming Prince of Capua, but the most dynamic was Robert Guiscard (c. 1015-85), the sixth of the 10 sons of Tancred d'Hauteville, a poor Norman noble, all of whom sought their fortune in southern Italy. In 1059 Pope Nicholas II recognised him as Duke of Apulia in return for the promise of Norman support against the Holy Roman Emperor. In 1060 Guiscard drove the Byzantines from Calabria; in 1071 he captured Bari and Brindisi, the main centres of Byzantine power in Italy. The Lombard principality of Salerno followed in 1077 and in 1081 Guiscard crossed the Adriatic, captured Corfu and defeated the Byzantine Emperor, Alexius Comnenus, at Durazzo. He died while preparing to attack Constantinople. The youngest of Robert's brothers, Roger, completed the conquest of Sicily: Messina had already fallen in 1061 and Catania in 1071, but the conquest was only completed in 1090. He also captured Malta. The basis of a powerful state had now been created. Roger II of Sicily (1105-54) gained control of the whole of southern Italy as well and in 1130 created a kingdom that united his dominions.

Where the Normans seized power they replaced the social elite, but there was no mass-displacement of the original population and much of the earlier administrative structure – whether Old English, Byzantine or Arab – continued. This was especially so in England, where a recognised political unit already existed, unlike southern Italy and Sicily, where one had to be created.

Normandy and the British Isles, 1062-92

2 In 1066, Duke William of Normandy ("the Conqueror") invaded England on the death of Edward the Confessor, claiming that Edward had bequeathed him the throne. He defeated the English forces at the Battle of Hastings in October, and 10 weeks later was acclaimed King of England in Westiminster Abbey. The previous unification of the country by the House of Wessex ensured that it fell rapidly to William the Conqueror, in contrast to the more lengthy conquest of the Iron Age and Romano-British kingdoms by the Romans and Anglo-Saxons respectively. Even so, the conquest did not run entirely smoothly, and William did not crush the entire Anglo-Saxon elite: there was widespread rebellion, particularly in the north in 1068-70.

After 1066 England was part of a state that spanned the Channel, which found itself obliged to ward off the ambitions of other expanding territories. The Duchy of Normandy had a long land frontier and, in the Kings of France and Counts of Anjou, aggressive neighbours. The continuous military effort that this entailed was to be a central theme, instrumental both in the development of government and in the domestic political history of the period. Though the Anglo-Norman realms were less a single state than a fortuitous conglomeration that had little in common in economic, administrative or legal terms, they were given common political direction by the interests of their ruler.

On the borders with their Celtic neighbours within Britain, the Normans faced a much less well-defined position. There were no clear geographical boundaries capable of preventing political expansion, and ethnicity could not serve as the basis for states. What eventually became Scotland was ethnically, geographically, economically and culturally diverse, and included Scots, Picts, the Britons of Strathclyde and the Angles of Lothian. Until the mid-12th century it was unclear whether much of what is now northern England, in particular Cumbria and Northumbria, would be part of England or of Scotland. The great ethnic and linguistic mixture of the population in both Cumbria and Lothian ensured that there was no obvious frontier in either respect. William II's conquest of Cumbria in 1092 played a major role in fixing the frontier.

In Wales, Gruffyd ap Llywelyn (see map 2, page 74) had been killed in 1063 as a result of the invasion of the country by Earl Harold of Wessex. It was not to be united again until the 13th century. William I did not seek to conquer Wales, but individual Norman adventurers seized land. These Normans were operating outside the kingdom of England and the "march" they created was a kind of no-man's-land between Wales and England. Initially the Normans advanced with great momentum, along the lowlands near the south and north coasts, and up the river valleys. The Welsh, however, benefited not only from their terrain, much of which offered little advantage to the feudal cavalry of the Normans, but also from the military skills honed by incessant conflict within their own ranks.

Iberia: Successor States of the Caliphate of Cordova, 1086

3 On the death of Abd ar'Rahman, Muslim Spain suffered two decades of civil war. The Caliphate of Cordova broke up into numerous independent kingdoms or ta'ifas. The most important of these was based on Seville, which gradually became pre-eminent in southern Spain. Elsewhere the ta'ifas were weakened by constant strife. They were forced to pay heavy tributes to the Christians, and this burden undermined them further. Their weakness led to the loss of Toledo to Castile in 1085. In order to resist the Christian advance, the Muslims called in the Almoravids, Saharan Berbers who had overrun Morocco in the 1060s. They defeated Alfonso VI of León at Sagrajas (1086) and put a temporary end to the Christian offensive.

1095

Crusader Europe

In March 1095 an embassy from the Byzantine Emperor Alexius I asked Pope Urban II for help against the Seljuk Turks who had overrun most of the eastern provinces of the Byzantine empire following the Battle of Manzikert in 1071 (*see* page 76) and who were threatening Constantinople itself. Urban responded by summoning Western European knights to come to the aid of the Christians in the East. So began the First Crusade, spurred on by the aim of retaking the holy city of Jerusalem, which had been in Muslim hands for over 400 years. The Crusader ideal of fighting holy wars against the external or internal foes of Christendom remained a potent one into the 15th century and beyond.

The First Crusade led to the capture of Antioch and Edessa in 1098 and Jerusalem 1099, and to the establishment of four states, the Kingdom of Jerusalem, the County of Tripolis, the Principality of Antioch, and the County of Edessa. These gains were expanded with the capture of Tyre (1124) and Ascalon (1153), but in 1144 most of the County of Edessa was lost to the Muslims under Zangi, Atabeg of Mosul. This inspired the Second Crusade, but that led only to an unsuccessful attack on Damascus in 1148. In 1187 Jerusalem and most of the Crusading states were lost by the Christians after the Muslim leader Saladin's crushing victory at Hattin.

The Crusades also inspired a novel form of monastic organisation that had political overtones: the Military Orders. The Templars and Hospitallers had troops and castles and were entrusted with the defence of large tracts of territory in Palestine. The Crusades also contributed to an expansion of Byzantine control in western and southern Anatolia, but this faltered with the victory of the Seljuks of Rum at Myriocephalum (1176).

The Crusades demonstrated that Christendom could take the initiative: they were as important for relations with Eastern Europe, especially Byzantium, as for those with the Islamic world. Crusading activity played a crucial role at the margins of Europe. Crusading in Spain was the central theme of the Reconquista, while activity against pagan peoples in the Baltic was seen in the context of a Crusade: in 1147 the Wends, a Slavic people of northeast Germany, were attacked by the Danes, Saxons and Poles. Here, however, the campaigns were as much spurred on by demographic pressures as by religious idealism. In the period as a whole, German peasant settlement expanded eastward, especially in Saxony and Brandenburg, putting pressure on the Slavic peoples.

Elsewhere in Europe, monarchs struggled to expand their power. In southern Italy Roger II of Sicily created a powerful state. The death of a cousin led to his acquiring Apulia in 1127 and in 1130 he took the title of King. Louis VI (1108-37) and Louis VII (1137-80) struggled to expand the power of the Capetians in France, but a major setback occurred in 1152 when Louis VII allowed his divorced wife Eleanor of Aquitaine to marry Henry, Count of Anjou, soon to be Henry II of England, thereby losing effective control of a large portion of southern France. In northern Italy the Emperor, Frederick Barbarossa, was defeated by the Lombard League of Cities at Legnano (1176).

Further east, the centre of Rus activity continued to move towards the forest belt. A new principality, Suzdal, developed in this area, while in 1126 Novgorod became a republic: it soon extended its power to the White Sea. In 1169 Kiev was sacked by Suzdal and the title of Great Prince was transferred to the ruler of the latter, commonly known as Great Prince of Vladimir, after Suzdal's capital.

NORWAY

SWEDEN

Nidaros

Oslo

Uppsala

Åbo

Finns

NOVGOROD

FINNO-UGRIANS

Estonians

Pskov

Livs

BALTIC
SEA

Lithuanians

Polotsk

Vitebsk

SMOLENSK

Smolensk

Tula

VLADIMIR-SUZDAL

Vladimir

Suzdal

MUROM-
RYAZAN

Volga

Bulgar

VOLGA
BULGARIA

Aarhus

Roskilde

Malmö

DENMARK

POMERELIA

Prussians

POLOTSK

Minsk

CHERNIGOV

Hamburg

POMERANIA

Bremen

Hanover

GREAT
POLAND

Poznań

MAZOVIA

Oder

Wrocław

SILESIA

LITTLE
POLAND

Vistula

Brest

TUROV-
PINSK

VOLHYNIA

KIEV

NOVGOROD-
SEVERSK

PEREYASLAVL

Don

…s

Volga

...GDOM

...OF

Elbe

Nuremberg

KINGDOM OF
BOHEMIA

Prague

Brno

MANY

Munich

Danube

Vienna

Salzburg

Innsbruck

Graz

Pozsony

Esztergom

GALICH

Galich

GALICH

Kiev

Dnieper

Dniester

C   u   m   a   n

C   u   m   a   n   s

Trieste

Venice

VENETIAN
REPUBLIC

Verona

Legnano

Bologna

...isa

Florence

Perugia

Zara

HUNGARY

Pécs

Szeged

Temesvár

Zágráb

Spalatum

Mostar

Cumans

Belgrade

Danube

(to Kiev)

(to Kiev)

Cherson

Alans

BLACK   SEA

GEORGIA

BYZANTINE

Naissus

Serdica

Odessus

Rome
PAPAL
STATE

Naples

Bari

Taranto

KINGDOM OF SICILY

Palermo

Messina

Catania

Salonica

Janina

Scupi

Philippopolis

Adrianople

Constantinople

Smyrna

Athens

EMPIRE

RUM
(ICONIUM)

Myriocephalum

Iconium

**Armenian
rulers**

PRINCIPALITY
OF ANTIOCH

Trapezus

Seljuk

rulers

Local
dynasties

Tigris

Euphrates

...SEA

Malta

Nicosia

COUNTY OF
TRIPOLIS

KINGDOM OF
JERUSALEM

(Saladin)

...ascus

Beirut

Bedouins

DENMARK

NORTH SEA

FRIESLAND

o Bremen

DUCHY OF SAXONY

o Utrecht

DUCHY OF LOWER LORRAINE

o Münster

Brunswick o

POMERANIA

MARGRAVATE OF BRANDENBURG

o Magdeburg

MARGRAVATE OF LUSATIA

POLISH STATES

Antwerp o
Cologne o
Aachen (Aix-la-Chapelle)
Namur o

MARGRAVATE OF LANDSBERG
Merseburg o
Meissen o

LANDGRAVIATE OF THURINGIA

PLEISSNER-LAND VOGTLAND
MARGRAVATE OF MEISSEN

Erfurt o

KINGDOM OF BOHEMIA

MARGRAVATE OF MORAVIA

Trier o
Mainz o

DUCHY OF FRANCONIA

Würzburg o

Nuremberg o

DUCHY OF LORRAINE
Metz o
UPPER
Toul o

DUCHY OF SWABIA

Ulm o
Augsburg o

DUCHY OF BAVARIA
Ratisbon o

Passau o

DUCHY OF AUSTRIA
Vienna o

FRANCE

Munich o

Salzburg o

Constance o

DUCHY OF STYRIA

HUNGARY

KINGDOM OF BURGUNDY (ARLES)

Brixen o

DUCHY OF CARINTHIA

Trent o

KINGDOM OF ITALY

VENETIAN REPUBLIC

MARGRAVATE OF CARNIOLA

GERMANY: EMERGING DYNASTIES, 1179 [4]

- Guelph lands
- Ascanian lands
- Wettin lands
- Babenberg lands
- Hohenstaufen Lands
- Other parts of the Holy Roman Empire
- — Frontiers, 1179

KING DOM OF MAN (to Norway)

SCOTLAND
Edir o
Glasgo o

IRELAND

Dublin o

Cork o

WELSH STATES

B r i t

FRANCE

Montpellier o

Provence

Santander o
Oviedo o

Béarn

Carcassonne

Santiago o

LEON *(separated from Castile in 1157)*

León o

NAVARRE

Pamplona o

A R A G O N
(united with Catalonia from 1137)

Gerona o

Huesca o

Burgos o

Saragossa o

Lérida o

Barcelona o

Oporto o

Zamora o
Salamanca o
Ávila o

Valladolid o

CASTILE
(separated from Leon in 1157)

Segovia o

Calatayud o

Tarragona o

Coimbra o

Ciudad Rodrigo o

Coria o

Guadalajara o

Toledo o

Cuenca o

Teruel o

Tortosa o

PORTUGAL *(fully independent from 1143)*

Santarém o

Badajoz o
Maridah o

Calatrava o

Valencia o

Palma o

MUSLIM KINGDOM OF MALLORCA

Lisbon o
Évora o

Beja o

EMPIRE OF THE ALMOHADS

Qurtubah o

Mursiyah o
Cartagena o

Ishbiliyah o

Gharnatah o

Qadis o

Malaqah o

Almería o

IBERIA: THE RECONQUISTA, 1085-1180 [1]

- Temporary Christian conquests at the end of the 11th century
- Controlled by El Cid, 1094-1102
- Northern limit of the Almoravid Empire, 1115
- Southern limit of areas temporarily held by Christians before 1180
- Catalan-Aragonese fiefs
- — Frontiers, 1180

BALTIC SEA

Kołobrz o

Szczecin o

Pomer

Slavs

Grea

Lubusz o

Poznań o

Pola

HOLY ROMAN EMPIRE

Głogów o

Wrocł

Si

HO
RO
EMP

HOLY ROMAN EMPIRE

Cambridge · London · erbury · HOLY ROMAN EMPIRE · NEL · Rouen · Paris · nandy · ne · Tours · jou · RANCE · noges · eaux · Aquitaine · HOLY ROMAN EMPIRE · cony · VARRE · ARAGON

THE FRAGMENTATION OF POLAND FROM 1138 **2**

Frontiers, 1138

Possessions of Bolesław III, 1138

Lands of the seniorate

Areas inherited by Bolesław's sons

Władysław

Mieszko

Bolesław

Henryk

Gdańsk · Prussians · a · Wyszogród · Masovia · Pultask · Włocławek · Płock · no · KIEVAN RUS · Łęczyca · Vistula · Kalisz · Radom · Tarnów · Lublin · Sandomiria · Sandomierz · a · Opole · Bytom · Cracowia · Cracow · (Little Poland) · HUNGARY

Iberia: the Reconquista, 1085-1180

1 The Christian advance into Spain which led to the capture of Toledo in 1085 had prompted the intervention of the Moroccan Almoravids in Spain (*see map 3, page 79*). The Almoravids took over most of the Muslim emirates in the early 1090s, Badajoz falling to them in 1095. The Almoravids, however, suffered a reverse when El Cid, a Christian soldier of fortune, captured Valencia in 1094.

Under Yusuf ibn-Tashfin and his son Ali (caliph 1106-43), the Almoravids overran the rest of Muslim Spain (1110-15) and recaptured Valencia from the Christians (1102), but, thereafter, the Christian states regained the initiative and expanded considerably. Under Alfonso VI and Alfonso VII León was particularly strong. In the 1140s Alfonso VII expanded his power to the Tagus and in 1147 he captured Almeria on the Mediterranean coast. Aragon and Catalonia united in 1137 and then captured the lower Ebro (1148-9). Portugal expanded greatly with the capture of Lisbon (1147). This owed much to help of a fleet of Flemings, Rhinelanders, Normans and English which was taking part in the Second Crusade. They pressed on to take Faro (1147) and to help Aragon and the Genoese in the successful siege of Tortosa (1148).

From the 1150s the Almoravids were replaced by the Almohads, Shi'ite sectaries who had already conquered Morocco in the 1140s. They lent new energy to Muslim resistance and the Christians were further hindered by the division of León into three kingdoms: León, Castile and Portugal. Navarre had broken away from Aragon in 1134. Despite these divisions, Alfonso VIII of Castile took Cuenca in 1177.

The Fragmentation of Poland from 1138

2 The power of the Polish monarchy was gravely affected both by the rise in the power of the magnates and by the granting of provinces to members of the ruling Piast dynasty. In his will, Boleslaw III Krzywousty ("the Wrymouthed", 1102-38), divided Poland between his sons, a process that made it harder to resist the rise of the magnates. This began the so-called "Period of Fragmentation" which lasted until the coronation of Wladyslaw I in 1320. During this time, politics revolved around the efforts of the regional princes to conquer the capital province of Cracowia and with it the title of *princeps* (senior prince). Fighting against each other, the princes were unable to mount effective resistance to German advances or to retain control over Pomerania.

The Growth of the Angevin Empire, 1154-80

3 Henry II (1154-89) of England created a powerful empire spanning the English Channel. His marriage to Eleanor of Aquitaine brought him control over most of southwest France. Combined with the Norman and Angevin (Anjou) inheri-

tances, this made him the most powerful ruler in France, more so than his suzerain (feudal lord) for these French territories, Louis VII, king of France. In his first 12 years Henry used this power to resolve inheritance disputes in his favour, gaining control of Brittany and more of southern France. Angevin power was also dynamic in Britain. The Scottish frontier was settled in 1157, with Cumbria and Northumbria definitively part of England, and Henry campaigned actively in Wales.

Following initiatives by some of his nobles, particularly Richard de Clare, "Strongbow", who were creating powerful lordships for themselves, Henry intervened in Ireland in 1171. This was in order to establish his rights in accordance with a papal bull of 1155 from the English pope, Adrian IV. Like Wales, Ireland was far from unified, and this provided opportunities for aristocratic and royal ambitions. Henry successfully established the new lordship of Ireland, based on Dublin, created a large royal demesne for himself and bound the Anglo-Norman barons and most of the native Irish kings to him.

Germany: Emerging Dynasties, 1179

4 The unification of the kingdom of Germany with those of Italy (951) and Burgundy (1033) created a potentially powerful unit, although the Investiture Controversy with the papacy in the late 11th century (*see page 76*) exacerbated the natural difficulties of attempting to maintain authority over such a wide area. The Empire, however, regained its dynamism in the 12th century. The Salian dynasty had come to a close with the death of Henry V (1106-25) who settled the Investiture Controversy and was replaced by the Hohenstaufen dynasty, named after the Swabian castle of Staufen.

The first Hohenstaufen Emperor, Conrad III (1138-52), was succeeded by his nephew Frederick I Barbarossa (1152-90). He was a vigorous ruler, but his position was affected by the growing power of many of the leading aristocratic families, especially the Guelphs in Saxony. Henry the Proud, the head of the Guelphs, had resisted Conrad III, and his son, Henry the Lion, was a crucial figure in Barbarossa's reign. Duke of Saxony (1142-80) and Bavaria (1156-80), he helped to expand Germany eastwards and also founded Munich in 1158. Henry broke with Barbarossa in 1176, was deprived of his lands and exiled. The commitment of Frederick to maintaining and expanding Imperial power in Italy weakened his position in Germany, although the extent of the territorial power there of his family, the Hohenstaufen, remained considerable.

The Empire was altered by these dynastic rivalries on its eastern frontier too, where the Babenburg rulers of Austria were drawn in on the side of the Hohenstaufen. Even so, the Empire managed to expand: the Duchy of Pomerania was added in 1181.

1180

The Eve of the Mongol Invasions

The period after 1180 saw the Christians in Spain at first under severe pressure from the Almohads, but the victory of Alfonso VIII of Castille over the Muslim forces at Las Navas de Tolosa in 1212 opened the way for significant inroads into Almohad territory over the next 50 years. The Third Crusade (1190-1), in contrast, failed to regain more than a part of the conquests made by Saladin. The Fourth Crusade (1202-4), under Venetian influence, in fact attacked not the Muslims, but first Zara, which the Hungarians had captured in 1186, and then Constantinople: Alexius Angelus, the son of the deposed Byzantine Emperor Isaac II (1185-1195), offered 200,000 marks, help with the crusade and the union of the Orthodox Church with Rome if his uncle was removed. This was effected by the Crusaders in July 1203, but the new Emperor, Alexius IV, was unable to fulfil his promises and was deposed in an anti-Western rising. This led the Crusaders to storm the city, crown Count Baldwin of Flanders as first Latin Emperor of Constantinople and partition the Byzantine Empire between them.

Even before 1204, the Byzantine Empire had been severely weakened in the Balkans. Bulgaria, under Tsars Peter and Asen, had re-asserted its independence after 1185, and by 1204 had captured large areas of Thessaly, Macedonia and Thrace. Serbia, too, under Stepan Nemanja (d. 1196) and Stepan II (1196-1228), gained Byzantine recognition of its independence and steadily expanded its territory to the south and east. Both Serbia and Bulgaria for a time recognised the religious authority of the Pope, so diluting Byzantine and Orthodox influence even further.

The Byzantine Empire was dealt a shattering blow, if not a fatal one, by the Latin occupation of its capital. The Latins did not succeed in occupying the entire Empire, and centres of resistance grew up around the Trebizond (the Empire of Trebizond), Arta (the Despotate of Epirus), and Nicaea (the Empire of Nicaea). The Nicaean Empire under Theodore Lascaris prevented the Latins from gaining a permanent foothold in Anatolia, and ultimately proved the most successful focus for Byzantine opposition to the western invaders.

Further north the Swedes gained a foothold in Finland, while a crusading military order, the Sword Brothers, from a base on the river Dvina established in 1199, conquered Livonia. Meanwhile, in Italy, Emperor Henry VI (1190-7), the son of Frederick I Barbarossa (*see* map 4, page 83), married the heiress to the Kingdom of Sicily. Hohenstaufen authority was established in southern Italy in 1190-4 and in 1194 Henry's Genoese and Pisan fleet ensured control of Sicily: the Hohenstaufen became the wealthiest rulers in Europe.

To the east, the Mongols under Genghiz Khan (1206-27) were extending their sway and raiding on the Eurasian steppe. Fortunately for Christendom, Genghiz had concentrated on China and then the Muslim states of Central Asia, but the successful campaign against the Khwarizm Shah of Persia (1220-1) led Mongol forces to move west into the Caucasus, defeating the kingdom of Georgia, the Alans and Cumans to the north of the Caucasus, and the south Russian princes. This was achieved by a subsidiary Mongol force, and it indicated the vulnerability of Europe to the mobile peoples of Central Asia. The European states were ill-placed to resist the wave of invasion which was about to engulf them from the east, lacking the population, military resources and technology to face this new foe.

Lapps

NORWAY

Nidaros

gen

Oslo

SWEDEN

Finns

Uppsala

Åbo

Reval (to Denmark)

Estonians

ORDER OF THE SWORD BROTHERS

Pskov

NOVGOROD

Novgorod

(To Rostov)

VLADIMIR-SUZDAL

ROSTOV

YURIEV

Suzdal

Vladimir

Moscow

VOLGA BULGARIA

Bulgar

Volga

Aarhus

Roskilde

Lund

BALTIC SEA

Curonians

Riga

Lithuanians

Polotsk

Vitebsk

SMOLENSK

Smolensk

Tula

MUROM-RYAZAN

PEREYASLAVL

DENMARK

Hamburg

Bremen

Elbe

Stettin

POMERELIA

Prussians

POLOTSK

Minsk

Don

Hanover

CUJAVIA

MAZOVIA

TUROV-PINSK

CHERNIGOV

NOVGOROD-SEVERSK

NGDOM

GREAT POLAND

Poznań

Vistula

Meissen

SILESIA

Wrocław

Oder

LITTLE POLAND

VOLHYNIA

KIEV

Kiev

PEREYASLAVL

OF

Prague

KINGDOM OF BOHEMIA

kfurt

Nuremberg

MANY

Brünn

Cracow

Dnieper

Volga

Munich

Danube

Galich

GALICH

Salzburg

Pozsony

Dniester

Vienna

Pest

Esztergom

C

Graz

HUNGARY

Kolozsvár

u

m

a

n

s

(to Kiev)

Pécs

Szeged

(to Kiev)

Alans

OM

Zágráb

Temesvár

Brassó

(to Venice)

Bologna

Florence

Zara

BOSNIA

Belgrade

ly

Spalato

VENETIAN REPUBLIC

BLACK SEA

PAPAL STATE

Rome

SERBIA

Nish

BULGARIA

Danube

Varna

Serdica

GEORGIA

Trebizond

EMPIRE OF TREBIZOND

Naples

Bari

Taranto

Philippopolis

Scupi

Adrianople LATIN

Constantinople

RUM (ICONIUM)

Angora

KHWARIZM

Palermo

Messina

KINGDOM OF SICILY

Catania

DUCHY OF ATHENS

PRINCIPALITY OF ACHAIA

KINGDOM OF SALONICA

Salonica

EMPIRE (ROMANIA)

DESPOTATE OF EPIRUS

Janina

Athens

EMPIRE OF NICAEA

Nicaea

Iconium

LESSER ARMENIA

Tigris

Mosul

PRINCIPALITY OF ANTIOCH

AYYUBIDS

SEA

VENETIAN REPUBLIC

(to Venice)

(Gabalas)

KINGDOM OF CYPRUS

Nicosia

COUNTY OF TRIPOLIS

Beirut

Damascus

Bedouins

The map at top left shows Eastern Europe with labels:

VOLHYNIA, KIEV, Lvov, rzemyśl, GALICH, Galich (under intermittent Hungarian control, 1208-34), Cumans, Kolozsvár, Brassó, Szörény, C u m a n i a, BULGARIA, Trnovo, Varna, Sredets, Philippopolis, Adrianople

THE EXPANSION OF DENMARK, c.950-1223

Legend	
Denmark, c.950	to Denmark, 1185
Brought under Danish rule by Cnut the Great (with dates)	to Denmark, early 13th century (with dates)
to Denmark, 1168	Frontiers, 1223

Map of Scandinavia and the Baltic with labels: L a p p s, Trondhjem, F i n n s, NORWAY (1028-35), Oslo, S W E D E N, B A L T I C   S T A T E S, Estonia (1219), Estonians, ORDER OF THE SWORD BROTHERS, DENMARK, Aarhus, BALTIC SEA, Lund, Ribe, Roskilde, Copenhagen, (1025), (1202), Hamburg, Baltic Peoples, POLISH STATES, HOLY ROMAN EMPIRE, R U S S I A N

The Expansion of Denmark, c. 950-1223

1 The Empire of Cnut (*see* page 72) and his successors had seen the king of Denmark also ruling England (1016-42) and Norway (1028-35). In the 1180s Denmark resumed an expansive role, this time in the Baltic. By 1185 the Danes, had occupied Pomerania, Mecklenburg and Holstein. King Valdemar Sejr (1202-41) captured the area around Lübeck and Hamburg, and during his reign the Danes played a major role in the crusading advance along the southern and eastern shores of the Baltic. In 1219-20 Denmark gained control of northern Estonia with their major base at Reval (Tallinn).

France: the Growth of the Royal Domain to 1223

2 The 12th century saw great expansion in the royal domain in France, that part of the kingdom under the direct control of the king rather than powerful feudal vassals. This growth was particularly at the expense of the Angevin monarchy. The determination and military success of Philip Augustus (1180-1223) led to King John of England's loss of most of his father's vast continental possessions, including Normandy and Anjou, in 1203-4. John's attempt to recover this continental inheritance ended in failure when his allies were defeated at Bouvines (1214). John's domestic opponents then offered the English throne to Philip's son Louis. His attempted invasion of England in 1217 was defeated by supporters of John's infant son, Henry III. French intervention in England was a logical consequence of the post-Conquest cross-Channel nature of the English monarchy. It was now plausible to attack England, or to support its rivals within the British Isles, in order to undermine the policy of England's monarchs, specifically their defence of their continental interests.

Whereas in Britain there were natural frontiers for most of the realm – the Anglo-Scottish and Anglo-Welsh land frontiers were far shorter than the marine frontiers – this was not the case to anywhere near the same extent on the continent. While the overlapping nature of feudal jurisdictions militated against the development of a national consciousness, within areas with a common sovereign, such as France, there were also important cultural, not least linguistic, divides.

In southern France the crusade against the Cathar (Albigensian) Christian heresy led eventually to an increase in royal power. Innocent III proclaimed a crusade in 1209, and Simon de Montfort overran much of Languedoc: Carcassonne fell after a short siege. In 1213 King Peter II of Aragon intervened. An orthodox Catholic, he was concerned about de Montfort's rising power, and backed Count Raymond VI of Toulouse with whom de Montfort was at war. Their united forces were defeated at Muret in September 1213. Peter was killed and the crusaders occupied Toulouse. Raymond regained the city in 1217 and his son was not forced to make peace until 1229. The war was important because expeditions in 1219 and 1226 by Louis, first as prince and then as Louis VIII, helped to strengthen royal influence in the region while the defeat of Aragon decisively weakened a long-lasting link between southern France and Catalonia.

Hungary and the Northern Balkans before the Mongols, 1140-1240

3 The growth in the power of Hungary was the most important development to the north of the Byzantine Empire in the 12th century. After having successfully fended off the attempts of Emperor Manuel I to conquer her, Hungary counterattacked following his death in 1180. The Hungarians gained not only southern Croatia and Bosnia, but also seized a frontier zone in the vicinity of Belgrade. At the start of the 13th century, the Hungarian kings extended their rule over the area known as Cumania (later Wallachia). The Hungarian kings also made attempts to take control of the Russian principality of Galich, but the enterprise proved too costly to sustain. The southern gains were more long-lasting. These areas were not annexed directly to Hungary, but administered by "bans", officials answering to the King of Hungary.

To the south Serbia regained her independence under Stefan Nemanja (1168-96). A successful revolt against Byzantium led to the restoration of Bulgarian independence in the mid 1180s too: the "Empire of Vlachs and Bulgars", or the Second Bulgarian Empire, had its capital at Trnovo. With the collapse of the Byzantine empire in 1204, both Bulgaria and Serbia made gains.

The Latin Empire, 1190-1212

4 The Latin Empire, known as "Romania", was created in 1204 after the Fourth Crusaders took Constantinople (*see* page 84), and comprised a number of feudal territories: the Principality of Achaia, the Duchy of Athens and the Kingdom of Salonica or Thessaly. The Venetians gained many of the Aegean islands, Candia (Crete) and a number of strategic points on the mainland that helped to give them command of coastal waters: the large crews required to man the oars of galleys needed a chain of bases to supply them. Part of the structure of a successful naval system was the existence of such bases, and it was these that Venetian expansion secured.

The Greeks were left with more peripheral parts of the Byzantine empire: the Empires of Nicaea and Trebizond, and the Despotates of Epirus and Rhodes (under the Gabalas). Nicaea, first under Theodore Lascaris (1206-22), was best placed to act as the Greek successor state as it was most able to challenge the Latins. The Latin empire rapidly encountered problems. Nicaea, which absorbed Rhodes, overran its Asian territories, while in 1223 Epirus took Salonica and made it the capital of the Empire of Salonica. The land route from Constantinople to Athens was therefore lost and the Latin Empire became dependent on maritime links.

1223

1270

The High Middle Ages

Eastern Europe suffered great turmoil in the 13th century, undergoing significantly greater territorial changes than occurred in Western Europe in the period. The Mongol invasions devastated the area: the northern principalities of Rus were overrun in 1233-9; Kiev was stormed and razed in 1240; in 1240-4 the Mongols tore through Hungary, taking Pest, while smaller forces poured into Poland, took Cracow and defeated a German-Polish army at Wãhlstatt in 1241. Only the death of the Great Khan Ogedai in December 1241 granted a respite to Europe as the Mongol hordes were recalled. The Byzantine Empire, meanwhile, had been restored with the capture of Constantinople from the Latins in 1261.

Another area of major change was the eastern Baltic, where the crusading movement still retained its vitality. The Teutonic Knights overran Prussia, their sovereign rights protected by Imperial (1226) and papal recognition (1234), the latter making their territory a papal fief. Königsberg was established as a base in 1255, Memel in 1252. The Knights of the Sword, however, were less successful. After their defeat by the pagan Lithuanians in 1236, they were absorbed by the Teutonic Knights. The latter, however, faced revolts in Prussia: their advance on Pskov was stopped by Prince Alexander Nevsky of Novgorod, who then defeated them on the frozen surface of Lake Peipus (1242); and they were defeated by the Lithuanians at Durben in 1260.

In Western Europe, the Muslims continued to lose ground in Spain, while the English Plantagenet kings were similarly on the defensive in France. Henry III (1216-72) failed to defeat the French and regain the lands lost by his father, John. In 1224 war with France resumed and Louis VIII successfully invaded Poitou and Gascony, though Bordeaux remained faithful to Henry, in part because of its commercial links with England. By the Treaty of Paris (1259), Henry III renounced his rights to Normandy, Anjou and Poitou.

Norway, too, suffered a reverse in its interests across its maritime empire. It obtained the submission of the Icelanders (1248), but lost territory to Scotland. In 1098 Magnus Barelegs had secured by treaty Norwegian rule of the islands to the west of Scotland. By the Treaty of Perth (1266), however, the Western Isles were regained by Scotland, a consequence of the failure of Hakon IV of Norway to overcome Alexander III of Scotland at Largs (1263), and the general failure of the entire campaign.

The increasing assertiveness of the Scottish kings provides a good example of the role of able monarchs, improved administrative and military mechanisms and the support of the Church in the formation of states, rather than of ethnic homogeneity. Though the authority of the kings over much of their kingdom, especially Galloway, the Highlands and the Isles, was limited, the fertile central belt was under secure control. Although ethnically diverse, Scotland was more politically united than Wales or Ireland. This was related to the introduction of Norman administrative methods and feudal tenures by David I (1124-53), who had been educated at the court of his brother-in-law, Henry I of England. Normanization also affected the Church, leading to new monastic foundations, the appointment of Anglo-French bishops, and thus to stronger Continental links. The Norman military machine of knights and castles, improved administrative mechanisms (especially the use of sheriffs), the skill of the rulers, and economic expansion served as the bases for an extension of royal power in the 13th century.

Lapps

NORWAY

Nidaros

gen

Oslo

SWEDEN

Åbo

DENMARK

Aarhus

Roskilde

Hamburg

Bremen

Hanover

MALL

Meissen

Stettin

Elbe

BALTIC
SEA

Riga

(to Denmark)
Reval

Lake
Peipus

Pskov

ORDER

Dünaburg

Königsberg

POMERELIA

TEUTONIC

Vilnius

LITHUANIA

Polotsk

Vitebsk

POLOTSK

Novgorod

N O V G O R O D

SMOLENSK

Smolensk

BELOOZERO

VELIKI USTYUG

GALICH

YAROSLAVL

KOSTROMA

UGLICH
PEREYASLAVL

ROSTOV

YURIEV

SUZDAL-
NIZHEGOROD

TVER

Suzdal

Vladimir

Volga

DMITROV

MUSCOVY

Moscow

VLADIMIR

STARODUB

MUROM

VLADIMIR

(to Novgorod)

Tula

RYAZAN

CHERNIGOV

NOVGOROD
SEVERSK

Don

Sarai

Volga

GREAT
POLAND

Poznań

CUJAVIAN
PRINCIPALITIES

MAZOVIA

Vistula

SILESIAN

Wahlstatt

PRINCIPALITIES

Wrocław

Meissen

BERESTIE

LITTLE
POLAND

VLADIMIR

Oder

TUROV-PINSK

KIEV

Kiev

PEREYASLAVL

Prague

BOHEMIA

Nuremberg

MORAVIA

Brünn

Cracow

ISYA-
SLAVL

SVIZH-
DEN

KREMENETS

Galich

GALICH

Dniester

Dnieper

TES

Munich

AUSTRIA

Danube

Salzburg

Innsbruck

Vienna

STYRIA

Graz

Pozsony

Buda

Eger

Kassa

Debrecen

Kolozsvár

HUNGARY

Pécs

Szeged

Temesvár

Brassó

Zágráb

VENETIAN REPUBLIC

Bologna

Florence

Zara

Spalato

BOSNIA

Belgrade

PAPAL

STATE

Rome

Naples

Bari

Taranto

Palermo

KINGDOM OF SICILY

Messina

Catania

Malta

SERBIA

Nish

Danube

Tirnovo

BULGARIA

Varna

Serdica

Scupi

Philippopolis

Adrianople

BYZANTINE

Constantinople

Salonica

DESPOTATE OF EPIRUS

DUCHY
OF
ATHENS

Athens

PR. OF ACHAIA

(to Venice)

Crete

SEA

BLACK   SEA

Caffa
(to Genoa)

GEORGIA

Trebizond

EMPIRE OF TREBIZOND

EMPIRE

RUM

(ICONIUM)

Angora

Smyrna

LESSER
ARMENIA

ILKHAN

EMPIRE

Tigris

Mosul

COUNTY OF
TRIPOLIS

MAMELUKES

KINGDOM
OF CYPRUS

Nicosia

KINGDOM OF
JERUSALEM

Beirut

Damascus

Bedouins

Euphrates

G O L D E N   H O R D E

89

THE AEGEAN: THE DECLINE OF THE LATIN STATES, 1212-70 2

- The Latin Empire, 1212
- The Empire of Nicaea, 1214
- Added by 1247 (with dates)
- Added in 1246
- Added later (with dates)
- The Despotate of Epirus 1224-30
- Southern boundary of Bulgaria from 1230
- Latin States
- Venetian possessions and dependencies
- Frontiers, 1270

THE EXPANSION OF THE PAPAL STATE, 1178-1278 1

- The Papal State, 1178
- Added by 1219
- Added by 1278
- Frontiers, 1278

The Expansion of the Papal State, 1178-1278

1 The struggle between the Hohenstaufens and their opponents (*see* map 4, page 83) allowed the papacy to expand its territory in Italy. The Emperor Frederick II (1212-50) sought to consolidate Imperial power in Italy, but was excommunicated by the papacy and opposed by the Lombard cities. In Sicily, however, Frederick bloodily suppressed a Muslim rebellion that had begun in 1189, and which had left the mountainous interior of the island in practice an independent state that resisted the Christians and sought help from Muslim powers elsewhere. Between 1220 and 1246 Frederick launched a series of campaigns which destroyed the Muslim community of Sicily. His opponents elsewhere in Italy were more successful. Frederick's son Conrad IV (1250-4) continued the struggle with the papacy, but the position of his son Conradin was usurped by Frederick's second son Manfred, allowing the Pope to declare the throne forfeit and to offer it to Louis IX of France who passed it on to his brother, Charles of Anjou. As part of a crusade Charles defeated Manfred in 1266 and Conradin at Tagliacozzo (1268), ending the Hohenstaufen state in southern Italy and transferring the kingdom of Sicily to the Angevins. That transfer lasted only until 1282 when, in the Sicilian Vespers, Sicily revolted and turned to the house of Aragon. Thereafter Sicily and Naples were different states.

The papacy was able to benefit from the weaknesses of its Italian opponents to expand northwards, first into the Duchy of Spoleto and the March of Ancona, and then into the Romagna. The Frankish rulers had granted the papacy much of central Italy in the 8th century, but it had proved very difficult for the popes to wield effective control outside the area near Rome, and the lands to the east of the Apennines were in effect independent. Similar problems arose with the lands bequeathed to the papacy by the pious Countess Mathilda of Tuscany, who died in 1115. Under Innocent III (Pope, 1198-1216) there was a major attempt to give meaning to papal territorial claims and this was continued under his successors. This was achieved by obtaining Imperial renunciation of territory and by granting papal "bulls" of protection. The popes began to organize their territory more effectively, creating provinces governed by rectors.

The Aegean: the Decline of the Latin States, 1212-70

2 The Latin Empire created after the Fourth Crusade in 1204 faced Greek opposition divided between the Despotate of Epirus and the Empire of Nicaea. At first it seemed as if Epirus would be the most serious threat to the Latins. Epirus, however, was decisively defeated by the Bulgarians in 1230, leaving the way clear for the Empire of Nicaea to claim the Byzantine mantle.

Emperor John III Vatatzes (1222-54) played the crucial role in the firm establishment of the Empire of Nicaea. In 1225 he decisively defeated the Latins and occupied almost all their territory in Asia Minor. The Nicaean fleet then took the Aegean islands of Lesbos, Chios, Samos and Icaria. Vatatzes's army also captured much of eastern Thrace.

The Byzantines were soon able to recapture more land in the Balkans. The Mongol invasion in 1241 (*see* page 88) severely weakened the Bulgarians, and the Byzantine Emperor took advantage of this to extend his territory deep into Thrace and Macedonia: in December 1246 he entered Salonica; in 1252, as a result of an unsuccessful campaign against the Nicaean Emperor, the Despot of Epirus, Michael II, was forced to cede the eastern portion of his domains to Nicaea. It was the Nicaean Emperor Michael VIII (1258-82), who finally retook Constantinople in 1261, restoring it to Byzantine rule after the 45-year Latin occupation. As part of the surrender he acquired the area around Mistra in the Peloponnese.

Latin rule, however, still clung on in places. Venice retained many of its gains, particularly Crete which increased its power in the eastern Mediterranean, while the surviving Latin principalities, Athens and Achaia, were driven to seek the support of Charles of Anjou, the brother of Louis IX of France, who in 1266 had conquered southern Italy, killing its Hohenstaufen ruler at the battle of Benevento. With that base he wished to create a second Latin empire in the eastern Mediterranean. He gained Corfu and the Latin kingdom of Achaia (1267) and then conquered much of Epirus, being crowned King of Albania.

The loss of Constantinople marked a major defeat for Western Christendom, for the Latin Patriarch who had been installed in Constantinople was replaced by the Greek Patriarch, now returned from Nicaea. The Armenian Church remained faithful to the Papacy, but the Bulgars, who had agreed to transfer their allegiance to the Papacy in return for a patriarch of their own at Trnovo, reverted to Orthodoxy in 1235.

Bohemian Expansion under Ottakar II, 1250-69

3 The kingdom of Bohemia expanded greatly in the 13th century. Ottokar II (1253-78) did not become king until 1253, but in 1251 he had already been elected Duke of Austria and Styria. He suffered a setback when he lost Styria to Hungary in 1254. He regained it, however, in 1260, and, funded by the silver mines of Bohemia and Moravia, he continued his southward expansion, gaining Carinthia and Carniola. However, the new Holy Roman Emperor, Rudolf II (1273-91), drove him from all but the original provinces of the crown of Bohemia by 1276, and Ottokar's successors looked to the north and east instead. Wenceslaus II (1278-1305) was elected King of Poland (1306) and his son Wenceslaus III (1305-6) King of Hungary (1301).

1270

BOHEMIAN EXPANSION UNDER OTTOKAR II, 1250-69 **3**

- Lands of the Bohemian crown, 1250
- Acquired by Ottokar, 1251
- Acquired by Ottokar, 1260
- Acquired by Ottokar, 1266
- Acquired by Ottokar, 1269
- Western limit of Hungarian control, 1254-60
- Frontier of the Holy Roman Empire
- Frontiers, 1270

The Consolidation of England

The fall of Acre in 1291 marked the end of the crusading presence in Palestine and Syria, but not the end of the crusading movement. The Knights of St John (Hospitallers) established a new base on Rhodes (1309), while Cyprus – which had been captured from its Byzantine ruler by Richard I of England and sold by him to his friend Guy of Lusignan, the former king of Jerusalem – remained under the Lusignan kings until acquired by Venice in 1489. Crusading also continued in the eastern Baltic. The Swedes proceeded with their conquest of southern Finland, where their position was recognised by Novgorod in 1323, while the Teutonic Knights moved their headquarters from Acre to Marienburg (1309) and waged war with the pagan Lithuanians. Meanwhile the French monarchy continued to expand, adding Flanders and several areas in the south to the royal domain by 1328.

The revived Byzantine Empire was unable to resist Ottoman advances in Anatolia, while there was also pressure on its northern frontier: under Tudor Svetoslav (1300-21), Bulgaria revived, after a period as a tributary of the Mongol Golden Horde, and expanded to include most of Macedonia and much of Serbia. These gains were, however, lost to the Serbs under Stefan Uros II (1282-1321) and Stefan Uros III (1321-31). The latter gained control over much of the strategic Vardar valley from Bulgaria and Byzantium.

Further north the power of the rulers of Hungary was greatly limited by the growth of aristocratic power. The native Arpad dynasty died out in 1301 and the first of the Angevin rulers was elected king in 1308. From his capital at Visegrád, Charles I (1308-42) reduced the power of the magnates, but it proved difficult to retain control of frontier areas: northern Serbia and Dalmatia were lost. In 1310, meanwhile, John of Luxemburg was elected king of Bohemia (1310-46). He held much of Poland too, particularly Mazovia (1329-51) and most of Silesia. John also expanded in other directions, gaining Upper Lusatia (1319) and, temporarily, the Tyrol (1335-42). Under Wladyslaw I (1305-33), Poland successfully resisted rule by kings of Bohemia, but lost territory to both Bohemia and Brandenburg. To the east, Lithuania under Gediminas (1316-41) was emerging as an important power, expanding into the Rus principalities, which were greatly weakened by the Golden Horde (the Mongols who settled the steppes of Russia after the invasion of 1240).

In Britain, the English rulers consolidated their position by the conquest of Wales. In 1277 Edward I (1272-1307) invaded with massive force and the support of other Welsh rulers: Llywelyn, who had been recognised by Henry III as Prince of Wales in 1267, was made to cede much of his territory. He rebelled and was killed in 1282. English power was then anchored by the building of a series of massive castles, while the independent Welsh principality was brought to an end. Edward I was less successful in Scotland. The death in 1286 of Alexander III of Scotland led to the succession of his young granddaughter, Margaret, the Maid of Norway. The Treaty of Salisbury (1289) secured Margaret's marriage to the heir of Edward I, the future Edward II. The rights and laws of Scotland were to be preserved, but 1289 prefigured the 1603 Union of the crowns. Margaret was succeeded in 1290 by John Balliol, chosen by Edward I as king and who swore fealty and did homage to him. For a while, the hegemony of the King of England over the British Isles seemed established. However, the eventual failure of his son, Edward II, to consolidate this position led to the recognition of Scottish independence (1328).

NORWAY

Trondhjem

Oslo

SWEDEN

NOVGOROD

Lapps

Stockholm

Åbo

(to Denmark)
Reval

Novgorod

VELIKI USTYUG

BELOOZERO

GALICH

YAROSLAVL
KOSTROMA

Kazan

DENMARK

Aarhus

Roskilde

Königsberg

Danzig

Marienburg

Riga

Pskov

UGLICH

ROSTOV

SUZDAL-NIZHEGOROD

Volga

STARO-
DUB

Dünaburg

TVER
DMITROV

YURIEV
VLADIMIR

Hamburg

Stettin

BALTIC
SEA

Vilnius

Vitebsk

Moscow
MUSCOVY

MUROM

Bremen

Hanover

BRANDENBURG

TEUTONIC

ORDER

Minsk

NOVGOROD

SMOLENSK

Smolensk

RYAZAN

Don

MALL
ATES

Leipzig

Dresden

UPPER
LUSATIA

Breslau

POZNAŃ

Vistula

MAZOVIA

LITHUANIA

CHERNIGOV

Sarai

NOVGOROD-
SEVERSK

Oder

Warsaw

Elbe

Prague

Cracow

VLADIMIR

KIEV

Kiev

PEREYASLAVL

Volga

BOHEMIA

Nuremberg

MORAVIA

Brünn

ISYA-
SLAVL

SVIZH-
DEN

Dnieper

Astrakhan

frurt

BAVARIA

Munich

Salzburg

AUSTRIA

Vienna

KREMENETS

GALICH

Dniester

GOLDEN HORDE

nnsbruck

STYRIA

Graz

Pozsony

Buda

Visegrád

HUNGARY

Kassa

Debrecen

Kolozsvár

(to Genoa)

Venice

VENETIAN REPUBLIC

Zara

Spalato

BOSNIA

Pécs

Szeged

Temesvár

Brassó

Caffa

(to Genoa)

San Marino

PAPAL

STATE

Zágráb

Belgrade

WALLACHIA

BLACK SEA

GEORGIA

ome

NAPLES
0

Naples

Bari

Taranto

SERBIA

Nish

Danube

Tirnovo

BULGARIA

Sofia

Varna

Burgas

(to Genoa)

Trebizond

EMPIRE OF TREBIZOND

Skopje

Philippopolis

Adrianople

ÇANDAR

alermo

SICILY
(to Aragon)

Messina

Catania

BYZANTINE EMPIRE

Constantinople

OSMAN
(OTTOMAN)

Angora

ILKHAN EMPIRE

Salonica

KARASI

GERMIYAN

Malta

SEA

DESPOTATE OF EPIRUS

DUCHY
OF
ATHENS

(to
Genoa)

Smyrna

AYDIN

SARUHAN

LADIK

HAMID

SAHIPATA

Tigris

LESSER
ARMENIA

Mosul

Euphrates

PRINCIPALITY OF ACHAIA

Athens

MENTESE

TEKE

KARAMAN

KNIGHTS OF ST JOHN

VENETIAN

REPUBLIC

Crete

KINGDOM
OF CYPRUS

Nicosia

MAMELUKES

Beirut

Damascus

Bedouins

93

Montpellier
F R A N C E

(to England)

Béarn (to Foix)

Santander
Santiago
Oviedo
Bilbao
Léon
Pamplona
NAVARRE
ANDORRA
(condominium of the
County of Foix and the
Bishopric
of Urgel)
Urgel
Burgos
Gerona
KGDM. OF
MAJORCA
Zamora
Valladolid
Huesca
Saragossa
Lérida
Barcelona
CASTILE
(united with León, 1230)
Calatayud
Tarragona
Oporto
Salamanca
Segovia
Tortosa
Ávila
Madrid
Guadalajara
Ciudad Rodrigo
Coria
Cuenca
Teruel
Coimbra
Toledo
Palma
Santarém
Lisbon
Badajoz
Mérida
Calatrava
KINGDOM OF MAJORCA
Évora
Alicante
Beja
Cordova
Las Navas de Tolosa
Murcia
Seville
Cartagena
KGDM. OF GRANADA
(to Castile by 1492)
Granada
Málaga
Almería
Algeciras
Tangier
Ceuta
MARINIDS
Z A Y Y A N I D S

Como
Viscont…
SAVOY
Milan
Turin
Asti
DAUPHINÉ
SALUZZO
NIZZA
Genoa
PROVENCE
Nizza
L I G U R I A N
SEA
G E N O …

IBERIA: **1**
THE RECONQUISTA AFTER 1180

──── Northern limit of Muslim
control, 1180

──── Eastern boundary of
Portuguese North African
possessions from 1471

──── Frontiers, 1328

CATALAN-ARAGONESE EXPANSION TO THE MID-15TH CENTURY **2**

──── Aragon, including fiefs, c. 1210

▨ Under varying degrees of Catalan or Aragonese
dependency or influence to the mid-13th century

▨ Aragonese possessions, 1382

▨ Acquired by Aragon in the
15th century

☐ Temporary Aragonese fiefs,
mid-15th century

──── Frontiers, 1382

(to England)

F R A N C E

BÉARN
Toulouse
VENAISSIN
NAVARRE
Montpellier
(to 1349, and 1365-82)
Provence
(to 1258)
Marseilles
Nice
Rousillon
PRINCIPALITY
OF CATALONIA
GULF OF
LIONS
Saragossa **(united**
in 1137)
KINGDOM
OF
ARAGON
Barcelona
C A S T I L E
KINGDOM
OF
Valencia
VALENCIA
(acquired
1233-1304,
mainly in
1238)
B a l e a r i c s
(acquired from 1229,
Kingdom of Majorca
1276-1344)
GRANADA

HOLY
ROMAN
EMPIRE

SAN
MARINO
PAPAL
STATE
ADRIATIC
SEA
REPUBLI…
OF RA…
Corsica
Rome
KINGDOM
O
OF
Naples
NAPLES
(acquired 1435)
SARDINIA
(conquered
1322)
Alghero
(conquered
1420)
TYRRHENIAN
SEA
Cagliari
Messina
Palermo
SICILY
(acquired 1282)
Catania

M E D I T E R R A N E A N   S E A

Z A Y Y A N I D S

H A F S I D S

Iberia: the Reconquista after 1180

1 The Reconquista gathered pace again in the early 13th century, recovering the energy that had been shown in the late 11th century. The Almohads had displayed considerable vitality in the 12th century, heavily defeating Alfonso VIII of Castile at Alarcos (near Calatrava) in 1195. However, in 1212 Alfonso commanded the united armies of Castile, Aragon and Navarre and some crusaders in an advance south from Toledo which captured Calatrava and then crushed Caliph al-Nasir at Las Navas de Tolosa (16 July 1212), the crucial victory of the Reconquista. The exploitation of the victory was helped by the collapse of the Almohad Empire as a result of succession disputes. Most of southern Spain was overrun by 1275: Alfonso IX of León captured Badajoz in 1230; his son, Ferdinand III, King of Castile since 1217, inherited Léon in 1230. He captured Cordova in 1235 and Seville in 1248; his forces recaptured the valley of the Guadalquivir. Ferdinand's son, Alfonso X, conquered the emirates of Murcia and Niebla, leaving only the kingdom of Granada under the Muslims which, while in theory a vassal of Castile, was in practice independent. Meanwhile, James I of Aragon had captured the Balearic Islands (1229-35) and the Kingdom of Valencia, while the Portuguese advanced south to conquer the Algarve.

After this burst of activity, the Christian monarchs devoted most of their energies to attempting to resettle the lands they had conquered, from which many Muslims had fled or, as in the case of Andalusia and the cities of Valencia, been expelled; and to conflict with each other. This conflict was exacerbated by foreign intervention during the Hundred Years War between England and France (*see* map 3, page 103). English archers played a significant part in the battle of Aljubarrota (1385), where the Portuguese defeated a Castilian attempt at conquest. In 1386-87 Anglo-Portuguese forces jointly invaded Castile.

The Marinid Sultanate of Morocco, meanwhile, which had supplanted the Almohads in 1269, began attacking Christian Spain in 1275 and had some successes, but in 1340 Alfonso IV of Portugal and Alfonso XI of Castile decisively defeated the Marinids. The fall of Algeciras on the Straits of Gibraltar (1344) prevented further Moroccan intervention.

The advance against the Muslims resumed in the late 15th century. The Portuguese, who had expanded into Morocco, capturing Ceuta in 1415, added Arzila and Tangier in 1471. The marriage of Ferdinand of Aragon and Isabella of Castile in 1469 helped to unify Spain. Isabella inherited Castile in 1474, Ferdinand Aragon in 1479 and the two then ruled jointly. They turned against Granada from 1482 using artillery to capture the Muslim strongholds. Muslim disunity helped. One by one the remaining Muslim cities were taken. In 1492 the city of Granada itself fell. Spain no longer had a Muslim state. In 1497 a Spanish expedition captured Melilla on the Moroccan coast and the Reconquista was thus extended into Africa and the Mediterranean.

Catalan-Aragonese Expansion to the mid-15th Century

2 The opportunities for territorial expansion round the Mediterranean were demonstrated first by the expansion of Angevin power in the 13th century, and then by the house of Aragon. The Reconquista brought it Valencia and Majorca, the revolt known as the Sicilian Vespers (1282) led to the gain of Sicily, and in 1311 the Catalan Grand Company took the Duchy of Athens, which became a fief of Aragon in 1379. Meanwhile Aragon lost territory to the north of the Pyrenees. Provence was lost to Anjou, while James I renounced lands in France in 1258. The defeat of Peter I by Simon de Montfort at Muret in 1213, and the consolidation of French power in the Toulousain in the 1220s blocked any Aragonese hopes of expansion north of the Pyrenees. In 1435, on the death of the last Angevin ruler of Naples, Louis II, Naples passed to Alfonso of Aragon.

Northern Italy, 1336

3 Northern Italy owed nominal allegiance to the Holy Roman Empire. However, the cities of the region had for long had considerable rights of self-government and in some this had led to the development of republican communes. Other cities had fallen under the control of seignorial families. This was largely due to a need for stronger government, which led to a leading figure being given greater powers, or to an individual seizing these powers. Thus the Visconti came to dominate Milan, the Gonzaga Mantua, the Este Ferrara and Modena, and the della Scala Verona.

The della Scala family, which had ruled Verona since 1263, was at the height of its power in the mid-14th century. Cangrande I della Scala (d. 1329) extended their sway until, with the Visconti, they dominated Lombardy. Mastino II della Scala (1329-51) added control over Lucca, and later Parma, but fatally over-extended his resources, leading to the family's ultimate downfall. For the Visconti, Ottone Visconti, Archbishop of Milan (d. 1295), established the foundations of family power and from 1395 they were hereditary Dukes of Milan. Azzo D'Este (1205-64) established Este authority in Ferrara and the office of Signore of Ferrara was made hereditary in the family. Modena and Reggio were annexed by the Este. As yet, Venice had not begun to expand on the Italian mainland: her efforts were concentrated on the Dalmatian coast and in the Aegean. Only in 1339 did they change this policy with the annexation of Treviso.

This fragmented power structure of northern Italy contrasted with the more consolidated position in southern Italy. In the north the "state" was essentially a city or group of cities, while in the south the kingdoms of Naples and Sicily matched the governmental range, power and structure of developed states elsewhere in Europe.

1328

1382

The Ottoman Advance

The Ottoman Empire was the most dynamic military power in Europe, western Asia and North Africa in the 14th, 15th and 16th centuries. Originating in Anatolia in the 13th century, this Muslim Turkish state expanded rapidly, helped by the ability of its ruling family, the house of Osman, and by the weaknesses of its opponents. The Byzantine Empire was unable to contest control of Anatolia and the Balkans effectively with them.

The Ottoman state originated as a frontier principality in the Byzantine-Seljuk frontier zone in northwestern Anatolia. Under Osman I (*c.* 1281- *c.* 1324), the Ottomans expanded to the south of the Sea of Marmora. Under Orkhan (*c.* 1324-62) Bursa was conquered in 1326, becoming the Ottoman capital, and in 1354 Gallipoli, their first European foothold, was captured. From there, the Ottomans expanded in 1361 to capture Adrianople (Edirne), where they moved their capital in 1402. Under Murad (1362-89), expansion continued in Europe, particularly into Thrace, while in Anatolia the Ottomans expanded south towards the Mediterranean, completely absorbing the Emirates of Germiyan and Hamid by 1390 and 1392 respectively.

Further north, Moscow became the seat of a growing Russian principality, while Lithuania also expanded. To the west, the Danes sold Estonia to the Teutonic Knights (1346), and pawned their provinces in southern Sweden to the King of Sweden (they did, however, subsequently regain them), while King Valdemar Atterdag of Denmark conquered the Baltic island of Gotland from the Swedes (1360-1). The Danes were, however, defeated in 1370 by the cities of North Germany, who had joined together in the Hanseatic League . Meanwhile, France expanded its power in the Rhône valley, and in 1349 purchased the Dauphiné, a major gain to the east of the river. Further north, however, the Duchy of Burgundy, in theory a French fief, became more independent and powerful under Duke Philip the Bold (1363-1404), who gained the counties of Burgundy (1363) and Flanders (1384), both fiefs of the Empire. In the south of France, the Kingdom of Naples lost control of Provence in 1382.

Elsewhere, England and France were involved in the Hundred Years War from 1337 and the Scots became active as allies of the French. English power ebbed in Ireland. Though Edward Bruce's invasion of 1315 was crushed at the battle of Faughart (1318), and the scheme for a Scottish conquest of Ireland was thus wrecked, English lordship there did not recover. Despite major expeditions from England in the 1360s, 1370s and 1390, the situation continued to deteriorate. By the following century, direct English control was limited to the Pale, the area around Dublin, while the semi-autonomous Anglo-Irish lords and the independent Gaelic chieftains controlled most of the island.

Quite apart from the growing Ottoman threat, the 14th century was a period of crisis. The Black Death, an outbreak of bubonic plague which devastated Europe from 1346 to 1353, killed at least 20 million out of a European population of about 80 million. Further outbreaks later in the century prevented new population growth. This helped to exacerbate social and economic tensions: the socio-economic system of the "High Middle Ages" broke down, helping to cause a wave of rural and urban disorder. There was a sense of crisis in the Church, too: the transfer of the papacy to Avignon (1305-77) and the Great Schism (1378-1417) in western Christendom between areas owing allegiance to rival popes in Rome and Avignon challenged patterns of authority and obedience, contributing to a sense of fragmentation.

Trondhjem

NORWAY (in personal union with Denmark)

gen

Oslo

SWEDEN

Åbo

Stockholm

Reval

Estonia

NOVGOROD

Novgorod

VELIKI USTYUG

MUSCOVY

Kazan

Pskov

MUSCOVY

YAROSLAV

ROSTOV

SUZDAL-NIZHEGOROD

Volga

Gotland

BALTIC SEA

Riga

PSKOV

Tver

MUSCOVY

Moscow

Nizhniy Novgorod

Aarhus
Copenhagen
Roskilde
Malmö

ORDER

Dünaburg

(to Novgorod)

MUROM

Königsberg

Vitebsk

SMOLENSK

Smolensk

SMALL PRINCIPALITIES

RYAZAN

GOLDEN HORDE

Hamburg
Bremen
Hanover
BRANDENBURG
Berlin

Stettin

TEUTONIC

Vilnius

Minsk

DENMARK

MALL
ATES

Leipzig
Dresden

Danzig

Vistula

Poznań

Warsaw

LITHUANIA

Sarai

Oder

SILESIA

POLAND

Kiev

Volga

nkfurt
Prague
BOHEMIA
Nuremberg
Brünn
Elbe

Breslau

MORAVIA

Cracow

GALICH

Lvov

VLADIMIR

Don

Dnieper

Astrakhan

ttgart
BAVARIA
Munich
Salzburg
Danube
AUSTRIA
Vienna
STYRIA
Innsbrück
Graz
TYROL

Kassa

Pozsony

Buda

HUNGARY

Debrecen

Suceava

Dniester

Szeged

Kolozsvár

MOLDAVIA

(to Genoa)

(to Genoa)

Caffa

Venice

VENETIAN REPUBLIC

Pécsc

Zágráb

Temesvár

Brassó

Târgovişte

WALLACHIA

ce

SAN MARINO

PAPAL

Zara

BOSNIA

Belgrade

Danube

BULGARIAN STATES

Varna

BLACK SEA

GEORGIA

STATE

Rome

REPUBLIC OF RAGUSA

Spalato

Local rulers

SERBIAN

Nish

Sofia

(to Genoa)

EMPIRE OF TREBIZOND

Trebizond

NAPLES

STATES

Skopje

Philippopolis

Adrianople

BYZANTINE EMPIRE

CANDAR

Naples
Bari

Taranto

MEGALO-VLACHIA

Salonica

OTTOMAN EMPIRE

Gallipoli

Constantinople

Bursa

Angora

ERETNA

Mosul

DULKADIR

JALAYRIDS

Palermo
Messina

Catania

SICILY (to Aragon)

BYZANTINE EMPIRE

DUCHY OF ATHENS

Athens

(to Genoa)

SARUHAN

Smyrna

GERMIYAN

AYDIN

HAMID

KARAMAN

RAMAZAN

Tigris

Euphrates

(Tocchi)

PRINCIPALITY OF ACHAIA

BYZANTINE EMPIRE

VENETIAN REPUBLIC

KNIGHTS OF ST JOHN

MENTEŞE

TEKE

MAMELUKES

Malta

SEA

Crete

KINGDOM OF CYPRUS

Nicosia

Damascus

Bedouins

97

NORTHERN ITALY AT THE PEAK OF VISCONTI POWER, 1390

- Held temporarily by the Viscontis (with dates)
- Small states vassal to the Papacy
- Other church states
- Small Italian states and other states within the Holy Roman Empire
- Frontier of the Holy Roman Empire
- Frontiers, 1390

THE BALKANS ON THE EVE OF THE OTTOMAN CONQUEST, 1360

- The Byzantine Empire, 1340
- The Serb Empire, 1355
- Frontiers, 1360
- States surrounded by the colour of Hungary were Hungarian fiefs

CENTRAL EUROPE: THE GROWTH OF ANJOU POWER TO 1382

- Hungarian vassals, 1382 (with dates of final acknowledgement of Hungarian suzerainty)
- Hungarian provinces governed intermittently by Bosnian and Wallachian vassal rulers
- In personal union with Hungary, 1348-51
- In personal union with Hungary from 1370
- Frontiers, 1382

The Balkans on the Eve of the Ottoman Conquest, 1360

1 On the eve of the Ottoman advance the most dynamic Balkan power was Serbia. Under the Nemanja dynasty, the role of the aristocracy was subordinated to royal power and territorial aggrandisement. Under Stefan Dušan (1331-55), Serbia expanded south and west to gain the rest of Macedonia, Albania, Epirus and Thessaly. Dušan also gained control of part of Herzegovina. He proclaimed himself Emperor of the Serbs, Greeks, Bulgarians and Albanians (1346), established a self-governing Serbian Orthodox Church with its own patriarch at Peć and moved his capital south to Skopje. Dušan had ambitions to supplant Byzantium in the Balkans and the expansion of his state clearly gained from its weaknesses. However, as so often in an age of hereditary monarchy, the fortunes of Serbia were compromised by weak successors, whose power was only nominal and under whom Serbia quickly disintegrated into local principalities, some of which became vassals of Hungary. At the same time Bulgaria fell into decline, and broke into three independent states.

The Balkans were now covered by more than 20 mini-states – including the Byzantine Empire in its terminal state of decline – all quarrelling with each other and ill-prepared to face the growing challenge of the Ottomans. Byzantium's remaining strength, in particular, was sapped by a bitter civil war which broke out on the death of Emperor Andronicus III in 1341. The loss of Epirus and Thessaly to the Serbs and Chios to the Genoese in 1346 left the Empire shrunken and unable to resist the Turkish advance. In 1354 the Ottomans seized Gallipoli, their first significant European foothold.

Central Europe: the Growth of Anjou Power to 1382

2 Charles I, the first of the Angevin rulers of Hungary (1308-42), had greatly increased royal authority and had also strengthened the economy. His successor, Louis the Great (1342-82), considerably extended Hungarian territorial power, greatly helped by the weakness of Serbia after the death of Stefan Dušan in 1355. To the east, Moldavia emerged under the suzerainty of Hungary (1372), which then gradually expanded its power towards the Dniester and the Black Sea. To the south suzerainty was again acknowledged by Wallachia and also, temporarily, by parts of Serbia and Bulgaria, and, reluctantly, by Bosnia. On the Adriatic the Republic of Ragusa accepted Hungarian sovereignty in 1358, while a bitter Hungarian war with Venice left Louis in control of Dalmatia.

Louis led two campaigns to Naples to revenge the murder of his brother, who had been King of Naples. He then took the crown for himself, and Naples was united with Hungary in a personal union (1348-51). To the north, Galich was gained by Hungary in 1370 and that year Louis succeeded the childless Casimir the Great as King of Poland. This amalgamation was not long to survive the death of Louis in

1382, an indication of the essentially transient nature of state-building, especially in Eastern Europe. Louis' authority had reached from the Adriatic to the Black Sea, from the Serbian valley of the Vardar to the frontier of Prussia, but there was no political, strategic, economic, geographical or ethnic logic to such a conglomeration and no real constituency of interest or opinion behind it. Louis left no son to maintain the union, but, instead, two daughters. The elder, Mária, married Sigismund, the son of the Holy Roman Emperor, Charles IV, heir to the Luxemburg lands in Germany, and brought the Hungarian Crown lands as her inheritance; but Poland remained apart from this under Louis' other daughter, Hedvig. Her marriage to the Lithuanian Jagiello united Poland and Lithuania and proved a crucial influence on Polish history until the 16th century.

Northern Italy at the Peak of Visconti Power, 1390

3 Venice with its far-flung foreign empire was the most successful of the Italian powers, which by 1390 ruled Crete, Euboea, Zara, Dubrovnik and most of Istria. As yet, however, Venice ruled little on the mainland bar Treviso, acquired in 1339. In 1378-81 Venice and Genoa fought a war over Chioggia, a city just to the south of the Venetian lagoon. Venice regained the city and thus drove Genoa from the northern Adriatic. The basis for Venetian expansion on the mainland had been laid.

However, the most powerful Italian state at this time was Milan under its Visconti dukes. The most dynamic was Gian Galeazzo Visconti (1351-1402). In 1378 he succeeded his father, Galeazzo II, as joint ruler with his uncle Bernabò, but in 1385 he had Bernabò seized and became sole ruler: Bernabò was killed the following year. Gian Galeazzo then rapidly expanded his inheritance, in particular by seizing Verona and Padua, which made him the most powerful ruler in northeast Italy. Visconti power was then extended into Tuscany. Bologna was temporarily captured, taking advantage of the weakness of Papal power to the east of the Apennines. The title Duke of Milan, purchased from the Emperor in 1395, confirmed Visconti power, but it was really based on the large army he built up. Gian Galeazzo compared himself to Julius Caesar, but his opponents saw him as a tyrant like Nero.

Neighbouring city-states, particularly Florence and Venice, feared Visconti expansion and when Gian Galeazzo died unexpectedly in 1402 they used the opportunity to increase their territories at the expense of Milan. Smaller city-states, such as Pisa, Lucca and Siena, which had survived as independent republics into the 14th century, increasingly became unable to preserve their status without powerful protectors. Pisa, for example, fell to Florence in 1406, in the aftermath of Gian Galeazzo's death.

1382

The Hundred Years' War

In 1430 the Hundred Years' War between England and France was at its height and with it the struggle for primacy in Western Europe. Edward III's mother, Isabella, was the daughter of Philip IV of France. As already tense Anglo-French relations deteriorated over Gascony, Edward broadened his challenge to Philip IV's nephew, Philip VI, by claiming the French throne (1337). The fortunes of the ensuing war were mixed, but the use of longbowmen helped to bring victory at Crécy (1346) and Poitiers (1356), leading to the Peace of Brétigny (1360), in which Edward promised to renounce his claim to the French throne, to Normandy and to Anjou, but was recognized as duke of the whole of Aquitaine, as well as ruler of Calais. Edward's acquisitions proved difficult to maintain and, by the Truce of Bruges (1375), he was left with little more than Calais, Bordeaux and Bayonne.

The initiative was not regained by the English until Henry V invaded France in 1415: at Agincourt his longbowmen blunted the successive advances of the French, with very heavy losses. On his second expedition, in 1417, Henry conquered much of Normandy, and in 1419 its capital Rouen. He was helped by serious divisions in the French camp, and in 1419 he won the alliance of the powerful Duke of Burgundy. Throughout the conflict, the successes of the kings of England owed much to the existence of French allies. The Hundred Years' War was, indeed, in part an international dimension to a series of French civil wars. The Kings of England had supporters in Normandy, Brittany, Navarre and, in the early 15th century, Burgundy, without whose support they would have fared much less well. Henry's victories led in 1420 to betrothal to Catherine, the daughter of Charles VI of France (1380-1422), and, by the Treaty of Troyes, he was recognized as Charles's heir and as regent during his life. The French Dauphin, from 1422 Charles VII, continued to resist, and Henry V died in 1422, possibly of dysentry, while on campaign near Paris.

Meanwhile in the east, the Ottomans continued to push forward into the Balkans. The Christians seemed powerless in the face of the relentless tide of their advance. Bulgaria succumbed rapidly: in 1385 Sofia fell to the Turks; the next year they took Nish; in 1388 what remained of Bulgaria was forced to accept Ottoman overlordship. In 1389, the Serbian army of King Lazar was defeated by the Ottomans at Kosovo, breaking the back of Serbia's resistance. The Byzantine Empire was reduced to a rump area around Constantinople and the Peloponnese. The most bitter blow was the fall of Salonica to the Turks in 1387. In 1396 a Hungarian-French crusade sent to relieve the Byzantines was destroyed at Nicopolis: the Empire was only saved by the intervention of the Mongol leader Timur, who destroyed the Ottoman army near Ankara (Angora) and imprisoned Sultan Bayezid. The Ottoman hold on Thrace was weakened and the Byzantines even recovered some territory, most notably Salonica, which they held until 1423, when, with Imperial troops unable to secure its defence, it was handed over to the Venetians.

In Scandinavia, the late 14th century saw the emergence of the Union of Kalmar (1397). Eric of Pomerania had been recognized as king of Norway in 1389 and of Sweden and Denmark in 1396, and in 1397 the notables of the three countries gathered at Kalmar to agree the framework for a permanent Union. Although they did draft an agreement setting out measures to secure the unification, in practice the Union remained a personal one.

NORWAY

Lapps

Nidaros

Oslo

SWEDEN

Åbo

NOVGOROD

Stockholm

Reval

Novgorod

MUSCOVY

ROSTOV

Nizhniy
Novgorod

Kazan

(Union

Pskov

Volga

TVER

SUZDAL

Kalmar)

Aarhus

Copenhagen

Roskilde

Malmö

BALTIC

Königsberg

Riga

Dünaburg

PSKOV

Smolensk

Moscow

Tula

Ryazan

SMALL
PRINCIP-
ALITIES

RYAZAN

Sarai

SEA

DENMARK

 O
R
D
E
R

Vilnius

Vitebsk

Don

GOLDEN HORDE

burg

Bremen

Stettin

Danzig

TEUTONIC

Minsk

Hanover

Berlin

Elbe

Vistula

Poznań

Oder

Warsaw

L I T H U A N I A

Volga

Astrakhan

MALL

Leipzig

Dresden

Breslau

LANDS OF

POLAND

Kiev

Dnieper

nkfurt

Nuremberg

Prague

THE BOHEMIAN

CROWN

Cracow

Lwów

Dniester

Tana

(to Genoa)

uttgart

Brünn

Danube

Kassa

Munich

Salzburg

AUSTRIA

Vienna

Pozsony

Buda

Debrecen

Suceava

Jassy

(to Genoa)

Caffa

Innsbruck

TYROL

Graz

STYRIA

H U N G A R Y

Pécs

Szeged

Kolozsvár

MOLDAVIA

Venice

VE

Zágráb

Temesvár

Brassó

BLACK   SEA

GEORGIA

NE

SAN
MARINO

ce

PAPAL

Zara

Spalato

TI

Bosnian
rulers

SERBIA

Belgrade

Nish

Târgoviște

WALLACHIA

Danube

Nicopolis

Varna

EMPIRE OF
TREBIZOND

AN

STATE

Rome

REPUBLIC
OF RAGUSA

NAPLES

OTTOMAN

Sofia

Kosovo

Üsküb

Tirnovo

Philippopolis

BYZANTINE
EMPIRE

(to Genoa)

Trebizond

Local
rulers

Naples

Bari

Taranto

Local
rulers

EMPIRE

Adrianople

Constantinople

Angora

AK KOYUNLU

DULKADIR

Mosul

Palermo

Messina

SICILY

Catania

(to Aragon)

R

Janina

BYZANTINE
EMPIRE

DUCHY
OF
ATHENS

Athens

Salonica

Smyrna

KARAMAN

RAMAZAN

Local
rulers

KARA
KOYUNLU

Malta

E

SEA

P

U

(Tocchi)

(to
Genoa)

KNIGHTS OF ST JOHN

Euphrates

Tigris

Malta

B

L

BYZANTINE
EMPIRE

I

KINGDOM
OF CYPRUS

Nicosia

MAMELUKES

Beirut

Damascus

Bedouins

Crete

101

Map labels

NOVGOROD

MUSCOVY
ROSTOV

PSKOV
MUSC-OVY
TVER
SUZDAL

MUSCOVY

Polotsk

Vgazma

SMALL PRINCIPALITIES *(vassals)*

RYAZAN

L I T H U A N I A

Novgorod Severski

Lyubech
Chernigov

Zhitomir
Kiev

...hynia

...olia

...VIA

G O L D E N   H O R D E

THE GROWTH OF LITHUANIA TO 1430

- Lithuanian core area
- Added by 1263
- Added by 1341
- Added by 1377
- Added by 1430
- Areas held temporarily before 1430
- Frontier of Lithuania and the Teutonic Order, 1392
- To Lithuania, 1398
- To the Teutonic Order, 1398-1411
- In union with Lithuania from 1386
- Vassal of Poland
- Frontiers, 1430
- Western frontier of areas controlled by the Golden Horde, mid-13th century

Kassa

MOLDAVIA
(Polish vassal)

Várad
Kolozsvár

G A R Y

1387
Temesvár
Brassó

Belgrade
WALLACHIA
(Hungarian vassal)

SERBIA
(Ottoman vassal)
BULGARIA
(Stratsimir)
Nicopolis
OTTOMAN EMPIRE

The Growth of Lithuania to 1430

1 The damage done to the Rus principalities by the Mongols and the continued pressure of their successors, the Golden Horde, created an opportunity for Lithuania to thrive. Founded in the 13th century by Mindaugas (d. 1263), this pagan state could not expand towards the Baltic because of the activity of the Teutonic Knights. Instead it expanded east, particularly in the earlier 14th century which saw the seizure of Polotsk as well as Podlasia. During the joint reign of Algirdas (1345-77) and Kestutis (1345-82), the southern lands of Kievan Rus were overrun: Novgorod-Severski fell in 1363 and Kiev in 1362-3. The Lithuanians thus expanded up to the lands of the Golden Horde. The Horde were then pushed back, so that by 1392 the Lithuanians had reached the Black Sea to the west of the Dnieper.

In 1385 a succession crisis in Poland led to a treaty at Krevo with Lithuania by which the Lithuanian Grand Duke, Jogaila, became King of Poland as Wladyslaw II Jagiello (1386-1434). In return the Lithuanians converted to Catholicism, although the two states continued to function as separate units. They united to fight the Teutonic Knights, who had been at war with Lithuania for much of the previous century. In 1410 the Polish-Lithuanian forces advanced into Prussia. At Tannenberg they crushed the Knights, killing the Grand Master, Ulrich von Jungingen, all but one of the commanders and 400 of the knight brothers. The Knights were greatly weakened, their period of expansion brought to a definitive close.

The Holy Roman Empire: the Growth of Habsburg Possessions

2 The Habsburgs were originally one of the second rank German princely families whose power expanded as the authority of the Holy Roman Emperor diminished. Their name is derived from the Habichtsburg (Hawk's Castle), built in about 1020 by the Bishop of Strassburg: the title Count of Habsburg first occurred in 1090. Initially, Habsburg power centred in Swabia, Alsace and northern Switzerland. In 1276, however, Rudolf I acquired Austria and Styria and this established the Habsburgs in the southeast of the Holy Roman Empire which, thereafter, was to be their centre of power. This advance was made at the expense of King Přemysl Ottakar II of Bohemia, who had been elected Duke of Upper and Lower Austria and had gained Styria, Carinthia and Carniola (*see* map 3, page 91). These were, however, only recent gains and thus the Habsburgs were able to advance into an area where there was no long-established state or dynasty to challenge their position. Rudolf's victory in battle in 1276 led, therefore, to a rapid transfer of control. From Austria and Styria the Habsburgs expanded to acquire Carinthia, Carniola and the Tyrol (in 1363). The Habsburgs also rose sufficiently in prominence for Rudolf I (1273-91) and Albert I (1298-1308) to become Holy Roman Emperors. In 1438 Albert II became Emperor and thereafter the Habsburgs held the title with only one short break until the end of the Empire in 1806.

In their Swiss heartland, however, the Habsburgs lost control to the demands of the Swiss cantons for autonomy. The Habsburgs had continued to expand their Swiss base in the 13th century, buying the lordship of Freiburg (1277), the town of Lucerne (1264) and Zug. In 1315, however, rising tension between the Habsburgs and the forest cantons led to warfare. Frederick of Habsburg's brother Leopold was routed at Morgarten. The Swiss cantons then rejected Habsburg seignorial rights. In 1385 Lucerne declared its independence. The Habsburg Leopold III was killed in battle against the Swiss near Zug in 1386, and a truce agreed in 1389 marked a permanent weakening of the Habsburg position in Switzerland as well as the creation of a strong Swiss confederation.

France: the Hundred Years' War

3 After the death of Henry V (*see* page 101), the tide of the Hundred Years' War turned against the English. Henry V's only son, Henry VI, became king when only nine months old and on the death of Charles VI was proclaimed King of France. The English strove to maintain Henry V's impetus and had some success until 1429. Charles VII, uncle of Henry VI, was, however, energized in 1429 by the charismatic Joan of Arc. That year, the English siege of Orléans was lifted by an army under Joan and Charles was crowned at Rheims. The balance of military advantage had shifted crucially and in 1435 the Burgundians abandoned Henry. Paris was lost in 1436 and the English were outmanoeuvred by the French, politically and militarily. In 1449-51, Normandy and Gascony fell swiftly to Charles VII's superior army, not least his artillery, and in 1453 an English riposte in Gascony was crushed at Castillon. The English were left holding only Calais.

The Growth of Luxemburg Power

4 The end of the Přemyslide dynasty in Bohemia (1306) was followed by an interregnum, and then by the election of John of Luxemburg (1310). Under John and his son Charles IV (1346-78) the power of the Luxemburg dynasty grew greatly. Charles was also Holy Roman Emperor and, by the Golden Bull outlining the imperial constitution (1356), the King of Bohemia was given precedence among the electors of the Empire. Charles also made Moravia, Silesia and Lusatia indissoluble parts of the Bohemian crownlands and acquired the Upper Palatinate (1353-73), Brabant and Limburg (1355), and Brandenburg (1373). His successor, Wenceslaus IV (1378-1419), lost Brandenburg (1411), however, and was opposed in Bohemia by the Hussites: a radical religious movement which gained support from Czech hostility to the Germans. Sigismund (1387-1437) became King of Hungary in 1387, Emperor in 1410 and King of Bohemia in 1419. He also conquered Bosnia. Sigismund took Luxemburg power to its greatest heights, but as with other dynastic accumulations, this was not to serve as the basis of a long-lasting state.

1430

The Age of the New Monarchies

The later 15th century was in some senses the age of the "new monarchies" – consolidated states such as England, France and Scotland – where a number of changes helped to make political authority more clearly defined. One such was the general European trend towards more definite frontiers. This was partly responsible for much of the warfare of the 14th and 15th centuries, since lands whose status had been ill-defined for centuries were claimed and contended for by rival states. The implementation of firm frontiers was bound up with the existence of more assertive states and growing state bureaucracies, which sought to know where exactly they could impose their demands for resources and where they needed to create their first line of defence.

By 1466, the kings of England had lost virtually all their possessions in France, save Calais. The final stages of the Hundred Years' War saw the loss of Paris (1436), the surrender of Maine to the French (1448) and the French capture of Normandy by 1450. England became a typical "New Monarchy", based on a more-or-less precise territory, with an increasingly assertive central authority. This did not, however, mean that multiple kingdoms were redundant, more that the French empire of the English kings had been unsuccessful. There were a whole series of composite states or multiple kingdoms in Eastern Europe, for example Bohemia under Charles IV (1333-78), Poland-Lithuania from 1386, and Hungary under Matthias Corvinus (1458-90). At a lesser level, the marriage of James II of Scotland and Margaret of Denmark in 1469 led to the incorporation of Orkney and Shetland within the Scottish realm.

Central and Eastern Europe, however, experienced a time of particular turmoil, with the ever-present threat of the Ottoman forces diverting much-needed resources to the defence of Christendom. Bohemia, moreover, was rent by religious dissent. The followers of the Czech religious reformer, Jan Hus, who had been burnt at the Council of Constance in 1415, seized power in Bohemia in 1419. It was not until 1436 that Sigismund, the Hungarian king, was able to re-assert his authority there. In 1457, the Bohemians elected the Hussite George of Poděbrady as King of Bohemia. Pope Paul II preached a crusade against him, which led to an unsuccessful Hungarian invasion in 1468.

The danger posed by Turkish encroachments had grown so great that in 1443 a crusade set out, under the leadership of Wladislaw I, king of both Poland and Hungary. Initially the crusaders had great success, storming Nish and Sofia. The Ottoman Sultan was forced to agree a truce with the Christians in July 1444, but within a month Wladislaw had again advanced beyond the Danube as far as Varna. There Wladislaw perished and his army was routed. After this the Turkish advance recommenced. Setbacks such as the Ottoman failure to overcome Albania, defended resolutely by George Castriota (Skanderbeg) from 1443 to 1468, meant it was more difficult for them to tolerate the independence of Byzantine territory to their rear. In 1453, Mehmet II finally captured Constantinople, causing great consternation in the west. His army laid siege to Belgrade in 1456, but the siege was raised by the brilliant Hungarian leader, Janos Hunyadi. By 1460, the remaining Byzantine strongholds in the Morea had fallen and with the capture of Trebizond on the Black Sea in 1461, the last remnant of Byzantium was finally extinguished.

NORWAY

Nidaros

Oslo

Stockholm

SWEDEN

Åbo

Reval

Novgorod

NOVGOROD

MUSCOVY

Nizhniy
Novgorod

Kazan

KHANATE OF
SIBIR

KHANATE OF
KAZAN

BALTIC
SEA

Pskov

PSKOV

Riga

Dünaburg

TVER

ROSTOV

Moscow

Volga

DENMARK

Aarhus

Copenhagen

Malmö

(Union
of
Kalmar)

Königsberg
Gdansk

Wilno

Vitebsk

Smolensk

Tula

Ryazan

SMALL
PRINCIP-
ALITIES

RYAZAN

Hamburg

Stettin

Minsk

GREAT KHANATE
(GOLDEN HORDE)

TEUTONIC ORDER

Elbe

Hanover

Berlin

Poznań

Warsaw

Don

SMALL

Dresden

Breslau

POLAND

LITHUANIA

Sarai

SAXONY

LANDS OF
THE BOHEMIAN
CROWN

Oder

Kiev

Volga

KHANATE OF
ASTRAKHAN

Prague

Brünn

Cracow

Lwów

Dnieper

Astrakhan

Danube

Munich

AUSTRIA

Vienna

Pozsony

Kassa

Dniester

KHANATE

OF

CRIMEA

Salzburg

Graz

STYRIA

Buda

Debrecen

Suceava

(to Genoa)

Jassy

(to Genoa)

TYROL

HUNGARY

Kolozsvár

MOLDAVIA

Caffa

VENETIAN

Trieste

Mantua

Venice

FERRARA

Pécs

Szeged

Temesvár

Brassó

Târgoviște

BLACK SEA

GEORGIA

SAN
MARINO

Zágráb

Zara

Belgrade

WALLACHIA

Bucharest

PAPAL

Bosna
Seray

HERZEGOVINA

Danube

Ruschuk

STATE

Spalato

Nish

Varna

Rome

REPUBLIC
OF RAGUSA

Mostar

OTTOMAN

Sofia

NAPLES

Üsküb

Philippopolis

Adrianople

Trebizond

Naples

Bari

Janina

Constantinople

KARA

Palermo

Taranto

Salonica

EMPIRE

Angora

Tigris

KOYUNLU

SICILY

(to Aragon)

Messina

Catania

Athens

(to
Genoa)

Smyrna

DULKADIR

RAMAZAN

Mosul

Morea

KNIGHTS OF ST JOHN

KINGDOM
OF CYPRUS

Nicosia

MAMELUKES

SEA

Crete

Beirut

Bedouins

105

THE OTTOMAN CONQUEST OF THE BALKANS, 1359-1500 **2**

Ottoman Empire, 1359	Added by 1464
Added by 1389	Ottoman vassal intermittently after 1456
Ottoman vassal from the end of the 14th century, thereafter intermittently a Hungarian vassal	Ottoman vassal from the end of the 15th century
Added by 1402	Added by 1500
Lost in 1402 and recovered later	Frontiers, 1500
Ottoman area under Hungarian control 1443-4; uncontested Ottoman control, 1459	

The Growth of Muscovy to 1466

1 The expansion of Muscovy was a slow process that owed much to the determination of its ruling house. Though the rulers of Rus were for long under the shadow of the Mongols and their descendants, the Muscovites were able to use this to their advantage: Ivan Kalita I (1328-41) gained the right to act as the tax collector of the Tatars and thus benefited from their power. This was not, however, a relationship free from tension and in 1445 the Tatars took Vasili II prisoner. Muscovy also faced challenges from other Rus rulers, such as the princes of Tver, who were not subdued until 1485. Other Rus states were unable to resist its expansion. Novgorod fell in 1478, Pskov in 1510. Ivan III, "the Great" (1462-1505), who conquered both Tver and Novgorod, refused to pay tribute to the Golden Horde and defied its attempt to intimidate him into doing so (1480). In 1493 he took the title "Sovereign of all Russia".

The Ottoman Conquest of the Balkans, 1359-1500

2 The crushing Turkish victory over the Serbs at Kosovo (1389) was the crucial triumph which anchored the Turks in the Balkans. The victor, Murad I (1360-89), added Rumelia (Thrace, Macedonia and southern Bulgaria) to the Ottoman Empire. After Kosovo, Serbia became a vassal state, the rest of Bulgaria was annexed (1389) and Wallachia, too, became a vassal state (1390). Constantinople was now completely surrounded, and from 1394 it was blockaded. Thessaly was then conquered. In 1396 a crusade to rescue Constantinople failed when a Hungarian-French army of 10,000 was routed at Nicopolis.

The move of the Ottoman capital to Adrianople (Edirne) in 1402 symbolised a shift in emphasis to Europe. Constantinople was reprieved for longer as a result of the advance of Timur (Tamberlaine) from Central Asia. Timur attacked and routed Bayezid in 1402 at Ankara. With Bayezid in captivity, the Turks made concessions to other opponents: Byzantium regained Salonica, and Wallachia, Serbia and Bosnia recovered their independence. Murad II (1421-44, 1446-51) restored the Turkish position. Wallachia, Serbia and Bosnia were subdued in the 1420s and 1430s, and Murad also expanded Turkish power into Epirus. In 1443 another crusade was launched. The Hungarians, under Janos Hunyadi, captured Nish and Sofia, Christians throughout the Balkans rebelled, particularly in Albania, and in 1444 an army of 20,000 under King Ladislas of Hungary advanced to Varna, only to be defeated by Murad II.

In 1453 Mehmet II (1451-81) laid siege to Constantinople, and finally took the city, putting an end to more than 1000 years of Byzantine history and inflicting a bitter psychological blow on Christendom. He then advanced on Belgrade in 1456, but his siege was broken by Hunyadi. Caffa in the Crimea was captured in 1475 and Albanian resistance was overcome in 1478. Mehmet also added the Morea (1458-60), the rest of Serbia (1459), southern Bosnia and Herzegovina (1463-82), and some of the islands in the Aegean. Wallachia became a permanent vassal state in 1476. In 1480 the Turks besieged Rhodes and landed at

Otranto in southern Italy. Both initiatives were cut short by Mehmet's death, and under his successor, Bayezid II (1481-1512), the dynamism of Turkish expansion greatly slackened, although he conquered the important ports of Kilia and Akkerman (Maurocastro) on the Black Sea in 1484.

Italy: the Treaty of Lodi, 1454

3 Venice was the principal beneficiary of the collapse of Visconti power in northern Italy. After Gian Galeazzo Visconti died in 1402, Venice seized Belluno (1404), Vicenza (1404), Padua (1405) and Verona (1405). In another forward advance, Venice took Bergamo and Brescia in 1428. Ravenna was added in 1441. Milanese power was revived by Gian Galeazzo's son, Filippo Maria (1412-47), and the latter's son-in-law, Francesco Sforza, (1450-66), a *condottiere* (mercenary leader), who used his military strength to establish himself in Lombardy.

Further south, Florence expanded its power in Tuscany, acquiring Arezzo (1384) and the formerly powerful independent republic of Pisa (1406). The competing ambitions of these states led to much warfare, the costs of which encouraged peace negotiations, as did the Turkish challenge to Italy after the fall of Constantinople in 1453. This threat encouraged Pope Nicholas V to try to bring peace and form an anti-Turkish league. By the Peace of Lodi (1454) Italy's leading powers – Milan, Venice, Florence, Naples and the Pope – recognized each other's boundaries and laid the basis for over two decades of peace.

The Growth of Burgundy to 1477

4 The dynamism of its Dukes and the weakness of neighbouring states allowed Burgundy to expand greatly in the 15th century. The basis of its power was the marriage in 1369 of Margaret, the heiress of the County of Flanders, to Philip the Bold, Duke of Burgundy (1363-1404), the younger brother of Charles V of France, who had been established in Burgundy in 1363. Margaret brought Flanders, Artois and Nevers to Burgundy.

Philip the Bold's grandson, Philip the Good (1419-67), expanded Burgundian power in the Netherlands, acquiring Luxemburg (1451), Holland, Hainault, Friesland and Zeeland (all in 1433), Brabant-Limburg (1430) and the Somme towns with Ponthieu and Boulogne (1435). Most of this was by conquest or force, although Philip also bought Namur and obtained the reversion to Alsace from his aunt. His son, Charles the Bold (1467-77) gained Alsace, conquered Guelders and Zutphen (1472) and became involved in Lorraine. Burgundy was an expanding power, buoyed up by the commercial growth of the Low Countries which threatened France, but the Burgundian army was defeated by the Swiss at Nancy in 1477. Charles was killed, his army routed. The Burgundian inheritance was partitioned in the aftermath between the Habsburgs and Louis XI of France, who made important gains, including Burgundy and Picardy.

1466

The Later Middle Ages

The late 15th century saw a consolidation of many European states and a coalescence of Europe into the contours which were to shape it for almost 400 years, until the crisis of nationalism in the 19th century. In the southwest, the Spanish state emerged with the final conquest of Granada from the Muslims in 1492 and the Union of the crowns of Aragon and Castille. The French kings continued the process of expanding the royal domain, until by 1483 only the Duchy of Brittany remained more or less independent, and even this was to be absorbed early in the 16th century (*see* map 3, page 115). England, too, although she had lost her lands in France – except for Calais – by the Treaty of Arras in 1453 and was racked by a bitter civil war from 1453 to 1471, would begin to emerge under the Tudor dynasty from 1485 onwards as a maritime power, whose interests in terms of territorial expansion lay outside Europe.

Italy, after the Treaty of Lodi (1454, *see* map 3, page 107), experienced 20 years of relative calm, until the Venetians went to war with Ferrara from 1480. Although it faced a coalition of almost all the other Italian states, the settlement which ended the war in 1484 did leave Venice with some minor gains. More ominously, the Venetians had tried to induce the French king, Charles VIII, to invade Italy with the promise of their help to conquer Naples, an attempt which foreshadowed the French intervention in the catastrophic Italian wars of the next decade (*see* map 2, page 115).

In the east, Muscovy had emerged by the end of the 15th century as the predominant principality in Russia. The capture of Novgorod in 1478 and the adoption by Ivan III of the title "Sovereign of all Russia" marked the emerge of a new power in the east, and one which, with the disappearance of the Byzantine Empire in 1453, could claim to be the champion of Orthodox Christianity. The Ottoman advance which had swept away Byzantium slackened somewhat after the 1470s. A Turkish siege of Rhodes and the temporary occupation of Otranto in southern Italy in 1480-81 proved, however, that the threat was by no means over.

Throughout Europe in the Middle Ages, national boundaries were hardened and the concept of "statehood" was emergent, becoming politically more significant than the "nation", in its original meaning of a people of common descent. This development is most marked in the consolidation of England, France and Spain. The growth of national consciousness was not, however, dependent on the authority of a unitary state. The strong consciousness of Germanness and German nationhood evolved in a very different political context from that of England, France and Scotland. States which had developed by inheritance and conquest, such as Burgundy, while they were in theory subject to an individual ruler, in practice were too diverse to function as individual units. Their fragility was demonstrated by the partitioning of Burgundy after the defeat by the Swiss of Duke Charles the Bold at Nancy in 1477. The growth of the Swiss Confederation, too, demonstrates that national consciousness did not always develop hand-in-hand with a strong state, for the Swiss had no central authority, but still defended their lands tenaciously against threats from the Habsburgs and Burgundians, and extended the scope of the Confederation steadily in the last half of the 15th century.

NORWAY

Lapps

SWEDEN

Nidaros

Oslo

Åbo

Stockholm

Reval

BALTIC SEA

(Union of Kalmar)

Aarhus

Copenhagen

Malmö

DENMARK

Königsberg

Gdansk

TEUTONIC ORDER

Riga

Dünaburg

Pskov

PSKOV

Novgorod

MUSCOVY

Moscow

Nizhniy Novgorod

Kazan

Volga

KHANATE OF KAZAN

Stettin

Berlin

BRANDENBURG

Hanover

Poznań

Wilno

Vitebsk

Smolensk

Tula

Ryazan

SMALL PRINCIP-ALITIES

RYAZAN

Don

GREAT KHANATE (GOLDEN HORDE)

Dresden

Breslau

Oder

POLAND

Warsaw

Minsk

LITHUANIA

Kiev

Sarai

Volga

SMALL

Prague

LANDS OF THE BOHEMIAN CROWN

Brünn

Elbe

Danube

Cracow

Lwów

Dniester

Dnieper

KHANATE OF ASTRAKHAN

Astrakhan

Munich

Salzburg

Vienna

Graz

AUSTRIA

Pozsony

Buda

Kassa

Debrecen

Kolozsvár

MOLDAVIA

Jassy

KHANATE OF CRIMEA

Trieste

Venice

FERRARA

SAN MARINO

HUNGARY

Szeged

Temesvár

Pécs

Zágráb

Belgrade

Brassó

WALLACHIA

Bucharest

Kefe

Local rulers

GEORGIAN STATES

PAPAL STATE

Rome

Zara

Bosna Serai

Spalato

Mostar

REPUBLIC OF RAGUSA

MONTENEGRO

Nish

Sofia

Ruschuk

Danube

Varna

BLACK SEA

Trebizond

Naples

Bari

NAPLES (to Aragon)

Taranto

Otranto

Üsküb

Philippopolis

Adrianople

Constantinople

Janina

Salonica

OTTOMAN EMPIRE

Angora

Tigris

DULKADIR

AK KOYUNLU

Mosul

Euphrates

Palermo

SICILY (to Aragon)

Messina

Catania

REPUBLIC

Smyrna

Athens

(to Genoa)

Rhodes

KNIGHTS OF ST. JOHN

RAMAZAN

MAMELUKES

Nicosia

Beirut

Bedouins

SEA

Crete

Map 1

THE GROWTH OF THE SWISS CONFEDERATION, 1291-1486

HOLY ROMAN EMPIRE

Schaffhausen · Lake Constance · Thurgau *1460* · Zurich · Zurich *1415* · St Gall · *1451* · Appenzell *1411* *1444* · Aargau · *1481* · Solothurn *1353* · Solothurn · *1365/1409* · *1436/38* · *1386/1415* · Zug · *1485* · *1332* · Lucerne · Lucerne · *1458* · Neuchâtel · *1388* *1353* · Biel · *1486* · Schwyz · (*1352*) · *1401/06* · *1475* · Berne · Unterwalden · *1386* · *1480* · Fribourg · *1353* · *1425* · Glarus · *1475* · *1481* · Uri *1317* *1407* · *1475-78* · *1475* · *1475* · SWISS CONFEDERATION · *1439* · Sion · Maggia *1411-22* · Riviera *1403/07-22* · *1475* · Valais · *1403/11-22* · Eschental · Lake Locarno · VENETIAN REPUBLIC

Legend:
- The Swiss Confederation, 1291
- Added by 1353 (with dates)
- Added by 1417 (with dates)
- Added by 1486 (with dates)
- Areas held temporarily (with dates)
- Frontier of the Holy Roman Empire
- Frontier, 1486

Map 2

HUNGARY UNDER MATTHIAS CORVINUS, 1458-90

SWEDEN · Union of Kalmar · BALTIC SEA · TEUTONIC OR[DER] · DENMARK · Wilno (Vilnius) · Königsberg · Gdańsk · Toruń · HOLY ROMAN EMPIRE · Lusatia · Silesia · POLAND · Warsaw · LANDS OF THE BOHEMIAN CROWN · Bohemia · Prague · Moravia · Cracow · Lwów · Brünn · Kassa · HABSBURG POSSESSIONS · Pozsony · Buda · HUNGARY · Kolozsvár · VENETIAN REPUBLIC · Zágráb · Mohács · Temesvár · Bras[só] · Belgrade · Târgoviş[te] · WAL[LACHIA] · OTTOMAN EM[PIRE]

Lower map:
POLAND · Lusatia · Boroszló · Silesia · HOLY ROMAN EMPIRE · Prague · Bohemia · Troppau · Moravia · Olmütz · Brünn · Kassa · LITHUANIA · Austria · Nyitra · Vienna · Pozsony · Bécsújhely (Wiener Neustadt) · Esztergom · Sopron · Győr · Buda · Debrecen · Fehérvár · Várad · Suceava · MOLDAVIA · HABSBURG POSSESSIONS · Styria · Graz · HUNGARY · Kalocsa · Kolozsvár · Transylvania · Zágráb · Pécs · Szeged · Gyulafehérvár · Szeben · Temesvár · Brassó · (Ottoman 1484) · VENETIAN REPUBLIC · Slavonia · Croatia · FERRARA · *1480* · (Venetian) · Belgrade · Târgovişte · SAN MARINO · *1463-64* · Szabács · *1471-76* · Bosnia · Jajca · Szendrő · Galambóc · *1458* · WALLACHIA · PAPAL STATES · Ancona · (Hungarian protectorate in 1488) · *1459* · OTTOMAN EMPIRE · Varna

Legend:
- to Hungary, 1477/79
- to Hungary from 1485
- Hungarian fief 1475-85, and briefly at other times during Matthias's rule
- Hungarian fief for brief periods during Matthias's rule
- Northern limit of temporary Hungarian losses (with dates)
- Lost by Hungary (with dates)
- Frontier of the Holy Roman Empire
- Frontiers, early 1490

The Growth of the Swiss Confederation, 1291-1486

1 By the beginning of the 15th century the Swiss Confederation comprised eight *Orte* (territories): Berne, Glarus, Lucerne, Schwyz, Unterwalden, Uri, Zug and Zurich. Having freed itself from the abbey of St Gall, Appenzell joined in 1411. A truce with the Habsburgs negotiated in 1389 expired in 1415 and the Habsburgs were then driven from the Aargau. This did not become a canton, but instead a dependency. In the 15th century the Swiss Confederation expanded further, particularly to the southeast, northeast and west. Some of these gains were temporary: the expansion into Eschental, Maggia and Riviera, and thus to the shores of Lake Locarno, was reversed in 1422 as the Duchy of Milan recovered from the crisis caused by the death of Gian Galeazzo Visconti (*see* map 3, page 99), and the Swiss were not to advance in that area again until the 1510s. To the northeast Appenzell gained Rhinetal in 1444, St Gall became an allied district in 1451, Schaffhausen was acquired in 1454 and Thurgau occupied in 1460: Lake Constance had been reached; the Rhine crossed. In 1466 Berne made a defensive alliance with the Alsatian city of Mülhausen, a major extension in the territorial scope of Swiss commitments. The crucial Swiss role in the defeat of Charles the Bold of Burgundy in 1476-7 led to greater attention being paid to Swiss wishes and in the volatile situation created by the collapse of Burgundian power the Swiss Confederation made major gains. In 1481 Fribourg and Solothurn were accepted as additional members of the Confederation by the Agreement of Stans. In 1499 the Swiss were to force the Emperor Maximilian to acknowledge their effective independence. Their determination and fighting qualities had reaped their reward.

Hungary under Matthias Corvinus, 1458-90

2 Matthias Corvinus was the second son of Janos Hunyadi, the successful defender of Belgrade against the Turks (1456). From 1458 until 1490 he was King of Hungary. Corvinus was a renaissance ruler who promoted learning greatly, but also had to resist the Turkish advance. He maintained a largely defensive attitude, seeking to preserve his kingdom, without trying, as his father did, to push back the Ottomans to any great extent. He was, nonetheless, successful in retaking northern Bosnia from the Turks after they had conquered it in 1463.

Corvinus's main attention, however, was directed towards the west. With the standing (permanent) army he developed, he hoped to gain the crown of Bohemia and become Holy Roman Emperor. Bohemia was divided as a result of the Hussite troubles and in 1468 Corvinus obtained Papal support to conduct a crusade against its Hussite ruler, George of Poděbrady. This led to the partition of the Bohemian kingdom. Corvinus gained Moravia, Silesia and Lusatia as well as the title "King of Bohemia", though not Bohemia itself. Corvinus was opposed by the Emperor, the Habsburg Frederick III (1440-93), who had been elected ruler of Hungary in 1439 by a group of nobles. Corvinus was successful, gaining Lower Austria and Styria from Austria, and transferring his capital to Vienna. Under Corvinus the Hungarian state developed considerably, but he faced opposition from nobles concerned about their privileges.

East Central Europe: the Growth of Jagiello Power, 1440-1526

3 The Polish Jagiellonian dynasty had a long-standing connection with Hungary. Wladislaw I had been King of Hungary as well as Poland-Lithuania, ruling the countries in a personal union from 1440 until his untimely death in battle against the Turks at Varna in 1444. After the death of Matthias Corvinus in 1490, the Hungarians chose Wladislaw of the Polish Jagiellonian dynasty as their king, who had already been elected King Ladislav II of Bohemia in 1471. He rejoined to Bohemia those areas which had been conquered by Hungary under Matthias Corvinus (*see* map 3, below), namely Moravia, Silesia and Lusatia. The Habsburgs reversed Corvinus's conquests and regained Lower Austria and Styria. Hungary and Bohemia remained separate kingdoms, and it is unclear whether their joint rule by the Jagiellonians would have produced a closer union. After Wladislaw died he was succeeded in both by Louis II (1516-26; Ludvik I in Bohemia), but his reign was cut short, as was so much else in Eastern Europe, by the Turks. He was killed in 1526 when the more numerous and powerful invading forces of Suleiman the Magnificent destroyed Hungary's army and independence on the battlefield of Mohács. Although Suleiman set off for Hungary in April 1526, bad weather delayed him so that he did not cross the river Drava until late August. The Hungarians, however, divided, poorly led and short of infantry, failed both to contest the Drava crossing and to retire to Buda and allow the Turks to exhaust their resources in a difficult siege. Instead they deployed behind the Borza, a small tributary of the Danube. The Hungarian heavy cavalry pushed back the Turkish *sipahis* (Cavalry) of Rumelia, but stopped when Turkish troops advanced on their flank. Louis II then led the remainder of the cavalry in a second attack which pushed through the *sipahis* of Anatolia, but was stopped by the janissaries and cannon. Louis and most of his aristocracy died on the battlefield or in the nearby Danube marshes, though some of the army escaped north under the cover of darkness. Suleiman swept on to Buda. The days of independent Hungary were numbered. Louis had no children, and his inheritance was to be contested by his brother-in-law, Archduke Ferdinand, the brother of the Habsburg Charles V, and the Turks.

1493

The Habsburg Ascendancy

In 1530, the triumph of the nation-state, whose beginnings are now conventionally traced to the start of the 16th century, would have seemed improbable. The most successful states appeared, instead, to be multinational ones, such as the Ottoman Empire in the east, or the "universal monarchy" built up by Charles V, which encompassed Spain, the Netherlands and the Austrian dominions of the Habsburgs. Small states prospered, too: the patchwork of hundreds of states which made up the Holy Roman Empire contained some of the most affluent parts of Europe. By contrast, the territorial kingdoms to the west, such as France and Spain, had seen their economic position badly affected by prolonged warfare and civil strife. The disparate inheritance of Charles of Habsburg seemed to represent the most acute threat to other monarchs in 1530 (*see* map 1, page 115). Charles had inherited, by quirks of marriage alliances and early deaths, the Burgundian Netherlands (1506), the united Spanish crowns (1516) and finally (in 1519), the lands of his grandfather Maximilian of Austria, after which he obtained the title of Holy Roman Emperor. The Imperial title, the secular counterpart of the Papacy, still carried immense prestige, giving its holder pre-eminence over other, lesser monarchs. Charles won it only in the face of a bitter challenge from Francis I of France, who saw the danger of Charles V, as Emperor, ruling a ring of territories around France (in Spain, Italy and Germany). The French king considered himself the legitimate successor of the first Emperor, Charlemagne, and tried unsuccessfully to play on this sentimental claim.

Having become Emperor, Charles V faced an immense task in keeping his domains united. The rise of Protestantism in the first half of the 16th century placed an additional strain on the Empire. Charles V failed to suppress it by force, despite temporary success in 1547-52, but held firm to Catholicism even though, in Germany at least, it might have been politically expedient to convert to Lutheranism. His power-base gradually shifted as a result, relying increasingly on Spain and her overseas empire to provide money and manpower for his wars against France and to counter the threat of the Turks in the Mediterranean and against Hungary. Overburdened, he could not support his brother-in-law, Christian II of Denmark, when in 1523 Gustavus Vasa led a successful rebellion in Sweden and founded an independent state.

The Ottoman Empire faced no such problems of religious dissent, and after 50 years in which the Sultans had consolidated their 15th-century Balkan conquests (*see* map 2, page 107), under Suleiman the Magnificent (1520-66) they renewed their drive against Christian territory. In 1521 Turkish forces captured Belgrade, and in 1526 Suleiman invaded Hungary, inflicting a crushing defeat on the Hungarian nobility at Mohács, and killing Louis II, the Hungarian king. In 1529, the Sultan's army besieged Vienna. This was a high-water mark of their advance. Though they failed to take Vienna, the Turks' gains confined the Habsburgs to Slovakia, Croatia and a thin strip of territory along the west bank of the Danube. This border area was to be the scene of battles between the Turks and Habsburgs for centuries to come, and the need to safeguard it meant that although the successors of Charles V enjoyed vast resources, they would have to fight on several fronts, against the infidel Muslim threat in the east and the heretical Protestant challenge in the west.

Habsburg Possessions

━━━ The Holy Roman Empire

N O R W A Y (Danish)

Lapps

Nidaros

Oslo

S W E D E N

Åbo

Stockholm

Reval

Novgorod

M U S C O V Y

Nizhniy Novgorod

Kazan

LIVONIAN ORDER OF THE BROTHERS OF THE SWORD

Pskov

Volga

Aarhus

Copenhagen

Malmö

BALTIC SEA

Riga

Dünaburg

Moscow

KHANATE OF KAZAN

D E N M A R K

Königsberg

Wilno

Vitebsk

Smolensk

Tula

Hamburg

Stettin

Gdansk

PRUSSIA

L I T H U A N I A

Minsk

Don

Kazakhs

BRANDENBURG

Berlin

Poznań

Visrula

Wild fields

KHANATE OF ASTRAKHAN

Hanover

Breslau

SILESIA

Oder

Warsaw

Elbe

Dresden

P O L A N D

Kiev

Volga

Prague

BOHEMIA

Danube

MORAVIA

Cracow

Lwów

Dnieper

Astrakhan

Nuremberg

Brünn

Munich

AUSTRIA

Vienna

Pozsony

Kassa

Winnica

Dniester

KHANATE OF CRIMEA

Salzburg

Buda

Debrecen

Jassy

Azov

Graz

H U N G A R Y

(National King)

Mohács

Szeged

Kolozsvár

(Habsburg King)

MANTUA

VENETIA

Trieste

Zágráb

Temesvár

Brassó

M O L D A V I A

Kefe

Venice

FERRARA

Belgrade

W A L L A C H I A

B L A C K   S E A

GEORGIAN STATES

Tiflis

Bologna

SAN MARINO

DUCHY OF URBINO

Zara

Bosna Saray

Bucharest

LUCCA

Spalato

Mostar

Ruschuk

Danube

PAPAL

PONTECORVO

REPUBLIC OF RAGUSA

Nish

Varna

Trebizond

PERSIA

STATES

Rome

BENEVENTO

MONTENEGRO

Sofia

O T T O M A N

Naples

Bari

Üsküb

Philippopolis

Adrianople

Angora

NAPLES

Taranto

Salonica

E M P I R E

Palermo

Messina

Janina

Smyrna

Mosul

Euphrates

SICILY

Catania

REPUBLIC

Athens

(to Genoa)

Adana

Tigris

P E R S I A

SEA

MALTA

(Knights of St. John)

Crete

Nicosia

Beirut

Damascus

Bedouins

Map labels (top map — Western/Central Europe):

ATLANTIC OCEAN · NORTH SEA · IRELAND · WALES · ENGLAND · DENMARK · PRUSSIA · NETHERLANDS · Antwerp · Ghent · SMALL STATES · HOLY ROMAN EMPIRE · WÜRTTEMBERG · *Lost by 1551* · COUNTY OF BURGUNDY · FRANCE · COUNTY OF CHAROLLES · VENAISSIN · AUSTRIA · STYRIA · TYROL · CARINTHIA · CARNIOLA · DUCHY OF MILAN · VENETIAN REP. · LANDS OF THE BOHEMIAN CROWN · POLAND-LITHUANIA · MOLDAVIA · *Eastern Hungary held only nominally after 1526, secured 1551* · HUNGARY · *Held only briefly and/or nominally after 1526* · WALLACHIA · OTTOMAN EMPIRE · PAPAL STATES · SAN MARINO · DUCHY OF URBINO · MONTENEGRO · REPUBLIC OF RAGUSA · DUCHY OF CASTRO · KINGDOM OF NAPLES · NAVARRE · ARAGON · PORTUGAL · SPAIN · CASTILE · KINGDOM OF SARDINIA · MEDITERRANEAN SEA · KINGDOM OF SICILY · MOROCCO · ALGIERS (Ottoman vassal) · HAFSIDS (disputed by Spain and Ottomans) · MALTA (Knights of St. John)

FRANCE: THE GROWTH OF THE ROYAL DOMAIN TO 1530   3

- The Royal Domain, 987
- Added by 1154
- Added by 1226
- Added by 1530
- Areas of France outside the Royal Domain in 1530
- Frontiers in 1530

Map labels (bottom-left map — France):

ENGLAND · Calais · ENGLISH CHANNEL · HOLY ROMAN EMPIRE · Picardy · Rouen · Senlis · Rheims · Paris · Normandy · Île-de-France · Champagne · Troyes · Rennes · Brittany · Angers · Orléans · Orléans · Burgundy · Blois · Nevers · Dijon · Besançon · Anjou · Tours · Nevers · Nantes · Bourges · Poitou · Poitiers · Bourbonnais · Limoges · Limousin · Lyons · Grenoble · Angoulême · Auvergne · Dauphiné · Valence · Périgord · Bordeaux · ORANGE · Guienne · VENAISSIN · Albi · Provence · Gascony · Marseille · Pau · Toulouse · Carcassonne · Foix · Béarn · Languedoc · Rhône · Seine · Loire · BAY OF BISCAY · MEDITERRANEAN SEA · SPAIN · ANDORRA

ITALY, 1499-1559   2

- Frontiers in 1500
- Boundary of areas brought under French control, 1499-1512
- Under French control from 1515 (with dates of termination)
- to France under agreement with Spain, 1500
- Attempted French conquest
- Added to France (with dates)
- French occupied, 1536-59
- to Swiss Confederation, 1512
- to Swiss Confederation by 1536
- Added to Florence (with dates)
- to Savoy, 1529
- Papal control re-established or established by 1513
- Frontier of areas lost by Venice (with dates)
- Frontier of temporary Venetian control (with dates)
- Autonomy or independence from Papal States re-established (with dates)
- Habsburg possessions, 1520
- The Holy Roman Empire, 1550

Map labels (right map — Italy):

1523 · Franche Comté · DUCHY OF SAVOY · FRANCE · SWISS CONFEDERATION · MARGRAVIATE OF MONTFERRAT · DUCHY OF MILAN (1525, to Habsburgs 1535) · MARGRAVIATE OF SALUZZO · Turin · ASTI · 1548 · MONACO · REPUBLIC OF GENOA (1528) · Genoa · PARMA · Massa · 1527 · REP. OF LUCCA · REP. OF PISA · Pisa · 1509 · DUCHY OF PIOMBINO · to Spain 1557/59 as Stato dei Presidii · DUCHY OF CASTRO 1537 · KINGDOM OF SARDINIA (to Spain) · Cagliari · HAFSIDS · KINGDOM OF SICILY (to Spain)

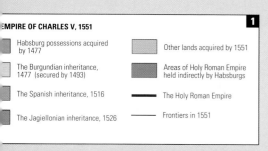

The Empire of Charles V, 1551

1 What other dynasties achieved by conquest, the House of Habsburg gained through marriage. The emergence of an empire straddling the western half of Europe from the Netherlands to Gibraltar owed more to judicious marriages and opportunely timed deaths than to conquest. By the age of 20, the future Charles V had added the Holy Roman Empire and the various Spanish crowns to the 17 separate Netherlandish provinces of the Netherlands which he inherited on the death of his father Philip the Handsome in 1506. After his grandfather, Ferdinand of Aragon, died in 1516, Charles V inherited the Spanish kingdoms of Aragon and Castile.

Although he was elected Emperor in succession to Maximilian in 1519, the main source of Charles V's power increasingly lay not in Germany, but in Spain and his possessions in the Netherlands. The great commercial wealth of the Netherlanders made their taxes particularly valuable, even if their independent-mindedness meant Charles V had to treat them cautiously.

Charles V added Milan, Mexico, Peru and several Dutch provinces, notably Gelderland, to the territories he had inherited. However, his main aim was to preserve his disparate territories intact, although he subsequently divided his legacy between his son Philip (who received Spain), and his brother Ferdinand (who inherited the Imperial title), regarding the unity of his family as more important than that of his domain. He was able to retain and pass on such diverse territories to his successors in part because he had not encroached too far on their particular rights, a precaution Philip unwisely ignored, contributing to the Revolt of the Netherlands in the 1560s (*see* map 1, page 123).

Italy, 1499–1559

2 The late 14th and early 15th centuries saw a shift in the interests of the major Italian powers, which became less concerned with internal struggles, and sought instead to expand their territorial authority. Venice, for example, carved out an empire in Lombardy, seeking a secure food supply to offset Turkish advances against her Adriatic dominions. It was only a matter of time before the increased rivalry between states sucked in foreign powers.

In 1494, Ludovico il Moro, uncle of the legitimate Sforza duke of Milan, courted French assistance to seize control of the duchy. Charles VIII of France was all-too-pleased to intervene, as he himself had a family claim to both Milan and Naples. In October 1494, Charles invaded with a massive army of 30,000 men. Sweeping aside feeble resistance, he marched south and in 1495 occupied the Kingdom of Naples. The Spanish Habsburgs (in alliance with the Papacy, the Emperor and Venice) intervened, however, to halt the French advance. The struggle lasted nine years, and saw, in 1501, an attempt to partition the Kingdom of Naples, with France receiving the north (including Naples itself) and Spain the south. By 1504, however, the French had been dri-

ven out, and the whole of southern Italy lay under the Habsburg shadow.

Even Milan, which the French had occupied in 1499, could not be held for long. At the Battle of Pavia (1525), the Emperor Charles V drove out the French and restored the duchy to the native Sforza duke. But when he died in 1535, the Habsburgs took Milan, too. Even states such as Florence and the Papacy had to employ careful diplomacy to retain their independence. Charles V's troops sacked Rome in 1527, a devastating psychological blow to the Italians, and temporarily occupied Florence in 1529. The Florentines made a virtue out of necessity and in 1552-7, allied with Charles V, Duke Cosimo de Medici, they conquered the pro-French republic of Siena, traditional enemy of Florence. The Habsburgs, however, kept five Sienese seaports for themselves, organised as the "Stato dei Presidi."

Although Florence expanded her territory, the Papacy imposed its authority on areas of the Papal States which had become semi-autonomous, and Venice retained most of her land empire (save the Romagna, lost in 1530), the continued existence of these independent Italian states could not disguise the fact that after the Treaty of Cateau-Cambrésis (1559), it was a foreign dynasty, the Habsburgs, who were the real masters of the peninsula.

France: the Growth of the Royal Domain to 1530

3 One of the key sources of renewed French power after the Hundred Years' War was the growth of the royal domain – that part of the kingdom directly controlled by the king and not through feudal vassals – which made more money and men available to the King, resources which in turn helped him to assert his dominance. Victory in the Hundred Years' War against England gave the French king the opportunity to re-incorporate large areas, previously part of the royal domain built up in the early 13th century by Philip Augustus (*see* map 2, page 87). Two important territories, however, Brittany and the Bourbonnais, remained under their own dukes, owing only vague loyalty to the French kings.

Charles VIII set in motion the incorporation of Brittany by marrying its heiress, Anne in 1491. In order to keep Anne's duchy on Charles VIII's death in 1498, his successor, Louis XII, divorced his first wife and married her instead. Charles, Duke of Bourbon, controlled a compact bloc of land in central France, in which he was in effect in control of royal powers. However, he had inherited half the lands through his wife and on her death in 1521, Francis I used a dispute about her legacy to seize the lands of his over-mighty subject. By his death in 1547, only Calais (under English control), the county of Orange, the Papal enclave of Avignon (the Venaissin) and the south remained outside the French king's jurisdiction.

The Wars of Religion

On 24 August 1572, the French Regent Catherine de Medici, despairing of attempts to find a *modus vivendi* with her Protestant subjects, ordered a policy of savage repression instead. The resulting St Bartholomew's Day Massacre, in which many French Protestant grandees perished, plunged France into a generation of religious warfare. It was a potent symbol of a Europe where Catholic-Protestant divisions were hardening, fuelled by the determination of Catholic rulers inspired by the Counter-Reformation to establish religious conformity within their lands.

If the spread of Calvinism through key sections of the French nobility (and towns such as La Rochelle) had alarmed Catherine, Philip II of Spain faced a similarly grave Protestant challenge in the Netherlands. The rebels were inspired not only by religion, but also by hatred of Philip's attempts to impose an absolutist system of government on the Seventeen Provinces he had inherited. Philip II had been fatally distracted from this task by the need to fend off Turkish incursions in the Mediterranean. This was particularly so in 1565, when an outbreak of anti-Catholic Calvinist rioting and growing dissent even amongst Catholic nobles could not be contained because all available forces were deployed in the Mediterranean to protect southern Italy from the Turks and to lift the Turkish siege of Malta (1565). Only in 1567 could Spanish troops be sent northwards up the thin strip of Habsburg territory known as "the Spanish road" from Italy to Brussels.

Philip II's viceroy in the Netherlands, the Duke of Alva, enjoyed considerable success in pacifying the Dutch rebels, even defeating an invasion organised by one of their leaders, William of Orange, in 1568; but the taxes required to pay his troops soon caused more unrest. In 1572 Orange persuaded the French Calvinist leaders to join him in a new invasion: while he led an army from Germany in the east, his navy launched an assault on Holland in the north, and French forces captured Mons in the south. The St Bartholomew's Day Massacre cut off further aid from France, however, and allowed Alva to drive Orange back into Holland. There a long and expensive war of siege and counter-siege began, which failed to dislodge the rebels. Spain nevertheless refused to concede toleration to the Dutch and persisted in fighting a war it could not win.

Meanwhile, although the Turks failed to capture Malta from the Knights of St John in 1565, the Sultan's nominal subjects in North Africa continued to drain Spanish resources with their constant pirate raids on Spain and other Christian states. Even the Christian victory over the Sultan's fleet at Lepanto (1571) offered only temporary respite: in 1574 a new Turkish navy captured Tunis and enslaved all its Spanish defenders. Moreover, the Turks still posed a serious threat to the Habsburgs in the Balkans, although their efforts were in practice largely directed to the east.

Although Eastern Europe escaped the intense religious wars that plagued the west, stability eluded the rulers even there. The death of the last Jagiellonian king of Poland, Sigismund II, in 1572, left no obvious successor and set off a quarrelsome debate amongst the nobility as to who should become king. This left Poland, in particular Polish Lithuania, vulnerable to interference from Russia to the east. Even here, the spectre of religious difference as a tool of dynastic politics arose, as many of the inhabitants of Polish Lithuania were Orthodox, and Muscovy saw them as potential subjects.

SWEDEN

RUSSIA

KHANATE OF SIBIR

Trondhjem

Oslo

Helsingfors

Stockholm

Åbo

Reval

Estonia

Novgorod

Nizhniy Novgorod

LANDS OF PRINCE MAGNUS

Livonia

Pskov

Riga

Moscow

Volga

Aarhus

Copenhagen

Malmö

COURLAND

Dyneburg

Baltic Sea

Tula

Kazakhs

Hamburg

Stettin

Königsberg

Wilno

Vitebsk

Smolensk

Gdansk

LITHUANIA

Bremen

PRUSSIA

Minsk

Hanover

Vistula

BRANDENBURG

Berlin

Poznań

Warsaw

Leipzig

Elbe

Dresden

Breslau

Kiev

Volga

ALL

kfurt

SILESIA

POLAND

Oder

Nuremberg

Prague

BOHEMIA

MORAVIA

Cracow

Lwów

Astrakhan

TES

Brünn

Danube

Munich

AUSTRIA

Vienna

Pozsony

HUNGARY

Kassa

Winnica

Dniester

Azov

Salzburg

Eger

Debrecen

KHANATE OF CRIMEA

Graz

Buda

Kolozsvár

MOLDAVIA

Jassy

Verona

Trieste

Pécs

Szeged

TRANSYLVANIA

Dnieper

Venice

VENETIA

Zágráb

Temesvár

Brassó

Circassians

Daghestan

FERRARA

MODENA

Bologna

Zara

Bosna Seraio

Belgrade

WALLACHIA

Bucharest

SAN MARINO

DUCHY OF URBINO

Spalato

Danube

Ruschuk

Varna

BLACK SEA

PERSIA

ANY

PAPAL

Mostar

Nish

Perugia

REPUBLIC OF RAGUSA

MONTENEGRO

Üsküb

Sofia

Philippopolis

Adrianople

Trebizond

STATES

Rome

PONTECORVO

Benevento

Naples

Bari

Constantinople

NAPLES

Taranto

Janina

Salonica

OTTOMAN

EMPIRE

Angora

Palermo

Messina

Smyrna

Adana

Mosul

SICILY

Catania

Athens

Tigris

Euphrates

SEA

Nicosia

MALTA
(Knights of St John)

Beirut

Damascus

Bedouins

117

POLAND AND LITHUANIA: THE UNION OF LUBLIN, 1569 **3**

- Poland before 1569
- Lithuania, 1562
- Added to Poland under the Union of Lublin, 1569
- Added to the Polish-Lithuanian state 1561/85
- Lithuania in the Polish-Lithuanian state, 1582
- Polish fief from 1466
- Polish fief from 1561
- Added to Prussia 1560 (1609 to Courland)
- In personal union with Poland-Lithuania 1576-1586
- Polish land pledged to Pomerania 1466-1637
- Western limit of Russian control within Poland-Lithuania, 1570
- Frontiers, 1585
- Frontier of the Holy-Roman Empire

HUNGARY, 1510-70 **1**

- Frontiers, 1510
- Area under Ottoman control following battle of Mohács, 1526
- Occupied by Ottomans by 1538
- Controlled by King János Szapolyai under the Treaty of Várad, 1538
- Under Habsburg control, 1538
- Northern frontier of Ottoman Empire under the Treaty of Adrianople, 1568
- Frontier between Habsburg Kingdom of Hungary and principality of Transylvania under Treaty of Speyer, 1570
- Frontier of the Holy Roman Empire

SWEDEN

DENMARK

Dorpat

Livonia

Riga

COURLAND

RUSSIA

Połock

PRUSSIA

Kowno

Wilno

Mogilev

Gdańsk
Königsberg

Minsk

POMERANIA-
STETTIN

Elbląg

Grodno

LITHUANIA

BRANDEN-
BURG

Toruń

Podlasia

Gomel

Poznań

Brest-Litovsk

Warsaw

HABSBURG

Silesia
(to
Brandenburg)

P O L A N D

Volhynia

Lublin

Kiev

Częstochowa

Żytomierz

Czerkasy

Cracow

Przemyśl

Lwów

U k r a i n e

Moravia

KINGDOM OF HUNGARY POSSESSIONS

Bracław

OTTOMAN
EMPIRE

MOLDAVIA

OTTOMAN
EMPIRE

KH

TRANSYLVANIA

CR

(Hungary map)

LANDS OF THE
BOHEMIAN CROWN
(to Habsburgs, 1526)

POLAND

Kassa

HABSBURG
POSSESSIONS

Pozsony
(Habsburg king elected Dec. 1526,
crowned Nov. 1527)

MOLDAVIA

Sopron

Győr

Eger

Köszeg

Buda

Debrecen

H U N G A R Y

Szolnok

Várad

Gotland

Fehérvár
(national king elected
and crowned Nov. 1526)

Kolozsvár

DENMA

Szigetvár

Pécs

Szeged

T r a n s y l v a n i a

Zágráb

Slavonia

Mohács

Temesvár

Gyulafehérvár

Me

Croatia

Bosnia

Eszék

Szeben

Jajca

Pétervárad

Belgrade

W A L L A C H I A

Köni

VENETIAN REPUBLIC

O T T O M A N   E M P I R E

Gdańsk

(P

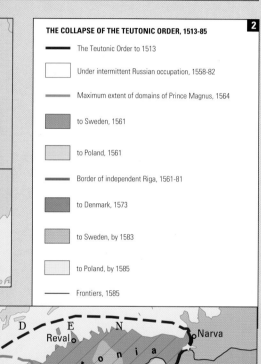

THE COLLAPSE OF THE TEUTONIC ORDER, 1513-85

— The Teutonic Order to 1513

☐ Under intermittent Russian occupation, 1558-82

— Maximum extent of domains of Prince Magnus, 1564

▨ to Sweden, 1561

☐ to Poland, 1561

— Border of independent Riga, 1561-81

▨ to Denmark, 1573

▨ to Sweden, by 1583

☐ to Poland, by 1585

— Frontiers, 1585

Hungary, 1510-70

1 Their crushing defeat by the Turks at Mohács in 1526 resulted in a split among the surviving Hungarian nobility about who should be elected in place of the dead king, Louis II. Although some opted for Ferdinand of Austria, others preferred a local candidate, János Szapolyai, who had led resistance to the prospect of a Habsburg succession as far back as 1505, when the Hungarian diet had ruled that a "foreigner" could not be elected. It was obviously convenient for the Ottoman sultan, Suleiman II, to recognise Szapolyai to prevent the Habsburgs from succeeding to the throne of Hungary. In the crisis after 1526, however, many of the Hungarian nobles felt they needed the foreigner Ferdinand – and the presumed assistance of the Empire against the Ottomans – more than he would gain by becoming their king.

For more than a decade, the forces of Hungary were caught in a civil war between the two kings, even after the Treaty of Várad (1538), when mutual acceptance was agreed on the basis of a dubious status quo. On Szapolyai's death, his supporters declared his infant son, John Sigismund, king. Ferdinand responded by laying siege to Buda, hoping to reclaim the east of Hungary, but this provoked Suleiman II into a counter-invasion. The Ottoman forces captured Buda, and a central strip of lowland leading to it from the south.

Hungary was now effectively divided into three parts. In the west, Ferdinand continued to rule less than one-third of the old kingdom (so-called "Royal Hungary"). In the east a new state of initially uncertain nature was emerging. This was at some times a Hungarian vassal kingdom of the Ottomans, at others it was united with Royal Hungary. With the Treaty of Speyer (1570), it crystallised into a new state of Hungarian character – Transylvania – loosely controlled by the Ottoman Empire. The third part of Hungary, the central plain, was ruled directly by the Sultan. He gradually extended the area he held directly until 1568, when new frontiers were agreed by the Treaty of Adrianople.

The Collapse of the Teutonic Order, 1513-85

2 The Teutonic Order had never entirely recovered from its defeat by Polish and Lithuanian forces at Tannenberg (Grünwald) in 1410. In 1513 the Grand Master of the Livonian Order of the Brothers of the Sword (which had been united with the Teutonic Order since 1237) purchased independence, leaving the latter with just East Prussia. In 1525 the Teutonic Grand Master, Albrecht von Hohenzollern, converted to Protestantism and secularised the remaining Teutonic lands as the Duchy of Prussia, the largest Protestant fief in the kingdom of Poland.

Meanwhile, the lands ruled by the Livonian Order remained independent and Catholic until, in 1556-7, a civil war came close to making the Order a Polish client. This outcome was unacceptable to Tsar Ivan IV of Russia, who invaded in 1558 and captured most of Livonia and Estonia. However, this proved equally unacceptable to the other states of the area, which fought over the territory for the next two decades. The last Grand Master of the Order managed to secularise Courland, which became a Polish fief; Sweden gained most of Estonia; Poland wrested most of Russia's conquests from Ivan; and Denmark (which initially exercised her influence indirectly through Magnus Prince of Holstein, brother of the Danish king, and which began as a close ally of Russia) found her role reduced significantly by the end of the 16th century, losing all except the island of Ösel.

No hereditary German state survived in the Baltic lands, though noblemen of German origin played a central role in the region until 1918 and provided many of the civil servants of future rulers of the Baltic region.

Poland and Lithuania: the Union of Lublin, 1569

3 For nearly two centuries following the marriage between the Grand Duke of Lithuania, Jogaila, and the Polish Queen, Jadwiga, in 1386, the union between Poland and Lithuania was a personal one. However, by the 1560s it was clear that Sigismund II Augustus would be the last of the Jagiellonian line. For the Lithuanians, the prospect of the dissolution of the link with Poland was dire. Lithuania had been under threat from both the Ottomans, who had seized her territory on the lower Dnieper, and the Muscovites, who were pressing westwards under Ivan the Terrible (1533-1584). Only Polish support could guarantee Lithuania, while union with her offered the Polish nobility the prospect of fresh lands for settlement.

In 1569 at Lublin, a Lithuanian Parliament specially called into existence agreed with the traditional Polish Sejm to form an "indissoluble" union or "commonwealth" and to elect a common monarch after the childless Sigismund II Augustus's death. Initial resistance from the Lithuanian magnates, concerned that the proposed union would diminish their own power, was overcome. Poland and Lithuania remained distinct states, each with its own army, administration and laws.

In order to persuade the Poles to take on the burden of defending them in future, Lithuania agreed to turn Podlasia, Volhynia and the Ukraine over to Polish administration. Polish settlers, noble and common alike, moved into these territories, establishing new farms and great estates, and extending the influence of the Catholic Church. In turn, this helped to fuel conflicts with the other (Orthodox) groups living in these areas, especially the Cossacks of the Ukraine.

1572

1618

The Eve of the Thirty Years' War

The period following 1572 was characterised by continuing religious and dynastic wars, many of them exacerbated by foreign meddling such as that of Spain and England in the French Wars of Religion, and of England and France in the Revolt of the Netherlands. These also helped to reinforce nascent national identities, although the religious division of Europe following the Reformation had tended to cut across linguistic or ethnic lines. In places such as the Netherlands, where there was no clear-cut religious or ethnic divide and constitutional issues clouded the struggle, the conflict to determine who might believe what, and where, dragged on for years.

Indeed, because Philip II could bring to bear in the Netherlands so many of the resources of his vast trans-Atlantic and Mediterranean empire, Spain was able to fight for decades in the remote Netherlands rather than permit the revolt against Spanish rule, which began in 1566, to set the dangerous precedent of successful religious and political rebellion.

Ironically, it had been Philip II's efforts to impose a standard system of absolutist rule on the 17 provinces of the Netherlands in the face of their mutual rivalries which forced them together. It was to take his more diplomatically gifted generals, above all Parma, much effort and many years to split the French-speaking Catholic provinces from the Protestant Dutch-speaking areas. By identifying rebellion with religion, Parma and his successors were able to win back the bulk of the southern provinces, which had formed the Union of Arras in 1579. The decision of the Protestants in the northern Union of Utrecht to attack the south caused the southerners to appeal to Spain for troops to protect them and gave Philip II the excuse to carry through their re-Catholicisation.

The threat of a French invasion of the Spanish Netherlands in 1572 had distracted Philip II's soldiers from their campaign there and allowed the rebels to gain firm footholds in fortified towns. Philip's general, Parma, invaded France in 1589. But 10 years of war ended in 1598 without a clear victory for either side. Increasingly it was Elizabeth I's England which sent troops and money to support the Dutch. In 1604, however, Spain made peace with England, too. On each occasion no land changed hands. Only the war in the Netherlands dragged on. By 1609, the Spanish had recovered the great port of Antwerp as well as Flanders. Mutual exhaustion then persuaded Philip III to accept a 12-year truce with the rebels.

In Bohemia a movement of religious and political dissent against the Habsburgs similar to that in the Netherlands had developed during the early 17th century. By 1618, the largely Protestant Bohemian aristocracy was in open revolt. The decision to choose a non-Habsburg, Frederick V of the Palatinate, as King of Bohemia was seen as a challenge on the Dutch model to what the Habsburgs considered their divinely ordained right to rule. Control over wealthy and strategically central Bohemia, with its vote in choosing the emperor, was vital to the Austrian Habsburgs. With the Habsburgs' principal rivals – the Ottomans, France and England – unwilling or unable to restrain him, Ferdinand II, the new Emperor, was encouraged to undertake an ambitious war of reconquest to restore his authority to areas which had been lost to Protestantism since 1570. By 1620, Ferdinand had conquered Bohemia and installed himself as King there.

Spanish Habsburg possessions

Austrian Habsburg possessions

The Holy Roman Empire

Trondhjem

Christiania

SWEDEN

Åbo   Helsingfors

Stockholm   Reval   Novgorod

Gothenburg   Pskov

RUSSIA

Archangel

Perm

Nizhniy
Novgorod

Volga

Aarhus

Copenhagen   Malmö

Riga   Moscow

BALTIC
SEA

COURLAND

Dyneburg

Samara

DENMARK

Hamburg   Stettin

Bremen

Königsberg

Gdansk

PRUSSIA

Wilno   Vitebsk   Smolensk

Tula

Don

LITHUANIA

Minsk

Kursk

Kazakhs

Saratov

BRANDENBURG

Berlin

Poznań

SAXONY   Breslau

Dresden   SILESIA

Hanover

Frankfurt

Nürnberg

Warsaw

POLAND

Kiev

Vistula

Oder

Elbe

Volga

Astrakhan

Prague

BOHEMIA

Brünn

MORAVIA   Cracow

Lwów

Dnieper

Winnica

BAVARIA

Munich

AUSTRIA

Salzburg

Vienna

Pozsony

Graz

Danube

HUNGARY

Kassa

Buda

Debrecen

TRANSYLVANIA

Kolozsvár

MOLDAVIA

Jassy

Dniester

Azov

KHANATE OF
CRIMEA

Bakhchisaray

Circassians

Daghestan

Trieste

Venice

VENETIA

MANTUA
MODENA

Bologna

LUCCA

FLORENCE

SAN MARINO

PAPAL

Zágráb

Zara

DUCHY OF
URBINO

Spalato

Bosna
Serai

Pécs

Szeged

Temesvár

Belgrade

WALLACHIA

Bucharest

Brassó

Danube   Ruschuk

Varna

BLACK SEA

Tiflis

PERSIA

Erivan

REPUBLIC OF RAGUSA

Mostar

MONTENEGRO

Nish

Sofia

Burgas

Rome

DUCHY
OF
ISTRO

STATES

Naples

Bari

NAPLES   Taranto

Üsküb

Janina

Philippopolis   Adrianople

Salonica

OTTOMAN

Constantinople

Angora

EMPIRE

Tigris

Mosul

Palermo

SICILY   Messina

Catania

SEA

REPUBLIC

Smyrna

Adana

Athens

Euphrates

MALTA
(Knights of
St John)

Crete

Nicosia

Beirut

Damascus

Bedouins

HOLY ROMAN EMPIRE

Trier ○ Frankfurt ○
FRANCE
PALATINATE

Nuremberg ○   UPPER PALATINATE

Augsburg ○

BAVARIA

Munich ○

Ratisbon ○

SILESIA

Prague ○

BOHEMIA

MORAVIA

Brünn ○

Linz ○   AUSTRIA   Vienna ○

Salzburg ○

Innsbruck ○

TYROL

STYRIA   HUNGARY

Graz ○

CARINTHIA

Klagenfurt ○

VENETIAN REPUBLIC

NORTH SEA

THE HABSBURG LANDS AND THE PALATINATE: RELIGIOUS AFFILIATIONS IN 1600

—— Possessions of the Palatinate line of the Wittelsbachs

—— Habsburg possessions

—— Bavaria

▨ Protestant

▢ Catholic

━━ Frontier of the Holy Roman Empire, 1618

—— Frontiers, 1618

DENMARK

BALTIC SEA

NORTH SEA

Lübeck ○

Kamm... ○

PRUSSIA

Bremen ○ Verden ○

Osnabrück ○

Münster ○ Minden ○

Hildesheim ○ Magdeburg ○

Paderborn ○ *(to Magdeburg)*

(to Cologne) Halberstadt ○ *(to Mainz)*

(to Mainz)

Liège ○ *(to Mainz)*

Cologne ○ Fulda ○

POLAND

Trier ○ Mainz ○

Worms ○ Würzburg ○ Bamberg ○

Spires ○

Ratisbon ○

Eichstätt ○

Strassburg ○ Augsburg ○

Basle ○ Freising ○ Passau ○

HUNGARY

Salzburg ○

Constance ○

Brixen ○

FRANCE

Trent ○ *(to Brixen)*

(to Freising)

VENETIAN REPUBLIC

VENAISSIN ○

OTTOMAN EMPIRE

ENGLAND

Zeeland
LANDS O...

Bruges ○ Ghent ○

Flanders

Br...

Artois

Tournai ○

Arras ○

Haina...

FRANCE

The Hag...

THE HOLY ROMAN EMPIRE : CHURCH STATES , 1618

▨ Bishopric

▢ Archbishopric

Some northern church states were Protestant or lay administered

—— Frontiers, 1618

━━ The Holy Roman Empire

THE NETHERLANDS, 1566-1648

▨ The Union of Utrecht, 1579	▢ Added to the United Netherlands, 1648
— The Union of Arras, 1579	▨ Spanish Netherlands, 1648
▨ Joined Union of Utrecht by 1581	— Frontier of the Holy Roman Empire
Boundary of United Netherlands according to 1609 truce	— Frontiers, 1648

The Netherlands, 1566-1648

1 The revolt of the Netherlands against their Habsburg rulers after 1566 was a pivotal development in European history. Although William, Prince of Orange, played a major role in the revolt, its primary result was the creation of a republican regime drawing its strength from the mercantile wealth of Dutch cities such as Amsterdam. The rebellion was sparked by Philip II's attempts in the 1560s to centralise the government of the 17 provinces of the Netherlands. The rebels originally demanded a reversal of this and only turned to republicanism when it became clear that Philip II himself was personally behind the schemes to reduce the provinces' independence. Of course, Philip II's religious intolerance played a major part in promoting rebellion, because the Protestants in the north of the Netherlands could not compromise with him, whereas many Catholics were eventually bought off with concessions.

Renewed fighting began between the Dutch, led by Orange, and Spanish forces in 1572. In 1576 the royal army mutinied and Orange's supporters temporarily took over almost all the 17 provinces, but within three years unity among the rebels evaporated. In January 1579, the Union of Arras, committed to Catholicism and loyalty to the king, was formed in the south. In the same month the anti-Habsburg northern Union of Utrecht, which evolved into the United Provinces of the Netherlands, was formed.

Only in 1609 was Philip III prepared to accept a 12-year truce. The United Provinces of the Netherlands became *de facto* independent and France, England and other states hurried to recognise them as such. However, the Habsburgs still hoped to stifle the "rebels" and fought until 1648 to conquer them, only then finally recognising their independence.

If they failed with the seven northern provinces, by dint of military effort, religious zeal and playing on local identity, the Habsburgs managed to reconcile the 10 southern provinces to their rule. Dutch naval power and control of the islands at the mouth of the Scheldt meant, however, that the trade of Antwerp (recaptured by the Spanish in 1585) was strangled. In an attempt to stabilise the 10 loyal provinces, Philip II bequeathed them to his daughter Isabella, who was married to her cousin Albert of Austria, while the rest of his empire went to Philip III. At Albert's death in 1621, his possessions were returned to Spanish rule, but subsequent attacks, by both the Calvinist Dutch and the Catholic French, forged a new national identity in the South Netherlands, ancestor of modern Belgium.

The Habsburg Lands and the Palatinate: Religious Affiliations in 1600

2 The Austrian Habsburg lands had been devolved to various members of the family who had pursued the Catholic Counter-Reformation with varying degrees of intensity. It was the most vigorous persecutor of Protestants, Ferdinand of Styria, who became the family's champion as the more relaxed

rule of Matthias waned. It was one thing to crack down on heresy in compliant Austria, but Bohemia had its own assertive local institutions which were strongly infiltrated by Protestantism.

By 1617, the Habsburg authorities were trying to push back the tide of Protestantism by ordering the closure and demolition of reformed churches in Bohemia, and the seizure of Protestant Church funds. This antagonised the Bohemian nobility, which prided itself on its independence. The fact that Bohemia had a Protestant neighbour in the Elector Palatine, whose eastern territories bordered Bohemia at Eger, meant that in the event of an election to the Bohemian throne there was a clear local Protestant counter-candidate to the Habsburgs.

Although the Bohemian estates had agreed to "accept" Ferdinand of Styria as their king in 1617 when Matthias died in 1619, the Bohemians chose Frederick V of the Palatinate to succeed him. Ferdinand of Styria ignored their choice and proclaimed himself king by hereditary right, using the Bohemian electoral vote to support his candidacy for the Empire and proceeded to invade and expel Frederick after only one winter as king. Ferdinand could rely on the equally staunch Catholic, Maximilian of Bavaria, to help him, not least because the Bavarian Duke coveted Frederick V's Upper Palatinate.

The Holy Roman Empire: Church States, 1618

3 Whereas even Catholic territorial monarchies such as France or Habsburg Spain had succeeded in abolishing separate ecclesiastical jurisdictions within their borders, many Church states survived as parts of the Holy Roman Empire. More controversially, one of the key consequences of the Reformation inside the Empire had been the secularisation of Church states by Protestant rulers. Both Catholic clerical rulers (such as the three clerical Electors of Cologne, Mainz and Trier) and Catholic lay rulers disliked such arbitrary secularisation (as they saw it) and wished to reverse it, while Protestant rulers who had benefited from it naturally resisted any reversion to the old order which could cost them land and income.

Neither the Catholics or Protestants accepted as definitive the Peace of Augsburg (1555), which brought a temporary halt to the first phase of the religious wars that followed the Reformation in Germany, and by 1618 they were manoeuvring for their own advantage. Conflict over the right of Protestants to build churches in Bohemia excited passions that spilled over into Germany and began the Thirty Years' War. The complexity of the Empire meant that there were always disputes over jurisdiction and historical rights, but the religious issue in particular and its European-wide implication meant that conflicts within the Empire soon spread and drew in other states.

1618

The Peace of Westphalia

The Thirty Years' War came to an end in 1648 after the most savage and destructive warfare yet seen in Europe. Peace was signed in the Westphalian towns of Osnabrück and Münster, where the Emperor negotiated separately with his Protestant and Catholic enemies. Yet whatever the convulsions of the long years of more or less general warfare, in the event strikingly few changes were made to the political map. The treaties, too, marked the final recognition that Catholic princes inspired by the Counter-Reformation would not be able to roll back entirely the gains that Protestantism had made in Europe since the early 16th century.

Although both France and Sweden gained lands inside the Empire, it was largely at the expense of minor princes and not the House of Habsburg. Of the Habsburgs' losses, the most important were those to the west of the Holy Roman Empire, where France gained Sundgau on the Rhine and Philippsburg, as well as a number of smaller territories. The result was that the Habsburg hold on the Spanish Road, the narrow strip of Habsburg controlled territory which linked Spain and the Spanish Netherlands, was cut.

Spain was forced to accept the independence and sovereignty of the seven United Provinces of the Netherlands some 80 years after the start of their revolt against Philip II. His grandson, Philip IV, retained the Southern Netherlands with their mixed Flemish and French-speaking populations and re-established Catholicism, which, despite linguistic differences within the newly reconquered territories, marked their identity for centuries afterwards and made even the southern Flemish-speakers reject the idea of unification with their Dutch-speaking cousins in the Protestant-dominated United Provinces.

From the mid-1630s Franco-Spanish conflict had been the central element of the Thirty Years' War. The war had begun as a battle for supremacy within the Empire between Catholic and Protestant in which outside powers had taken sides according to their dominant faith. Thus, first Lutheran Denmark, then Sweden supported the Protestant princes, while Catholic Spain backed the Emperor. But Catholic France's sympathies with the Protestant side changed the composition of the struggle. The pragmatic Cardinal Richelieu identified breaking Spain's ring of territories around France's land borders as the key to the rise of French power, overruling the arguments of a pro-Catholic *dévot* faction in France. Richelieu attempted to weaken the Habsburgs by subsidising their Protestant enemies, but after the catastrophic defeat of Sweden in 1634, France entered the war against Spain directly in 1635. Despite her previous disastrous set-back, Sweden emerged a victor from the war, largely as France's major ally. Her territorial gains in a girdle of lands to the south of Denmark put her traditional enemy at a disadvantage, but made further struggle between Denmark and Sweden for control of key trade routes through the Baltic much more likely. Sweden's position was additionally strengthened by her conquest of Livonia from Poland in 1629.

It soon became clear that Richelieu's successor, Mazarin, had overrated both the weakness of Spain and the capacity of the French population to support the expensive burden of the war. Mazarin's expectations of rapid victories against Spain were to be thwarted as the war dragged on for more than a decade.

Spanish Habsburg possessions

Austrian Habsburg possessions

The Holy Roman Empire

N O R W A Y
Trondhjem
(Danish)
gen
Christiania

S W E D E N

Åbo
Helsingfors
Stockholm
Reval
Gothenburg

BALTIC
SEA

Aarhus
Copenhagen
Malmö

ENMARK

SWEDISH
POMERANIA

Hamburg
Stettin
BRANDENBURG
Bremen
rück
ter
HANOVER
Berlin
Elbe
SAXONY
Breslau
Leipzig
Dresden
SILESIA
nkfurt
White
Mountain
mberg
BOHEMIA
tes
MORAVIA
Brünn
BAVARIA
Danube
Munich
AUSTRIA
Vienna
Pozsony
Salzburg
Graz

LITHUANIA

Livonia
Riga
Pskov

COURLAND
Dyneburg

Königsberg
Gdansk
PRUSSIA
Vistula

Poznań

Warsaw

P O L A N D

Cracow
Lwów

KASSA
HUNGARY
Debrecen
Kolozsvár
Buda
TRANSYLVANIA
MOLDAVIA
Jassy
Pécs
Szeged
Brassó
Temesvár
Belgrade
WALLACHIA
Bucharest

R U S S I A

Nizhniy
Novgorod
Kazan
Volga

Moscow
Samara

Tula
Kazakhs

Vitebsk
Smolensk
Wilno
Minsk

Kursk
Saratov

Don

Kharkov
Tsaritsyn

Kiev

Winnica
Volga

Dniester
Astrakhan

Dnieper

Azov
KHANATE OF
CRIMEA
Circassians
Daghestan
Bakhchisaray

BLACK SEA
PERSIA

Varna
Ruschuk
Danube
Nish
Sofia

Philippopolis
Adrianople

Constantinople

Trebizond

Janina

Angora

Smyrna

Athens

Adana

Mosul
Tigris
Euphrates

Trieste
VENICE
Venice
MANTUA
MODENA
Bologna
Lucca
SAN MARINO
ce
PAPAL
CANY
STATES
Rome
DUCHY
OF
ASTRO

Zágráb
Zara
Bosna
Seray
Spalato
Mostar
REPUBLIC OF
RAGUSA
MONTENEGRO
Üsküb
Salonica

OTTOMAN EMPIRE

VENETIA

Naples
Bari
NAPLES
Taranto

Palermo
Messina
SICILY
Catania

REPUBLIC

Nicosia

SEA

MALTA
(Knights of
St John)

Crete

Beirut
Damascus
Bedouins

125

NORTH SEA

BALT[IC]

DENMARK

ENGLAND

COUNTY OF EAST FRIESLAND

COUNTY OF OLDENBURG

PRINCIPALITY OF BREMEN

Hamburg

Lübeck

DUCHY OF MECKLENBURG SCHWERIN GÜSTROW

SWEDISH POMERANIA

Stettin

NETHERLANDS

B. OSNABRÜCK

DUCHY OF BRUNSWICK-LÜNEBURG

DUCHY OF BRUNSWICK-KALENBERG

ELECTORATE OF BRANDENBURG

Bremen

Osnabrück

Hanover

Brunswick

Berlin

Antwerp

DUCHY OF KLEVE

B. OF MUNSTER

Münster

D. OF BR.-WOLF.

A. MAGDEBURG

Magdeburg

Brussels

SPANISH NETHERLANDS

A. COLOGNE

DUCHY OF BERG

Cologne

C. OF MARK

C. OF LIPPE

DUCHY OF WESTPHALIA (to Cologne)

B. PADERBORN

D. OF BR.-WOLF

COUNTY OF WALDECK

B. OF HILD.

D. OF BR.-KAL

PRINCIPALITY OF ANHALT

Leipzig

ELECTORATE OF SAXONY

Aix-la-Chapelle

DUCHY OF JÜLICH

PRINC. OF NASSAU

LANDGRAVIATE OF HESSE-KASSEL

Dresden

A. TRIER

LAND. OF HESSE DARMSTADT

FULDA

SAXON DUCHIES

Trier

Frankfurt H-L

Mainz

A. MAINZ

WÜRZBURG

B. WÜRZBURG

PR. OF BAYREUTH

Prague

KINGDOM OF BOHEMIA

H-L

LOWER PALATINATE

B. BAMBERG

UPPER PALATINATE

COUNTY OF HANAU-LICHTENBERG

PR. OF BAYREUTH

Nuremberg

PR. OF

Nancy

B. SPIRES

MARG. OF BADEN

DUCHY OF WÜRTTEMBERG

Stuttgart

ANSBACH

B. EICHSTÄTT

B. RATISBON

Ratisbon

Strassburg

B. STRASSBURG

H.L

H.L.

ELECTORATE OF BAVARIA

B. PASSAU

DUCHY OF LORRAINE

B. S.

Munich

B. FREISING

Linz

FRANCE

FRANCHE COMTÉ

Besançon

B. BASEL

SWISS CONFEDERATION

B. AUGSBURG

A. SALZBURG

Salzburg

ARCHDUCHY OF AUSTR[IA]

Innsbruck

COUNTY OF TYROL

B. BRIXEN

DUCHY OF STYRIA

Graz

DUCHY OF CARINTHIA

Klagenfurt

B. TRENT

Trent

VENETIAN REPUBLIC

DUCHY OF CARNIOLA

MANTUA

FRANCE

HOLY ROMAN EMPIRE

Rottweil
1519-1632

Mülhausen
1515
FRANCE
Basle
1579
Schaffhausen
1579

Bishopric of Basle
1579

1501

Zurich

St Gallen

Franche-Comté

Biel

Solothurn

Lucerne

Berne

SWISS CONFEDERATION

Fribourg

1497/99

Grisons

Bormio

1475-78

1536

Vaud

Lausanne

1495

1512

1536

Chiavenna

Valtellina

Gex
1536-67/69

Chablais
1536-67/69

Sion

1513
Ticino

1500

Geneva

1526

1536-39

Eschental
1512-15

1513-15

Lugano

1512

1512-24

SAVOY

DUCHY OF MILAN

VENETIAN REPUBLIC

THE SWISS CONFEDERATION TO 1648

	The Swiss Confederation, 1486
	Added by 1500 (with dates)
	Added during the 16th century (with dates)
	Areas held temporarily (with dates)
▬▬	Frontier of the Holy Roman Empire, 1648
—	Frontiers, 1648

THE HOLY ROMAN EMPIRE IN 1648

	Austrian Habsburg possessions
	Spanish Habsburg possessions
	Possessions of the Wittelsbachs of Bava[ria]
	Other Wittelsbach possessions
	Possessions of the Hohenzollerns of Bran[denburg]

PRUSSIA

POLAND

R. OF
HLAU

Breslau

PR. OF
BRIEG

PR. OF BRIEG

DUCHY OF SILESIA

ATE OF MORAVIA

Brünn

DOM OF HUNGARY

OTTOMAN
EMPIRE

2

Other Hohenzollern possessions	Other states within the Holy Roman Empire
Swedish possessions	—— Frontiers, 1648
Danish possessions (Oldenburgs)	—— The Holy Roman Empire
Church lands	
Imperial Cities	

The Swiss Confederation to 1648

1 Although the Emperor had in effect given up trying to bring the Swiss cantons back under his control as early as 1499, it was only in 1648 that the Holy Roman Empire renounced all claims over the 13 cantons and the city of Basle which together formed the "Community of the Oath" (*Eidegenossenschaft*).

At the same time that the Peace of Westphalia accorded independence to the Swiss cantons, by releasing their legal obligations to the empire, the generally poor Swiss cantons continued their involvement with Imperial politics by providing recruits to the great powers of Europe. Swiss mercenaries passed through the Gex corridor between Franche-Comté and Savoy into France, while others continued to serve the Pope and, from the Grisons in particular, the King of Spain.

The Holy Roman Empire, 1648

2 Historians have always found it difficult to define exactly what the Holy Roman Empire was. The very vagueness of the Empire's definition was part of its identity. It was clearly not a centralised absolutist state of the sort which France had become under the Bourbons. Unlike England, for instance, with its unified system of justice, the Empire contained more than 2,300 different jurisdictions. Given that the Empire was made up of somewhere between 294 and 348 different states after 1648 (historians disagree), it is clear that many of these jurisdictions were overlapping. This had been a source of conflict for centuries, and following the Reformation the issue of whether a prince could determine the faith of his subjects had been the cause of immense strife. Nonetheless, after 1648 most rulers were weary of using religion as the occasion of quarrel – a clear break with the past.

The most important and influential figures in the Empire were the seven Electors who chose the Emperor. Three of them were the Catholic Prince-Archbishops of the clerical states of Cologne, Mainz and Trier, while the other four were lay rulers. Until 1648, three of these were Protestants: the Electors of Brandenburg, the Palatinate and Saxony. Catholic Bavaria was granted the Electoral dignity in 1623. (In 1692, Protestant Hanover was added to the list of Electoral states, while in 1803, in the dying years of the Empire, Baden and Hesse acquired electoral status though neither had the chance to exercise their rights before the Empire's abolition in 1806.)

Despite the best efforts of Ferdinand III, the Habsburgs failed to preserve much real authority for the holder of the Imperial dignity. As a result, the idea that the different princes and states were subservient to the Emperor withered away. It was agreed that majorities in the Imperial Diet could not bind minorities, so no effective legislation was possible. Furthermore the Imperial "circles" (which authorised the raising of taxation) operated only by consent and with no effective means of coercion, which should not, however, mask the occasions on which the members of given "circles" agreed on the need for common action. In addition, the multitude of weaker states looked to the Emperor as the guarantor of their status and rights. After all, their own standing depended on the same legal basis as that of the Emperor.

Voltaire's famous gibe that the Holy Roman Empire was neither holy, nor Roman, nor an empire applied especially well to the situation after 1648. Nonetheless, after the bloodletting within the Empire during the previous 30 years, it is perhaps more surprising that any Imperial institutions survived at all rather than that shadow instead of substance tended to predominate following the Thirty Years' War. For the Holy Roman Empire to survive more than 150 years after Westphalia suggests that its very vagueness served the purposes of its members (including the more powerful ones) rather better than a clear-cut definition of sovereignty on what was becoming the "modern" model for 17th-century Europe.

Out of the wreckage of the great Habsburg effort to assert Imperial predominance under Ferdinand II from 1618, his son, Ferdinand III, was able to preserve the continuity of the idea of the Empire and from his point of view, perhaps more importantly, to confirm the assumption that a Habsburg should be automatically elected to the throne. Partly because France was convulsed by the civil disorders known as the Frondes, Mazarin was unable to block Ferdinand III's nomination of his own successor, but a sudden death left the position of "King of the Romans" open at Ferdinand's death in 1656 and a bitterly contested election followed in 1657. The Habsburg Leopold I defeated his Bourbon rival, Louis XIV, but only at the cost of renouncing some of his father's rights.

In effect, a balance of power inside the Empire was established in 1648 by the Peace of Westphalia which was to last almost a century. The Habsburg lands did not give the Emperor a strong enough power base to seek to dominate the other rulers (as Ferdinand II had tried with Spanish help). The survival of the Habsburgs on the Imperial throne was offset by the expansion of Brandenburg – to include the Rhine duchies (1609), Prussia (1618) and much of Pomerania – and the acquisition of territories still formally inside the Empire by Sweden and France, as well as the acquisition of land by Bavaria in southern Germany.

The centre of gravity of Habsburg power shifted as a result of these changes towards their Austrian lands. Bohemia, which had been a centre of Protestant dissent, was almost wholly reclaimed for the Catholic Church, while in 1627 the Bohemian crown went from being elective to hereditary within the Habsburg family.

1648

1683

The Siege of Vienna

The failure of the vast Ottoman army to capture Vienna in 1683 was a decisive event in European history. The victory of a mixed force of Imperial and Polish troops over the Sultan's army marked the point after which Christian Europe was never again threatened with conquest by an external enemy. Although the northwestern European powers played no part in the crisis and some German princes, like the Great Elector of Brandenburg-Prussia, studiously ignored the Emperor Leopold I's requests for help, it mattered a great deal to them who won. If the Sultan's forces had captured Vienna, the whole European balance of power would have been shattered. In the event, though 1683 saw the Ottoman Empire at the height of its European conquests, the Turks were already weakened by domestic divisions. Defeat served only to magnify them. Although Polish troops led by their king, Jan Sobieski, played a decisive part in raising the siege of Vienna in September 1683, it was not Poland but the Austrian Habsburgs who ultimately benefited most from the defeat of the Turks. The threat of rebellion in Habsburg-controlled Hungary was reduced, as the border with the Turks was pushed forwards to the south and east.

Yet however momentous the defeat of the Ottomans, the most significant change in the European balance of power after 1648 was the emergence of France as the mightiest country in western Europe. Following the Treaty of the Pyrenees (1659), Spain, formerly the pre-eminent European power, lost any vestiges of her previous position. By 1683, Louis XIV's France was nearing the peak of her power, and aggressively seeking to acquire land along her frontiers. France's power was based on her large population, which at 20 million far outstripped that of her neighbours. Numbers meant power: they provided large tax revenues and a rich source of recruits. Louis XIV's able ministers built on the legacy of Richelieu and Mazarin to create a large standing army, able to intervene swiftly against less well-prepared and well-funded enemies.

Although Louis XIV's France was seen as the arch-absolutist state, in fact it was smaller countries such as Brandenburg-Prussia and Sweden which exemplified the trend away from medieval constitutions to unified and centralised government. With only about two-million subjects, Sweden achieved much more, proportionately, than heavily populated France. In the later 17th century, an absolutist model of rule was imposed on Sweden by Charles XI (1660-97). Unlike his belligerent predecessor, Charles X, Charles XI concentrated on building up the financial power of the monarchy. Charles X's victories had marked the height of Swedish power, but his son's suppression of much of the influence of the nobility was vital in providing the secure base for Sweden's long struggle during the Great Northern War after 1700 (see page 136).

Large-scale wars in Eastern Europe, too, particularly involving Poland, had a major effect on the continental balance of power. In 1655, Charles X of Sweden invaded and temporarily took most of Poland, save Gdańsk and Lwów, in the Northern War. By the Truce of Andrusovo (1667), furthermore, Poland lost much of the Ukraine to Russia. By 1668, Poland had a population of only four million, down 45 per cent on that in 1618, while her economy had suffered devastating damage. Her increasing weakness opened up a tempting vacuum which drew in states such as Sweden and Moscow, as well as German princes, all eager for territorial acquisitions.

Trondhjem

gen

N
O
R
W
A
Y
(Danish)

Christiania

SWEDEN

Åbo

Helsingfors

Stockholm

Reval

Gothenburg

Riga

Pskov

Archangel

Kazan

Nizhniy
Novgorod

Moscow

Samara

Aarhus

Copenhagen
Malmö

COURLAND

Dyneburg

Smolensk

Tula

R U S S I A

Saratov

DENMARK

BALTIC
SEA

Wilno

Vitebsk

Minsk

Kursk

Hamburg

Stettin

SWEDISH
POMERANIA

Gdańsk

Königsberg

PRUSSIA

LITHUANIA

Bremen
abrück

Hanover

BRANDENBURG

Berlin

Poznań

Vistula

Warsaw

Tsaritsyn

ALL
nkfurt

SAXONY

Leipzig

Dresden

Elbe

Breslau

Oder

SILESIA

P O L A N D

HETMANATE

Kharkov

Don

Volga

BOHEMIA

Prague

MORAVIA

Brünn

Cracow

Lwów

Kiev

Dnieper

Astrakhan

ES

Nuremberg

Danube

Y

Kassa

Winnica

Zaporogian Cossacks

BAVARIA

Vienna

Munich

Salzburg

AUSTRIA

H
U
N
G
A
R
Y

Pozsony

PRINC. OF THÖKÖLY
(in revolt against
Habsburgs)

Buda

Debrecen

Dniester

MOLDAVIA

Jassy

Azov

KHANATE
OF
CRIMEA

Bakhchisaray

Circassians

Daghestan

Graz

Pécs

Szeged

Temesvár

Kolozsvár

TRANSYLVANIA

Brassó

MANTUA

Trieste

Venice

Zágráb

Zara

Bosna
Saray

Belgrade

WALLACHIA

Bucharest

Ruschuk

Danube

Varna

BLACK SEA

Tiflis

SAN MARINO

Spalato

Mostar

Nish

MONTENEGRO

Sofia

Philippopolis

Adrianople

Erivan

Trebizond

PERSIA

ENCE
PAPAL

Perugia

STATES

Rome

REP. OF
RAGUSA

Üsküb

Salonica

Constantinople

Ankara

Naples

Bari

Taranto

NAPLES

Janina

Smyrna

O T T O M A N   E M P I R E

Adana

Mosul

Palermo

Messina

SICILY

Catania

SEA

Athens

Euphrates

Tigris

MALTA
(Knights of
St John)

Crete

Nicosia

Beirut
Damascus

B e d o u i n s

129

HUNGARY, 1606-83

- Ottoman Empire in 1606
- Added by 1620 (with dates)
- Added, 1664
- Added, 1672
- Transylvania 1621-29 and 1645-48
- Extent of Thököly's Hungarian Principality in 1683 (in revolt against Habsburgs)
- Habsburg possessions
- Frontiers in 1683

SWEDEN TO 1683

- Sweden from 1523
- Added, 1561
- Added, 1582
- Added by c.1600
- Added, 1617
- Added, 1629
- Added, 1645
- Added, 1648
- Added, 1654
- Added, 1658
- Areas held temporarily (with dates)
- Frontiers in 1683
- The Holy Roman Empire

THE GROWT...

- Co... Fra...
- Ad...
- Ad...
- Ad...

County of Charolle: 1674-78, 16...

Y R O M A N   E M P I R E
Cologne
Rhine
Aix-la-Chapelle
Liège
Coblenz
Frankfurt
Mainz
Treves
Luxemburg   Palatinate
1679   *1688*   Spires
Duchy of Bar
1635-61
1670
Metz
Duchy of Lorraine
1681
Toul
Nancy   Strassburg
1681
1635-59   *1684*
1670   Freiburg
1679
Alsace
Basle
1676
Franche
Besançon

Comté
SWISS CONFEDERATION

Geneva

SAVOY

LOUIS XIV   [1]

Added 1668, lost 1678/9   —— Frontiers, 1648

Added 1678/9   —— The Holy Roman
                                         Empire, 1648

Occupied and/or claimed by
c.1690 (with dates of occupation)

Other annexations (with dates)

The Growth of France under Louis XIV

[1] After the death of Mazarin in 1661, Louis XIV pursued a policy of diplomatic aggression. But it was only in 1667 that he first went to war. Claiming parts of the Spanish Netherlands by virtue of his Habsburg wife's rights as the elder sister of the new Spanish king, Carlos II, Louis XIV's troops quickly occupied the territory. Peace in 1668 gave France 12 fortresses along her borders with the Spanish Netherlands (to add to Dunkirk, bought from England in 1662).

Then, in 1672, Louis XIV turned on his former Dutch allies. They were saved from defeat only by opening the dykes as they had done a century earlier in their war against the Spanish. Although the Dutch survived until peace in 1678 and even recovered Maastricht by the Treaty of Nijmegen (1678-9), it was their weak Spanish allies who paid the price: France took more border fortresses plus the Franche-Comté and remained in occupation of the Duchy of Lorraine. France also kept Freiburg on the Rhine.

Louis XIV now adopted a complicated and essentially fraudulent legal procedure to claim sovereignty over many pockets of Imperial territory along his eastern border whose status after the Peace of Westphalia (*see* page 124) was ambiguous. Using his ever-growing army to back up the decisions of the so-called *chambres des réunions*, Luxemburg was repeatedly besieged and threatened as Louis nibbled at one part then another of the Duchy before seizing the fortress itself in 1684. Using the clerical jurisdiction of three bishoprics, Metz, Toul and Verdun, granted to France definitively at Westphalia, Louis XIV claimed political sovereignty over other places in their sees. Similarly, in Alsace French judges annulled the traditional rights of the German-speaking towns, seizing the great trading city of Strassburg in 1681.

Sweden to 1683

[2] Sweden had expanded significantly from her core areas even before her gains from the Peace of Westphalia. By 1595, Sweden controlled the whole of Estonia. In 1617, under the Peace of Stolbovo, she added Karelia, cutting off Russia from all access to the Baltic. Sweden took Livonia from Poland in 1629, and occupied a string of Baltic ports on the Polish coastline between 1629 and 1635. In 1645 Denmark was forced to cede the Baltic islands of Ösel and Gotland to Sweden, as well as Jämtland and Härjedalen on the border with Norway. Although the peace settlement in 1648 gave her a string of territories around the southern borders of her old enemy Denmark, the Scania peninsula remained in Danish hands until 1658. Charles X waged a brilliant set of campaigns against a coalition of enemies, Denmark, Poland and Muscovy, and captured much of the remaining Danish territory on the northern side of the Baltic. In addition to Scania, Denmark had to cede parts of Norway around Trondheim and the island of Bornholm in the Baltic. Charles X how-

ever grew over-ambitious and tried to seize Copenhagen itself in a renewed war, hoping Sweden could control the traffic into the Baltic and therefore its tolls. But his sudden death and stiff Danish resistance led to a modified settlement in 1660, in which Denmark recovered Bornholm and parts of Norway. Sweden also had to renounce her demand that Denmark prevent foreign warships entering the Baltic.

During the minority of Charles XI (until 1672), Denmark started a war to recover Scania but the young king asserted himself and defeated the Danish invasion. Sweden fared less well against Brandenburg-Prussia, which had imitated some of her military and administrative measures, and put them to the test in a war in 1675. Only Louis XIV's pressure prevented Sweden losing more than small areas of Pomerania to Brandenburg. As the wars of the 1650s and 1670s showed, Sweden's Baltic empire was surrounded by envious neighbours and it was only a matter of time before the numerically weak Swedes lost the advantage of better organisation.

Hungary, 1606-83

[3] By the early 17th century, the Turkish hold on central Hungary was weakening. Transylvania emerged during this period as an important and prosperous European power, ruled by Prince Bethlen Gábor (1613-29). He doubled the territory's revenues and acted as a staunch defender of Calvinism in Central Europe. His influence, and that of his successor Györgi I Rákóczi, meant that the Habsburgs could not enforce the Counter-Reformation as brutally in the parts of Hungary they controlled (Royal Hungary) as they did elsewhere.

Transylvania's brief flowering ended after 1657, when the army of Györgi II Rákóczi was destroyed by Tatars while attempting to seize the crown of Poland. Mehmet Köprülü, the Turkish Grand Vizier, took this chance to invade Transylvania, and seized important parts of the principality in the west, including Várad. The Habsburgs intervened and won a surprise victory against the Turks, but the peace settlement of Vasvár (1664) ratified most of the Ottoman gains.

The apparent increase in Turkish power encouraged anti-Habsburg plotting in Royal Hungary in the 1670s. A savage Habsburg reaction had the effect of driving the malcontents to more extreme measures. In 1678, Imre Thököly, a young Transylvanian, raised the standard of revolt and occupied a large part of central Hungary. The Turks took this opportunity to intervene and sent a huge army into Hungary in 1683. This laid siege to Vienna, putting the whole European balance of power in peril. By September, however, the siege had been lifted, in part through the intervention of King Jan Sobieski of Poland, and by 1699 Imperial forces had swept the Turks out of most of Hungary.

1683

The Ascendancy of France

The defeat of the Ottoman army at Vienna in September 1683 by the Habsburgs was followed by the rapid advance of Emperor Leopold I's forces into Hungary, Transylvania and the Balkans. The Emperor formed the Holy League in 1684 with Poland and Venice to pursue the struggle against the Turks. Russia joined in 1686. However, war in the west gave the Turks a breathing space, as the Emperor, fearing a switch in the traditional pro-Habsburg majority in the Electoral College which chose Holy Roman Emperors, was forced to send soldiers westwards to the Rhine to resist a French threat to the Electorates there. Nonetheless, fighting dragged on until 1699 and the Turkish Sultan, who had recovered all of the Northern Balkans, was forced to cede Transylvania and most of Hungary to the Emperor by the Treaty of Carlowitz in 1699. His allies acquired territory, too. Poland regained Podolia and part of the Ukraine west of the Dnieper, while Venice took the Peloponnese and most of Dalmatia.

In Western Europe, Louis XIV's relentless nibbling away at the Spanish Netherlands and at the Imperial fringe territories turned his neighbours against him. In 1686, Catholic and Protestant German princes formed the League of Augsburg to resist further French penetration into the Holy Roman Empire. Louis XIV's revocation of the rights of French Protestants in 1685 also pushed traditionally pro-French, but firmly Protestant, Sweden into the League along with Catholic Austria, Bavaria and Spain.

France was already feeling the strain of enormous military expenditure even before the outbreak of war in 1688 (the Nine Years' War), when Louis XIV sent his troops into the Rhineland to secure his authority there. The war cost France dear. Famine and peasant discontent compounded the failure of the French armies to achieve victory. Instead, the improved forces of the German princes, backed by Anglo-Dutch troops and financial power, wore France down.

With the French in 1688 committed to their assault on the Rhineland, the Dutch were able to spare troops to assist in the overthrow of the Catholic James II of England. The Dutch Prince William of Orange gained the British crown, and the anti-French coalition was thereby greatly strengthened.

On the other hand, as the French threat declined, so rivalries between the allies grew. On the political horizon, the vital question of who would inherit the Spanish Habsburg throne when the childless Carlos II eventually died was becoming acute. William III (of England and the Netherlands), although in alliance with the Austrian Habsburgs from 1688, was anxious to avoid either a clear-cut French or Austrian succession. Peace in 1697 was meant to buy all the participants time to prepare for the next crisis.

In the east, another European succession crisis loomed when Charles XI of Sweden died in 1697, leaving his 15 year-old son, Charles XII, as king. Sweden's neighbours eyed her territory greedily, and none more so than Augustus the Strong of Saxony, who had additionally ruled Poland in personal union since 1697. By 1699, Augustus was preparing for a campaign to seize Sweden's territories to the south of the Baltic, despite bitter opposition from the Polish Diet (parliament).

Meanwhile, the young Tsar of Muscovy, Peter I, had captured Azov on the Black Sea from the Turks in 1696, giving his previously land-locked empire an outlet to the sea. Peter managed to retain Azov, despite the weakening of his strategic position when Austria and Venice, his Holy League allies, made peace with the Sultan by the Treaty of Carlowitz in 1699.

NORWAY (Danish)

Trondhjem

Christiania

SWEDEN

Gothenburg

Stockholm
Åbo
Helsingfors
Reval

RUSSIAN EMPIRE

Archangel

Perm

Nizhniy Novgorod
Volga

Moscow
Samara

DENMARK
Aarhus
Copenhagen
Malmö

BALTIC SEA

Riga
Pskov

Smolensk
Tula

DUCHY OF SCHLESWIG HOLSTEIN-GOTTORP

SWEDISH POMERANIA

Königsberg

PRUSSIA

Gdańsk

LITHUANIA

Wilno
Vitebsk

Minsk

Kursk

Saratov

Hamburg
Stettin

BRANDENBURG
Berlin
Poznań

Vistula

Warsaw
Brześć-Litewski

Don

Hanover
Bremen

Elbe

SAXONY
Leipzig
Dresden

SILESIA
Breslau
Łódź

Oder

POLAND
(in Personal Union with Saxony)

HETMANATE

Kiev
Kharkov

Volga

Frankfurt

BOHEMIA
Prague

MORAVIA
Brünn

Cracow

Winnica

Dnieper

Astrakhan

Danube

BAVARIA
Munich

Vienna

AUSTRIA
Salzburg

Pozsony

Buda Pest

Graz

Dniester

Zaporogian Cossacks

Azov

KHANATE OF CRIMEA

Venice
Trieste

Zágráb

(Military administration)

HUNGARY

Debrecen

Szeged

Kolozsvár

TRANSYLVANIA

Temesvár
Brassó

Jassy

MOLDAVIA

Bakhchisaray

Great Kabardia

Circassians

Daghestan

MODENA
Bologna
SAN MARINO

TUSCANY
PAPAL
Rome

Zara

Bosna Saray

Belgrade

WALLACHIA
Bucharest

Danube

Ruschuk

Varna

BLACK SEA

PERSIA

VENETIAN REPUBLIC

Spalato

Mostar

REP. OF RAGUSA

MONTENEGRO

Nish

Sofia

Philippopolis

Üsküb

Adrianople

Trebizond

STATES

Naples
Bari
Taranto

NAPLES

Janina

OTTOMAN EMPIRE

Salonica

Constantinople

Angora

Mosul

Palermo
Messina
Catania

SICILY

Patras
Athens

Smyrna

Adana

Tigris

Euphrates

SEA

MALTA
(Knights of St John)

Crete

Nicosia

Beirut
Damascus

Bedouins

33

NORTH
SEA

SWEDEN

DENMARK

BALTIC
SEA

(to Sweden)

SWEDISH
POMERANIA

1679
Kolberg °
1663
1657

1720
P o m
e r
1657

1679
Stettin

NETHERLANDS

Lingen
1702

Tecklenburg
1707

Minden

Cleves

Mörs
1702

Ravensberg

Mark

Upper
Guelders
1715

Hohnstein
1699

B r a n d e n b u r g

1680
Magdeburg °

° Berlin

Frankfurt on
the Oder

Schwiebus
1686-95

1680

P O

AUSTRIAN NETHERLANDS

G E R M A N

S T A T E S

HABSBURG

POSSESSIONS

Rhine

Limpurg
1713

HABSBURG

POSSESSIONS

Danube

FRANCE

NEUCHÂTEL

1707

SWISS
CONFEDERATION

POLAND

° Żytomierz

° Winnica

ENGLAND

NETHERLANDS

Rhine

Dunkirk °
Calais °

Flanders

Ghent °

° Cologne

Artois

Tournai

° Brussels

° Aix-la-Chapelle

Namur °

° Liège

Amiens °

HOLY ROMAN

Coblenz °

E M P I R E

Trier °

° Frankfurt

Luxemburg °

° Mainz

Palatinate

Spires °

Paris °

Rheims °

Duchy of Bar

Metz °

Toul °

Nancy °

Alsace

1
2

3

MOLDAVIA

OTTOMAN

FRANCE

Orléans °

Duchy of Lorraine

Basle °

Dijon °

SWISS
CONFED-
ERATION

1691

1691

oKönigsberg

P r u s s i a

land
6-7

N   D

THE RISE OF BRANDENBURG-PRUSSIA, 1640-1720 **1**

Brandenburg-Prussia, 1640

Additional territory agreed by Peace of Westphalia, 1648

Territory added in late 17th century (with dates)

Territory added by 1720 (with dates)

Temporary acquisitions (with dates)

Frontiers, 1721

Holy Roman Empire

THE UKRAINE: THE ZAPOROGIAN COSSACKS **2**

Eastern frontier of Poland, to 1667

Autonomous Grand Duchy of Ruthenia (according to aborted Polish-Ukrainian Treaty of Hadiach, 1658)

The Hetmanate (autonomous within Russia under Treaty of Andrusovo, 1667)

Ukraine under Mazappa, prior to Battle of Poltava, 1708-9

Sub-autonomous within Hetmanate in periods when both banks united and not under Ottoman control

Northern limit of Ottoman control, 1711-33

Frontiers, 1700

Glukhov

R   U   S   S   I   A

Hadiach
tmanate
nomy abolished 1764)
av   oPoltava

Z a p o r o g i a
rino   (under increasing Russian control in the 18th
century: autonomy abolished 1775)

Right Bank   Old Sech   Left Bank
ous after Treaty of Andrusovo:
ternating Polish and Ottoman
ntrol in the 17th century   New Sech

K H A N A T E

O F

C R I M E A

The Rise of Brandenburg-Prussia 1640-1720

1 When Frederick William inherited the Electorate of Brandenburg in 1640, it was one of the most devastated parts of the Holy Roman Empire. During the negotiations leading up to the Peace of Westphalia in 1648 he showed skillful obstinacy which eventually persuaded the other great powers, France and Sweden, to accept some of his ambitious demands in order to get a peace settlement agreed within the Empire. Although Sweden took the bulk of Pomerania, Brandenburg received Eastern Pomerania plus pockets of territory such as Minden and the reversion of Magdeburg on the death of its "administrator" (who died in 1680), which helped to link the core lands east of the Elbe with the possessions in the Rhineland, Cleve and Mark.

Frederick William recognised that without a standing army and therefore without the tax revenue to pay for it, he could never hope to assert himself in his inherited quarrels with dynastic rivals or to pursue his ambitions against what had become Swedish Pomerania after 1648. The Elector had first to make himself master over his own subjects. The two decades after 1648 were largely taken up with Frederick William's imposition of absolutist rule on each of his territories in turn. He persuaded or cajoled the local estates into granting him taxes to maintain a standing army, which in turn served to intimidate the local elites into obeying him.

In 1657, as a by-product of Poland's humiliation in the Northern War with Sweden, the Elector was able to make himself sovereign Duke of East Prussia instead of owing fealty to Poland. It was a significant step towards his son's assertion of the royal title of King in Prussia in 1701. At his death in 1688, the "Great" Elector's regular army numbered 30,000 – more than England's – and Brandenburg-Prussia was well on the way to being "an army with a state" rather than a state with an army. Prussia's position was further strengthened in 1720, with the acquisition of much of western Pomerania from Sweden by the Peace of Stockholm.

The Ukraine: the Zaporogian Cossacks

2 In the second third of the 17th century, Polish noblemen established great estates and even endowed Catholic (Uniate) churches well to the east of the Dnieper as far as Poltava. The Ukraine appeared set to become an integrated part of the Polish Commonwealth.

Local Cossacks were subordinated in theory to the Polish authorities but their obedience was often bought by encouraging them to raid their Tatar and Turkish enemies to the south. Most peasants found themselves enserfed. In 1648, thousands of peasants rose in revolt against their masters, encouraged by a simultaneous dispute between the Polish authorities and the leaders of the "free" Cossacks. Kiev fell to the rebels and was declared Orthodox again, while the Catholic clergy were driven out.

After winning dramatic victories, the Cossack leaders settled with the new King of Poland, Jan Casimir, much to the disgust of the peasantry. Fresh quarrels ensued. The Poles gradually whittled down the area of Cossack control as the Cossacks turned to Muscovy for support.

The Northern War (1655-60) left Poland much weakened and her control over the Ukraine, particularly in the south and east, was never secure after 1648. Wars with Russia (1654-6 and 1658-67) saw the Cossacks side with the Tsar against the Poles. The Treaty of Hadiach (1658) left Ukraine and Poland rejoined in a personal union, but renewed Russian-Polish fighting meant its terms were never effectively implemented. By the Treaty of Andrusovo (1667), Muscovy gained Smolensk and the Ukraine up to the Dnieper as well as ancient Kiev on the west bank. An autonomous region, the Hetmanate, was created on part of the territory added to Russia. The Cossacks of Zaporogia had autonomy within this area, which applied to their lands when they were not under Polish or Ottoman control.

The Cossacks proved almost as unruly as subjects of the Tsar as they had under the Poles. Under Peter the Great, Mazappa, the Hetman (commander) of the Tsar's Cossacks, tried to create an independent Cossack state in the Ukraine in alliance with the Swedes and the Zaporogian Cossack Host. Peter's victory in 1709 marked the conquest of the Cossacks. Many of the survivors were deported to distant parts of the Tsar's empire.

French Losses in 1697

3 Although the Nine Years' War (1688-97) soon reached stalemate, it took many years before Louis XIV was prepared to make sufficient concessions to buy peace from his enemies. In 1696, he gave up some areas in southern France around Nice to Savoy, in effect admitting that the duchy of Savoy could not be made into a French satellite.

By the Treaty of Rijswijk (1697), France returned Lorraine to her duke, but with the duchy surrounded by Louis XIV's territory, France retained effective military control. However, both Flanders and Luxemburg were returned to Spain (as was occupied Catalonia), probably because Louis was already manoeuvring for Madrid's favour over who would succeed to the Spanish throne when Carlos II died. Other parts of Imperial territory, including a section of the Palatinate, were also given up, though France kept Alsace and Strasbourg.

A key cause of the war after 1688 was Louis XIV's evident determination to dominate the key clerical electorates in the triangle between Trier, Cologne and Mainz. This would have made France dominant along the vital trade arteries of the Rhine and Main. By 1697, however, the greater problem of who would inherit the vast Spanish empire was looming on the horizon.

1699

The Rise of Russia

Though Spanish Habsburg power was in decline by the late 17th century, control of their vast empire in Europe and in the Americas remained a crucial prize. The death of the childless last Spanish Habsburg, Carlos II, in 1700 led to a struggle between his French and Austrian relatives for the succession. Europe's strategic balance was at stake, and the determination of the Austrian Habsburgs and their Anglo-Dutch allies to thwart Louis XIV's ambitions for French expansion led to the bitterly-contested War of the Spanish Succession (1701-14). Louis XIV's acceptance of Carlos II's will, which granted his entire empire to his grandson, the Bourbon Philip of Anjou, made war with Britain inevitable, as she could not tolerate the strategic Barrier Fortresses on the border with the Spanish Netherlands falling into French hands. Leopold I of Austria, meanwhile, sought to place his younger son, Charles, on the Spanish throne and fighting spread across western Europe from Italy, into Spain itself, and up the Rhine into the Low Countries.

After a decade of war, France engineered a compromise peace. Philip of Anjou retained the Spanish throne (as Philip V), but he and his heirs were denied the right to succeed Louis XIV in France. Leopold I's son, now Charles VI, had to accept the loss of Spain, particularly as his erstwhile British and Dutch allies saw little purpose in fighting to prevent a Bourbon hegemony only to restore a Habsburg version of it. The treaties of Utrecht (1713), Baden (1714) and Rastatt (1714) brought the conflict to an end. Charles VI did not, however, formally recognise the Bourbon Philip V as King of Spain until 1720.

The Austrian Habsburgs made up for this serious reverse in the west by continuing their advances into Ottoman territory in the east. By the Treaty of Passarowitz (1718), they gained Belgrade, the Banat of Temesvár, and parts of Serbia and Wallachia. The Turks were not entirely on the defensive, however, as in 1715 they forced the Venetians out of the Peloponnese.

In northern Europe, the young Charles XII faced a coalition of Sweden's neighbours intent on taking advantage of his minority. Unfortunately for Denmark, Saxony-Poland and Russia, the young king inherited a well-trained and officered army and possessed military genius, which came to the fore in the Great Northern War (1700-1721). He routed an ill-prepared Russian army at Narva in 1700 and then scattered his Danish and Polish/Saxon enemies, but his invasion of Russia led to disaster at Poltava (1709). Sweden lacked the resources to make up its heavy losses and afterwards was forced back into a defensive strategic position.

Britain and Russia emerged the winners from the two great wars at the start of the 18th century. Although in territorial terms, Britain gained little, only the fortress of Gibraltar and Minorca, her influence after Utrecht was still enormous because of her wealth from commercial gains outside Europe. France, though defeated, was too populous and wealthy to be reduced from her status as the greatest single power, but her long-term prospects of dominating the Continent were damaged by the financial exhaustion which Louis XIV bequeathed his infant successor in 1715.

Peter the Great of Russia (1682-1725) decisively altered the estimation of the previously vast but ill-organised Tsarist empire. By combining Western techniques with ruthless autocratic methods, he created a military system for Russia capable of wearing down his gifted Swedish rival. By 1721, Russia overshadowed the Baltic region: she gained greatly from the Treaty of Nystad (1721), taking Estonia, Livonia, Ingria, most of Karelia and part of Finland. A defeat by the Turks, however, led to the loss of Azov on the Black Sea in 1711.

NORWAY (Danish)

Trondhjem

Christiania

SWEDEN

en

Gothenburg

DENMARK
Aarhus
Copenhagen
Frederiksborg
Malmö

BALTIC SEA

Stockholm

Nystad
Åbo
Helsingfors

KARELIA

St. Petersburg

Narva **Ingria**
Revel
Estonia

Livonia
Riga
Pskov

COURLAND

Dyneburg

Königsberg

PRUSSIA

Wilno
Vitebsk

Smolensk

RUSSIAN EMPIRE

Archangel

Perm

Nizhniy
Novgorod

Volga

Moscow

Samara

Tula

Saratov

HAMburg
SWEDISH POMERANIA
Stettin

HANOVER
Hanover
kfurt

PRUSSIA
Berlin

Elbe
Oder

Gdansk

LITHUANIA

Minsk

Poznań

Vistula

Warsaw
Brześć-Litewski

Łódź

SAXONY
Dresden
SILESIA
Breslau

BOHEMIA
Prague

MORAVIA
Brünn

Cracow

POLAND
(in Personal Union with Saxony)

HETMANATE

Kiev

Kharkov

Kursk

Don

Volga

Astrakhan

BAVARIA
Munich

Danube

Vienna
Pozsony

AUSTRIA
Salzburg
Graz

HABSBURG POSESSIONS

Buda Pest

Debrecen

Dniester

Winnica

Poltava

Dnieper

Zaporogian Cossacks

Azov

Trieste

VENETIAN

ANTUA

MODENA
Bologna
SAN MARINO
CANY PAPAL
STATES
Rome

Zágráb

HUNGARY
(Military administration)

Szeged
Temesvár

Kolozsvár
TRANSYLVANIA
Brassó

MOLDAVIA

Jassy

KHANATE OF CRIMEA

Bakhchisaray

Great Kabardia

Circassians

Daghestan

Zara
Spalato

Bosna Saray

Nish

WALLACHIA
Belgrade
Bucharest

Danube
Ruschuk

BLACK SEA

PERSIA

Mostar

REPUBLIC
OF RAGUSA
MONTENEGRO
Üsküb

Sofia
Phillippopolis

Varna
Burgas

Trebizond

Naples
Bari
Taranto

Adrianople

Constantinople

Angora

Mosul

KINGDOM OF
NAPLES AND SICILY

Palermo
Messina
Catania

Janina

Salonica

OTTOMAN EMPIRE

Smyrna

Adana

Tigris

Patras
Athens

MALTA
(Knights
of St John)

SEA

Crete

Nicosia

Beirut
Damascus

Bedouins

Euphrates

137

DENMARK

Friesland
Holland
NETHERLANDS
Zeeland
AUSTRIAN NETHERLANDS
Hainaut

(to Sweden)

Brandenburg

POLAND

Cologne
JÜLICH BERG

G E R M A N
S T A T E S

Bohemia

FRANCE

Würzburg
Bayreuth
Bamberg
PALATINATE
Spires
Nuremberg

Ratisbon
BAVARIA
Passau
Munich
Salzburg
Tyrol

H A B S B U R G   P O S S E S S I O N S

Austria

HUNGARY

NEUCHÂTEL
SWISS CONFEDERATION

Carinthia

KINGDOM
OF
SARDINIA

MILAN

V E N E T I A N

MANTUA

R E P U B L I C

VENAISSIN

PARMA
MODENA
PAPAL
STATES

MILITARY
FRONTIER

1

**BAVARIA TO THE END OF
THE 18TH CENTURY**

— Bavaria, 955

⬚ Wittelsbach possessions,
  c. 1350

— Frontiers, 1721

▢ Bavaria, 1721

▢ 18th-century additions to
  Bavarian territory

⬚ Bavarian territory lost in 1779

━ The Holy Roman Empire

SWISS CONFEDERATION

Tyrol

Savoy
MASSERANO
KINGDOM
OF
SARDINIA
Piedmont

DUCHY OF
Milan
MILAN

BISHOPRIC OF

Verona
Mantua
DUCHY
OF
MANTUA

FRANCE

SABIONETTA
Parma
GUASTALLA-
NOVELLARA
PARMA
Módena
MODENA

Bolo

Genoa
FOSDINOVO
MASSSA
LUCCA

Nizza
MONACO

R E P U B L I C   O F   G E N O A

Lucca
Florence

TUSCANY

PIOMBINO
STATO DEI
PRESIDI

STA

Rome

PRUSSIA

Bohemia

Moravia

GERMAN
STATES

Austria
Vienna
Pozsony

Kassa

POLAND

m

MOLDAVIA

Styria

Sopron

Buda

Nagyvárad

H U N G A R Y

Carinthia

Carniola

Zágráb
Croatia

Pécs

Szeged

Temesvár
Zenta
BANAT OF TEMES
(to Hungary 1779)

Kolozsvár

TRANSYLVANIA

Gyulafehérvár

Nagyszeben

Brassó

Eszék
Slavonia

Carlowitz

WALLACHIA

VENETIAN REPUBLIC

PAPAL STATES

Belgrade
Passarowitz

O T T O M A N   E M P I R E

M E D I T E R R A N

TUNIS
*(Ottoman
vassal)*

3

Sassari
KINGDOM
OF SARDINIA
*(held by Habsburgs,
1714-20)*

(to Pa

THE HABSBURG REORGANISATION OF HUNGARY

— Hungary, c.1500

— Ottoman frontier, 1683

╌ Ottoman frontier, 1699

⬚ Status undecided until 1732,
  when united with Hungary

▢ Status undecided until 1732,
  when united with Transylvania

⬚ Returned to Hungary from military administration in 1744 but then
  united with Croatia: status subsequently disputed

▢ Hungary by 1745

▢ Returned to Hungary from military administration, 1750

▢ Lands acknowledged by Habsburgs as part of the
  Hungarian Crown but administered separately

⬚ Autonomous within Hungary

▢ Temporary Habsburg acquisition, 1718-39

▢ Other Habsburg territory

— Frontiers, 1752

2

ITALY, 1714-21

▢ Habsburg possessions

━ The Holy Roman Empire

— Frontiers, 1721

Bavaria to the End of the 18th Century

1 The origins of the Bavarian duchy lay in a 4th-century barbarian incursion into the Roman Empire. The Bavarians were ruled by the native Agilolfing dynasty until their last duke, Tassilo, was defeated by Charlemagne in 788 and his lands incorporated into the Frankish Empire. After the partitions of the Frankish empire in the 9th century, the Duchy of Bavaria became an East Frankish territory with a royal residence at Regensburg.

By the 11th century Bavaria came to be ruled by the Wittelsbach family, who held it until 1918. At first they ruled only the southeastern part of present-day Bavaria and political divisions in the 14th and 15th century led to a fragmentation of the duchy. Bavaria was only reunited by Duke Albert IV (1467-1508) with Munich as its capital.

During the Wars of Religion of the 16th century and in the Thirty Years' War, the Bavarian Dukes were staunch defenders of the Catholic cause. They were rewarded for their loyalty to the Imperial cause by the transfer of the Upper Palatinate to Bavaria in 1648, and with it the title of Elector. Bavarian influence was further enhanced by the acquisition of Julich-Berg, inherited by Charles Theodore of the Palatinate, Elector of Bavaria from 1777 to 1799. By the late 18th century, the duchy had become a serious rival to the Habsburgs in southern Germany.

The Austrian Habsburgs, indeed, sought repeatedly to draw Bavaria into their sphere of influence. In the War of the Spanish Succession, the Elector Max Emmanuel sided with Louis XIV, and was, for his pains, expelled by the Austrian Habsburgs, and only restored at French insistence. In 1777 the Elector Max Joseph II died and the Austrian Habsburg Emperor Joseph II put forward a distant claim of his own to the Bavarian crown. The Prussians reacted with large-scale troop movements to prevent this disturbance in the European balance of power. The Bavarian War of Succession which resulted between Austria and Prussia was not a long fought struggle, and from the Treaty of Teschen which ended it in 1779 no clear victor emerged, and only a small area of land to the north of Salzburg passed to the Austrians.

Italy, 1714-21

2 Despite the peace settlement which concluded the War of the Spanish Succession, the Habsburg Charles VI of Austria was still unwilling to accept the Bourbon Philip V as King of Spain, and the Mediterranean became the scene of tension and clashes after 1714 as the Emperor manoeuvred, apparently to pursue his claims to Spain, while Philip V and his Italian wife, Elizabeth Farnese, devoted much effort to interference in Italy and seeking to establish their children there as a way of reversing Vienna's hegemony.

An eventual compromise was reached, which granted Don Carlos, Elizabeth's son, the succession to Parma, while Sicily and Sardinia were swapped between the Austrian emperor and Victor

Amadeus of Savoy in 1720. The Austrian Habsburgs now had a cohesive southern Italian kingdom of Naples and Sicily, while Savoy ruled over more distant Sardinia. Austria also possessed the key Tuscan ports (and the island of Elba) which had given their Spanish cousins dominance over much of Central Italy's trade for two centuries. Milan and Mantua, too, were Austrian Habsburg territory from 1714, although Savoy had received some border areas from Milan in 1713.

These uneasy compromises were the result of an unusual alliance between France and Britain which came into being in 1716 to force Spain into line. Philip V announced that Spain had no ambitions in Italy – even though his children by Elizabeth Farnese still had aspirations to rule in Parma.

The Habsburg Reorganisation of Hungary

3 The potential of Austrian Habsburg power was often diminished by the division of its attention between two fronts. In the west, the struggle against Louis XIV dragged on for decades, while in the east Leopold I and his successors pursued their ambitions against the Sultan. Only when Austria had support in the west from powerful allies like Britain and the Netherlands and when her own armies, under the generalship of Prince Eugene of Savoy, achieved levels of military efficiency comparable with the best in Europe, could she hope to overcome this division of her forces.

After the defeat of the Turks outside Vienna in 1683, Leopold I pursued the war against the Sultan and found new allies to join in his latter-day crusade. While the Venetians seized the Morea and Athens in 1690, Habsburg forces occupied Hungary and Transylvania. In 1687, the Hungarian Diet agreed that the Hungarian Crown should pass by hereditary right to the Habsburgs.

Although the Turks had recovered Belgrade in 1690, they suffered a crushing defeat by Prince Eugene at Zenta in 1697, and the Sultan made peace with the Emperor at Carlowitz in 1699. The land taken from the Ottomans was put initially under military administration. During the next half century it was gradually re-absorbed into Hungary, save for a strip by the Ottoman frontier which remained under military administration as the Military Frontier (*see* map 2, page 143). The War of the Spanish Succession distracted the Habsburgs from the Balkans, but between 1716 and 1718 Prince Eugene waged his most devastating war of conquest. By the Treaty of Passarowitz, the Sultan was forced to cede northern Serbia, Little Wallachia and the Banat to the Emperor. Charles VI lost much of this territory in 1739, but at the end of the second decade of the 18th century, the Habsburgs seemed set to make further inroads into the Balkans, gains which in the event eluded them.

1721

The Eve of the French Revolution

An uneasy peace covered much of Europe at the start of 1789. Relations between most of the Great Powers were tranquil, although not cordial, following the deaths of Frederick II of Prussia (1786) and Maria Theresa of Austria (1780), the two principal protagonists of the Habsburg-Hohenzollern wars of 1740-8 and 1756-63.

The major development of the first half of the 18th century had been Brandenburg-Prussia's emergence from a subordinate position within the Holy Roman Empire to the status of principal rival to the Austrian Habsburgs. This led to bitter wars between them, particularly over the problem of the succession to Charles VI of Austria. Charles had only daughters, and needed acceptance by the other Great Powers of the Pragmatic Sanction (1713) by which he left his lands to his daughter Maria Theresa. He was especially vulnerable as Austria's war with Turkey had gone badly wrong and the Treaty of Belgrade in 1739, by which Austria ceded to the Turks much of the land gained at the Treaty of Passarowitz (1718), made clear the real weakness of the Habsburg armies.

Frederick II of Prussia refused to acknowledge the settlement and launched a surprise attack on Austria after the succession of Maria Theresa in 1740, seizing Silesia. Britain sided with Austria, hoping to prevent the Prussians' French allies gaining too much influence in central Europe. The Prussian success against Maria Theresa also encouraged the other Electors in 1742 to choose Charles Albert of Bavaria as the first non-Habsburg Emperor for 300 years.

In 1743, Charles Albert tried, with French assistance, to seize Maria Theresa's hereditary lands. Maria Theresa bought off Prussia with the concession of Silesia, and instead concentrated Austria's forces on recovering Bohemia and Austria from Franco-Bavarian occupation. By 1748, a classic war of coalitions had led to general exhaustion and a willingness to make peace. In 1756, the Austrians reversed a 250-year old policy of enmity towards France, and the old rivals performed a "diplomatic revolution" which was intended to allow Austria to recover Silesia while France concentrated on her colonial rivalry with Britain. The ensuing Seven Years' War (1756-63) almost shattered Prussia, but Frederick II earned his title "the Great" by defeating the combined forces of France, Austria and Russia.

France did gain Lorraine in 1766, which had been ruled since 1738 by Stanislaw Leszczyński, the candidate for the Polish crown whom the French had unsuccessfully supported during the War of the Polish Succession (1733-8), and who was also the father-in-law of Louis XV.

Russia, meanwhile, continued to expand around the Black Sea. The Treaty of Belgrade gave Russia Azov and the lands of the Zaporogian Cossacks. A further Russo-Turkish war in 1768-74 brought Russia Kerch and Yenikale in the Crimea and Kherson. The Treaty of Kutchuk-Kainardji which ended the war also gave the Tsar a vague duty to protect the Sultan's Christian subjects, the cause of much future Russo-Turkish friction.

Although Prussia and Austria did spar again over the issue of who should rule Bavaria in 1778 (*see* map 1, page 138), the Great Powers avoided another great land war after 1763 for more than 25 years. It seemed as if a balance between France, Austria, Prussia and Russia had been established, with Britain holding the ring offshore. Even small states seemed protected by the arrangement, although the First Partition of Poland in 1772 between Prussia, Russia and Austria was a taste of how cynically the Great Powers could treat their weaker neighbours.

NORWAY

Trondhjem

rgen

Christiania

SWEDEN

Danish

DENMARK

Aarhus

Copenhagen • Malmö

BALTIC
SEA

Gothenburg

Stockholm

Åbo

Helsingfors

Revel

St. Petersburg

Pskov

Riga

COURLAND

Dvinsk

SWEDISH
POMERANIA

Vilna

LITHUANIA

Vitebsk

Minsk

Smolensk

Moscow

Tula

Kursk

Archangel

Nizhniy
Novgorod

Volga

Saratov

Perm

Samara

Small
Hord

RUSSIAN EMPIRE

Hamburg

HANOVER

Hanover

Berlin

P R U S S I A

Stettin

Königsberg

Gdańsk

Poznań

Warsaw

Łódź

Brest-Litovsk

P O L A N D

Kiev

Kharkov

SMALL

kfurt

ERMAN

TES

gart

SAXONY

Dresden

BOHEMIA

Prague

Nuremberg

MORAVIA

Brünn

BAVARIA

Munich

Silesia

Breslau

Cracow

GALICIA

Oder

Vistula

Elbe

Danube

AUSTRIA

Salzburg

Vienna

Pozsony

HABSBURG POSSESSIONS

Buda

Debrecen

HUNGARY

Szeged

Temesvár

Kolozsvár

TRANSYLVANIA

Brassó

Vinnitsa

Dnieper

Ekaterinoslav

Dniester

Jassy

MOLDAVIA

Ekaterinoslav

Don

Volga

Astrakhan

Kerch

Crimea

Sebastopol

Great Kabardia

Circassians

Daghestan

GEORGIA

Graz

Trieste

Venice

Zágráb

NETT

Military

Frontier

Belgrade

WALLACHIA

Bucharest

Ruschuk

Danube

Varna

BLACK SEA

Trebizond

MODENA

Bologna

SCANY

SAN MARINO

Zara

Bosna Saray

Spalato

Mostar

REPUBLIC
OF RAGUSA

MONTENEGRO

Nish

Sofia

Philippopolis

Üsküb

Salonica

PERSIA

PAPAL

rence

STATES

Rome

DEI

DI

Naples

Bari

Taranto

KINGDOM OF NAPLES
AND SICILY

Palermo

Messina

Catania

REPUBLIC

SEA

MALTA
(Knights
of St John)

Janina

Patras

Athens

Crete

O T T O M A N   E M P I R E

Adrianople

Constantinople

Smyrna

Ankara

Adana

Beirut

Damascus

Burgas

Nicosia

Mosul

Tigris

Euphrates

Bedouins

141

NETHERLANDS
Utrecht
Antwerp
1714
Brussels
Aachen
AUSTRIAN
NETHERLANDS
Luxemburg

GERMAN STATES
SAXONY
Breslau

PRUSSIA

POLAND

Lemberg

FRANCE
Rastatt
Blenheim

Bohemia
Prague
Olmütz
Brünn
Moravia
1770

Galicia
1772

BAVARIA

Austria
1779
Linz
Vienna
Salzburg
Innsbruck
SWISS CONFEDERATION
NEUCHÂTEL
Tyrol
Styria
Graz
Klagenfurt

Pressburg
(Pozsony)
Ofen Pest
(Buda)

HUNGARY

Kaschau
(Kassa)

Bukovina
1775

MOLDAVIA

Grosswardein
(Nagyvárad)
Klausenburg
(Kolozsvár)
TRANSYLVANIA
Kronstadt
(Brassó)

Moravia
Vienna
Pozsony

KINGDOM OF SARDINIA
1714-38/48
MILAN
1714
1748
Milan
1714-38/48
1708
MANTUA
PARMA
1735-48
MODENA
GUASTALLA
MASSA
LUCCA
MONACO
REPUBLIC OF GENOA

Croatia
Agram
(Zágráb)

Fünfkirchen
(Pécs)
Esseg
(Eszék)

Temeschwar
(Temesvár)
Banat
1718

Military Frontier
Belgrade Passarowitz
Serbia
Little Wallachia
1718-39

WALLACHIA

Zágráb
Pécs
Croatia
Esseg (Eszék)
Slavonia
Brod
OTT

Florence
SAN MARINO
TUSCANY
1737
PAPAL STATES
PIOMBINO
STATO DEI PRESIDI
1714-35

VENETIAN REPUBLIC
ADRIATIC SEA

OTTOMAN EMPIRE

REPUBLIC OF RAGUSA
MONTENEGRO

VENETIAN REPUBLIC
PAPAL STATES
ADRIATIC SEA
REPUBLIC OF RAGUSA
MONTEN
OTT

Sassari
KINGDOM OF SARDINIA
1714-20
Cagliari

Naples
NAPLES
1714-35
Bari
Taranto

VENETIAN REPUBLIC
NAPLES

MEDITERRANEAN SEA

Palermo
SICILY
1720-35
Catania

ALGIERS

TUNIS
(Ottoman vassal)

MALTA
(Knights of St. John)

NORTH SEA

SWEDEN

DENMARK

SWEDISH POMERANIA
Kolberg

East Friesland
1744
(to Sweden)
Lingen
Tecklenburg
Minden

Pomeran
Stettin
U

GREAT BRITAIN

NETHERLANDS
Upper Guelders
Cleves
Mark
Aachen
AUSTRIAN
NETHERLANDS

Ravensberg
Sayn
1741-83
Mansfeld
1780

Brandenburg
Magdeburg
Berlin
Potsdam
Rossbach
SAXONY
Dresden
Pirna

Frankfurt on the Oder
PR
U

FRANCE

GERMAN STATES

Limpurg

NEUCHÂTEL
SWISS CONFEDERATION
Tyrol

BAVARIA

Prague
Kolin
Bohemia
Austria

Mora
HABSB

1

HABSBURG EUROPE, 1699-1789

- Habsburg territory, 1699-1789
- Church lands under Habsburg control
- Added by 1714 (with dates)
- Added by 1775 (with dates)
- Temporary acquisitions (with dates)
- Territory lost, 1742
- Frontier of Poland to 1770
- Frontier of Holy Roman Empire
- Frontiers, 1789

Habsburg Europe, 1699-1789

1 Following the Treaty of Carlowitz (1699), the Austrian Habsburg advance into the Balkans was slowed down by domestic difficulties. In 1703, Ferenc II Rákóczi, of the old ruling house of Transylvania, led a peasants revolt to drive out the Habsburgs. Hoped for assistance from the French failed to materialise, however, because of their defeat in 1704 at Blenheim by the Anglo-Austrian coalition in the War of the Spanish Succession. Any chance of a reconciliation with Vienna was destroyed by Rákóczi's election as Prince by the Transylvanian nobles in 1704. For a while Transylvania was effectively freed from Habsburg rule, until the revolt finally fizzled out in 1711.

Charles VI's reign (1711-40) saw the Austrian Habsburgs reach unparalleled heights of power, but by the end Austria's position was actually much weakened. Distant territories like the southern Netherlands and Naples (obtained in 1714) and Sicily (acquired in 1720) proved expensive to defend and administer. By the 1730s, it became clear that the triumphs of Prince Eugene had not led to any long-term increase in the strength of the Habsburg army. By the Treaty of Belgrade (1739) Charles VI had to give the city itself and those parts of Serbia gained by Eugene back to the Sultan, although he was able to preserve the territories in the Banat of Temesvár gained in 1718.

As for any dynastic state, the absence of a male heir to Charles VI opened the Habsburg lands to the threat of aggression from its neighbours. Charles's daughter, Maria Theresa, managed, however, to preserve the bulk of her father's legacy, despite a Prussian invasion at the start of her reign which led to the loss of Silesia.

After 1763, it was clear that Austria could not hope to recover Silesia from Prussia so Vienna turned instead to plans to acquire other territories to "compensate" for its loss. In 1772, Maria Theresa participated in the partition of Poland, gaining Galicia – although she "wept as she took", as Frederick of Prussia commented – and acquiring Bukovina from the Ottomans in 1775. However, for much of the 18th century, the Habsburgs and their advisers had regarded the acquisition of Bavaria as a natural strategic goal. The addition of Catholic and German-speaking Bavaria would round off the core Habsburg lands of Bohemia and Austria. In return for Bavaria, Vienna was prepared to offer the Southern Netherlands. However, when the crisis of Bavarian Succession arose in 1777, the spectre of revived Imperial authority in Germany proved sufficient to bring Prussian intervention on the side of the Bavarians. Out of a bloodless war, Austria had to be satisfied with the acquisition of a small area of land to the northwest of Salzburg.

In Italy, a re-division of territory saw the Habsburgs gain Tuscany in 1732 in exchange for Sicily, Naples and Parma, which went to the children of the Bourbon Philip V of Spain.

The Military Frontier from 1700

2 The land taken from the Ottomans by the Treaty of Carlowitz was initially put under military administration. Over the next half century much of it was reabsorbed back into Hungary, but a strip by the Ottoman frontier remained permanently under military administration. Its eastern section was, however, returned to Hungary when further lands were gained from the Ottomans by the Treaty of Passarowitz (1718). The Habsburgs freed another part of the frontier from military rule in 1751, but sought to prevent its incorporation into Hungary by organising the territory as a new crownland, which they named the Banat of Temesvár. In 1775, however, the Hungarian Diet persuaded the Habsburgs to return this land to Hungarian civil administration.

Transylvania retained a separate status, although strongly Hungarian in character. The old borderlands of Hungary proper were governed by Transylvania, and were the subject of a dispute with Hungary until 1732, when an agreement (the "Carolina Resolutio") allowed both countries to retain a share. The Transylvanian borderlands remained under military administration until 1851.

The Growth of Prussia under Frederick the Great

3 Unlike his father, Frederick William I (1713-40), Frederick II of Prussia (1740-1786) preferred to use his armies rather than just play at soldiers. Frederick William I had built up Prussia's military potential and left his son a standing army of 80,000 but had only fought in one major war (against Sweden from 1715 to 1721). Frederick II opened his reign by launching a surprise attack on neighbouring Silesia in 1740 and seizing it from the new Austrian ruler, Maria Theresa.

Frederick II's behaviour meant that Prussia's traditional alliance with the Habsburgs was completely reversed. Despite two great wars with Maria Theresa and her allies, Frederick II kept Silesia, although at enormous cost to Prussia. Frederick's state only survived by concentrating its resources on the army, and by emphasising the militarisation of life.

Out of the War of the Austrian Succession, Frederick gained not only Silesia but East Friesland in northwestern Germany. He was lucky to preserve his gains after the Seven Years' War (1756-63). He succeeded, however, in his ambition to link his East Prussian lands with his core territories around Brandenburg. Prussia's share of the first Partition of Poland in 1772 gave him West Prussia and the elbow of Ermeland, though not yet the strategic port of Danzig.

1789

The Rise of Napoleon

Given the domestic political chaos in France after the outbreak of the Revolution in the summer of 1789, few observers would have predicted that French troops would dominate the western half of Europe only a few years later. In fact, although the monarchs of Russia, Austria and Prussia were alarmed by the collapse of Louis XVI's authority and outraged by his subsequent deposition and execution, they consistently underrated the power of revolutionary France well into the 1790s. Ironically, Louis XVI's lavish expenditure on the French army and navy, which had done so much to bankrupt the monarchy and precipitate the Revolution, provided his revolutionary successors with the military resources to wage a successful war of conquest, or "liberation" as they called it. However, as long as the French were content to maintain a defensive posture, the response of the Great Powers was half-hearted. In 1792, Prussia despatched a relatively small force to intimidate the French authorities and particularly the people of Paris into not harming the king or his wife Marie-Antoinette. In fact this bungled invasion – defeated at Valmy in September – spurred on the radicalisation of the revolutionaries and encouraged them to spread their creed of "liberty, equality and fraternity" by force into the dominions of what they saw as hostile monarchs.

The neighbouring lands of Louis XVI's Austrian in-laws, plus the clerical states of the Holy Roman Empire along the Rhine, made natural targets for "liberation", though even the republican Swiss were not immune to French attack. The youthful Napoleon Bonaparte made his name thwarting British assistance to the counter-revolutionaries based at Toulon, but it was his role as the youngest general in the French army in Italy in the mid-1790s which made his reputation as the most able and feared commander of his day.

Mutual rivalries continued to prevent a united monarchist front and many sovereigns hoped that others would bear the burden of restoring the divinely ordained order in France while they pursued their own interests elsewhere. Poland became a victim of this policy, gradually disappearing from the map as her lands were divided up between Austria, Prussia and Russia in three successive partitions (1772, 1792 and 1795); *see* map 1, page 147.

Meanwhile, Austria's army, which had hardly covered itself in glory in the war against Turkey after 1788 (fought in alliance with Russia), proved itself unable to withstand the French, either in the Netherlands or in Italy, where the Habsburgs lost the dominant position which they had spent so much of the 18th century securing.

For Russia, Austria's growing preoccupation with the French threat was quite convenient. It meant that she was in a position to dictate terms to Turkey after what had been a joint campaign with Austrian troops, who were then redeployed to the west. By the Treaty of Jassy (1792), Russia gained the Black Sea coast between the Bug and the Dniester and was able to establish the port of Odessa.

The Treaty of Campo Formio (1797), imposed by France on the Austrians, brought to a conclusion the first phase of the revolutionary wars. France gained Venice and the Ionian Islands in the Adriatic, and took control of Austria's former Belgian provinces. Northern Italy fell more firmly into the French sphere of influence, too, as the Cisalpine and Ligurian Republics were set up to replace former monarchical regimes.

NORWAY

Trondhjem

(Danish)

SWEDEN

Christiania

Åbo

Helsingfors

St. Petersburg

Stockholm

Revel

Archangel

Perm

Gothenburg

Riga

Pskov

Moscow

Nizhniy
Novgorod

Volga

Samara

DENMARK

Aarhus

Copenhagen

Malmö

BALTIC
SEA

Dvinsk

R U S S I A N

SWEDISH
POMERANIA

Königsberg

Danzig

Vilna

Vitebsk

Smolensk

Tula

Saratov

Small
Horde

Hamburg

HANOVER

Bremen

Stettin

P R U S S I A

Vistula

Minsk

E M P I R E

Astrakhan

Hanover

Berlin

Posen

Warsaw

Bug

Oder

SAXONY

Dresden

Breslau

Lodz

Kursk

Volga

Frankfurt

STATES

Nuremberg

BOHEMIA

Prague

Cracow

Lemberg

Vinnitsa

Kiev

Kharkov

Dnieper

Ekaterinoslav

MORAVIA

Brünn

GALICIA

Stuttgart

BAVARIA

Danube

Vienna

Pozsony

H A B S B U R G   P O S S E S S I O N S

Dniester

Munich

AUSTRIA

Salzburg

Buda

Pest

Debrecen

Odessa

Innsbruck

Campo Formio

Graz

HUNGARY

Kolozsvár

Jassy

Szeged

TRANSYLVANIA

MOLDAVIA

Trieste

Venice

Zágráb

Pécs

Temesvár

Great Kabardia

CISALPINE
REP.

Bologna

Zara

Bosna Saray

Military

Frontier

Belgrade

WALLACHIA

Bucharest

Circassians

Daghestan

Florence

TUSCANY

SAN MARINO

PAPAL

Spalato

Mostar

Nish

Ruschuk

Danube

Varna

GEORGIA

STATES

REPUBLIC
OF RAGUSA

MONTENEGRO

Sofia

Burgas

B L A C K   S E A

Loreto

Rome

Üsküb

Philippopolis

Adrianople

Trebizond

PERSIA

Naples

Bari

O T T O M A N

Constantinople

KINGDOM OF NAPLES
AND SICILY

Taranto

Corfu

Janina

Salonica

E M P I R E

Ankara

Mosul

Palermo

Messina

Ionian Islands
(Fr.)

Smyrna

Adana

Tigris

Euphrates

Catania

Athens

SEA

MALTA
(Knights of
St John)

Crete

Nicosia

Beirut

Damascus

Bedouins

145

The Partitions of Poland, 1772-95

1 By the mid-18th century, Augustus the Strong's ambitions to create a great Saxon-Polish power under his dynasty had come to nothing. The elective nature of the Polish monarchy combined with the fractious behaviour of much of the Polish nobility meant that the vast and strategically valuable lands between Poznán and Kiev were an attractive target for other states' ambitions.

In 1772, Russia and Austria, the erstwhile enemies of Prussia, joined Frederick II of Prussia in detaching significant territories from the Polish Commonwealth. Prussia took West Prussia, though without the valuable port of Gdańsk, which she only acquired in 1793. Catherine obtained a large tract of land around Witebsk, while Maria Theresa of Austria received the valuable province of Galicia.

Poland could only survive so long as her independence did not threaten to reverse the three powers' gains. But when serious reforms, including Europe's first written constitution (of May 1791), got underway, Prussia and Russia acted to forestall any chance of a revitalised Poland re-asserting herself.

Austria was distracted by the fate of the Emperor's sister, Marie-Antoinette, in France, but in 1793 Prussia and Russia seized further extensive territories in Poland. Influenced by French revolutionary success, the Poles revolted in 1794. They were swiftly and brutally defeated by the combined powers. Austria and Prussia in particular were anxious to compensate themselves for their losses to France, sharing out what remained of Poland with Russia in 1795. Even Warsaw passed into Prussian hands.

French Revolutionary Conquests, 1789-97

2 Using Louis XVI's military build-up as a basis for their own army, the French revolutionaries showed a genius for organisation after 1792. Conscription (*levée en masse*) was introduced, and the advantage in numbers this gave, combined with revolutionary élan and outstanding generalship, quickly led to the French conquest of neighbouring states.

By 1793, France had annexed the Venaissin (including Avignon), Savoy, Montbéliard, and an area north of Nizza, as well as a patchwork of clerical electorates and other territories in the Rhineland. The occupied territories were, in due course, mostly annexed to the French empire, so that by 1797, when the Austrian Netherlands were annexed, France had acquired her "natural frontiers" from the Channel coast down the Rhine. The Netherlands were allowed nominal independence as the Batavian Republic, while Piedmont was occupied in 1796, although not yet annexed to France.

Venice on the Eve of Napoleon's Conquest

3 Even though Venice had lost much of her former commercial wealth by the late 18th century, she still remained a valuable prize for any conqueror. Ironically, after centuries of defying would-be conquerors, Venice fell even though she was not formally at war with France. Napoleon decided to eradicate Venice's independence along with that of her ancient rival, Genoa, as part of the Campo Formio settlement which he imposed on Austria in 1797. In order to persuade Austria to accept his creation of French-controlled republics elsewhere in northern Italy, Bonaparte granted Venice herself to the Habsburgs.

Venice's rise to occupy the position of the most powerful republic in Italy and a Mediterranean power in her own right owed everything to her position as an easily defended but highly accessible entrepôt for trade between the European mainland and the Mediterranean. Through her participation in the Fourth Crusade (1204) and the conquest of commercially valuable Constantinople rather than the holy city of Jerusalem, Venice gained a significant empire in the Aegean and the Morea.

Rising Ottoman power and the decline in Venetian wealth due to the shift to trans-Atlantic trade had led, by the start of 1797, to the loss of all but the Ionian Islands (Corfu, Cephalonia and Zante), and several footholds on the Adriatic. Crete had been lost by 1669 and the whole of the Morea by 1715. But Venice clung on to much of Dalmatia (around Zara and Spalato) as well as Istria until 1797. They then fell to Austria before Napoleon incorporated them into his French Empire. Already in 1797, Napoleon had taken the Ionian Islands for France as a stepping stone for his attempted conquest of Egypt.

Italy: the Revolutionary Republics

4 French victories over the Austrians in the 1790s led to a dramatic reordering of the map of Italy. Just as in the Low Countries and Switzerland, Bonaparte re-drafted the constitutional as well as the political map of Italy. In fact, he went much further than the Directory in Paris had expected or desired. His Italian settlement of 1797 was the first sign that he intended to pursue his own political goals, albeit still under the guise of serving the French state.

Genoa became the Ligurian Republic, while a Cisalpine Republic was created out of the former duchies of Milan, France's share of the Venetian Republic plus Modena and the Papal territories in the Romagna, including Bologna. At first, the south of the Italian peninsula was left in monarchical hands, but the French soon moved to suppress that compromise. The Kingdom of Naples was turned into the Parthenopean Republic in 1799 while the Papal States around Rome became a republic, too – though both lacked sufficient local republican enthusiasm to make them anything other than French satellites. In 1801, the Kingdom of Etruria was formed out of Tuscany, as compensation for the Bourbon rulers of Parma, which Napoleon planned to annex (and did so in 1805). Only the kingdoms of Sardinia and Sicily remained outside the French republican system of satellites.

1797

1812

Napoleonic Europe

In mid-June 1812, Napoleon's empire dominated Europe, but even as he invaded Russia, cracks were showing in the hastily established edifice of French imperial power. Napoleon found it far easier to conquer than to control the vast territories which his military genius and the superior organisation of the French armies had secured. Yet as his troops advanced on Moscow, Wellington's British forces, with local Portuguese and Spanish allies, were already gnawing away at French control of Spain.

Napoleon's rise to power would have been impossible without the forces unleashed by the French Revolution, but after he had established himself as a dictator (in November 1799), he was confronted by the challenge of making his power permanent. Within five years, he rose from revolutionary consul to self-proclaimed Emperor. Although he staged a referendum to legitimise his accession to the throne and insisted that he was "Emperor of the French" rather than "King of France", his regime increasingly aped old monarchical ways.

Furthermore, whatever his support inside French-speaking Europe, Napoleon insisted on installing his brothers and his sister on the thrones of occupied territories. This old-fashioned dynastic policy backfired most badly in Spain where the brutal deposition of the Spanish Bourbons in 1808 provoked a popular revolt and the first so-called guerrilla war in Europe. Elsewhere, Napoleon placed his brother Louis on the throne of Holland and Jerome on that of the specially created Westphalia. His brother-in-law, Joachim Murat, became King of Naples. These novel monarchies did much to destabilise Napoleon's power-base without legitimising it in the eyes of new subjects.

While Napoleon concentrated on Central Europe and Italy, the Tsar asserted Russian power in the Baltic and against Turkey. Alexander I, who became Tsar after the assassination of his father Paul I in 1801, at first opposed France, but after the drubbing received by the Austro-Russian army at Austerlitz in 1805, and the defeat of a Prussian-Russian force at Friedland in 1806, his mood changed. Following a meeting with Napoleon at Tilsit, the boundary between French conquest and Russia, Europe was divided into spheres of influence. In 1809, Sweden was forced to cede Finland to the Russian Tsar, though Alexander and his successors ruled it as a separate Grand Duchy with its own laws. The Tsar's forces occupied largely Romanian-speaking Bessarabia and forced the Sultan to give it to Russia in 1812.

In 1807, Napoleon was still primarily concerned with his plans for the re-ordering of Germany and Italy (*see* map 2, page 151). He was content to leave Russia alone, particularly as he hoped that Alexander's evident ambitions with regard to Turkey might bring Russia into conflict with France's most persistent enemy, Britain. Russia's war with Turkey was a distraction for Alexander I, but nothing could disguise Napoleon's determination to draw Russia into his Continental System, designed to choke off British trade to Europe. Alexander did not wish to be used as cannon-fodder in France's quarrel with Britain, but nor could Russia afford to be cut off from trade through the Baltic with Britain. Finally, in 1812, Napoleon lost patience and invaded Russia.

Jealousy of Napoleon's unprecedented empire and the humiliation of ancient families serving as his unwilling allies combined to create an unstable situation in 1812, as Prussia and Austria bided their time to see how the invasion of Russia would turn out.

Trondhjem

NORWAY

(Danish)

SWEDEN

FINLAND

Åbo · Helsingfors · St. Petersburg

Christiania

Stockholm · Revel

Gothenburg · Riga · Pskov

Aarhus · BALTIC · Dvinsk

Copenhagen · Malmö · SEA · Vilna · Vitebsk · Smolensk

DENMARK · REPUBLIC OF DANZIG · Tilsit · Königsberg · Minsk

amburg · Danzig · Friedland · Brest-Litovsk

Bremen · Stettin · PRUSSIA · Poznań GRAND DUCHY

Berlin · OF · Warsaw

FEDERATION · Dresden · Oder · Breslau · WARSAW

nkfurt · Prague · Cracow

Nuremberg

THE RHINE · Austerlitz

ttgart · Danube · Vienna · Pozsony

Munich · Salzburg · AUSTRIAN EMPIRE

Innsbruck · Buda · Pest · Debrecen · Kolozsvár

Graz · HUNGARY · TRANSYLVANIA · MOLDAVIA

NGDOM · Zágráb · Szeged · Temesvár · Brassó

TALY · Trieste · Military · WALLACHIA

Verona · Venice · Frontier · Belgrade · Bucharest

Bologna · Bosna · Saray

SAN MARINO · Zara · Mostar · Nish · Ruschuk

OMBINO · Spalato · Sofia · Philippopolis

RENCH · MONTENEGRO · Üsküb · Adrianople

MPIRE · KINGDOM · Salonica

Rome · OF · Bari

PONTECORVO · Taranto

BENEVENTO · Naples · Janina

NAPLES

Palermo · Corfu

Messina · Patras · Athens

Catania · Ionian Islands (Br.)

INGDOM OF · Smyrna

SICILY · SEA · Crete

MALTA (Br.)

RUSSIAN EMPIRE

Archangel

Nizhniy Novgorod · Volga · Perm

Moscow · Samara

Tula · Small Horde

Kursk

Kharkov

Kiev · Don · Saratov

Vinnitsa · Ekaterinoslav · Volga · Astrakhan

Dniester · Rostov

Kishinev · Bessarabia

Jassy · Odessa

Sebastopol · Great Kabardia · Daghestan

Circassians

BLACK SEA · Tiflis

Varna · Erivan

Burgas · Trebizond

Constantinople · PERSIA

Angora

OTTOMAN EMPIRE

Tigris

Adana · Mosul

Euphrates

Nicosia

Beirut · Bedouins

Damascus

149

1 CENTRAL EUROPE AND ITALY, 1806

Holy Roman Empire, 1797-1806

Small German states outside the Confederation of the Rhine

Map 1 labels:
Copenhagen
DENMARK
Jever (to Russia)
Amsterdam
KINGDOM OF HOLLAND
Hamburg · Lübeck
Bremen
Hanover
PRUSSIA
SWEDEN
Danzig
Stettin
Belostok
RUSSIA
Berlin
Warsaw
Brussels
Leipzig
Dresden
Breslau
Cracow
Luxembourg · Mayence
Frankfurt
Prague
Bohemia
FRENCH EMPIRE
CONFEDERATION OF THE RHINE
Nuremberg
Stuttgart · Ratisbon
Moravia
Austerlitz
PR. OF NEUCHÂTEL
Munich
Salzburg
Vienna
AUSTRIAN EMPIRE
Hungary
Berne
HELVETIA
Buda · Pest
Transylvania
REP. OF VALAIS
Milan
Venice
Trieste
Military Frontier
Wallachia (occupied by Russia)
Genoa
KINGDOM OF ITALY
PR. OF LUCCA
Florence
SAN MARINO
KGDM. OF ETRURIA
Zara
Dalmatia
OTTOMAN EMPIRE
Belgrade
PR. OF PIOMBINO
PAPAL STATES
Ragusa
REP. OF RAGUSA
Montenegro
(occupied by Russia)
Rome
KINGDOM OF NAPLES
KINGDOM OF SARDINIA
PR. OF PONTECORVO
PR. OF BENEVENTO

2 CENTRAL EUROPE AND ITALY, 1807

Added to the Confederation of the Rhine

Small German states outside the Confederation of the Rhine

Added to French Empire

Under French administration

Annexations by other states

Map 2 labels:
DENMARK
Hamburg
Bremen
Hanover
CONFEDERATION
Erfurt
Frankfurt
Luxembourg · Mayence
FRENCH EMPIRE
Stuttgart
Nuremberg
OF THE RHINE
Ratisbon
Munich
PR. OF NEUCHÂTEL
Berne
HELVETIA
REP. OF VALAIS
Milan
Venice
Genoa
KINGDOM
PR. OF LUCCA
Florence
SAN MARINO
PAPAL STATES
Rome
PR. OF PONTECORVO

3 CENTRAL EUROPE AND ITALY, 1809

Added to the Confederation of the Rhine

Added to French Empire

Under French administration

Annexations by other states

Map 3 labels:
Copenhagen
DENMARK
Hamburg · Lübeck
Amsterdam
Bremen
Hanover
KINGDOM OF HOLLAND
SWEDEN
REP. OF DANZIG
Danzig
Stettin
PRUSSIA
Belostok
RUSSIA
Brussels
CONFEDERATION
Erfurt
Berlin
Leipzig
Dresden
GRAND DUCHY OF WARSAW
Warsaw
West Galicia
Luxembourg · Mayence
Frankfurt
OF
Breslau
Prague
Cracow
FRENCH EMPIRE
Stuttgart
Nuremberg
Ratisbon
THE RHINE
Munich
Austerlitz
Wagram
Vienna
PR. OF NEUCHÂTEL
Berne
HELVETIA
Tyrol
Salzburg
Buda · Pest
AUSTRIAN EMPIRE
Hungary
REP. OF VALAIS
Milan
Venice
Trieste
KINGDOM OF ITALY
Transylvania
Genoa
Military Frontier
Wallachia (occupied by Russia)
FRENCH EMPIRE
PR. OF LUCCA
Florence
SAN MARINO
Zara
Belgrade
OTTOMAN EMPIRE
PR. OF PIOMBINO
FRENCH EMPIRE
Ragusa
Montenegro
Rome
KINGDOM OF NAPLES
PR. OF PONTECORVO
PR. OF BENEVENTO

4 CENTRAL EUROPE AND ITALY, 1810

Added to the Confederation of the Rhine

Added to French Empire

Map 4 labels:
DENMARK
Hamburg
Bremen
Hanover
Amsterdam
Netherlands
CONFEDERATION
Erfurt
Brussels
Frankfurt
Luxembourg · Mayence
OF
FRENCH EMPIRE
Stuttgart
Nuremberg
Ratisbon
THE RHINE
Munich
PR. OF NEUCHÂTEL
Berne
HELVETIA
Tyrol
Valais
Milan
Venice
KINGDOM OF ITALY
Genoa
PR. OF LUCCA
Florence
PR. OF PIOMBINO
FRENCH EMPIRE
Rome
PR. OF PONTECO

Central Europe and Italy, 1806

1 Like many shadowy institutions, the Holy Roman Empire served a purpose even during long decades of decline: its institutions provided a pan-German forum for diplomatic discussions without imposing any effective control on the individual states. However, by the beginning of the 19th century, the Empire had become a dangerous political vacuum on the edge of the French state.

Despite their long hold on the Imperial Crown, the Habsburgs recognised that their own collection of personal dominions might prove fragile if they lost the Holy Roman title, with the result that Francis I of Austria tried to reform in a bid to pre-empt Napoleon's threat of abolition. Already in 1803, the Emperor had accepted a radical revision of the old Imperial order. Only three Church states survived out of 81 and the number of free cities sank from 51 to six. In 1804 Francis declared himself "Emperor of Austria", although in doing so he at least clung to a territorial identity for the Habsburg lands, a contrast with Napoleon's title as "Emperor of the French."

On 26 December 1805, just three weeks after Napoleon's crushing victory over an Austrian and Russian army at Austerlitz, Francis agreed to cede all Habsburg territory south of the Alps to France. Napoleon gained Venice and Dalmatia, which he incorporated into the newly formed Kingdom of Italy. The Emperor also had to recognise the rulers of southern Germany as independent sovereigns (though they were in fact puppets of Napoleon). In the meantime, Napoleon had established his own Confederation of the Rhine to co-ordinate his puppets and allies in the German-speaking lands between the Rhine and Prussia. This marked the effective death of any Holy Roman Empire. Francis I formally abrogated its existence on 6 August 1806, at French insistence.

Central Europe and Italy, 1807

2 While he had to confront the Austro-Russian alliance, Napoleon had been willing to bribe Prussia to remain neutral (with, for instance, the offer of George III of England's other kingdom, Hanover), but after his victory over the Austrians and Russians at Austerlitz, he was more willing to dictate terms to the Prussians. Foolishly, Prussia declared war on France in August 1806, even though she was diplomatically isolated.

The shattering defeat of Prussia's much-vaunted army at Jena in October, 1806, left Napoleon free to dispose of Prussian territory and other northern and central German states at will. Napoleon left the Prussian king, Frederick William III, his traditional territories in the east, but took away Prussia's western provinces to provide the core of his brother Jerome's new kingdom of Westphalia. Saxony became a member of the Confederation of the Rhine in 1807, while several of the German states (including Hamburg) were brought under French administration, although not annexed. Prussia also lost the bulk of its gains from the partitions of Poland to the newly created French puppet-state, the Grand Duchy of Warsaw. Danzig, too, was removed from Prussian control and became an independent republic.

At Tilsit, Russia lost some recently gained outposts on the Adriatic to France, though Napoleon gave the Tsar the district around Belostok. In return, the Tsar accepted the existence of the Grand Duchy of Warsaw, a potential threat to Russia's Polish lands. Napoleon also consolidated his position by annexing the Kingdom of Etruria directly to France, and adding East Friesland to the French client kingdom of Holland.

Central Europe and Italy, 1809

3 After his establishment of an informal alliance with the Russian Tsar at Tilsit in 1807, Napoleon turned to mopping up the smaller states which bordered his empire. In May 1809 he annexed the bulk of the Papal States directly to the French empire. His brother, Joseph, already ruled southern Italy from Naples, while his stepson, Eugene de Beauharnais, acted as Viceroy of the Kingdom of Italy.

Napoleon's confiscation of so many Austrian states and properties after Austerlitz encouraged plans for revenge. After 1805, the Austrian military system was much reformed. Austria resumed her war effort against France in 1809, but despite inflicting severe losses on Napoleon's increasingly raw recruits, the Habsburgs' army was defeated at Wagram and Francis I forced to make peace.

Napoleon obliged Austria to cede her remaining Adriatic territories to his puppet Kingdom of Italy and her Polish lands (West Galicia) to the Grand Duchy of Warsaw. He rewarded his ally Bavaria with a swathe of Austrian territory stretching southwards into the Tyrol and including Salzburg. Apart from Britain, Portugal, Sweden and the Ottoman Empire, and a few offshore islands such as Sicily and Sardinia, all of Europe was either ruled by Napoleon or in alliance with him.

Central Europe and Italy, 1810

4 Napoleon's allies were rarely reliable once he faced difficulties. Even his brother Louis sided too often with his Dutch subjects for Napoleon's liking, so in 1810 he was unceremoniously deposed and his Kingdom of Holland incorporated directly into the French Empire, along with a large section of northwest Germany.

Napoleon's attempt to blockade Britain through the enforcement of his "Continental System", designed to destroy British commerce by closing the entire European continent to British trade, led him to occupy even the Duchy of Oldenburg in 1810. This offended the Tsar, since the Duchy was ruled by the family of his grandmother, Catherine the Great. Russia, like France's other unwilling allies, was not prepared to forego the benefits of trade with Britain and war became inevitable.

1812

The Treaty of Vienna

From 1812, with Napoleon's catastrophic defeat in Russia, in which an army of 600,000 vanished into the steppe and the snow, the defeat of Napoleonic France became suddenly probable. Driven out of Spain and then defeated by a coalition army at Leipzig in 1813, in 1815 the revolutionary French forces suffered their final defeat at Waterloo.

Since 1789, Europe had undergone a generation-long convulsion which had left nothing untouched. Old states had been abolished, the world of the *ancien régime* was gone for ever. Yet though the representatives of the victorious powers who assembled in Vienna in 1815 to determine the future of Europe were joined by a common desire to restore the world lost after 1789, they were forced to recognise that no such course was in practice open to them. Thus the the Holy Roman Empire and its constellation of feudal principalities and mini-states summarily abolished by Napoleon in 1806 (*see* map 1, page 150) was not restored. Instead, they drafted the boundaries of a 39-member German Confederation, which paid lip-service both to the defunct Holy Roman past (even as it pronounced the last rites over the vast majority of its members) and to the notion of a common German identity so strongly displayed during the war of liberation against Napoleon after 1812.

At the same time, not least under the persuasive prompting of the central architect of the new order, Prince Metternich of Austria, the new order was profoundly conservative. At Vienna, the victorious allies agreed to meet periodically to settle disputes which might threaten the peace. This "Congress System" proved inadequate for dealing with the crises which arose after 1815. It soon became clear that it was only the overwhelming threat of Napoleonic France which had kept the Allies united. The disappearance of that threat after Waterloo revealed the rivalries and differing interests of the four Great Powers who had defeated the French. Britain's primary concern was to prevent the revival of a French threat to her own independence. So long as the danger of any power exercising hegemony across the continent of Europe was kept in check, Britain was satisfied. Her continental Allies had ideological concerns, too. Francis I's chief minister, Metternich, was determined to prevent any kind of constitutional changes, let alone revolutionary developments, which might threaten the Vienna settlement. By making opposition to internal political change a key principle of the post-Vienna system, Metternich risked committing the Allies to constant police actions and interference in the internal developments of states anywhere in Europe. Particularly after the suicide of the British Foreign Minister Castlereagh in 1822 and his replacement by Canning, the British government was out of sympathy with Metternich's ambition to hinder all change.

At first, Metternich had the support of Russia and Prussia in establishing the Holy Alliance – although Britain refused to join – which was committed to the maintenance of the Vienna settlement in its entirety. The Alliance even wanted to intervene to prevent successful rebellions in Spain's Latin American colonies, but were prevented from doing so by the logistical difficulties involved in such an undertaking, compounded by British and US opposition. The boundaries established between the Great Powers in Europe in 1815, however, proved remarkably stable over the next century by comparison with the 20 years of turbulence which had preceded the Congress of Vienna.

NORWAY

SWEDEN

FINLAND

Trondhjem

Christiania

jen

Åbo   Helsingfors   St. Petersburg

Stockholm   Revel

Gothenburg   Pskov

Riga

Aarhus

Copenhagen   Malmö
DENMARK

BALTIC
SEA

Dvinsk

Vitebsk   Smolensk

Vilna

Königsberg

Danzig

Hamburg

Bremen   Stettin

ANOVER   PRUSSIA

Hanover   Berlin   Posen

Leipzig   Oder   Lodz   Warsaw   Brest-Litovsk

kfurt   Dresden   Breslau   POLAND

SAXONY   Vistula

Nuremberg   Prague   REPUBLIC
OF CRACOW

BAVARIA   Brünn   Cracow

tgart   WÜRTTEMBERG   Vienna   Pozsony

Munich   Salzburg   AUSTRIAN EMPIRE

Innsbruck   Debrecen

STEIN   Buda   Pest

Graz   HUNGARY   Kolozsvár

RDY-VENETIA   Zágráb   Szeged   TRANSYLVANIA   MOLDAVIA   Jassy

Trieste   ILLYRIAN KINGDOM   Temesvár   Brassó

PARMA   Venice

MODENA   Military   Frontier

Bologna   Zara   Bosna Saray   Belgrade   WALLACHIA   Bucharest   Ruschuk

rence   SAN MARINO   Spalato   Mostar   Nish   Danube

CANY   PAPAL
STATES   MONTENEGRO   Sofia   Philippopolis   Adrianople

Rome   Üsküb   Burgas

Naples   Salonica   Varna

Taranto

KINGDOM OF THE
TWO SICILIES   Janina

Palermo   Messina   Corfu

Sicily   Catania   Patras   Athens

MALTA
(Br.)   Crete

Ionian Islands
(Br.)   Smyrna

SEA

Archangel

Perm

Nizhniy
Novgorod   Volga

Moscow   Samara

Tula

R U S S I A N

Minsk   Saratov

Kursk   Small
Horde

E M P I R E

Kiev   Kharkov

Vinnitsa   Don

Dnieper   Ekaterinoslav   Volga

Kishinev   Rostov   Astrakhan

Odessa   Dniester

Sebastopol   BLACK   SEA   Kabardia

Circassians   Daghestan

Tiflis

O T T O M A N   E M P I R E

Constantinople

Angora   Trebizond   Erivan

PERSIA

Adana   Tigris   Mosul

Nicosia

Beirut   Bedouins

Damascus

Danube

153

Map 1 — Saxony and Poland

SWEDEN

BALTIC SEA

DENMARK

Riga

Lithuania

Polock

Wilno

Minsk

MECK-LENBURG

HANOVER

PRUSSIA

Gdańsk

Grodno

Białystok

RUSSIAN

Berlin

Toruń

Poznań

Warsaw

EMPIRE

ANHALT

Cottbus

Lusatia

Leipzig

Dresden

POLAND

Lublin

Kiev

THURINGIA

Prague

REPUBLIC OF CRACOW

Żytomierz

Pau

Bohemia

Cracow

Przemyśl

Lwów

Ukraine

to Poland in 1699

BAVARIA

AUSTRIAN EMPIRE

HUNGARY

SAXONY AND POLAND, c.1600-1815

- The Electorate of Saxony, early 17th century

additions to Saxon territory:

- 1635
- 1659-1780
- 1807
- Saxony from 1815

- Poland in 1697; in personal union with Saxony, 1697-1706 and 1710-63
- Poland from 1699
- Grand Duchy of Warsaw (in personal union with Saxony), 1807
- Additions to Grand Duchy of Warsaw, 1809
- Border of the German Confederation, 1815
- Frontiers, 1815

1

Map 2 (inset top right)

DEN

Lüb

MECK

OLDENBURG

HANOVER

Hanover

HANOVER

NETHERLANDS

Cologne

Jena

Trier

BADEN

Bayreuth

FRANCE

WÜRTTEMBERG

BAVA

SWITZERLAND

AU

SARDINIA

PRUSSIA: LOSSES AND GAINS, 1806-15

- Prussia in 1806
- Prussia in 1807
- Additions to Prussia, 1815
- The German Confederation, 1815
- Frontiers, 1815

FRANCE, 1814-15

- Territories annexed 1789-1812 and retained by France after 1815
- Territories retained by France in 1814, lost 1815
- Frontiers, 1815

4

Map 4 (France)

ENGLAND

NETHERLANDS

PRUSSIA

Calais

Philippeville

Amiens

Saarbrücken

Landau

Rouen

Rheims

BAVARIA

Paris

Strasbourg

Rennes

Troyes

Mulhouse

Orléans

Montbéliard

AUSTRIAN EMP.

Angers

Dijon

Nantes

FRANCE

SWITZERLAND

Poitiers

Lyons

Savoy

Chambéry

LOMBARDY-VENETIA

Bordeaux

Grenoble

SARDINIA

PARMA

Venaissin

Avignon

MONACO

Pau

Toulouse

Marseille

Corsica

Carcassonne

ANDORRA

SPAIN

SARDINIA

Map 3 (Italy/Central Europe)

NETHERLANDS

PRUSSIA

HOLY ROMAN

PRUSSIA

Austrian Netherlands

Brussels

GERMAN STATES

PRUSSIA

Prague

Bohemia

FRANCE

EMPIRE

Br

Aus

RAURACIAN REPUBLIC

PRINCIPALITY OF NEUCHÂTEL (to Prussia)

SWISS CONFEDERATION

Salzburg

Linz

Vien

Austria

Tyrol

Styria

Campo Formio

Graz

Carinthia

KINGDOM OF SARDINIA

MANTUA

Venice

Carniola

Trieste

MILAN

Croat

Marengo

VENETIAN

PARMA

REP. OF GENOA

MODENA

DALMA

LUCCA

TUSCANY

REPUB

Florence

TUSCANY

SAN MARINO

PIOMBINO

PAPAL STATES

FRANCE

STATO DEI PRESIDI

KINGDOM OF NAPLES AND SICILY

Saxony and Poland, c. 1600-1815

1 In retrospect, the domination of German history by Prussia seems a quite natural development, but other principalities challenged her and fell by the wayside. The Electorate of Saxony was perhaps the strongest alternative contender for the title of champion of Protestant Germany, but its rulers failed to capitalise on its natural wealth and strategic position. This failure by Augustus the Strong (1694-1733) and his successor Augustus III (1733-63) to achieve the status of a major European power, was all the more striking because the Saxon monarchs ruled the vast territory of Poland, too, from 1697 to 1706 and from 1710 to 1763. They struggled, however, to turn their dual realm into a rival to the Austrian Habsburgs and the Hohenzollerns of Prussia. The Polish constitution limited the powers of the monarchs severely, exposing the folly of the two Augustuses in devoting so many resources to buying the throne of Poland. Saxony and Poland became, instead, the battleground in the struggles between Frederick the Great of Prussia and Maria-Theresa of Austria. Poland, in particular, suffered great depopulation and economic damage.

During the French Revolutionary wars, the Saxon rulers sided with Napoleon, and were rewarded with the acquisition of the Grand Duchy of Warsaw in 1807. Saxony, however, failed to change sides as deftly as some of the other German princes after Napoleon's débacle in Russia in 1812 and was punished by the victorious allies after the final French defeat in 1815. Although Austria and Britain refused to permit the total annexation of Saxony by the Prussians, the Hohenzollerns of Prussia did take the northern half of pre-war Saxony.

The Habsburgs: Losses and Gains, 1792-1815

2 The peace settlement of 1815 saw the restoration to Austria of some of the territories Napoleon had deprived her of. West Galicia, lost in 1809 to the Grand Duchy of Warsaw, was not regained, although the province of Tarnopol, awarded to Russia in 1809 after Napoleon's victory against the Austrians, was recovered by the Habsburgs. The Venetian territories, acquired by the Campo Formio settlement in 1797, but lost again in 1805, returned to Austrian rule. The Austrian Netherlands, lost in 1797, were attached to the Dutch state.

After the abolition of the Holy Roman Empire in 1806, the Habsburgs in effect renounced any ambitions to pursue territorial expansion to the northwest into Germany, relieving long-standing pressure on Bavaria, and opening the way for Prussia to assert its dominance within Germany.

In Italy, Francis I recovered Lombardy and Venetia, while his daughter Marie Louise ruled Parma and his brother Ferdinand restored Tuscany to Habsburg rule. Austrian political and military superiority also ensured the restoration of most of the non-Habsburg monarchs in Italy.

Prussia: Losses and Gains, 1806-15

3 Prussia's role in the Revolutionary and Napoleonic Wars had often been ambivalent, but her decisive participation in the final battle against Napoleon at Waterloo gave her considerable claims both to rewards for her share in the Allied war effort and to a new role as a guarantor of the peace settlement. The Hohenzollern family had long held possessions in western Germany between the Rhine and the Netherlands, but in 1815 Prussia received a large tract of territory, including Trier and Cologne as well as the Saarland. This gave Prussia a wedge of territory intended to back up the United Netherlands as a barrier to any future French attempts at expansion.

These western lands were separated from the rest of Prussia by other newly restored or created states belonging to the German Confederation. This corridor of non-Prussian territory offered a temptation to any ruler in Berlin anxious to consolidate and link his dominions. The key obstacle was the restored Kingdom of Hanover, which was still ruled in personal union by George III of England.

The integration of the western provinces into Prussia posed other problems than their physical separation from the centre. The Rhinelanders had often welcomed the French invaders, for example, and the legacy of prolonged French occupation was not easy to erase. The French-imposed legal system survived, as did metric weights and measures in Prussia to the west of the Rhine.

France, 1814-15

4 At first, the Allies assembled at Vienna in 1814 treated defeated France with remarkable moderation. The Treaty of Paris (30 May 1814) treated France very leniently, largely in the hope of stabilising the restoration of the Bourbons, but a more severe settlement was imposed in November 1815, after the final French defeat at Waterloo, as a retribution for the support given to Napoleon during "The Hundred Days" (his return from Elba).

In 1814, at the insistence of his erstwhile ally, Alexander I of Russia, Napoleon himself had been treated with remarkable clemency by his conquerors. He was exiled to the island of Elba as its nominal emperor, but after Waterloo the defeated Napoleon disappeared into captivity on the British island of St Helena in the South Atlantic.

France was now deprived of strategically important territories on her northeastern frontier, including Philippeville, Landau and part of Savoy. She was in effect pushed back to her borders in 1790, and had to submit to a temporary occupation of Paris, and to pay a large indemnity to the Allies.

THE HABSBURGS: LOSSES AND GAINS, 1792-1815

- The Holy Roman Empire, 1792
- Frontiers, 1792
- Habsburg possessions, 1792
- Under Habsburg cadet branch, 1792
- Lost by 1797
- Gained by 1797
- Gained, 1805
- Lost, 1805
- Lost, 1809
- Under Habsburg cadet branch, 1815
- The Austrian Empire, 1815

1815

1861

The Unification of Italy

The statesmen who gathered at Vienna in 1814-15 after Napoleon's final defeat had been guided by the ambition to stifle the threat of nationalism and revolution to the newly won European order as much as to ensure that France should never again be able to threaten Europe militarily. In practice, the capacity of France to dominate Europe again was already waning. At the start of the century, France's population of some 30 million had overshadowed its neighbours and provided Napoleon with the manpower for his *grande armée*. But thereafter the French population rose only slowly, to around 36 million, while other countries, most notably Prussia, saw their birthrates rise rapidly. France's stagnant birthrate, combined with her relatively slow industrialisation, meant that the threat of French expansion was growing ever weaker.

However, the experience of the French revolution and Napoleonic expansion had given enormous impetus to nationalism: the overthrow of traditional ruling élites in territories overrun by the French armies had a profound effect across Europe. In some states, such as Prussia, resentment of French influence had helped promote a militant patriotism. But whereas nationalism in these countries, in reflecting a reaction against French-imposed change, sought to reinforce existing social orders, in other parts of Europe, especially Italy and Poland, its effect was much more challenging to the status quo. Having tasted the social changes promoted by Napoleon following the French invasions, and in some cases having been granted a degree of autonomy by the invaders, nationalists there naturally reacted against the Vienna settlement, especially as it meant the restoration of traditional rulers (in Italy) and the loss of territory to the victors of the Napoleonic wars (in Poland). Likewise, in 1830, the Belgians revolted and won their independence the following year from the Dutch king, William I, who had been awarded Belgium by the Vienna settlement.

Even in the Balkans, where the slogan of "Liberté, Egalité et Fraternité" and the name of Bonaparte were distant echoes, the stirrings of nationalism appeared, above all in Greece, which achieved its independence from the Turks in 1830. This coincided with a further decline in the cohesion of the Ottoman Empire and with an inability on the part of Austria, faced with nationalist challenges to its own rule, to fill the growing political vacuum to the southeast. A series of revolutions in 1848 rapidly engulfed Austria and Hungary and spread throughout Central Europe. These, and the strains imposed on the Russians in fighting the Crimean War (1854-6) against a coalition of France, Britain and Turkey, showed that neither the Habsburgs nor the Russian Tsar remained strong enough to preserve the Vienna system by force. They had, however, retained sufficient power to hold the line in 1848-9, albeit at great cost and in part because of divisions within nationalist ranks, which in Germany centred on those favouring the inclusion of Austria within a greater German state and those wanting to exclude it.

But relations between Vienna and St Petersburg cooled rapidly, opening the way for the French emperor Napoleon III's campaigns against Russia (1854-56) and then Austria (1859), when neither supported the other against France. The Austrian defeat by the French in 1859 undermined the stability of the central Italian states, which voted for unification with Sardinia-Piedmont. Sicily and Naples were taken in 1860 by an Italian expeditionary force led by Garibaldi, and by 1861 a united Kingdom of Italy had emerged, excluding only the rump Papal States and Venice.

NORWAY

SWEDEN

FINLAND

Trondhjem

gen

Christiania

Gothenburg

Åbo

Helsingfors

Stockholm

Revel

St. Petersburg

Archangel

Perm

Aarhus

Copenhagen

Malmö

Pskov

BALTIC SEA

Riga

Dvinsk

Moscow

Nizhniy Novgorod

Volga

Samara

DENMARK

Königsberg

Vilna

Vitebsk

Smolensk

Tula

RUSSIAN

Saratov

Hamburg

Danzig

Bremen

Stettin

Minsk

Don

Kursk

Saratov

HANOVER

Berlin

PRUSSIA

Posen

Brest-Litovsk

EMPIRE

Hanover

Elbe

Oder

Vistula

Warsaw

ankfurt

Leipzig

Dresden

Lodz

POLAND

Kiev

Kharkov

SAXONY

Breslau

Volga

Nuremberg

Prague

Cracow

Lemberg

Dnieper

Ekaterinoslav

Astrakhan

ttgart

BERG

Brünn

Kaschau

Vinnitsa

Rostov

BAVARIA

Danube

AUSTRIAN

Dniester

Munich

Vienna

Pressburg

Kishinev

Odessa

EIN

Salzburg

Ofen

Pest

Debreczen

Jassy

Innsbruck

Graz

EMPIRE

Klausenburg

Circassians

Laibach

Szegedin

Kronstadt

0

Venice

Trieste

Agram

Fünfkirchen

Temeschwar

Sebastopol

Tiflis

Villafranca

ROMANIA

Bologna

Zara

Bosna Saray

Belgrade

Bucharest

BLACK SEA

Florence

SAN MARINO

SERBIA

Danube

Ruschuk

Varna

Erivan

Perugia

Spalato

Mostar

Nish

Sofia

Burgas

Trebizond

ITALY

MONTENEGRO

Üsküb

Philippopolis

Adrianople

PERSIA

Rome

PAPAL STATES

Gaeta

Constantinople

Naples

Bari

Salonica

OTTOMAN

Ankara

Mosul

Taranto

Janina

Smyrna

Adana

Euphrates

Palermo

Messina

Sicily

Catania

IONIAN ISLANDS (Br.)

Patras

Athens

GREECE

EMPIRE

Tigris

MALTA (Br.)

SEA

Crete

Nicosia

Beirut

Damascus

Bedouins

Poland, 1807-47

1 After Napoleon's crushing defeat of Prussia in the autumn of 1806 and his rapprochement with Alexander I of Russia at Tilsit in 1807, Poland's chances of regaining her independence barely a decade after her extinction by the Third Partition seemed strong. Napoleon did, indeed, establish a Grand Duchy of Warsaw (*see* map 2, page 151) composed of territories taken from Prussia's share of the last partition, but he showed no inclination to permit a genuinely independent Poland, preferring instead to punish his enemies among the former partitioning powers. Thus, after Austria's defeat by Napoleon in 1809, she lost West Galicia to the Grand Duchy.

Napoleon's defeat in 1815 meant a restoration of tripartite control of Poland by Russia, Austria and Prussia. The new division of spoils gave west Poland and Gdańsk to Prussia while Austria surrendered her claims to West Galicia, which in common with the remainder of the Grand Duchy came under Russian hegemony, in exchange for Tarnopol. Alexander ruled this so-called "Congress Kingdom" of Poland as just another part of his empire, despite its constitution which made it a personal union with Russia. The great Polish rebellion of 1831 was easily defeated by the powerful Russian army and provided Alexander's successor, Nicholas I, with an excuse to tighten his control.

The ancient university city of Cracow had survived 1815 as the Republic of Cracow, the last remnant of self-governed Polish territory. In 1847, Austria annexed it in agreement with Prussia and Russia, despite the protests of France and Britain.

Italy, 1815-61

2 The defeat of Napoleon brought most of the former ruling families of Italy back to their thrones. The role of Austrian troops in restoring the old dynasties, however, illustrated the fragility of the Italian state system. Ultimately the rulers' thrones now rested on the ability of Austria to prop them up.

The Kingdom of Sardinia, which became the driving force behind Italian unification, was ruled by a native Italian dynasty and so faced no nationalist challenges, such as those experienced by the Bourbon and Habsburg rulers in southern Italy. In 1849, Charles Albert of Sardinia unsuccessfully tried to seize Lombardy from the Austrians, but even failure established the Sardinian's credentials as the "natural" leader of Italy. In 1859, with the support of Napoleon III, he gained Milan and Lombardy from the Austrians. Part of Savoy and Nizza were handed over to France to repay her aid. The Austrian defeat destabilised the central Italian states, and under Sardinian pressure they voted for unification. Sicily and Naples were conquered by Garibaldi and his thousand volunteers in 1860 and then handed over to the Sardinian government. The Kingdom of Italy thus came into being in 1861. With the acquisition of Venetia from the Austrians in 1866, and the rump of the Papal States by 1870, unification was almost complete. San Marino, Corsica and some frontier zones of Austria were the only Italian-speaking areas remaining outside Italy's borders.

The Balkans, 1815-61

3 The decay of Ottoman power in Europe during the 19th century was perhaps the key factor in destabilising post-Napoleonic Europe. The emergence of Balkan nationalism occurred in territories far less ethnically homogeneous than those areas in Western Europe which had experienced nationalist movements. Furthermore, the Great Powers of Europe had some sympathy with the nationalist aspirations of the Christian subjects of the Muslim Sultan, above all with the Greeks, modern heirs of the classical civilization of ancient Greece, which outweighed their instinctive desire to maintain the existing order.

Moldavia and Wallachia were the first to rebel (with encouragement from Alexander I of Russia's Greek minister, Capodistria), in 1821. Despite the failure of these uprisings, the Greeks then started a more effective rebellion, backed by idealists such as the English poet Lord Byron. The British, French and Russians sought to temper Turkish reprisals for these revolts, leading to the annihilation of the Ottoman fleet at the decisive, if unintended, battle of Navarino in 1827. The way was cleared for an independent Greece, which emerged in 1830. Many Greek-speaking islands (including Crete), however, remained Ottoman possessions for decades.

Serbia achieved autonomous status after 1817, followed by Wallachia and Moldavia in 1829, the latter two emerging as the United Principalities in 1859 and as Romania in 1861. Serbia, despite further expansion in 1833, remained confined to a small territory north of Nish and south of the Danube.

Belgian Independence, 1831-39

4 The unification of the Low Countries under the House of Orange after 1815 had been intended as an obstacle to revived French expansionism. It was backed up by the garrisoning of the great fortresses at Luxembourg with Prussian troops.

The instability of the new state was revealed when the Belgians, encouraged by the July Revolution in Paris which toppled the Bourbons, rose up against the House of Orange in August 1830. The Belgian revolt combined liberal radicalism, local resentment of Dutch domination and Catholic anti-Orange feeling which united the French-speaking Walloons and the Flemings against the Dutch. The Dutch appealed to Prussia to send troops to crush the rebellion, but Britain persuaded the other Great Powers (France, Prussia, Austria and Russia) to accept an independent Belgium with the proviso that it would be perpetually neutral. The Dutch bitterly opposed the settlement and the new Belgian state achieved full international recognition only in 1839. The Netherlands, meanwhile, were reduced to their borders of 1790, while the Grand Duchy of Luxembourg became a personal union with the Dutch crown.

1861

The Unification of Germany

During the 1860s, Prussia experienced an astonishingly rapid transformation from the least of the five recognised Great Powers to become the motor of a united German state whose military and economic power overshadowed her neighbours. Prussia's rise was based on the rapid growth of her industrial base, which provided the revenues to fund an expanded conscript army equipped with the most modern weaponry. However, without the political genius of Otto von Bismarck, the Prussian Chancellor and architect of German unification, and the military skills of the Prussian General Staff, the unification of Germany to the exclusion of the Habsburg Austrian empire, much of it as "German" as Prussia, could not have come about.

Military reforms begun at the end of the 1850s meant Bismarck was able to elevate Prussia to a dominant position in the German Confederation. Allying himself with Austria against Denmark in 1864, Bismarck tested the new Prussian army successfully. In 1866, it was turned against Austria and those other German states – a majority of them – who opposed the Prussians. In only seven weeks, Prussia routed her enemies and created the North German Confederation.

The settlement which ended the war, the Treaty of Prague, saw Austria excluded from the new Confederation and forbidden to ally herself with the three southern German states (Bavaria, Baden and Wurttemberg). But Bismarck held back from humiliating Austria: Franz Josef did not lose any territory to Prussia (though he had to cede Venetia to Italy).

Bismarck's magnanimity meant that Austria was not inclined to attack Prussia in 1870, when she was at war with France. By contrast, Napoleon III's inept diplomacy left France without allies against the Prussians. Russia refused to help because of Napoleon's support for the Polish rebels against Russia in 1863, while Austria resented the French refusal to help her in 1866. Britain, meanwhile, distrusted the French Emperor's designs on the Low Countries. Italy similarly took advantage of Napoleon III's predicament, seizing French-garrisoned Rome. Bismarck's forces rapidly overran the French and encircled Paris. The following year, Napoleon III was obliged, humiliatingly, to sue for peace. The Treaty of Frankfurt, which followed the war, saw Alsace-Lorraine ceded to Germany, adding to French resentment.

France had for so many generations held the position of chief threat in the minds of other European rulers that the implications of a united Germany went largely unnoticed. The new nation-state had a population of 41 million, larger than any other country west of Russia. Furthermore, Germany's economy was growing as rapidly as her population. But while the new Germany was too large to be a comfortable neighbour, she was too small to exercise hegemony over the rest of Europe. The resulting tension was increasingly to dominate Great Power diplomacy in Europe.

To counter Prussian military success, the great Continental Powers sought to emulate what they perceived as the roots of German success. Instead of relying on a professional army, which the Germans had swept aside, France returned to her revolutionary tradition of conscription, which Prussia had adapted after 1859 to such deadly effect. Even relatively poor Austria and Russia followed the Prussian model. Mass armies became instruments of national power as well as, in states such as France and Italy, schools of nationalism for still largely illiterate peasant soldiers.

NORWAY
SWEDEN
FINLAND

Trondhjem
Christiania
Stockholm
Gothenburg

Åbo
Helsingfors
Revel
St. Petersburg
Archangel
Perm

DENMARK
Aarhus
Copenhagen
Malmö
Hamburg
Bremen

Pskov
Riga
Dvinsk
Moscow
Nizhniy Novgorod
Samara

GERMAN EMPIRE
Berlin
Leipzig
Dresden
Nuremberg
Munich
Stuttgart

Königsberg
Danzig
Stettin
Posen
Breslau
Königgrätz
Prague
Brünn

Vilna
Vitebsk
Smolensk
Tula
Saratov

Warsaw
POLAND
Lodz
Brest-Litovsk
Minsk
Kursk

RUSSIAN EMPIRE

Cracow
Lemberg
Vinnitsa
Kiev
Kharkov
Ekaterinoslav
Rostov
Astrakhan

AUSTRO-HUNGARIAN
EMPIRE
Kassa
Vienna
Pozsony
Buda Pest
Debrecen
Kolozsvár
Szeged
Temesvár
Brassó
Újvidék
Pécs
Zágráb

Kishinev
Odessa
Jassy
Sebastopol

Tiflis
Erivan

Salzburg
Graz
Innsbruck
LIECHTENSTEIN
Laibach
Venice
Trieste

ROMANIA
Bucharest
Ruschuk

ITALY
Bologna
Zara
SAN MARINO
Perugia
Rome
Spalato
Bosna Saray
Mostar
Belgrade
SERBIA
Nish
MONTENEGRO
Üsküb
Sofia
Philippopolis
Adrianople
Varna
Burgas

OTTOMAN EMPIRE

Constantinople
Angora
Trebizond
PERSIA
Mosul

Naples
Bari
Taranto
Salonica
Janina

Smyrna
Adana

Palermo
Messina
Sicily
Catania
Patras
Athens
GREECE

MALTA
(Br.)

Cyprus
Nicosia

Crete

Beirut
Damascus
Bedouins

161

1

Slovakian	Croatian	Ladin & Friulian
Ukranian	Slovenian	Romanian
Serbian	Italian	—— Frontiers, 1868

Austria-Hungary: Ethnic Divisions

1 Franz Josef's empire was a denial of the fashionable 19th-century doctrine of national self-determination. His subjects spoke at least 12 languages and adhered to four major religions (Catholicism, Protestantism, Orthodoxy and Judaism). The Habsburgs had long recognised that nationalism was their deadly enemy, but even an empire based on loyalty to a dynasty rather than a national ideal could not avoid the issue of language rights.

Although some Habsburg dominions possessed clear linguistic majorities, such as the overwhelmingly German-speaking provinces in the Alpine west or the Hungarian-speaking villages of the plains, most parts of the empire contained a mixture of peoples and faiths. As the 19th century progressed, the Habsburgs' Slav subjects began to assert their own identity through new national literatures, music and political organisations.

German-speaking Vienna's difficulties with Budapest over the Hungarians' rights to self-rule made dealing with the other peoples still more complicated. Although Hungarian liberals demanded that the crownlands of St Stephen should enjoy self-rule, they were not happy to extend equal political rights to their large Slovak, Romanian or Serb minorities.

The Habsburg Empire, 1849-68

2 Hungary's relationship with the Habsburg monarchy had always been voluntary – at least in Hungarian eyes. Vienna's efforts to Germanise the Magyars had been resisted both under Joseph II in the 1790s and his successors. 1848 saw a liberal-nationalist revolution in Hungary. For a few months Habsburg rule was overthrown, but in 1849 the Russian army intervened to restore the Habsburg monarchy. Having defeated Hungary, the Habsburgs detached Transylvania from her, augmented Croatia at Hungarian expense, created the new crownlands of Serbian Voivodina and the Banat of Temesvár from former Hungarian territory, and suppressed even nominal Hungarian autonomy. This situation continued until after the Austrian defeat in Italy in 1859, when the Habsburgs, aware of their vulnerable position, agreed a compromise with the Hungarians, by which Serbian Voivodina and the Banat of Temesvár were returned to Hungary and the jurisdiction of the Hungarian parliament was recognised.

Austria's defeat by Prussia in 1866 opened the way for renewed Hungarian demands for self-rule which Franz Josef in Vienna could not resist. The Emperor abandoned any aspiration for centralised rule from Vienna and restored self-government to Hungary by the so-called "Compromise" (*Ausgleich*) of 1867, which granted complete independence to Hungary, leaving only foreign affairs and military policy in common with the lands of the Austrian Crown. Transylvania and other areas were returned to Hungary, including Croatia, which enjoyed a relatively privileged status even in the newly re-founded Magyar national component of the Dual Monarchy (in which the reigning Habsburg was Emperor of Austria, but King of Hungary). The Croatian kingdom had been associated with the Crown of St Stephen for over 700 years and it was only briefly subject to Vienna after 1849. Ironically, Croatian military support for the Habsburgs against the Magyar rebels had been vital to saving the monarchy then, but the Habsburgs proved as ungrateful to the Croats as to the Tsar.

After 1867, the Hungarians conceded more: by the "Agreement" (*Nagoda*) of 1868, Budapest granted Croatia an assembly (*Sabor*) with limited local government powers. By 1882, the "Military Frontier" had been put under civilian administration. Mutual fear of disintegration kept Vienna and Budapest together after 1867, despite petty disputes about the title of the common army (Imperial or Royal according to where it was stationed) and the language of command.

Germany, 1864-66

3 Palmerston once remarked that only three people had ever understood the answer to the Schleswig-Holstein question: the first had gone mad; the second, Queen Victoria's Prince Consort, had since died; while the third, Palmerston himself, had forgotten it. This apparently obscure issue was a classic illustration of the tension between dynastic rights and national identity which became more and more acute during the course of the 19th century.

Danish ambitions to incorporate the two duchies of Schleswig and Holstein went against the grain of German nationalism. The bulk of the duchies' populations was German-speaking, and already by 1848 defending their rights against Danish encroachments had become a popular cause in Germany. Bismarck used the issue to divide his liberal opponents, many of whom felt unable to oppose military intervention on behalf of the Germans there. Austria went along with Bismarck's war against Denmark in 1864 and the re-drawing of boundaries which followed. Austria administered Holstein while Prussia held Schleswig. But friction rapidly developed between Vienna and Berlin leading to the Seven Weeks' War in 1866, after which Prussia annexed the Kingdom of Hanover, Nassau, the Electorate of Hesse and the free city of Frankfurt. In Hanover, political opposition to incorporation into Prussia was particularly persistent. Neither Luxembourg nor Limbourg, which belonged to the King of the Netherlands, joined the North German Confederation after 1866. Limbourg joined the Netherlands, while Luxembourg remained in personal union with the Dutch crown until 1890.

The Prussian dominated 23-state North German Confederation became the German Empire in January 1871 when the principal south German states – Bavaria, Wurttemburg, Baden and Hesse – joined it. Alsace and Lorraine were taken from France and added to the new Reich. The exclusion of the German-speaking Austrians from what was soon to become a united "little Germany" (*Kleindeutschland*) left an anomaly of national self-determination unfulfilled to haunt the 20th century.

1871

Imperial Europe

The years 1871 to 1914 saw Imperial Europe at its zenith. Outside Europe, all the Great Powers bar Austria-Hungary – Britain, Germany, France, Italy, and Russia – established empires that extended across the globe; within Europe, they co-existed uneasily. With none powerful enough to defeat the others unaided and with Britain, the most powerful of all, continuing her traditional concern with her colonies overseas rather than with Europe, each sought advantage in a system of complex and shifting alliances. The principal architect of this armed peace was Germany, concerned above all to safeguard her new territorial gains. But these alliances never included France. The humiliating defeat of 1870-71 and the loss of Alsace-Lorraine were hard enough for France to bear, but far worse was her loss of primacy in Europe. Between 1870 and 1914, Germany's population doubled (from 33 to 65 million; in the same period France's population remained static at around 40 million) and her industrial output quadrupled. She also built up impressive armed forces. Her army, at 95 divisions, was twice the size of France's and 12 times the size of Britain's, while her navy was second only to Britain's. Franco-German estrangement was the one fixed point among the shifting alliances of the Great Powers. For 20 years after 1871 Germany succeeded in convincing most of Europe of her conservative and pacific intentions, and France remained isolated. The balance of power that resulted in Western Europe preserved the peace for 43 years and for most governments territorial questions ceased to be a major issue.

Less intractable than the Franco-German rivalry but equally permanent and sometimes threatening to combine with it was the potential clash of Austro-Hungarian and Russian interests in the Balkans. Here, the combination of Ottoman misgovernment and insurgent nationalism speeded the erosion of Ottoman rule that had already seen Greece achieve independence in 1830, and which culminated in the Treaty of San Stefano in 1878, following a Russo-Ottoman war. The terms of the treaty were considered too favourable to Russia and Bulgaria for Austria-Hungary to accept, and were revised by the Treaty of Berlin the same year (*see* map 3, page 167). Ottoman control of the central Balkans was, though still much weakened, for the time being rescued.

Russia considered it essential that no other power achieved a position from which it could control the straits at Constantinople, through which passed most of the grain on which her economy (and hence her Great Power status) depended. Russia's fundamental motive may thus have been defensive but in practice she varied between attempting to stabilise Ottoman rule and to overthrow it in the hope of replacing the empire with a string of submissive satellites. To Habsburg Austria-Hungary, Russia's efforts seemed a dangerously threatening attempt to encircle the Habsburg monarchy with a crowd of irredentist Slav states under Russian protection. Britain, too, found itself drawn into the conflict. Many saw Russia's interest in the Ottoman Empire as a threat to the overland and Suez routes to India, already endangered in their view by Russian expansion towards Persia and Afghanistan. For the most part, however, as the Great Powers became aware of the complexities of the Balkans, the threats posed by emerging national movements, and of the dangerous incompatibilities of their own ambitions there, they clung stubbornly to the status quo.

SOUTHERN HUNGARY: THE DISSOLUTION OF THE MILITARY FRONTIER. 1873-82

Frontier, Hungarian crownlands
Military frontier, to 1873
Tributaries lost by Ottoman Empire, 1878
Territory lost by Ottoman Empire, 1878

Territory brought under civil administration, with date:
To Hungary, 1873
To Croatia-Slavonia, 1873
To Croatia-Slavonia, 1882
Frontiers from 1878

AUSTRIA

Klagenfurt

Zágráb
Croatia-
Fiume
Sziszek
Slavonia
Eszék
Zengg
CROWNLANDS
Dalmatia
Zara
Knin
Spalato
Banja Luka
Bosnia-Herzegovina
(Austro-Hungarian occupation from 1878)
Sarajevo
Mostar
Ragusa
MONTE-NEGRO

Pécs
HUNGARY
Temesvár
Újvidék
Pétervárad
Zimony
Pancsova
Belgrade

SERBIA

Sanjak of Novibazar
Novibazar
Nish

Scutari
Üsküb

OTTOMAN EMPIRE

ADRIATIC SEA

ITALY

AUSTRO-HUNGARIAN EMPIRE

Pécs
Eszék
Temesvár
Újvidék
Belgrade

Bosnia
Herzegovina
Spalato
Sarejevo
Mostar
Ragusa
Sanjak of Novibazar
Novibazar
Nish
Sofia

MONTENEGRO
Scutari
Durazzo
Tirana
Üsküb

ADRIATIC SEA

ITALY

SERBIA

Macedonia
OTTO

Janina
Sal

Thessaly
(to Greece, 1881)

SWEDEN
DENMARK
BALTIC SEA
NORTH SEA

Königsberg

Lübeck
Hamburg
GRAND DUCHY OF OLDENBURG
Bremen
GRAND DUCHY OF MECKLENBURG-SCHWERIN
Stettin
GRAND DUCHY OF MECKLENBURG-STRELITZ

NETHERLANDS

PRINCIPALITY OF SCHAUMBURG-LIPPE
PRINCIPALITY OF LIPPE-DETMOLD
DUCHY OF BRUNSWICK
DUCHY OF ANHALT

KINGDOM OF PRUSSIA

Berlin
Posen

RUSSIAN EMPIRE

BELGIUM

Cologne
PRINCIPALITY OF WALDECK
Leipzig
THURINGIAN STATES
KINGDOM OF SAXONY
Breslau
KINGDOM OF BAVARIA

GRAND DUCHY
Frankfurt
OF HESSE
LUXEMBOURG

ALSACE-LORRAINE Imperial Territory
KINGDOM OF BAVARIA
GRAND DUCHY OF BADEN
Stuttgart
KINGDOM OF WÜRTTEMBERG
Danube
KINGDOM OF BAVARIA
Munich

FRANCE

LIECHTENSTEIN
SWITZERLAND

AUSTRO-HUNGARIAN EMPIRE

RUSSIAN
EMPIRE

Brasso

Bessarabia

Bucharest

Dobruja

Ruse

Varna

GARIA

BLACK

EASTERN RUMELIA
(to Bulgaria in 1885)

Burgas

SEA

Plovdiv

Adrianople

*(to Ottoman
Empire, 1886)*

Constantinople

San Stefano

N

E

M

P   I   R   E

EGEAN

SEA

E BALKANS, 1878-1908   `2`

Tributary states of Ottoman
Empire, to 1878

New boundary of Russia, from 1878

Boundaries agreed by Treaty of
San Stefano, 1878

ritories lost by Ottoman Empire,
aty of Berlin 1878:

to Romania

to Serbia

to Montenegro

Under Austro-Hungarian
occupation

Independent tributary of
Ottoman Empire

Autonomous province of
Ottoman Empire

Notional boundary of Ottoman
Empire, from 1878

Areas under actual Ottoman
control, from 1878

Boundary of Ottoman-
controlled territory, from 1908

IAL GERMANY, 1871   `1`

Boundary of German Empire from 1871

Free cities

Imperial Germany, 1871

`1` The notion that unified Germany was no more than Prussia in another guise gained such rapid acceptance that it was easily and frequently overlooked that Imperial Germany was in fact a federal state in which the 26 individual states had an equal voice. That said, Prussia's remained the dominant influence. Not only was it the largest state, stretching across the whole of the north of the country from the Low Countries in the west to Russia in the east, with the lion's share of the new country's rapidly developing industrial base it had a decisive voice in decision-making.

Yet however inevitable the dominance of Prussia, Bismarck had nonetheless been fearful that the new state would erode Prussia's leading role and that a federal constitution was essential to maintain her identity. (At the same time, he similarly recognised that such an arrangement would allay fears on the part of the smaller states that they would be swallowed whole by Prussia.)

The constitutional arrangements of Prussia itself were significantly different in several important ways from those of the most other German states, not least in regard to the development of democracy. Prussia's parliament (*Landtag*), unlike those of the other German states (save defiantly feudal Mecklenburg-Schwerin), was not elected by universal male suffrage but by a three-tier voting system dating from 1849 and based on taxable income. In consequence, power was largely concentrated in the hands of Bismarck and his successors. Control of the *Landtag* in each state was important because only the local parliaments could raise direct taxes. The fiscal powers of the Imperial Parliament (*Reichstag*) were limited to indirect taxes, such as customs duties. Most important, the army was paid for at a state level and each state had its own army. Nonetheless, all but the Bavarian army were controlled by Prussian superiors, and even this was subordinate to the Prussian General Staff, which co-ordinated all military operations.

Ironically, the only part of the Reich which was not a federal state in its own right with its own constitution and monarch was the Imperial Territory (*Reichsland*) of Alsace-Lorraine, ceded by France under the Treaty of Frankfurt in 1871 (and returned to France at the end of the First World War).

The Balkans, 1878-1908

`2` As revolts against Ottoman rule spread through the Balkans in the mid-1870s, Austria was reassured by Russia's apparent lack of direct ambition there. St. Petersburg agreed that no new large-scale Christian state should be created which might thwart Austria's ambitions but that instead Turkey should reform itself.

But by 1877 Russian public opinion had pushed the Tsar into war in support of the Christian Slav rebels. Under the Treaty of San Stefano in 1878 which concluded the war, the Russians chose to create a "Big Bulgaria" stretching across the southern Balkans. This immediately sparked crisis among the Great Powers. Neither Austria-Hungary nor Britain would accept such a Russian puppet-state, particularly as it left Constantinople vulnerable to sudden attack. Playing on Germany's lack of interest in the Balkans, in the same year Bismarck, offering his services as an "honest broker", stepped in to separate his two imperial allies before a further war broke out.

The Treaty of Berlin (1878) overturned much of the San Stefano agreements. Instead, while it ratified the independent status of Serbia and Romania, it preserved the fiction of Ottoman suzerainty over a much-reduced Bulgarian principality. It also created a special status for Bulgarian-inhabited Eastern Rumelia, though this became wholly Bulgarian in 1885.

The decision to reduce Bulgaria and to restore Macedonia to Turkey (as well as to end the Austrian occupation of Bosnia-Herzegovina) proved a costly error in the long term. Bulgaria naturally aspired to recover what had been awarded to her by the Treaty of San Stefano, while Serbia similarly regarded Macedonia and other San Stefano territories as legitimate objects of her ambition. This brought her into direct conflict with Greece, which had, since her own independence in 1830, nursed claims to Macedonia on the ground that it was part of the historic territory of Greece. (Greece made partial amends with her seizure of Thessaly in 1881.)

Meanwhile, no one could agree the fate the Christian populations of the Balkans beyond a pious regret that they should have to remain under Muslim rule. However understandable the failure to grasp the Balkan nettle at Berlin in 1878, the problems of the region's numerous ethnic, nationalist, religious and imperial rivalries were to fester unchecked into the 20th century to everyone's disadvantage.

Southern Hungary: the Dissolution of the Military Frontier, 1873-82

`3` The border between Christian Europe and the Muslim Ottoman Empire – the Military Frontier – was one of the great fault lines of Europe. It was established by the Habsburgs in Croatia in the mid-16th century to guard the Habsburg lands against Ottoman incursion and then greatly expanded after 1699 following the expulsion of the Ottomans from the most of Hungary by Prince Eugene. By the mid-19th century, with the Ottoman Empire in terminal decline, Hungarian demands for the return of the Frontier lands to civilian administration increased and from 1873 the Military Frontier was accordingly parcelled among Hungary and Croatia-Slavonia.

1885

1914

The Eve of the First World War

The boundaries between the Great Powers changed little in the century after the Congress of Vienna (1815). Germany, although now unified, Austria-Hungary and Russia still shared largely the same frontiers established at Vienna, and most observers could be forgiven for regarding them as permanent. But in practice the emergence of small states on the periphery of the Powers, allied to tensions created by conflicting aspirations for autonomy and independence on the part of the many ethnic groups within the Austro-Hungarian and Russian empires, marked the beginning of a process that threatened the empires' territorial integrity. In tandem with Great Power rivalry, it created the conditions that were to lead to the cataclysms of the First World War.

Whatever its problems with nationalism, Russia at least had a majority ethnic group. Austria-Hungary lacked even this. The largest group in Hungary were the Magyars, who made up just under half the population. Slovaks, Romanians, Serbs and Croats as well as two-million Germans formed the other half. In the Austrian part of the empire, Germans amounted to only about 35 per cent of the population. Czechs, Poles, Slovenes, Italians and several smaller groups comprised the remainder. The very principle of national self-determination which had justified the unification of Germany was a threat to its Habsburg ally. Nationalist goals were satisfied in Norway, however, which in 1905 was granted full independence by Sweden.

But it was in the Balkans that nationalist aspirations were to prove most volatile. Newly independent Serbia, Bulgaria and Greece all saw the decline of the Turkish Ottoman Empire as an opportunity to extend their territories at the expense of the Turks. At the same, Austria-Hungary and Russia both sought to increase their influence in the region. With Britain's abandonment of its role as protector of the Turkish sultan (a policy intended chiefly to contain Russian ambitions), the way was left open for Serbia, Bulgaria and Greece in 1912 to attack the Ottomans. Dividing the spoils proved harder, however (*see* maps 2 and 3, page 171), and led to further fighting the following year. More threatening still, however, was the involvement of Austria-Hungary and Russia. While the former feared the destabilising effect Serbia might have on its large South Slav population, especially in Bosnia-Herzegovina (provocatively annexed by Austria-Hungary in 1908), the latter was determined to resume her role as protector of Orthodox Christians in the region – if necessary against Catholic Austria-Hungary rather than Muslim Turkey. With Austria and Russia members respectively of the Triple Alliance and the Triple Entente (*see* map 1, page 171), their rivalry in the Balkans increasingly threatened to suck the whole of Europe into conflict. Austria-Hungary's declaration of war against Serbia in July 1914 following the Serbian-sponsored assassination of the Archduke Ferdinand in Sarajevo the previous month was the spark that lit the the conflagration. Russia ordered a general mobilisation. Germany, Austria's ally, mobilised in turn, and on August 1 declared war on Russia. Three days later, Germany also declared war on France. The following day, the Germans invaded Belgium, determined to smash the Triple Entente. Britain promptly declared war on Germany and Austria on Russia. The First World War had begun.

NORWAY

SWEDEN

FINLAND

DENMARK

Narvik

Trondhjem

Christiania

Stockholm

Gothenburg

Åbo

Helsingfors

St. Petersburg

Revel

Archangel

Perm

BALTIC SEA

Aarhus
Copenhagen
Malmö

Hamburg

Bremen

Hanover

Berlin

RMAN EMPIRE

Königsberg

Danzig

Stettin

Posen

Warsaw

Brest-Litovsk

POLAND

Lodz

Pskov

Riga

Dvinsk

Vilna

Vitebsk

Minsk

Smolensk

Moscow

Tula

R U S S I A N

Kursk

Nizhniy
Novgorod

Volga

Samara

Saratov

E M P I R E

Don

Leipzig
Dresden

Breslau

Prague

Nuremberg

Brünn

Cracow

Lemberg

Kassa

AUSTRO-HUNGARIAN

Pozsony

Vinnitsa

Kiev

Kharkov

Vistula

Elbe

Oder

rt

Munich

HTENSTEIN

Innsbruck

Vienna

Salzburg

Graz

Budapest

EMPIRE

Debrecen

Kolozsvár

Jassy

Danube

Dniester

Kishinev

Dnieper

Ekaterinoslav

Rostov

Astrakhan

Volga

Tiflis

Laibach
Zágráb

Pécs

Szeged

Temesvár

Brassó

Odessa

Venice
Verona

Trieste

Újvidék

ROMANIA

BOSNIA-
HERZEGOVINA

Belgrade

Bucharest

Sebastopol

BLACK SEA

Bologna

rence

Zara

San Marino

Spalato

Sarajevo

SERBIA

MONTE-
NEGRO

Danube

Nish

BULGARIA

Ruse

Varna

Mostar

Sofia

Burgas

ITALY

Perugia

Rome

Naples

Bari

Taranto

ALBANIA

Tirana

Janina

GREECE

Skopje

Plovdiv

Adrianople

Constantinople

Salonica

Angora

OTTOMAN

Erivan

PERSIA

Trebizond

EMPIRE

Tigris

Smyrna

Adana

Mosul

Euphrates

Palermo

Messina

Sicily

Catania

Athens

Patras

MALTA
(Br.)

SEA

DODECANESE
(It.)

Crete

CYPRUS
(Br.)

Nicosia

Beirut

Damascus

Bedouins

169

Alliance Systems after 1892

1 By the latter part of the 19th century dynastic ties and fear of unrest had served to draw together the Great Powers to promote an essentially stable order across Europe through a multi-faceted series of diplomatic alliances and alignments. This was the apogee of the European state system. But whatever its apparent stability, the system was permanently threatened by French resentment of Germany's growing primacy among the Continental powers (even if for much of the period France was unable to challenge Germany's fast increasing industrial and military might) and by instability in the Balkans, where an already heady cocktail of dissatisfied and mutually antagonistic states was made more potent still by the rival ambitions of Austria-Hungary and Russia. Both exploited every opportunity to destabilise the new independent states and to occupy disputed frontier areas.

By 1894 Germany's expanding military strength caused France and Russia to become nervous allies. In 1904, alarmed by the equally rapid growth of German naval power, Britain abandoned its "splendid isolation" and also allied itself with France, despite previously strained relations. In 1907 Britain then patched up its differences with Russia to form, with France, the Triple Entente to assure mutual defence against German attack. In Berlin, these measures of alleged self-defence were viewed more as encirclement. Facing declared enemies to the west and the east, Germany drew closer to Austria, whose strained relations with Russia finally cracked in 1908 following the Austrian annexation of Bosnia-Herzegovina. Though Italy had claims on Habsburg territory up to the Alps and in Dalmatia – and was also secretly allied with France and Russia – she, too, was at least nominally allied with Germany and Austria-Hungary in the Triple Alliance, as was Romania. By 1914, Austria-Hungary was Germany's only reliable ally. In the crisis after the murder of the Archduke Ferdinand, Germany could not afford to abandon her even at the risk of a general European war. Furthermore, if war did come, the Kaiser's generals wanted it sooner rather than later: the German army was increasingly certain that it could defeat France and Russia.

The First Balkan War, 1912

2 The new Balkan states – Serbia, Bulgaria and Greece – were united only by their hostility towards the Ottoman Empire, which in 1912 still held Albania and Macedonia. The Italian defeat of the Ottomans in Libya in 1912 encouraged Serbia, Bulgaria and Greece to activate their anti-Ottoman alliance in the hope of dividing the Sultan's European territories between them. The Turkish armies were swiftly defeated. The Treaty of London (1913), mediated by a committee of the Great Powers and chaired by Britain, oversaw the division of the spoils. It left everyone dissatisfied. The great Aegean port of Salonica was coveted by all three victors. In the event, the Greek army had reached it just hours before the Bulgarians. To bitter Bulgarian resentment, Greek possession was confirmed in London. Bulgaria did, however, take possession of a large tract of land from the Black Sea to Kavala on the Aegean, including Adrianople. The province of Macedonia, which had a mixed population of Slavs, Turks, Jews and Greeks, was claimed by all three states, each with varying degrees of justice and all indifferent to the wishes of its inhabitants. Conquest confirmed its division between Serbia, Bulgaria and Greece. The Treaty of London also confirmed the creation of the independent principality of Albania, a development resented by both Greece and Serbia. Serbia wanted a port on the Adriatic at Albania's expense and feared moreover that an independent Albania would make her substantial Albanian minorities in Kosovo and Macedonia restive. Greece laid claim to northern Epirus (ie, southern Albania), basing her claim on the Greek Orthodox community there. Threatened by hostile neighbours, Albania was pushed into looking first to Austria-Hungary for protection and then to Italy.

The Sanjak of Novibazar, held by Austria-Hungary until 1908, was divided between Serbia and Montenegro. In thus closing the gap between them, their acquisition was crucial in increasing tension between Vienna and Belgrade. Serbia and Montenegro could now co-operate across a common border against their northern neighbour, Austria-Hungary, and seek to stir up the discontents of the South Slavs there. They also blocked further Austro-Hungarian expansion into the Balkans. The clash between Serbian nationalism in full flood and Habsburg expansion culminated in the assassination of the Archduke Ferdinand in Sarajevo in June 1914.

The Second Balkan War, 1913

3 Resentment with the Treaty of London quickly flared into a new war. Determined to right the wrongs done to it in London, in June 1913 Bulgaria attacked its erstwhile allies, Greece and Serbia. Bulgarian military optimism was soon shown to be misplaced. The Greeks and Serbians, aided by Romania and Turkey, who swiftly appreciated the opportunity the Bulgarian attack presented, had little difficulty repulsing the Bulgarians. Bulgaria was as rapidly defeated as Turkey had been the year before. Serbia partitioned much of the former Bulgarian-held areas of Macedonia with Greece. Greece kept Salonica and took western Thrace. Resentful Bulgaria was confined to a barren stretch of the Aegean coast while Turkey recovered Adrianople in Thrace, preserving the foothold in Europe she maintains today. Romania, a non-combatant in the first Balkan War, received southern Dobruja for her efforts in the second.

1914

The Aftermath of the First World War

Despite the defeat of Germany and her allies in the autumn of 1918 and the signing of a string of peace treaties in Paris between the victorious allies and the defeated states in 1919 and 1920, it was several years before the boundaries of the new Europe were clearly established. Revolution and civil war plunged Russia, Germany and much of what had been Austria-Hungary into chaos.

The Europe that emerged was radically different. Russia and Germany had shrunk dramatically; the Austro-Hungarian and Ottoman empires had disappeared; a host of mostly smaller states had appeared. And in Soviet Russia a communist government now ruled in place of the Tsar. The civil war of 1918-20 that followed the 1917 revolution in Russia found counterparts in Hungary (1919), and in Germany (1918-23), where the new democratic government faced threats from both extreme right and left. Until 1923 Germany and parts of central Europe were also afflicted by hyper-inflation, which further destabilised these already fragile regions. Italy, too, was effectively gripped by revolution between 1920 and 1922, when Mussolini's Fascist party seized power. Among the combatants, only in Britain and France was there no serious threat to the political order, though civil war preceded and followed the creation of the Irish Free State in 1922.

The principal treaties agreed at Paris were those of Versailles (1919, with Germany); St-Germain (1919, with Austria); Neuilly (1919, with Bulgaria); Trianon (1920, with Hungary, *see* map 5, page 175); and Sèvres (1920, with Turkey), this last modified after the Greek-Turkish war of 1920-22 by the Treaty of Lausanne (1923).

As members of the victorious alliance, France and Italy gained what nationalists had long regarded as their "natural" frontiers. France regained her Rhine frontier. Italy gained an Alpine frontier (as well as a substantial German-speaking minority). Italy also acquired Istria and the port of Fiume along with Zara (Zadar) on the Dalmatian coast.

The most obviously dramatic effects of the Paris Settlement were the resurrection of Poland as an independent state more than a century after its partition between Austria, Prussia and Russia (*see* map 1, page 147) and the establishment of two new states: Czechoslovakia and Yugoslavia. Yugoslavia was officially a new kingdom of "Serbs, Croats and Slovenes" but was dominated by its old Serbian core. Of equal importance, the Paris Settlement left every post-war state in central Europe with internal problems and potential border disputes. It proved easier to break up multi-national empires than to replace them with ethnically homogeneous states. Poland and Czechoslovakia both had large German minorities after 1919, as well as disgruntled Slav minorities. Czechoslovakia and Yugoslavia also had substantial Hungarian minorities. Furthermore, neither Czechs and Slovaks, nor Serbs, Croats and Slovenes had any experience of living under a common government. Romania, too, inherited large Hungarian and German minorities.

In 1925 the Treaty of Locarno put relations with Germany and the allies on a new basis. But Germany was a reluctant signatory, accepting only her western borders as defined at Locarno. The question of her eastern borders would fester until Hitler resolved them by force.

NORWAY

Narvik

Trondheim

SWEDEN

FINLAND

Murmansk

Archangel

gen

Oslo

Turku

Helsinki

Leningrad

UNION OF

Perm

Stockholm

Tallinn

ESTONIA

Gothenburg

Pskov

LATVIA

Riga

Moscow

Nizhniy
Novgorod

SOVIET

Aarhus

Copenhagen

Malmo

BALTIC
SEA

Daugavpils

LITHUANIA

Tula

Volga

Samara

DENMARK

FREE CITY
OF DANZIG

Königsberg

Wilno

Vitebsk

Smolensk

SOCIALIST

Saratov

Hamburg

Danzig

(Germany)

Minsk

Kursk

Bremen

Stettin

Elbe

Don

Berlin

Oder

Vistula

Poznań

Warsaw

Brześć

Hanover

Astrakhan

Leipzig

Dresden

Łódź

ERMANY

Breslau

POLAND

Kiev

Kharkov

Volga

kfurt

Prague

Nuremberg

CZECHOSLOVAKIA

Cracow

Lwów

Vinnitsa

Dnieper

Dnepropetrovsk

REPUBLICS

ttgart

Brno

Košice

Dniester

Rostov

Munich

Danube

Vienna

Bratislava

Salzburg

Debrecen

Iaşi

Chriştinău

Odessa

Innsbruck

AUSTRIA

Budapest

HUNGARY

Graz

Pécs

Szeged

Cluj

ENSTEIN

Ljubljana

Venice

Trieste

Zagreb

Novi Sad

Timişoara

ROMANIA

Braşov

Sebastopol

BLACK SEA

Tbilisi

Verona

Bologna

rence

SAN MARINO

Zara

Split

KINGDOM OF THE

Sarajevo

Bucharest

Danube

Ruse

Yerevan

Perugia

Mostar

SERBS, CROATS

AND SLOVENES

Nish

BULGARIA

Varna

ITALY

Belgrade

Sofia

Burgas

PERSIA

Rome

Skoplje

Plovdiv

Adrianople

Trabzon

Tirana

ALBANIA

Thessaloniki

Istanbul

Naples

Bari

Taranto

Ankara

TURKEY

Ioannina

GREECE

Izmir

Palermo

Messina

Sicily

Catania

Patrai

Athens

Adana

Mosul

Euphrates

IRAQ
(Br. Mandate)

MALTA
(Br.)

SEA

DODECANESE
(It.)

Nicosia

CYPRUS
(Br.)

Crete

SYRIA
(Fr. Mandate)

Beirut

Damascus

Tigris

POLAND, LITHUANIA AND RUSSIA, 1918-23

- Frontiers, 1924
- Poland under the Treaty of Brest-Litovsk, March 1918
- Lithuania under the Treaty of Brest-Litovsk, March 1918
- Curzon Line, December 1919
- Lithuania under the Peace of Moscow, July 1920
- Poland from the end of 1922
- Lithuania from the end of 1922
- Allied administration from 1918; annexed by Lithuania, 1923

THE TREATY OF BREST-LITOVSK, 1918

- Frontiers, 1914
- Lost by Russia (nominally independent; controlled by Central Powers)
- Independent under the Treaty of Brest-Litovsk

CENTRAL EUROPE: PLEBISCITES, 1920-35

- Post-war frontiers established by plebiscites
- Other frontiers, 1924

Outcome of plebiscites in favour of:
- Germany
- Poland
- Hungary
- Austria
- Belgium
- Denmark

174

*(Map, left column — labels)*

NETHERLANDS

(occupied to 1926)

Rhine

Essen   Dortmund

BELGIUM

Aachen   Düsseldorf

Eupen   Cologne

Malmédy   Bonn

GERMANY

(occupied to 1929)   Coblenz

(to Belgium 1920)

Wiesbaden   Frankfurt

Trier   Mainz

LUXEMBOURG   (occupied to 1930)

(to Germany 1935)   Saar   Mannheim

Saarbrücken

Metz

Alsace-Lorraine   Karlsruhe

Strasbourg   Stuttgart

FRANCE   Rhine

Mulhouse

SWITZERLAND

LIECHTENSTEIN

E RHINELAND: ZONES OF CUPATION AFTER 1919

- Added to France , 1919
- Areas of plebiscites
- Demilitarised zone
- Eastern boundary of allied occupation zone after 1918
- Eastern boundary of later allied occupations
- Boundaries between areas of different lengths of occupation

THE TREATY OF TRIANON, 1920

- Hungary, 1914
- Frontiers in 1924
- Hungarian-speaking areas lost by Hungary
- Areas with minority non-Hungarian populations who remained minorities in successor states
- Other areas lost by Hungary
- Autonomous region within Hungary until 1918
- Area of plebiscite

AND

KIA

ssa (ice)

Nagyvárad (Oradea)   Kolozsvár (Cluj)

Transylvania

Brassó (Brasov)

Temesvár (Timişoara)   ROMANIA

NES   BULGARIA

The Treaty of Brest-Litovsk, 1918

1 Russia's withdrawal from the First World War after the Bolshevik takeover was formalised by the settlement between Lenin's Russia and Germany and her allies on 3 March 1918 at Brest-Litovsk. The treaty, deeply unfavourable to Russia, revealed in part the Europe Berlin hoped would be the outcome of the war. Russia lost all its western provinces: Finland, the Baltic states, Poland and the Ukraine (as well as Georgia under the Treaty of Berlin of August 1918). Germany's subsequent defeat was to mean that little could be done to exploit the territories lost by Russia, all of which, other than Georgia and the bulk of the Ukraine, remained independent at least until 1939. Nonetheless, the German desire to lay claim to the resources of this vast region foreshadowed Hitler's obsession with it 20 years later.

The Rhineland: Zones of Occupation after 1919

2 The demilitarisation of Germany was among the key objectives of Versailles, with France in particular anxious that Germany should never again be able to launch an attack across its eastern frontier. In addition to restrictions on the size of the German army, German forces were banned permanently from a wide band of the Rhineland from the Netherlands to Switzerland. To enforce the demilitarisation, allied troops (predominantly French) were stationed in three zones in the demilitarised area, from which they were to withdraw at five-year intervals until 1935. The allied occupation was also intended to ensure that Germany met the huge reparations bill demanded by the allies in compensation for their war losses. It was at least in part the scale of these that accelerated the economic catastrophe that overtook Germany in the early 1920s, leading the country to renege on her payments in 1923. In response, French and Belgian troops occupied further areas, principally in the Ruhr. The following year, Germany accepted a compromise reparations package. A further settlement was reached in 1928. Confident that the question had been settled and anxious to renew good relations with Germany, the withdrawal of the occupying forces was accelerated and the last troops were withdrawn in 1930. In March 1936, Hitler marched his troops back into the Rhineland.

Central Europe: Plebiscites, 1920-35

3 In accordance with the doctrine of self-determination championed by US President Wilson at the Paris Peace Settlement, the victorious allies permitted plebiscites to be held in certain hotly disputed territories to allow their inhabitants to decide which country they wished to live in. This was a novel idea, largely untried before 1919, though even now the allies generally redistributed territory without reference to its inhabitants. In almost every case, the plebiscites were decided along language lines. But there were exceptions. The Protestant Masurians of southern East Prussia, for example, preferred to remain in Germany rather than join Catholic Poland. Furthermore, a simple majority of one group over another could often disguise considerable complications on the ground. In the southeast corner of Upper Silesia, for example, mainly German-speaking towns were surrounded by predominantly Polish-speaking rural areas. As it was clearly impossible to give the rural areas to Poland and the towns to Germany, the Polish majority ensured that the whole area went to Poland. This was a source of enduring German resentment, as was the decision to entrust Danzig to the control of the League of Nations despite its overwhelming German character. Just as economic reasons dictated much of the Polish-German border, so the coal-rich Saarland was also placed under League of Nations control, allowing France to exercise *de facto* economic control. The last of the plebiscites promised at Versailles took place in 1935 when the Saarlanders voted overwhelmingly to return to German rule.

Poland, Lithuania and Russia, 1918-23

4 The defeat of the Red Army outside Warsaw in 1920 ended any prospect of the spread of communism to the West by "armed missionaries". The settlement between Poland and Soviet Russia agreed at Riga in 1921 was surpassed in its harshness to Lenin's Russia only by Brest-Litovsk. Having been obliged to accept the independence of the Baltic States the previous year, Russia now found itself having to accept a greatly expanded Poland, whose eastern border was pushed 200 miles beyond the Curzon Line, the border proposed by Poland's allies at the Paris Peace Settlement. Thus encouraged, the following year Polish forces seized southern Lithuania. (Lithuanian resentment at Poland's gains was such that the two were technically in a state of war until 1939). Lithuania responded by seizing the formerly German port of Memel in 1923, giving rise to further German resentment of the post-war settlement.

The Treaty of Trianon, 1920

5 The truncation of the ancient kingdom of Hungary was one of the most significant results of the First World War. Post-war Hungary lost not only its non-Magyar regions but vast Hungarian-speaking areas as well. The country even lost territory to its former partner, Austria, though Hungary was allowed to retain territory around Sopron after a plebiscite (*see* map 3). Hungarian resentment at the loss of over two-thirds of its pre-war territory and at the fate of more than one-third of the Hungarian-speaking population now under foreign rule simmered throughout the inter-war period.

1925

The Nazi Conquests

Resentment against the terms of the Versailles Settlement was widespread in Weimar Germany. The failure of the new democratic governments there to achieve any significant change in its terms, combined with the effects of the Great Depression after 1929, facilitated the rise to power of Adolf Hitler and the Nazi Party in 1933, which used anti-Versailles rhetoric as an essential ingredient in its election campaigns.

For the first five years of his rule, the Nazi dictator confined himself to chipping away at the restrictions imposed on Germany at Versailles. He refused, for example, to resume the reparations payments imposed at Versailles, while in 1933 he took Germany out of the League of Nations, to which she had been admitted only in 1926. More seriously, in March 1935 Hitler reintroduced conscription and an airforce, both forbidden in 1919, while the following March, more provocatively still, he re-occupied the demilitarised Rhineland.

In March 1938, Hitler's pan-German ambitions became more apparent when, again in direct contravention of the Versailles Treaty, he engineered the unification (*Anschluss*) of his native Austria with Germany. By the following March, with the tacit blessing of Britain and France, who were anxious at all costs to avoid war, Hitler had also occupied the Czech lands (*see* map 2, page 179), using at first the excuse that the country's three-and-a-half-million German speakers had been persecuted by the Czechoslovakian government.

Alerted at last by this occupation of non-German-speaking territory to the real dangers posed by Germany, Britain and France pledged to defend Poland, Greece and Romania from similar Nazi aggression and embarked on crash programmes of military spending. Again, Hitler wrong-footed them. In August, he signed a non-aggression pact with the Soviet Union (*see* map 3, page 178), despite his previous unwavering hostility to communism, neatly sidelining the one country he took to be his most serious enemy. Thus guaranteed, on 1 September Hitler invaded Poland. When their demands that Germany withdraw were ignored, Britain and France declared war. Though taken somewhat by surprise by this new Anglo-French resolve, Hitler's invasion of Poland continued, indeed was augmented by the Soviet invasion of eastern Poland in mid-September. By 29 September, Germany and the Soviet Union had partitioned Poland between them.

Hitler had now to deal with his enemies in the west before they had time to gather strength. In April 1940, his forces rapidly overran Denmark and Norway. On 10 May, they opened a devastating offensive against Holland, Belgium and France. The inadequate defence mounted by British and French forces was brushed aside. Precipitately, the remnants of the British army withdrew to Dunkirk and were evacuated. By mid-June France had effectively been defeated. The Government, now led by Marshal Pétain (a hero of the First World War), requested an armistice and subsequently established itself at Vichy, while the Germans continued to occupy northern and western parts of France.

By July 1940, when Hitler held victory celebrations in Berlin, Germany and her ally, Italy – the "Axis" – were masters, directly or indirectly, of the whole of Western and Central as well as much of Eastern Europe. The Soviet Union, it is true, had made use of Hitler's western offensive in order to occupy Finland and the Baltic states. But the difficulties experienced by the Soviet army in attaining these objectives suggested that it posed no threat to Germany. Hitler's rhetoric about acquiring *Lebensraum* (living space) for German colonisation seemed about to become reality.

NORWAY

SWEDEN

FINLAND

Narvik

Trondheim

gen

Oslo

Stockholm

Gothenburg

DENMARK

Aarhus
Copenhagen
Malmö

Hamburg

Bremen

Hanover   Berlin

GERMAN EMPIRE

Leipzig   Dresden

Nuremberg

PROTECTORATE
OF BOHEMIA
AND MORAVIA

ttgart   Brünn

Munich

Innsbruck

ENSTEIN

Salzburg

Vienna

Graz

Venice

Verona   Trieste

Ljubljana

Zagreb

Bologna

orence

Zara

SAN MARINO

Perugia

ITALY

Rome

Naples   Bari

Palermo   Messina

Sicily   Catania

Taranto

MALTA
(Br.)

Murmansk

Archangel

Perm

BALTIC
SEA

Turku

Helsinki

Hangö

Tallinn

Vyborg

Leningrad

UNION OF

Nizhniy
Novgorod
Volga

Pskov

Riga

Moscow

Kuybyshev

SOVIET

Daugavpils

Vilnius   Vitebsk

Smolensk

Tula

Königsberg

Danzig

Stettin

Posen

Minsk

Kursk

Saratov

SOCIALIST

Odel

Vistula

Lodz

Warsaw

Brest

Elbe

Breslau

GENERAL
GOVERNMENT

Prague

Cracow

L'vov

Kiev

Kharkov

REPUBLICS

Vinnitsa

Dnieper

Astrakhan

Volga

SLOVAKIA

Bratislava

Kassa

Dniester

Dnepropetrovsk

Rostov

Danube

Debrecen

Budapest

HUNGARY

Kolozsvár

Iaşi

Kishinev

Odessa

Szeged

Pécs

Novi Sad

Timişoara

Braşov

ROMANIA

Sebastopol

BLACK SEA

YUGOSLAVIA

Belgrade

Bucharest

Danube Ruse

Tbilisi

Split

Sarajevo

Mostar

Nish

BULGARIA

Varna

Sofia

Burgas

Yerevan

Tirana

ALBANIA

Skoplje

Plovdiv Edirne

Istanbul

Trabzon

IRAN

Ioannina

Ankara

TURKEY

GREECE

Izmir

Mosul

IRAQ

Patrai

Athens

Adana

Euphrates

Tigri

SEA

DODECANESE
(It.)

SYRIA
(Fr. Mandate)

CYPRUS
(Br.)

Nicosia

Crete

Damascus

177

CZECHOSLOVAKIA, 1938–39

- Frontiers to 1938
- Czechoslovakia to 1938

Lost by Czechoslovakia in 1938:
- to Germany (Munich settlement)
- to Hungary (Vienna Award)
- to Poland

Lost by Czechoslovakia in 1939:
- Annexed by Germany
- Annexed by Hungary

THE NAZI-SOVIET PACT, 1939

- Frontiers, October 1938
- Annexed by Germany, March 1939
- German-occupied Slovakia (March 1939); nominally independent
- Line separating spheres of influence agreed by Nazi-Soviet Pact, 23 August 1939
- Annexed by Germany, September 1939
- Annexed by Germany, as 'General Government'
- Annexed by the USSR, September 1939
- Annexed by Lithuania, October 1939
- Annexed by the USSR, 1940

GERMAN EXPANSION, 1933–39

- Frontiers, 1937
- Land returned to Germany by plebiscite, 1935
- Eastern border of demilitarised zone

German annexations:
- March 1938
- October 1938
- March 1939
- September 1939

German Expansion, 1933-39

1 If the causes of the First World War were a complex and increasingly unstable series of Great Power rivalries which finally debalanced when Austria-Hungary and Russia clashed in the Balkans, the cause of the Second World War was far more clear-cut: Hitler's determination to ensure German domination of Europe. While Hitler, at any rate to begin with, sought only to overturn the punitive terms of the Paris Peace Settlement, his early successes – the overwhelming vote in favour of rejoining Germany by the Saarlanders in the 1935 referendum; rearmament; and the remilitarisation of the Rhine – rapidly persuaded him to widen his ambitions. Support from his fellow Fascist leader Mussolini in Italy, the distractions caused by the Civil War in Spain (1936-39), the chaos unleashed in the Soviet Union by Stalin's purges, and the reluctance of Britain and France to take seriously the threat of German expansion combined to make his task substantially easier.

Between March 1938 and March 1939, Hitler absorbed into his new *Reich* not only Austria and the Sudentenland, both of which could be claimed to be historically German, but, under its new name of the Protectorate of Bohemia and Moravia, the remainder of the Czech lands as well as the Lithuanian Baltic port of Memel with its surrounding lands. The bridging of the Danzig corridor in Poland, which separated East Prussia from the rest of Germany, was the logical next step, duly taken in September 1939.

Czechoslovakia, 1938-39

2 After 1918, the newly created Czechoslovak state was beset by the problems of incorporating successfully the ethnic groups who found themselves within its borders, above all the three-million-plus Germans in the prosperous industrialised Czech territories of Bohemia and Moravia. By 1938, the combination of economic depression and frustration with the Czech-speaking bureaucracy had produced a vigorous movement among them for unification with neighbouring Germany. At the same time, many Slovaks resented Czech domination of industry and government and the second-class status to which they felt inevitably relegated. Despite a mutually intelligible language, Czechs and Slovaks had little common history.

In September 1938, Hitler engineered the take-over of the Sudentenland as well as much of the south of the frontier lands of the Czech half of the country. As with the *Anschluss* with Austria the previous year, Hitler's was not a military operation. Rather, having co-opted Britain and France to approve his annexation in return for a promise of no further German expansion, it was an entirely peaceful manouevre. Its result, however, was to make what remained of the country effectively indefensible, depriving Czechoslovakia not only of her fortifications but, with her abandonment by her allies, of her will to resist. In

addition, the Munich Settlement, as it came to be called, greatly encouraged separatists in Slovakia to break away from the rump Czech lands. By March 1939, they felt secure enough to proclaim an independent Slovakia under German protection. By the middle of the month, Hitler had marched his troops into what remained of the independent Czech lands. Both Poland and Hungary found the prospect of grabbing parts of the dying Czechoslovakia irresistible. Poland seized Cieszyn (Teschen), while Hungary obtained parts of southern Slovakia and Ruthenia, which had substantial Hungarian minorities and had belonged to the Crown Lands of St Stephen before 1918.

The Nazi-Soviet Pact, 1939

3 Although he had loudly condemned appeasement of Germany before Munich, Stalin showed less enthusiasm for confronting Hitler once the Anglo-French capitalists had announced their guarantees of Polish, Romanian and Greek sovereignty following the Nazi occupation of Prague. However, such had been the vocal animosity between Nazi Germany and Soviet Russia that few people were prepared for the sudden reversal of policy announced on 23 August 1939. By then Hitler's demands that Poland agree to the incorporation into his Reich of the overwhelmingly German Free City of Danzig, along with the territory separating it and East Prussia from the rest of Germany, had produced a crisis. The Poles refused to negotiate and were backed up by London and Paris.

Unfortunately, the Western allies were in no position to offer Stalin inducements to co-operate and the Poles, remembering the war of 1919-20, showed no desire to allow Soviet troops into their country. Hitler, however, had no compunction about offering Stalin incentives to adopt a benevolent neutrality in the event of a German-Polish war. In fact, secret protocols to the Nazi-Soviet Non-Aggression Pact of 23 August envisaged the division of the Baltic states and Eastern Europe into German and Soviet spheres. On 1 September, Germany invaded and rapidly overran western Poland. On 17 September, the Red Army moved into the east of the country.

Unlike the German conquerors, the Soviet forces went through the motions of organising plebiscites to confirm the popular will to join the Soviet Union in the areas it occupied. Stalin also demanded that the three Baltic republics permit the entry of Soviet forces to protect them. The following June, as Hitler's troops entered Paris, Lithuania, Latvia and Estonia all "voted" to join the Soviet Union. A rump area of Poland was not annexed directly to the German Reich. Known as the General Government, it was ruled from Cracow.

1940

Hitler's Europe

By the autumn of 1942, Hitler's Germany was at the peak of its power. To the conquests of 1939-40 were added those of Yugoslavia and Greece in the spring of 1941, while in North Africa German troops reached the borders of Egypt, threatening Britain's vital links with India, the Far East and Australia and New Zealand. In June 1941, Hitler had also launched his most ambitious military offensive to date, Operation Barbarossa – the invasion of the Soviet Union.

Hitler's crusade against communism, temporarily shelved by the Nazi-Soviet Pact of 1939, made his invasion of the Soviet Union inevitable. Given his successes by 1941 and the almost complete disorganisation of the Soviet army after Stalin's purges, it must have seemed a realistic prospect, however daunting. Yet in the event the Germans were to be defeated by the immensity of the task they had set themselves: the enormous distances involved, the severity of the Russian winter, the seemingly limitless manpower of the Russians. To begin with, however, it was a remarkable success. The invasion was launched on 22 June with three-million men advancing along a 2,000-mile front. Heavily defended Smolensk, 400 miles behind the Russian frontier, fell within a month. By late November, having taken three-million prisoners and destroyed or captured 18,000 tanks and 20,000 planes, the Germans stood at the gates of Leningrad and Moscow. But as the winter set in, there they remained. In December, the Russians counter-attacked, driving the Germans back more than 100 miles and giving Stalin time to reorganise his shattered defences.

With the Japanese attack on the US Pacific naval base at Pearl Harbor and America's entry into the war against Japan, Hitler then declared war against America. For the first time, the tide was poised to turn against him. The immense resources America was able to deploy combined with the Soviet Union's rapidly increasing military muscle to stretch the Germans to breaking point and beyond. Despite a renewed German offensive against the Soviet Union in the spring of 1942, which saw four-million Axis troops thrust south and west, Hitler was by now fatally over-committed. By October, the German attack had faltered at Stalingrad. As winter closed in once more, half-a-million Axis troops struggled to take the city. By February, the battle had been lost and the starving survivors of 20 German divisions surrendered. It had been the greatest battle in history, claiming one million lives.

But if short-lived, the Nazi re-ordering of Europe was significant. Through a mixture of racial extermination, deportations and boundary adjustments, the Germans tried to establish a new system of states in Europe. The key difference to any previous system was that no freedom was to be permitted to Germany's allies or satellites even if they retained a nominal independence. Vichy France and Denmark, for example, were both permitted self-government, the former until November 1942, the latter until November 1943. Poland, by contrast, was permitted no trace of autonomy after 1939. But even territories with nominal self-government imposed Nazi measures, especially against Jews, which some (such as Vichy France) did with more enthusiasm than the Germans themselves might have expected. These states were also obliged to co-ordinate their economies with Germany's war effort and to provide forced labour in German factories to fill in for German soldiers at the front. These war-time measures foreshadowed the way in which Nazi planners expected to direct a Europe-wide New Order after their final victory.

10°   20°   30°   40°   50°   60°

NORWAY

Narvik

Trondheim

SWEDEN

FINLAND

Murmansk

Archangel

gen

Oslo

Turku   Viipuri

Helsinki   Leningrad

UNION OF

Molotov

60°

Stockholm

Reval

Gothenburg

Pskov

Gorkiy   Volga

SOVIET

Kuybyshev

Aarhus

Copenhagen

Malmö

BALTIC
SEA

Riga

REICHSKOMMISSARIAT

Dünaburg

Vitebsk

Smolensk

Moscow

Tula

SOCIALIST

Saratov

50°

DENMARK

Wilna

OSTLAND

Minsk

Königsberg

Danzig

Hamburg

Bremen

Stettin

Hanover   Berlin

Vistula

Posen

Odet

Warsaw   Brest

Kursk

Don

Stalingrad

REPUBLICS

Volga

Astrakhan

Leipzig   Dresden

nkfurt

ERMAN EMPIRE

Elbe

Lodz

Breslau

GENERAL
GOVERNMENT

REICHSKOMMISSARIAT

Kiev

Kharkov

Dnepropetrovsk

Rostov

Nuremberg

PROTECTORATE
OF BOHEMIA
AND MORAVIA

Prague

Cracow

Lemberg

Vinnitsa

UKRAINE

ttgart

Brünn

SLOVAKIA

Kassa

Dnieper

Munich

ENSTEIN

Danube

Vienna

Bratislava

Salzburg

Graz

Budapest

Debrecen

Dniester

Transnistria

Iași

Chișinău

Odessa

Innsbruck

Lubiana

Trieste

Pécs

HUNGARY

Szeged

Kolozsvár

Venice

Verona

Zagreb

Banat

Timișoara

Brașov

CROATIA

Újvidék

Belgrade

ROMANIA

Sebastopol

BLACK   SEA

Bologna

rence

Zara

SAN MARINO

Spalato

Perugia

Sarajevo

SERBIA

Bucharest

Danube   Ruse

Tiblisi

Rome

Mostar

MONTENEGRO

Nish

BULGARIA

Varna

Burgas

Yerevan

40°

ITALY

ALBANIA

Sofia

Plovdiv

Edirne

Istanbul

Trabzon

IRAN

Naples   Bari

Tirana

Skopje

Ankara

TURKEY

Mosul

IRAQ

Palermo   Messina

Sicily   Catania

Ioannina

GREECE

Thessaloníki

Izmir

Adana

Euphrates

Tigris

SEA

MALTA
(Br.)

Patrai

Athens

DODECANESE
(It.)

Crete

CYPRUS
(Br.)

Nicosia

SYRIA
(Fr. Mandate)

LEBANON

Damascus

ROMANIA, 1940-41

- Romania, late 1940

Territory lost by Romania in 1940:
- to Hungary
- to Bulgaria
- to USSR (regained 1941)
- Territory occupied by Romania, 1941
- German Empire and territories under German military administration
- Frontiers, 1942

2

THE BALKANS, 1941-42

- Yugoslavia, to 1941
- Greece, to 1941
- To Germany, 1941
- To Italy, 1941
- To Hungary, 1941
- To Bulgaria, 1941
- Governed by Italy, from 1941
- Under German military administration
- German-occupied
- Italian-occupied
- Frontiers,1942

3

THE GERMAN INVASION OF THE USSR, 1941-42

- Western frontier of the USSR in 1941 before German invasion

Territorial gains, 1941:
- to Finland
- to Romania
- to Germany
- Under German administration

Maximum extent of penetration into USSR:
- 1941
- 1942
- Frontiers, 1942

4

Italian Expansion from 1939

1 Following the Italian occupation of Albania on Good Friday 1939, Mussolini hoped for further Italian expansion into the Balkans. Playing on Italy's Roman heritage and the medieval empires of Venice and Genoa in the Adriatic and eastern Mediterranean, the fascist regime ringingly asserted the Mediterranean to be Mare Nostrum ("Our Sea"). It also hoped to link the Dodecanese, Italian since 1912, through a corridor of Italian-controlled islands with Italy proper.

However, Mussolini's ambitions could only be realised with German aid, as his bungled invasion of Greece in October 1940 made clear. In April 1941 the German army destroyed both Yugoslav and Greek resistance and placed western Croatia and much of Greece under Italian occupation. The following year, Italy also occupied a swathe of French territory between the Mediterranean and Switzerland as well as the island of Corsica.

Romania, 1940-41

2 Like other weak states in Eastern Europe, Romania came increasingly under German domination in the late 1930s. But German influence did little to diminish long-standing rivalries between these ostensible allies of Hitler. Hungary, for example, aspired to recover territories lost at Trianon (*see* map 5, page 175). The Nazi-Soviet Pact also conspired to weaken Romania: Hitler refused to support Romania when Stalin demanded that she cede Bessarabia to the Soviet Union in June 1940. Taking advantage of Romania's evident weakness, Hungary then demanded that Transylvania be returned. Germany and Italy mediated between their allies and on 30 August 1940 under the Vienna Award gave Hungary a finger of territory from the northwest towards Braşov. At the same time, Bulgaria also recovered southern Dobruja. The effect of these truncations was to leave Romania more dependent on Germany but anxious to recover territory where she could. Hitler's invasion of the Soviet Union gave Romania the chance not only to recover Bessarabia but to seize Transnistria, both of which she held until 1944.

The Balkans, 1941-42

3 The Balkan states had not figured greatly in Hitler's strategy. The role of minor satrapies in the future New Order was the best they could hope for. However, Italy's ambitions in the area, which considerably outstripped her abilities to put them into practice, forced Hitler's hand, though at the same time Hitler was conscious of the need to protect his flank for his invasion of the Soviet Union. In March 1941, a coup d'etat saw the overthrow of the Yugoslav government by one more favourable to the Allies. In April, Hitler ordered the invasion of Yugoslavia, which capitulated within 10 days. The German army went on to drive the British out of Greece.

Yugoslavia was divided into zones of occupation shared between Germany, Italy, Hungary and Bulgaria. Germany annexed northern Carinthia and Slovenia but Italy took the capital, Lubiana. Hungary recovered Bácska while Bulgaria occupied the bulk of Macedonia. The Germans established the so-called "Independent State of Croatia" led by the local Fascist leader, Ante Pavelić. Italy took over much of Croatia's coastal territories while Germany occupied the inland areas. Partisan warfare limited the effective control of Pavelić's government, which needed German and Italian forces to prop it up. Its savage atrocities against Serbs, Jews and other minorities made the Croatian regime notorious. A collaborative regime under Nedić was established in a rump Serbia. Greece was largely occupied by Italian forces, with the Germans controlling Athens and Thessaloniki as well as some Aegean islands and Crete. Nonetheless, the increasing success of partisan guerrilla forces coupled with the shortage of German troops to garrison the Balkans meant that large areas were effectively outside Axis control.

The German Invasion of the USSR, 1941-42

4 The occupation and exploitation of the western Soviet Union had long been the goal of Hitler's *Lebensraum* policy. Although German forces never reached the line from Archangel to Astrakhan which Hitler set as the eastern boundary of his future empire, the organisation and exploitation of the occupied territories was started. A fluid area immediately behind the front line was under military administration, but two Reichskommisariats were established: *Reichskommisariat Ostland* administered the territories of the three former Baltic States plus Belorussia; *Reichskommissariat Ukraine* administered the bulk of the Ukraine. (The Crimea remained under military administration.)

In practice, the wartime situation, partisan resistance and Soviet military recovery meant that the German plans to exploit these regions were hardly begun. Only the "negative" policy of mass extermination of Jews and other groups targeted as enemies by the Nazis was carried out on a huge scale. Apart from inflicting enormous loss of life and massive damage to property, the German occupation of Russia left no traces on the ground. After the expulsion of the Germans, the Soviet forces rapidly restored the former Soviet administration, albeit in areas racked by depopulation.

Like the Romanians, the Finns took advantage of the German invasion to recover territory lost to the Soviet Union in 1940, though they advanced only to the border as it had been before the Winter War of 1939-40 in which the Finns, though heavily outnumbered, successfully repulsed a Russian offensive before being obliged by sheer weight of numbers to sue for peace and yield the southeastern corner of the country to Stalin.

1942

Cold War Europe

The Allies had considered the question of the post-war order in Europe as early as 1943. At Tehran in November that year, Churchill and US President Roosevelt had agreed with Stalin that should Hitler be defeated the Soviet Union would be permitted to return to its 1941 borders, thus tacitly allowing Stalin to retain his gains under the Nazi-Soviet Pact of 1939. At subsequent Allied conferences – Yalta in February 1945 and, in the immediate aftermath of the war, Potsdam – Britain and the United States went further still, agreeing that the Soviet Union be allowed to treat the Eastern European territories its army had conquered as belonging to a Soviet sphere of influence. Whatever misgivings the Allies may have felt, and however much they may later have claimed that they were in no position to refuse Stalin's demands, in allowing the Soviet Union to dominate Eastern Europe, the map of the continent was radically transformed following Hitler's defeat.

The most striking result was the shrinking of Germany, with Poland the principal beneficiary, and the division of what remained into two countries. West Germany (the Federal Republic) was formed from the American, French and British areas of occupied Germany, East Germany (the Democratic Republic) from the Soviet occupied zone (see map 2, page 186). The former German capital, Berlin, followed this pattern in miniature. As significant, however, was the swallowing whole by the Soviet Union of practically all those states granted independence by the Versailles Settlement after the First World War. Thus Estonia, Latvia and Lithuania and the Ukraine were all incorporated into the Soviet Union, as was Bessarabia, given up by Romania (on Hitler's orders) to the Soviet Union in 1940, seized back by it in 1941 and retaken by Stalin in 1944. Both Poland and Czechoslovakia were revived, though where the latter was reformed largely as it had been in 1919, the former was granted Silesia and Pomerania, areas long inhabited almost exclusively by Germans, and the southern part of East Prussia and Danzig (Gdańsk); but Poland lost vast territories on her eastern border to the Soviet Union. At the same the Soviet Union occupied northern East Prussia, including Königsberg (Kaliningrad). But rather than incorporate the region into neighbouring Lithuania it became part of Russia itself, creating an anomaly of some strategic significance after the collapse of the Soviet Union in 1991 (see page 188). Hungary, meanwhile, was restored to the borders established by the Treaty of Trianon (see map 5, page 175). Yugoslavia, too, was reformed. Austria was detached from Germany and restored to independence, albeit initially under a Russian-sponsored government recognised only reluctantly by the western powers. In elections held in November 1945 a democratic government was returned and Austria gradually moved away from Soviet influence.

The two zones of Germany followed wholly divergent paths: while denazification in the west followed the Austrian model, with the first free elections permitted in January 1946, in the east the Soviets moved quickly to eradicate all pre-war political parties other than the communists, simultaneously stripping the country of industrial plunder for war reparation. Much the same was true of the rest of Eastern Europe. Indeed by 1949 it was clear that Stalin had created what was in effect a massive extension of the Soviet Empire, as well as a substantial buffer zone between the Soviet Union proper and the West. Western-Soviet relations were plunged into a freeze from which they would not emerge for decades: the Cold War. In escaping Nazi occupation, much of Europe had simply exchanged one tyranny for another.

NORWAY

Trondhjem

Narvik

SWEDEN

Oslo

Stockholm

Gothenburg

FINLAND

Turku

Helsinki
Porkkala

Tallinn

Murmansk

Archangel

Leningrad

Vyborg

Pskov

UNION OF

Perm

DENMARK

Aarhus
Copenhagen

Malmo

BALTIC
SEA

Daugavpils

Riga

Vilnius

Kaliningrad

Gdańsk

Moscow

Gorkiy
Volga

SOVIET

Kuybyshev

Hamburg

Bremen

Hanover

GERMAN
DEMOCRATIC
REPUBLIC

Berlin
(under four-
power control)

Poznań

POLAND

Warsaw

Brest

Minsk

Vitebsk

Smolensk

Tula

Kursk

SOCIALIST

Saratov

Leipzig

Dresden

Łódź

Wrocław

Elbe

Odra

Vistula

Prague

Nuremberg

tgart

unich

CZECHOSLOVAKIA

Brno

Danube

Vienna

Salzburg

AUSTRIA
(under four-
power control)

Graz

Bratislava

Budapest

Cracow

Lvov

Košice

Debrecen

HUNGARY

Szeged

Pécs

Kiev

Vinnitsa

Dnieper

Dnepropetrovsk

Kharkov

Dniester

Iaşi

Kishinev

REPUBLICS

Volga

Astrakhan

Rostov

Innsbruck

ENSTEIN

FREE STATE
OF TRIESTE

Venice

Verona

Ljubljana

Zagreb

Novi Sad

Trieste

Belgrade

YUGOSLAVIA

ROMANIA

Timişoara

Cluj

Braşov

Bucharest

Danube Ruse

Odessa

Sevastopol

BLACK SEA

Bologna

rence

Zadar

SAN MARINO

Perugia

Split

Mostar

Sarajevo

Niš

Sofia

Varna

ITALY

Rome

Naples

Bari

Taranto

ALBANIA

Tirana

Skopje

BULGARIA

Plovdiv

Edirne

Burgas

Thessaloniki

Istanbul

Ankara

Trabzon

Tbilisi

Yerevan

IRAN

TURKEY

Palermo

Messina

Catania

Sicily

Ioannina

GREECE

Patraí

Athens

Izmir

Adana

Euphrates

Tigris

Mosul

IRAQ

MALTA
(Br.)

SEA

Crete

CYPRUS
(Br.)

Nicosia

LEBANON

SYRIA

1 POST-WAR POPULATION MOVEMENTS

FINLAND

400
Finns and Karelians
1944

NORWAY
SWEDEN

60
Estonians
1944

40
Estonians
1944-45

(to the West)

90
Latvians
1944

100
Latvians
1944-45

50
Lithuanians
1944

80
Lithuanians
1944-45

(to Siberia and Central Asia)

DENMARK

U.S.S.R.

2500
Russians
1946-50

(to U.K., America, and South Africa)

8050
Germans
1944-45

POLAND

1850
Germans
1945-52

3500
Poles
1945-52

525
Germans
1943-44
(to Germany)

GERMANY

960
Displaced Persons
1947-51

2900
Germans
1945-47

1900
Czechs
1945-47

CZECHOSLOVAKIA

500
Ukranians
1946-47

1500
Poles
1945-46

(to Siberia and Central Asia)

600
Crimean Tartars
1944-45

AUSTRIA

100
Slovakians
1946-47

250
Germans
1945-47

200
Hung.
1946-47

HUNGARY

60
Slovaks
1946-47

300
Germans
1945-48

40
Serbs, Croats
1946

40
Hung.
1946

ROMANIA

375
Germans
1944-49
(to Germany)

300
Italians
1945-48

ITALY

YUGOSLAVIA

400
Serbs, Montenegrins
1945-47

BULGARIA

ALBANIA

160
Turks
1950-52

(to Israel)

GREECE

TURKEY

POST-WAR POPULATION MOVEMENTS **1**
— Boundaries in 1947
All numbers of peoples are in thousands

(Berlin inset, top right)

R. Havel

REINICKENDORF

Falkensee

Tegel

SPANDAU

TIE

CHARLOTTENB

Gatow

WILMERSDORF

ZEHLENDORF

S

BERLIN, 1945-90

- American sector
- British sector
- French sector
- Soviet sector
- — City borders
- — The Berlin Wall, 1961-89
- — Autobahn
- — International railway
- ✈ Airport
- ■ Headquarters
- ☐ Allied H.Q.
- → Air corridor

(Germany/Austria zones map, bottom)

USSR

Kaliningrad

Hamburg
Bremen

Szczecin

NETHERLANDS

Essen
Dortmund

Düsseldorf

Cologne

BELGIUM

Bonn

(Zones economically united in 1948)

Potsdam

Berlin

(German Democratic Republic from 1949)

P O L A N D

Leipzig

Dresden

Wrocław

GERMANY

LUXEMBOURG

Saar
(Added to economically united zones in 1949)

Frankfurt am Main

Nuremberg

C Z E C H O S L O V A K I A

FRANCE

Stuttgart

Munich

Linz

Salzburg

Vienna

SWITZERLAND

A U S T R I A

Graz

H U N G A R Y

ROMANIA

ITALY

YUGOSLAVIA

FREE TERRITORY OF TRIESTE

AUSTRIA AND GERMANY, 1945-55

- — Frontiers, 1947
- — Boundaries between zones of occupation
- American zones
- British zones
- French zones
- Soviet zones
- Jointly occupied cit
- Lost by Germany, 19
- — The Federal Republ of Germany from 19
- — The Saar, 1949

(locator inset with regions 1, 2, 3, 4)

Post-War Population Movements

1 The erasure of the Nazi map of Europe involved vast movements of populations. Germans were expelled from Czechoslovakia and Poland (making the latter an overwhelmingly Polish society for the first time), while many ethnic Germans fled from Yugoslavia, Hungary, Romania, the Baltic States and the Soviet Union. Large-scale German emigration also occurred from France, Belgium and Holland. In all, around 10 million Germans reached the Western zones of occupation, but as many as three million may have died en route. At the same time, several million Russians who had made their way westward during the war were returned to the Soviet Union, as had been agreed at Yalta, many to certain death. Similarly, many thousands of Yugoslavs who had chosen the wrong side in the Partisan war were returned to the new Communist Yugoslav government headed by the successful guerrilla leader, Tito. In Finland, around 400,000 Finns were displaced by the Soviet occupation of Karelia. In the Baltic states, the Soviet government forcibly uprooted 200,000 Balts – an equal number had fled to Germany – and compulsorily resettled or exiled minorities suspected of collaborating with the Germans. About one million "Displaced Persons" of many nationalities were resettled in a variety of western countries. Many Jewish survivors of the Holocaust made their way to Palestine (Israel from May 1948).

Austria and Germany, 1945-55

2 The original hope of the Western Allies was that Germany, once cleansed of Nazism, would be established as a united democratic state. As proposed at the Tehran Conference and agreed at the Yalta Conference in February 1945, the Allies divided Germany and Austria into zones of occupation. The plans, anticipating the advance of the Soviet army from the east and the British and Americans from the west, allotted the eastern part of Germany to the Russians, the north of Germany to the British and southern Germany to the Americans. Berlin was to be under tripartite control. An American proposal for a corridor linking Berlin to the British and American zones was not accepted. At Yalta, it was also agreed that France be allocated an occupation zone, with the British and American sectors reduced to accommodate it, and a sector of Berlin. Similar plans were agreed for the occupation of Austria.

It rapidly became clear, however, that Stalin's intentions toward eastern Germany were wholly at variance with the West's goals for western Germany. Stalin acted almost at once to ensure Communist dominance in his zone, sponsoring the German Communist party – which was relaunched as the Socialist Unity Party in April 1946 – and suppressing all other political organisations by November 1947. As it became clear that the western and eastern halves of the country were destined for separate futures, so relations between the former Allies deteriorated. Germany rapidly became one of the major theatres of conflict in the Cold War, as the growing hostility came to be called, with Berlin the focal point as Stalin strove in the winter of 1948-49 to force the Western Allies out of the city (*see* map 3, below). In September 1949, the Western Allies, abandoning for good hopes of rapprochement with Stalin, announced the creation of the Federal Republic of Germany. Not to be outdone, the next month the Soviet government sponsored the creation of the German Democratic Republic. Both claimed to be the sole legitimate government of Germany.

Austria fared better. Despite Soviet successes elsewhere in Eastern Europe in promoting Communism, they were unable do likewise in Austria. As democracy was re-established, so the occupying forces withdrew. Under the 1955 Treaty of Independence, the last of the occupying troops left, with Austria in turn, at Soviet insistence, accepting irrevocable neutrality and renouncing all rights to renewed *Anshcluss* with Germany.

Berlin, 1945-90

3 Although firmly within the Soviet zone of post-war Germany, Berlin, capital of Germany since 1871, was divided between all four occupying powers. The existence of a Western-controlled island in Soviet territory became an increasing anomaly in Stalin's eyes. Once the economic and monetary division of Germany was sealed in June 1948, Stalin acted to try to push the Western Allies out of their three city zones by blockading Berlin from June 1948 until the spring of 1949. In response, the Western Allies launched an airlift of fuel and food which saved their part of the city from starvation and surrender. West Berlin then entered a twilight period in which, though self-governing, it remained an occupied city. Its isolation increased with the building of the Berlin Wall in 1961. It was the breaching of the Wall in November 1989 that signalled not only the end of the divided city, but the death-knell of the GDR itself.

Trieste, 1947-54

4 In the spring of 1945, both British forces from northern Italy and Tito's partisan forces raced through the disintegrating German armies intent on seizing the port-city of Trieste at the head of the Adriatic. Although the city had an Italian majority, it contained a large Slav minority and its hinterland was largely Slovene-speaking. In the summer of 1945 there was a tense stand-off between the British and Tito's forces. The Partisans could see little reason why their Western ally was supporting the claims of their erstwhile Italian enemies. Trieste threatened to be the first flashpoint of the embryonic Cold War. Only in 1954 was a compromise grudgingly agreed granting the city and a narrow strip of land linking it to the rest of Italy but leaving Trieste still hemmed in by Yugoslav territory. A more amicable agreement was signed in 1979. With the outbreak of the Yugoslav War in 1991, however, some Serb militants announced a revived claim to Trieste.

1949

Map legend (TRIESTE, 1947-54)

- Yugoslavia to 1941
- Eastern frontier of Italy, 1941-43
- Gained by Yugoslavia, 1945/47
- Italy, 1947
- The Free State of Trieste, 1947-54
- Zona A
- Zona B
- Italian-Yugoslav frontier from 1954

2005

The Aftermath of the Soviet Union

The post-war borders of Europe proved remarkably resilient: for 40 years after 1949 there were no major changes to the European map. But the stability resulted not from affection but from mutual hostility, in the form of the Cold War. Eastern Europe was dominated by the communist Soviet Union, which imposed on it a repressive and economically backward rule. Western Europe, by contrast, was broadly democratic and economically vigorous. These divisions were underlined by rival military and economic blocs: NATO, the EEC and EFTA in the West; and the Warsaw Pact and COMECON in the East.

The most potent symbol of this division was Germany – democratic in the west, communist in the east – and above all its former capital, Berlin, since 1961 literally divided in two by the Berlin Wall. It was the fall of the Wall in November 1989 that heralded the end of the post-war division of Europe and the disintegration of the Soviet Union. In the wake of communist rule, no fewer than 22 new countries in eastern Europe and the former Soviet Union emerged, including the three Baltic states, Belarus, Ukraine, Moldova, Georgia, Azerbaijan and Armenia. Along with new freedom, however, the removal of the communist stranglehold allowed old hatreds to breathe. Armenia went to war with Azerbaijan over Nagorno-Karabakh, and Czechoslovakia split into the Czech Republic and Slovakia. Break-away movements also emerged: Transnistria declared independence from Moldova; Chechnya declared its independence from Russia; and Crimea sought to break away from Ukraine.

The pattern of strife and centrifuge was most extreme in Yugoslavia, which in 1991 simply disintegrated under pressure from the long-suppressed rivalries of its ethnic groups. In June of that year the republics of Slovenia and Croatia declared their independence, prompting Serbian forces to attack them both. The war in Croatia lasted for seven months. In April 1992 full-scale civil war broke out between Serbs, Croats and Muslims in newly independent Bosnia-Herzegovina. Peace was restored only in November 1995, leaving a fragile Bosnian state divided between the three races. In the Serbian province of Kosovo, NATO intervened in 1999 to halt the Serb slaughter of the majority ethnic-Albanian population. Kosovo was left in a state of limbo, in theory still part of Yugoslavia, in practice administered by the international community. Macedonia, too, which remained uneasily free of fighting after its declaration of independence in 1992, suffered an ethnic-Albanian insurgency in 2001.

While the euphoria following the fall of the Berlin Wall took only a few years to evaporate, the post-cold war experience of Europe has been marked by triumph as well as tribulation. The EU has added new member-states, eight of which were formerly within the Soviet sphere of influence, and is slated to add more. Between 2003 and 2005, two former Soviet satellites shook off corrupt and authoritarian governments by peaceful democratic means. During the same period, however, the process of ratifying the proposed EU constitution stalled.

By 2005, therefore, Europe had cause for both celebration and gloom. Open warfare had ended, but parts of Europe were beset by instability, poverty, and ethnic tensions. The east remained poorer than the west, but had made strides towards liberal democracy; the west had welcomed the east into the EU, but had not absorbed all immigrants into its societies. The wars were over, but peace proved difficult.

NORWAY

SWEDEN

FINLAND

Narvik

Trondhjem

Oslo

Turku

Helsinki

Vyborg

Murmansk

Archangel

Perm

St Petersburg

Stockholm

Tallinn

ESTONIA

Pskov

Nizhniy
Novgorod

Volga

Gothenburg

Riga

LATVIA

Daugavpils

Moscow

Samara

DENMARK

Århus

Copenhagen

Malmö

BALTIC
SEA

LITHUANIA

Vilnius

RUS.FED.
Kaliningrad

Vitsyebsk

Smolensk

Tula

RUSSIAN FEDERATION

Saratov

Hamburg

Gdańsk

Minsk

BELARUS

Kursk

Bremen

GERMANY

Berlin

Szczecin

Elbe

Hanover

POLAND

Poznań

Oder

Brest

Don

Leipzig

Dresden

Łódź

Warsaw

KAZAKHSTAN

Frankfurt

Wrocław

Vistula

Kiev

Kharkiv

Volga

Nuremberg

Prague

Cracow

Stuttgart

CZECH REPUBLIC

Brno

L'viv

UKRAINE

Dnieper

Astrakhan

Munich

Danube

Vienna

SLOVAKIA

Košice

Vinnytsya

Dnipropetrovs'k

Salzburg

Bratislava

Debrecen

Dniester

Rostov

Innsbruck

AUSTRIA

Budapest

MOLDOVA

LIECHTENSTEIN

Graz

HUNGARY

Szeged

Iaşi

Chişinău

Odesa

SLOVENIA

Zagreb

Pécs

ROMANIA

Crimea

Venice

Trieste

Ljubljana

CROATIA

Novi Sad

Timişoara

Braşov

Sevastopol

Verona

Bologna

Zadar

BOSNIA
HERZEGOVINA

Belgrade

Bucharest

Ruse

BLACK SEA

GEORGIA

CHECHNYA

Florence

SAN MARINO

Sarajevo

Danube

Varna

Tbilisi

AZERBAIJAN

ITALY

Perugia

Split

Mostar

SERBIA & MONTENEGRO

Niš

Sofia

Burgas

ARMENIA

Yerevan

Rome

KOSOVO

BULGARIA

NAGORNO-
KARABAKH

IRAN

Naples

Bari

Taranto

ALBANIA

Tirana

Skopje

MACEDONIA

Plovdiv

Edirne

Istanbul

Ankara

Trabzon

Palermo

Messina

Sicily

Catania

Ioannina

GREECE

Thessaloniki

Izmir

TURKEY

Euphrates

Tigris

Mosul

IRAQ

SEA

MALTA

Patra

Athens

Adana

Syria

SYRIA

CYPRUS

Nicosia

LEBANON

Crete

189

EUROPEAN ECONOMIC BLOCS, 1947-2005

— Benelux customs union, 1947

Council for Mutual Economic Assistance (COMECON)

COMECON members, 1947

subsequent members

YUGO. countries which broke up, 1990–93

The European Free Trade Association (EFTA)

— EFTA members, late 1972

The European Economic Area (EEA)

EEA members, April 1997

The European Union

EEC members, 1957

joined, Jan. 1973

joined, Jan. 1981

joined, Jan. 1986

admitted Oct. 1990 (East Germany)

joined, Jan. 1995

joined, Jan. 2004

★ scheduled to become members, Jan. 2007

★ official candidate countries

★ potential candidate countries

ICELAND

NORWAY SWEDEN FINLAND

ESTONIA
LATVIA
LITHUANIA
RUS. FED.

SOVIET UNION

DENMARK BELARUS

UNITED KINGDOM
IRELAND

NETHER-LANDS EAST GERMANY POLAND UKRAINE

GERMANY CZECH REP. *CZECHOSLOVAKIA* SLOVAKIA MOLDOVA

BELGIUM LUX.

FRANCE LIECT. AUSTRIA HUNGARY ROMANIA

SWITZ. SLOVENIA CROATIA

MONACO *YUGOSLAVIA* SERBIA & BULGARIA

ANDORRA SAN MARINO *BOSNIA & HERZ.* MONT. MAC.

TURKEY

ITALY ALBANIA GREECE

PORTUGAL SPAIN

customs union with EU effective from 1 Jan. 1996

GIBRALTAR MALTA CYPRUS

SERBIA Niš

Novi Pazar Leskovac Pirot

MONTENEGRO Mitrovica BULGARIA

Podgorica Priština

KOSOVO
(occupied by NATO forces administered by UN) Vranje

Shkodër Kumanovo

Kukës Tetovo Skopje Kočani

A L B A N I A MACEDONIA

Durrës Tirana Kičevo Strumica

Prilep

Elbasan Ohrid Bitola

Lake Ohrid *Lake Prespa* *Vardar*

ALBANIANS IN THE BALKANS, 1998-2005

Overwhelmingly Albanian-inhabited areas outside Albania

UN administered Kosovo since June 1999, ethnic Albanians seeking independence

Demilitarized zone since June 1999

— Notional frontier of Yugoslavia, 2001

Approximate extent of Albanian guerilla activity, 2001

— Frontiers, 2005

Korçë

Vlorë

G R E E C E

Gjirokastër

CENTRAL AND EASTERN EUROPE, 1990-2005

— Western border of the USSR to 1991

- - - Former satellite states of the USSR

Former GDR: to the Federal Republic of Germany, 1990

Independent, 1991

Independent, 1992

Independant, 1993

Yugoslavia to 1991

Czechoslovakia to 1993

Chechenia-Ingushetia, November 1991

Independence declared after 1990 but not recognised internationally

Independence asserted after 1990

Under foreign occupation (from May 2001)

— Frontiers, 2005

NORWAY Oslo SWEDEN FINLAND

DENMARK Tallinn ESTONIA

Riga LATVIA

(independence declared 1990, recognised 1991)

LITHUANIA Vilnius

RUSSIAN FED.

GERMANY **West Berlin (to 1990)** Berlin

POLAND Warsaw BELARUS Minsk

RUSSIAN FEDERATION Moscow

TATARSTAN

BASHKORTOSTAN

CZECH REPUBLIC Prague

SLOVAKIA Bratislava Kiev

AUSTRIA Budapest U K R A I N E KAZAKHSTAN

SLOVENIA HUNGARY

Zagreb MOLDOVA TRANSNISTRIA

CROATIA *SERBIAN REP. OF BOSNIA* ROMANIA GAGAUZIA

BOSNIA-HERZE-GOVINA Belgrade

Sarajevo Bucharest

HERCEG BOSNA SERBIA & KOSOVO **(occupied by NATO forces, administered by the UN)**

MONTENEGRO Sofia

MONTENEGRO (referendum on separation from Serbia to be held in 2006)

Skopje BULGARIA MACEDONIA

ALBANIA GREECE TURKEY

(at war with invading Russian forces 1994-96; partially successful Russian onslaught 1999, still at war in 2005)

(Ingushetia: joined Russian Federation, December 1992)

CHECHNYA

ABKHAZIA GEORGIA AZERBAIJAN NAGORNO-KARABAKH ARMENIA

(occupied by Armenian/Karabakh forces)

AUSTRIA

Maribor SLOVENIA Ljubljana

Karlovac

Rijeka Sisak

Zadar Knin

ITALY

190

THE BREAK-UP OF YUGOSLAVIA FROM 1991

Yugoslavia to mid-1991

Independent, October 1991

Croatia

Controlled by Croatia after Yugoslav/Serb attack following Croatian independence (October 1991)

Secured as "independent" Krajina by Serb forces, 1992; reoccupied by Croatian forces, 1993-95 (mainly August to October 1995)

Bosnia

Controlled by Bosnia-Herzegovina after Yugoslav/Serb attack following Bosnian independence (April 1992)

Secured as "independent" Serbian Republic of Bosnia (Republic Srpska) by Serb forces (February 1994)

Secured as "independent" Herceg-Bosna by Croat forces (February 1994)

Dividing line between Serb Republic component and Croat-Muslim Federation component of the Confederation of Bosnia-Herzegovina according to terms of the Dayton peace agreement, November 1995

Yugoslavia, (changed name to Serbia and Montenegro in 2003)

Yugoslavia, late 1992

Areas of Serbia and Montenegro where ethnic minorities constitute the majority

Serb majority area with significant minorities

Independent, November 1992

Frontiers, 2005

Central and Eastern Europe, 1990-2005

1 The opening of the Berlin Wall on 9 November 1989 marked the dramatic collapse of the East German regime. Faced with a massive wave of emigration to the west and the collapse of its economy, there was little alternative for the GDR but to unite with the West. The restoration of a united Germany on 3 October 1990 marked the end of the limitations on German sovereignty in force since 1945.

Thereafter events in Eastern Europe took increasingly dramatic turns. On 25 December 1991 the USSR came to an end after many of its constituent republics declared independence. This did not bring peace, however: Armenian forces occupied most of Nagorno-Karabakh, claiming it from neighbouring Azerbaijan; Chechnya declared its independence and suffered two invasions, in 1994 and 1999, aimed at reincorporating it into Russia; and the Russian majority in Transnistria (eastern Moldova) also declared its independence. Meanwhile, Czechoslovakia broke up into the Czech Republic and Slovakia in January 1993 following a Slovak nationalist election victory.

Notwithstanding the strife, there was also cause for cheer. In 2003, the Rose Revolution in Georgia resulted in the ouster of Eduard Shevardnadze's government, widely perceived as corrupt, and its replacement by Mikhail Saakashvilli's. In 2004-2005, the Orange Revolution in Ukraine successfully overturned fraudulent election results in favour of the rightful winner. Eight eastern and central European countries joined the EU, with more on the way. Taken together, these events constituted a westward turn away from the Soviet past.

Unrest in the Balkans after 1991

2 With the death of Tito in 1980 and the end of the Cold War a decade later, the authoritarian and ideological forces holding together the multi-ethic country of Yugoslovia weakened. A resurgence of Serb nationalism, promoted after 1987 by the leader of the Serbian Communist Party, Slobodan Milošević, alarmed the other republics. In Serbia (and Montenegro), the Communist Party repositioned itself as the guardian of national rather than class interests. In Slovenia, with its homogeneous population (90% Slovene), a non-communist nationalist opposition won power and declared independence in 1991.

After a half-hearted attempt to coerce Slovenia back into Yugoslavia at the end of June 1991, a much more serious war broke out in Croatia during that summer. The Serb minority (12%) which formed the majority in areas such as the Krajina refused to accept the idea of Croatian independence. Serbian forces took military action and conquered about one-third of Croatia's territory at the time of independence (June 1991). Unlike Serbia and Croatia, Bosnia lacked a numerically dominant group: Serbs constituted about 31% of the population, Croats 17% and Bosnian Muslims 44%. War broke out in 1992, and with it came the policy of "ethnic cleansing" of populations to create areas with a majority of one ethnic group.

The efforts of international bodies like the UN and EU to resolve the war could not halt the advance of Bosnian Serb forces. By early 1994, their army had occupied more than two-thirds of pre-war Bosnia. More than two million people had been displaced and over 100,000 killed. Against the odds, Bosnia survived. In March 1994 the Bosnian Muslims and Croats formed a fragile federation, and in 1995 Bosnian Serb atrocities against Muslim enclaves provoked NATO to intervene. In November 1995, facing military defeat, Milošević bowed to American-backed pressure to accept a settlement. Serbs, Croats and Muslims were joined in an uneasy federal system, while Bosnian Serbs and Croats sought closer ties with Serbia and Croatia proper.

European Unity, 1947-2005

3 The Second World War gave renewed impetus to the idea of uniting the European states in some form of federal arrangement. The European Recovery Program, begun in 1947, and NATO, established in 1949, represented partial first steps, but the most robust sign of commitment came with the establishment of the European Economic Community (EEC or EC) by the Treaty of Rome in 1957. In 1959, Britain attempted to set up an alternative, the European Free Trade Association (EFTA), but it gradually lost members to the EC. In the Single European Act (SEA), drafted in 1985 and adopted in 1987, the EC agreed to the creation of a single market under which Europe would become a single free-trade zone. Proposals for further integration bore fruit in the Maastricht Treaty (also known as the Treaty of Rome and the Treaty on European Union), which committed the EC to work towards economic and monetary union.

As it moved towards economic and monetary union, Europe moved more slowly towards political union. Along with their economic provisions, the SEA tentatively and the Maastricht Treaty firmly committed the EC to political union. Reflecting this commitment, the EC became the European Union (EU) in January 1994. In 1998-2000, the EU opened accession negotiations with ten formerly communist states; eight have become members and the remaining two are slated to enter in 2007. Meanwhile, the European Constitution, signed in 2004, stalled in the ratification process in 2005, when it was rejected by French and Dutch voters in referenda.

Albanians in the Balkans, 1998-2005

4 When Albania won independence from the Ottoman empire in 1912, over half the Albanian community was left outside its borders, largely in the Yugoslav-controlled regions of Kosovo and Macedonia. In 1998 an ethnic Albanian guerrilla group, the Kosovo Liberation Army (KLA), stepped up its campaign for an independent Kosovo. Serb forces responded with a campaign of ethnic cleansing against the Albanians in 1998-99, but a NATO-led bombing campaign in early 1999 forced the Yugoslav government to back down. Many Kosovo Serbs fled into Serbia proper. In 2001, another ethnic Albanian insurgent group occupied villages in northern Macedonia where much of the population is of Albanian origin; the insurgency ended with the imposition of a NATO ceasefire.

2005

BIBLIOGRAPHY

Listed below are a range of historical and thematic atlases which contain particularly useful maps, and a basic selection of works for further reading:

I. Historical and Thematic Atlases

Alexis, M.G. *Atlas de Géographie et Historique*, Brussels 1900

Atlante Enciclopedico, Storia Antica e Medievale, Milan 1989

Atlante Enciclopedico, Storia Moderna e Contemporanea, Milan 1990

Atlante Storico Illustrato, Novara 1977

Atlas Historiczny Polski, Warsaw 1973

Atlas Istoriya na Bulgariya, Sofia 1975

Atlas of Modern World History, Oxford 1989

Atlas of the Classical World, London 1959

Atlas zur Geschichte, 2 vols. Leipzig 1976

Atlas zur Universalgeschichte, Munich 1980

Bazilevsky, K.V., Golubtsov, A., Zinoviev, M.A. *Atlas Istorii SSR*, Moscow 1952

Beckingham, C.F. *Atlas of the Arab World and the Middle East*, London 1960

Bjørklund, O., Holmboe, H., Røhr, A. *Historical Atlas of the World*, Edinburgh 1970

Brice, C. (ed.) *An Historical Atlas of Islam*, Leiden 1981

Calmette, J. *Atlas Historique II*, Paris 1959

The Collins Atlas of World History, London 1987

Darby, H.C., Fullard, H. (eds.) *The New Cambridge Modern History* vol. XIV: Atlas, Cambridge 1970

Dockrill, M. *Atlas of Twentieth Century World History*, Glasgow 1991

Duby, G. *Atlas Historique Larousse*, Paris 1978

Edwards, R.D. *An Atlas of Irish History*, London 1973

Fox, E. (ed.) *Atlas of European History*, Oxford 1964

Freeman-Grenville, G.S.P. *Atlas of British History*, London 1979

Gilbert, M. *Russian History Atlas*, London 1993

Gilbert, M. *Recent History Atlas 1860-1960*, London 1966

Gilbert, M. *First World War Atlas*, London 1970

Gilbert, M. *Jewish History Atlas*, London 1973

Griess, T.E. (ed.) *Atlas for the Great War*, Wayne, New Jersey, 1986

Grosser Atlas zur Weltgeschichte, Braunschweig 1972

Grosser Historischer Weltatlas, 3 vols., Munich 1972-81

Hazard, H.W. *Atlas of Islamic History*, Princeton 1952

Hilgemann, *Atlas zur Deutschen Zeitgeschichte*, Munich 1986

Hill, D. *An Atlas of Anglo-Saxon England*, Oxford 1981

Keegan, J. *The Times Atlas of the Second World War*, London 1989

Képes Történelmi Atlasz, Budapest 1976

Kinder, H., Hilgermann, W. *DTV Atlas zur Weltgeschichte* 2 vols. Stuttgart 1964 (published in English as *The Penguin Atlas of World History*, London 1974 & 1978)

Kubijovyč, V. (ed.) *Atlas of Ukraine and Adjoining Countries*, Lviv 1937

Mackay, A., Ditchburn, D. (eds.) *Atlas of Medieval Europe*, London 1977

McEvedy, C. *The Penguin Atlas of Modern History*, Harmondsworth, 1979

McEvedy, C. *The Penguin Atlas of Recent History*, Harmondsworth, 1982

McEvedy, C. *The Penguin Atlas of Medieval History*, Harmondsworth, 1977

McEvedy, C. *The Penguin Atlas of Ancient History*, Harmondsworth 1967

Millî Tarih Atlası, Istanbul 1985

Milner-Gulland, R., Dejevsky N. *Cultural Atlas of Russia*, New York 1989

Nelson's Atlas of the Classical World, London 1959

Nelson's Atlas of the Early Christian World, London 1959

Nelson's Atlas of World History, London 1965

Palmer, R.R. (ed.) *Atlas of World History*, Chicago 1965

Parker, G. (ed.), *The Times Atlas of World History*, 4th edtn., London 1993

Pascu, S. *Atlas Istoric*, Bucharest, 1971

Riley-Smith, J.H. (ed.) *The Atlas of the Crusades*, London 1991

Roaf, M. *Cultural Atlas of Mesopotamia and the Ancient Near East*, Oxford 1990

Robinson, F. *Atlas of the Islamic World since 1500*, Oxford 1982

Scarre, C. (ed.) *The Times Atlas of Past Worlds*, London 1988

Scarre, C. *The Penguin Historical Atlas of Ancient Rome*, London 1995

Sellman, R.R. *A Historical Atlas 1789-1971*, London 1971

Shepherd, W.R. *Historical Atlas*, New York 1964

Sinclair, S. *Atlas de Geographie Historique de la Fance et de la Gaule*, Paris 1985

Školský Atlas Československých Dejín, Bratislava 1970

Stembridge, J.H., *The Oxford War Atlas*, London 1941

Talbert, R.J.A. (ed.) *Atlas of Classical History*, London 1985

The Times Atlas of the World, 9th Comprehensive Edition, London 1992

Tarih Atlası, Istanbul 1989

Toynbee, A.J., Myers, E.D. *A Study of History, Historical Atlas and Gazetteer*, Oxford 1959

Treharne, R.F., Fullard, H. (eds.) *Muir's Historical Atlas*, London 1966

Van der Heyden, A.M., Scullard, H.H. *Atlas of the Classical World*, London 1959

Van Der Meer, F., Mohrmann, C. *Atlas of the Early Christian World*, London 1958

Vermaseren, B.A. *Atlas Algemene en Vaderlandse Geschiedenis*, Groningen 1969

Verzameling, R. *Atlas der Algemene en der Belgische Geschiedenis*, Namen 1985

Vicens Vives, J. *Atlas de Historia de España*, Barcelona 1973

Westermann Grosser Atlas zur Weltgeschichte, Brunswick 1976

Whitehouse, D. & R. *Archaeological Atlas of the World*, London 1975

II. General Works

Clogg, R. *A Concise History of Greece*, Cambridge 1992

Cook, M.A. (ed.) *A History of the Ottoman Empire to 1730*, Cambridge 1976

Darby, H.C. (ed.) *An Historical Geography of England before AD1800*, Cambridge 1936 & 1960

East, W.G. *An Historical Geography of Europe*, London 1967

Freeman, E.A. *The Historical Geography of Europe*, London 1882

Grousset, R. *The Empire of the Steppes: A History of Central Asia*, New Brunswick N.J. 1970

Hearder, H. *Italy, A Short History*, Cambridge 1990

Jelavich, B. *History of the Balkans*, Cambridge 1983

Langer, W.L. *An Encyclopedia of World History*, London 1972

Malcolm, N. *Bosnia, A Short History*, London 1994

Mantram, R. *Histoire de l'Empire Ottoman*, Paris 1989

McNeill, W.H. *A World History*, New York 1971

Miquel, A. *L'Islam et sa Civilisation*, Paris 1968

Ostrogorsky, G. *History of the Byzantine State*, Oxford 1969

Parker, W.H. *An Historical Geography of Russia*, London 1968

Pitcher, D.E. *An Historical Geography of the Ottoman Empire*, Leiden 1973

Roberts, J.M. *The Hutchinson History of the World*, revised ed., London 1987

Seltzer, L.E. (ed.) *The Columbia Lippincott Gazetteer of the World*, New York 1952

Smith, C.T. *An Historical Geography of Western Europe before 1800*, revised ed., London & New York 1978

Wanklyn, W. *The Eastern Marchlands of Europe*, London 1941

III. Classical Europe

Boardman, J. (ed.) *The Oxford History of the Classical World*, Oxford 1989

Bury, J.B., Cook, S.A., Adcock, F.E. (eds.) *The Cambridge Ancient History*, Cambridge 1923, 2nd ed. 1982

Cary M., Scullard H.H. *A History of Rome down to the Reign of Constantine*, London 1975

Ferguson, J. *The Heritage of Hellenism*, London 1973

Jones, A.H.M. *The Late Roman Empire* (3 vols) Oxford 1964

Scullard, H.H. *From the Gracchi to Nero*, London & New York 1959

Snodgrass, A. *Archaic Greece*, London 1989

Tarn, W.W. *Alexander the Great*, Cambridge 1948

IV. Dark Ages Europe

Ahzweiler, H. *L'Asie Mineure et les Invasions Arabes, Revue Historique* 1962

Collins R., *Early Medieval Spain: Unity in Diversity 400-1000*, London 1983

James, E. *The Origins of France*, Oxford 1982

McKitterick, R. *The Frankish Kingdoms under the Carolingians 751-987*, London 1983

Musset, L. *Les Invasions: Les Vagues Germaniques*, Paris 1965

Musset, L. *Les Invasions: Le Second Assaut contre l'Europe Chrétienne*, Paris 1971

Thompson, E.A. *A History of Attila and the Huns*, 1948

Vernadsky, G. *Kievan Russia*, New Haven, Conn. 1972

Wallace-Hadrill, J.M. *The Barbarian West 400-1000*

Wood, I. *The Merovingian Kingdoms 450-751*, London 1994

V. Medieval Europe

Barraclough, G. *Medieval Germany*, Oxford 1938 & 1967

Bauml, F.H. *Medieval Civilization in Germany 800-1273*, London 1969

Brooke, C.N.L. *The Twelfth-century Renaissance*

Bury, J.B., Gwatkin, H.M., Whitney, J.P. (eds.) *The Cambridge Medieval History*, Cambridge 1911-

Christiansen, E. *The Northern Crusades*, 1980

Fowler, K. *The Age of Plantagenet and Valois*, New York 1967

Hay, D. *Europe in the Fourteenth and Fifteenth Centuries*, London 1966

Holmes. G. *Europe, Hierarchy and Revolt 1320-1450*, London 1975

Lomax, D.W. *The Reconquest of Spain*, 1978

McKitterick, R. (ed.) *The New Cambridge Medieval History II: 700-900*, Cambridge 1995

Moss, H. St. L.B. *The Birth of the Middle Ages*, Oxford 1935

Phillips, J.R.S. *The Medieval Expansion of Europe*, Oxford 1988

Southern, R.W. *The Making of the Middle Ages*, 1953

VI. Early Modern Europe

Boxer, C.R. *The Portuguese Seaborne Empire 1415-1825*, London 1991

Boxer, C.R. *The Dutch Seaborne Empire 1600-1800*, London 1965

Braudel, F. *The Mediterranean and the Mediterranean World in the age of Philip II*, London 1972

Elliott, J.H. *Europe Divided 1559-98*, London 1968

Elton, G.R. *Reformation Europe 1517-59*, London

Evans, R.J.W. *The making of the Habsburg Monarchy 1550-1700*, Oxford 1979

Fletcher, A. *Tudor Rebellions*, 3rd ed., London 1983

Hale. J.R. *Renaissance Europe*, London 1971

Hatton, R.M. *Europe in the age of Louis XIV*, London 1969

Inalcik, H. *The Ottoman Empire: The Classical Age 1300-1600*, London 1973

Koeningsberger, H.G., Mosse, G.L., Bowler G.Q. *Europe in the sixteenth century*, 2nd ed., London 1989

Lockyer, R. *Habsburg & Bourbon Europe*, Harlow 1974

Parker, G. *The Dutch Revolt*, Harmondsworth, 1977

Parker, G. *Europe in Crisis 1598-1648*, London 1979

Parker, G. *Spain and the Netherlands 1559-1659*, London 1979

Stoye, J. *The Siege of Vienna*, London 1964

Stoye, J. *Europe Unfolding, 1648-88*, London

VII. Modern Europe

Calvocoressi, P. *World Politics since 1945*, 6th edtn., London 1993

Churchill, Winston S. *The Second World War*, London 1948-53

Clark, M. *Modern Italy 1871-1982*, London 1984

Grenville, J. *Europe Reshaped 1848-78*, London

Hobsbawm, E.J. *The Age of Revolution*, London 1962

Hufton, O. *Europe: Privilege and Protest 1730-89*, London 1980

Liddell Hart, B. *History of the Second World War*, London 1970

Rudé, G. *Revolutionary Europe 1783-1815*, London, 1972

Stone, N. *Europe Transformed*, London 1983

Taylor, A.J.P. *The First World War*, London 1963

Thomson, D. *Europe Since Napoleon*, (revised edtn.) London 1966

INDEX

1 HISTORICAL PLACE NAMES

Geographical names vary with time and with language, and there is some difficulty in treating them consistently in an historical atlas which covers Europe from 900 BC to the present day. Over these nearly three-thousand years the same place will often have been known by many different names. We have aimed at the simplest possible approach to the names on the maps, using the index to weld together the variations.

On the maps, forms of names will be found in the following hierarchy of preference:

a English conventional names or spellings, in the widest sense, for all principal places and features, e.g. Moscow, Vienna, Munich, Danube (including those that today might be considered obsolete when these are appropriate to the context, e.g. Saragossa).

b Names that are contemporary in terms of the maps concerned. There are here three broad categories:

i names in the ancient world, where the forms used are classical, e.g. Latin or latinised Greek.

ii Names in the post-medieval modern world, which are given in the form (though not necessarily the spelling) current at the time of the map (e.g. Reval or Revel before 1920, not Tallinn) whose language reflects the sovereignty then existing, e.g. Üsküb (Turkish) rather than Skoplje (Serbian) or Skopje (Macedonian) in maps showing Ottoman rule.

iii Names in the present-day world, where the spelling generally follows that of *The Times Atlas of the World*.

Alternative names and spellings have occasionally been shown in brackets on the maps to aid identification.

2 THE INDEX

The index includes all names appearing on the main maps and all those on the subsidiary maps that are pertinent to the events and developments they illustrate. Names of important places which appear successively on main maps are indexed to their first occurrence only, e.g. "**Bremen** N Germany 48-" indicates that this name will be found on all main maps from page 48 onwards.

Where a place is referred to by two or more different names in the course of the atlas, there will be a corresponding number of main entries in the index. The variant names in each case are given in brackets at the beginning of the entry, their different forms and origins being distinguished by such words as *now*, *later*, *formerly* and others included in the list of abbreviations.

"**Vilna** (*Ger.* Wilna, *Pol.* Wilno, *mod.* Vilnius)" means that the page references to that city on maps dealing with periods when it was known as Vilna follow that entry, but the page references pertaining to it when it had other names will be found under those other names.

Places are located generally by reference to the country in which they lie (exceptionally by reference to island groups or sea areas), this being narrowed down where necessary by location as E(ast), N(orth), C(entral), etc. The reference will normally be to the modern state in which the place now falls unless there is a conventional or historical name which conveniently avoids the inevitably anachronistic ring of some modern names, e.g. Anatolia rather than Turkey.

Though page references are generally kept in numerical order, since this corresponds for the most part with chronological order, they have been rearranged occasionally where the

chronological sequence would be obviously wrong, or in the interests of grouping appropriate references under a single sub-heading.

All variant names and spellings are cross-referenced in the form "**Bourgogne** (Burgundy)", except those which would immediately precede or follow the main entries to which they refer. The bracketed form has been chosen so that such entries may also serve as quick visual indications of equivalence. Thus Bourgogne (Burgundy) means not only "see under Burgundy" but also that Burgundy is another name for Bourgogne.

Reference to the main maps is by page number(s), e.g. 85 or 97-109; to the subsidiary maps it is by page number/map number, e.g. 135/2. All main entries have been given sub-entries in the form of a relevant date or, where possible, of date + event, e.g. "conquered by Clovis, 507".

3 ABBREVIATIONS

a/c	also called
Alb.	Albanian
anc.	ancient
Ar.	Arabic
a/s	also spelled
Bas.	Basque
Bel.	Belorussian
Bibl.	Biblical
Bret.	Breton
Bulg.	Bulgarian
C	Century (when preceded by 17, 18, etc.)
C	Central
Cat.	Catalan
Cr.	Croat
Cz.	Czech
Dan.	Danish
Dut.	Dutch
E	East(ern)
Eng.	English
Est.	Estonian
f/c	formerly called
Finn.	Finnish
form.	former(ly)
Fr.	French
f/s	formerly spelled
Gal.	Galician
Geor.	Georgian
Ger.	German
Gr.	Greek
Hung.	Hungarian
Ir.	Irish
It.	Italian
Lat.	Latin
Latv.	Latvian
Lith.	Lithuanian
Lus.	Lusatian
Maced.	Macedonian
med.	medieval
mod.	modern
N	North(ern)
n/c	now called
Nor.	Norwegian
n/s	now spelled
obs.	obsolete
Pol.	Polish
Port.	Portuguese
Rom.	Romanian
Russ.	Russian
S	South(ern)
s/c	sometimes called
S.Cr.	Serbo-Croat
Serb.	Serbian
Slvk.	Slovak
Slvn.	Slovene
Sp.	Spanish
Sw.	Swedish
Turk.	Turkish
Ukr.	Ukrainian
var.	variant
W	West(ern)
Wel.	Welsh
WW1	First World War
WW2	Second World War

Aachen (*Fr.* Aix-la-Chapelle, *anc.* Aquis Granum) Frankish Kingdom 511, 54/1, 4
Aargau (*Fr.* Argovie) canton of N Switzerland added to Swiss Confederation 1417, 110/1
Aarhus (*n/s* Århus) C Denmark 60-
Abdera NE Greece Greek colony 9C-6C BC, 14/1; in Persian Empire 480 BC, 18/1; Athenian Empire 431 BC, 22/1
Abkhazia breakaway region of NW Georgia 1993, 190/1
Åbo (*Finn.* Turku) SW Finland 77-
Abydos (*a/s* Abydus) NW Anatolia Ionian revolt against Persians 5C BC, 19/2; Athenian Empire 431 BC, 22/1; Second Macedonian War 202 BC, 30/2
Acanthus NE Greece Greek colony 9C- 6C BC, 14/1
Acarnania region of NW Greece 900-800 BC, 10/4; Persian Wars 490-480 BC, 18/3; Corinthian League 337 BC, 22/3; Second Macedonian War 202 BC, 30/2
Achaea (*a/s* Achaia) region of S Greece 900-800 BC, 10/4; Persian Wars 490-480 BC, 18/3; Athenian Empire 431 BC, 22/1; conquered by Rome 146 BC, 30/1; Roman province AD 180, 38/3
Achaean League W Greece Pyrrhus's Empire 295-275 BC, 26/3; Second Macedonian War 202 BC, 30/2
Achaia, Principality of S Greece state of Latin Empire 1190-1270, 86/4, 90/1
A Coruña (Corunna)
Acragas (Akragas)
Adana S Turkey 85-
Adria (Hadria)
Adrianople (*mod.* Edirne, *anc.* Uskudama, *later* Hadrianopolis) NW Turkey Roman Empire 450, 45; 526, 49; Byzantine Empire 527, 54/2; Ottoman Empire 1389, 107/2
Aegae N Greece Athenian Empire 431 BC, 22/1
Aegean Sea Genoese possessions 500, 107/2; First Balkan War 1912, 170/2
Aegyptus Roman diocese of Egypt and Libya 324-337, 42/3
Aenus (*a/s* Aenos, *MGr.* Ainos, *a/s* Enos, *Turk.* Enez, *f/s* Inoz) NW Turkey Greek colony 9C-6C BC, 14/1; Ionian revolt against Persians 5C BC, 19/2; Athenian Empire 431 BC, 22/1; in Ptolemaic Empire 202 BC, 30/2
Aeolians people of Greece and W Anatolia 800 BC, 10/4
Aeolis region of NW Anatolia 900-800 BC, 10/4
Aetolia region of W Greece Persian Wars 490-480 BC, 18/3
Aetolian League W Greece Pyrrhus's Empire 295-275 BC, 26/3; Second Macedonian War 202 BC, 30/2
Africa Roman diocese of NW Africa 285-337, 42/2,3
Africa Proconsularis Roman province of N Africa AD 180, 38/3
Agathe (*mod.* Agde) S France Greek colony 9C-6C BC, 14/1
Agedincum (*mod.* Sens) NE France conquered by Rome 57 BC, 34/2
Agincourt (*Fr.* Azincourt) N France Hundred Years' War, 102/2
Agram (Zágráb)
Agri Decumates district of SE Germany abandoned by Rome 260, 46/1
Agrigento, Agrigentum (Akragas)
Ainos (Aenus)
Aix-la-Chapelle (*Ger.* Aachen, *anc.* Aquis Granum) in Kingdom of Soissons 481, 51/4; East Frankish kingdoms 870, 66/4; annexed by France 1792-3, 146/1
Akkerman (Cetatea Albă)
Ak-Koyunlu Turcoman principality of E Anatolia 1430, 101
Akragas (*a/s* Acragas, *Lat.* Agrigentum, *mod.* Agrigento, *f/c* Girgenti) Greek colony 9C-6C BC, 14/1; Syracusan rule 375 BC, 22/2; Pyrrhus's Empire 295-275 BC, 26/3
Alalia (*a/c* Aleria) E Corsica Etruscan city 6C BC, 14/3
Alans people of the N Caucasus 395-1003, 41-69
Alba region of N Scotland 908, 64
Alba Fucens (*a/c* Alba Fucentia, *mod.* Alba) Roman colony 300 BC, 26/2
Albania subdued by Macedonia 336 BC, 22/3; temporary Aragonese fief

Albanians minority within Serbia 1993, 191/2
Albarrazin district of NE Spain 1086, 79/3
Aldborough (Isurium)
Aldeigjuborg (*mod.* Staraya Ladoga) NW Russia Viking town 9-10C, 66/C
Alemannia S Germany 561 55/4; Frankish territory 565, 62/1
Alemans people of S Germany 565, 52; 54/1
Aleria (*a/c* Alalia) E Corsica Roman Empire 238 BC, 30/1
Alexander's Empire 323 BC, 21, 22/4; successor states 323, 24/4
Alexandria (*Ar.* Al Iskandariyah) N Egypt Ptolemy's Empire 301 BC, 26/1; Byzantine Empire 527, 54/2
Alexandria (*a/c* Alexandria Areion, *mod.* Herat) Afghanistan Seleucid Empire 301 BC, 26/1
Alexandria (*a/c* Alexandria ad Issum, *later* Alexandretta, *mod.* Iskenderun) SE Turkey Seleucid Empire 301 BC, 26/1
Alexandria Troas NW Anatolia Roman Empire 29 BC, 30/3; 55 BC, 34/3
Algecrias SW Spain 80-
Alger (Algiers)
Algeria (*Fr.* Algérie) French from1861-1961, 156-185; independence 1962, 189
Alghero NW Sardinia conquered by Aragonese 1322, 94/2
Algiers (*Fr.* Alger) N Algeria to France 1830, 158/2
Al Iskandariyah (Alexandria)
Allenstein (*Pol.* Olsztyn) NW Poland plebiscite 1920, 174/3
Almeria, Kingdom of Spain Seleucid Empire 301 BC, 26/1; Spain 1086, 79/3
Almohads, Empire of the S Spain 1180, 82/1
Almoravid Empire northern limits in Spain 1115, 82/1
Alpes Cottiae Roman province of France/Italy AD 180, 38/3
Alpes Graiae et Poeninae Roman province of France/Italy AD 180, 38/3
Alpes Maritimae Roman province of France/Italy AD 180, 38/3
Alpuente district of NE Spain 1086, 79/3
Alsace (*Ger.* Elsass) region of E France added to Burgundy by 1477, 106/1; controlled by France 1648, 131/1
Alsace-Lorraine (*Ger.* Elsass-Lothringen) region of E France in German Empire 1871, 166/1; added to France 1919, 175/2
Al Ushbunah (*mod.* Lisbon) C Portugal Muslim conquest by 732, 56; Muslim rule 60-76
Amalfi S Italy conquered by Normans 1127, 79/1
Amaseia (*a/s* Amasia, *mod.* Amasya) NE Anatolia Empire of Pontus 121 BC, 34/4
Ambracia (*mod.* Arta) NW Greece Greek colony 9C-6C BC, 14/1; Persian Wars 490-480 BC, 18/3; Athenian Empire 431 BC, 22/1; in Molossian Kingdom 334 BC, 22/3; Pyrrhus's Empire 295-275 BC, 26/3; Second Macedonian War 202 BC, 30/2
Amiens (Samarobriva)
Amisus (*mod.* Samsun) N Anatolia Greek colony 9C-6C BC, 14/2; Roman Empire 31 BC, 33; in Persian Empire 480, 17; in Alexander's Empire 323, 21
Amorgos island of S Aegean conquered by Persians 480 BC, 18/3
Ampurias (Emporiae)
Amsterdam C Netherlands 80-; 1648, 123/1
Anatolia Greek colonisation 9C-6C BC, 14/2; Kingdom of Antigonus 323 BC, 22/4; Turcoman principalities 14C, 93-97; Ottoman Empire 1390-1913, 98-170
Ancona C Italy ally of Rome by 270 BC, 26/2; acquired by Papal States 774, 62/3; 1219, 90/3; Hungarian protectorate 1488, 110/1
Ancyra (*mod.* Ankara, *f/c* Angora) C Anatolia Seleucid Empire 301 BC, 26/1; in Roman Empire 395, 41
Andorra condominium 1180, 94/1
Andros island of C Aegean conquered by Persians 480 BC, 18/3; Macedonian dependency 202 BC, 30/2; Venetian possession 1210, 146/3
Angevin Empire England and France growth 1154-80, 83/3
Angles settlement in Britain 350-450, 46/2
Angora (*anc.* Ancyra, *mod.* Ankara) C Turkey 81-

Cartagena (*anc.* Carthago Nova) SE Spain 72-

Carteia S Spain Roman Empire 55 BC, 34/3

Cartenna N Africa controlled by Carthage 149 BC, 30/1

Carthage state of W Mediterranean 550-270 BC, 12-24; colonised by Phoenicia 9C BC, 14/1; Sicily 375 BC, 22/2, 275 BC, 26/3; Punic Wars 264-146 BC, 30/1; Roman Empire 55 BC, 34/3; Byzantine Empire 535, 54/2

Carthago Nova (*mod.* Cartagena) SE Spain Roman Empire 197 BC, 30/1; 55 BC, 34/3; Empire of Postumus 259-274, 43/1; 46/1; Visigothic rule 476, 50/1,3; Byzantine Empire 554, 54/2

Carystos (*a/s* Carystus, *mod.* Karistos) E Greece Athenian Empire 431 BC, 22/1

Cassander, Kingdom of Alexander's Empire 323 BC, 22/4; 301 BC, 26/1

Cassandreia (*f/c* Potidaea) NE Greece Kingdom of Cassander 323 BC, 22/4

Castille, Kingdom of (*f/s* Castile) N Spain 718-1030, 74/1; separated from Leon 1157, 82/1; united with Leon 1230, 94/1; Spanish inheritance of Charles V 1516, 114/1

Castillon SW France Hundred Years' War, 102/2

Castra Batava (Passau)

Castra Regina (*Celt.* Radasbona, *mod.* Regensburg, *Eng.* Ratisbon, *Fr.* Ratisbonne) Roman Empire 15 BC, 38/1; Roman Empire 395, 40

Castro, Duchy of independence from Papal States 1537, 114/2

Catalan Counties NE Spain nominally French 1030, 74/1,3

Catalonia, Principality of NW Spain united with Aragon 1137, 94/2

Catana (*mod.* Catania) E Sicily Greek colony 9C-6C BC, 14/1; Syracusan rule 375 BC, 22/2; Greek city 275 BC, 26/3; Roman Empire 241 BC, 30/3; 55 BC, 34/3

Catania (*anc.* Catana) E Sicily 69-; Byzantine possession 1036-43, 79/1

Cataonia region of E Anatolia dependency of Ptolemaic Empire 301 BC, 26/1

Cattaro (*mod.* Kotor) W Montenegro occupied by Italy 1941, 182/3, 193/1

Cea (Ceos)

Čechy (Bohemia)

Celovec (Virunum)

Celtiberians early people of Spain 12-

Celts early people of W Europe 8-

Ceos (*a/s* Cea, *mod.* Kea) island of SW Aegean Macedonian dependency 202 BC, 30/2

Cenabum (*a/s* Genabum, *later* Aurelianum or Civitas Aurelianorum, *mod.* Orléans) N France conquered by Rome 57 BC, 34/2

Cephallenia (*mod.* Kefallinia, *Eng.* Cephalonia) island of W Greece Persian Wars 490-480 BC, 18/3; Second Macedonian War 202 BC, 30/2

Cephalonia (*mod.* Kefallinia, *anc.* Cephallenia) island of W Greece Venetian possession 1210, 146/3

Cerigo (*mod.* Kythira, *a/s* Kythera, Kithira, *anc.* Cythera) island of S Greece Venetian possession 1210, 146/3

Cernăuţi (*Ukr.* Chernivtsi, *Russ.* Chernovtsy, *Ger.* Czernowitz) W Ukraine occupied by USSR 1940, regained by Romania 1941, 182/2

Cerveteri (Caere)

Cetatea Albă (*anc.* Tyras, *f/c* Akkerman, *Ukr.* Bilhorod-Dnistrovs'kyy, *Russ.* Belgorod-Dnestrovskiy) SW Ukraine occupied by USSR 1940, regained by Romania 1941, 182/2

Cetinje (*It.* Cettigne) Montenegro 1860, 158/3

Ceuta (Sebtum)

Chablais region of SE France in Swiss Confederation 16C, 126/1

Chaeronea C Greece Corinthian League 337 BC, 22/3

Chalcedon NW Anatolia Ionian revolt against Persians 5C BC, 19/2; Athenian Empire 431 BC, 22/1

Chalcidice (*mod.* Khalkidiki) region of NE Greece subdued by Macedonia 336 BC, 22/3

Chalcis (*mod.* Chalkida, *f/s* Khalkis) SE Greece Greek mother-city 9C-6C BC, 14/1,2; Second Macedonian War 202 BC, 30/2; 135/2

Champagne region of NE France added to Royal Domain by 1530, 114/3

Champagne, County of NE France fief of French Crown 1030, 74/3

Chania (Cydonia)

Charlottenburg district of West Berlin 1945-90, 186/3

Charolles, County of E France Burgundian inheritance of Charles V 1477, 114/1; annexed to France 1674-8 and 1684, 131/1

Cheb (*Ger.* Eger) W Bohemia acquired by Ottokar II 1266, 91/2

Chechenia (*a/s* Chechnia, *Russ.* Chechnya) autonomous region of S Russia 1993, 190/1

Chełm (*Ger.* Cholm) S Poland to Habsburgs 1795, 146/2

Cherbourg N France 72-; English in 1380, 102/2

Cherchel (Iol)

Cherkasy, Cherkassy (Czerkasy)

Chernigov (*mod.* Chernihiv) N Ukraine in Kievan Rus 800, 70/1; 1030, 73; Lithuanian by 1377, 103/3

Chernigov, Principality of early principality of W Russia 1095-1328, 77-93

Chernivtsi, Chernovtsy (Cernăuţi)

Chersonesus (*a/c* Heraclea Chersonesus, Chersonesus Heracleotica, *later* Cherson, *mod.* Sevastopol', *Eng.* Sebastopol) S Ukraine Greek colony 9C-6C BC, 14/2; Greek city 301 BC, 26/1; Roman Empire 55 BC, 34/3; Ostrogothic Empire 370, 43/4; in Byzantine Empire 1031, 70/1; 1180, 81

Chester (*anc.* Deva) W England Mercian rule 625, 62/2

Chiavenna region of SE Switzerland added to Swiss Confederation 16C, 126/1

Chichester (Noviomagus)

Chigirin (*mod.* Chyhyryn) C Ukraine in Grand Duchy of Ruthenia 1658, 135/2

Chios (*a/s* Khios, *It.* Scio) island of C Aegean Ionian revolt against Persians 5C BC, 19/2; Second Macedonian War 202 BC, 30/2; Venetian possession 1210, 146/3; independence 1832, 159/3

Chişinău (*Russ.* Kishinev) C Moldova occupied by USSR 1940, regained by Romania 1941, 182/2

Chiusi (Clusium)

Chur (Curia)

Chyhyryn (Chigirin)

Christiania (Oslo)

Cibyra (*a/s* Kibyra) city-state of SW Anatolia 121 BC, 29, 34/4

Cieszyn (*Ger.* Teschen, *Cz.* Těšín) SE Poland to Poland 1938, 178/2; annexed by Germany 1939, 178/3

Cilicia region of SE Anatolia 550 BC, 13; region of Seleucid Empire 301 BC, 26/1; dependency of Ptolemaic Empire 301 BC, 26/1; Roman province of SE Anatolia AD 180, 38/3

Cimmerians early people of S Russia 9-

Circassians people of N Caucasus 1570-1861, 117, 129, 157

Cisalpine Republic N Italy 146/1,4

Cius (*mod.* Gemlik) NW Turkey Ionian revolt against Persians 5C BC, 19/2

Cividale del Friuli (Forum Julii)

Civitas Aurelianorum (*f/c* Cenabum, *mod.* Orléans) Roman Empire 180, 36

Civitas Nemetum (Spires)

Clermont (*anc.* Augustonemetum, *mod.* Clermont-Ferrand) C France conquered by Clovis by 507, 51/4

Clermont-Ferrand (*f/c* Clermont) C France 132-

Cleves (*Ger.* Kleve) NW Germany Duchy 1648, 126/2; in Prussia 1640, 135/1; 1720, 142/1

Cluj, Cluj-Napoca (Kolozsvár)

Clusium (*mod.* Chiusi) N Italy Etruscan city, 600 BC, 14/3

Cnidus (*Gr.* Knidos) SW Anatolia Dorian city 800 BC, 10/4

Cnossus (Knossos)

Coblenz (*a/s* Koblenz, *Fr.* Coblence, *anc.* Confluentes) W Germany annexed by France 1792-3, 146/1; Allied occupation 1918-29, 175/2

Colchester (Camulodunum)

Cologne (*anc.* Colonia Agrippina, *a/c* Colonia Agrippinensis, *Ger.* Köln) NW Germany Frankish kingdoms 526, 48-64; in Germany 1003, 68-; Archbishopric 1660, 122/3; 1648, 126/2; annexed by France 1792-3, 146/1; Allied occupation 1918-26, 175/2; British Occupation 1945, 186/2

Colonia Agrippina (*a/c* Colonia Agrippinensis, *mod.* Köln, *Eng.* Cologne) NW Germany Roman Empire AD 180, 36; Empire of Postumus 259-274, 43/1; abandoned by Rome by 3C, 46/1

Commagene region of E Anatolia 121 BC, 29; Roman dependency 31 BC, 33

Como (*anc.* Comum) N Italy under the Visconti 1390, 98/3

Condovincum (Nantes)

Confederation of the Rhine addition of states 1806-10, 150/1-4

Confluentes (Coblenz)

Connaught province of Ireland 1092, 78/2

Constance (*Ger.* Konstanz) S Germany Bishopric 1660, 122/3

Constanţa (Tomi)

Constantinople (*mod.* Istanbul, *anc.* Byzantium) added to Empire of Nicaea 1261, 90/1

Copenhagen (*Dan.* København) E Denmark 68-

Cora C Italy controlled by Rome 380 BC, 22/2

Corcyra (*mod.* Kerkira, *Eng.* Corfu) island of NW Greece Persian Wars 490-480 BC, 18/3; Pyrrhus's Empire 295-275 BC, 26/3

Cordova (*anc.* Corduba, *Sp.* Córdoba) S Spain 88-

Cordova, Caliphate of S Spain disintegration from 1010, 74/1; 1010, 79/3

Corduba (*Ar.* Qurtubah, *mod.* Córdoba, *Eng.* Cordova) S Spain Roman Empire 55 BC, 34/3; abandoned by Rome by 3C, 46/1; Visigothic rule 476, 50/1,3; 571, 58/1; Byzantine Empire 554, 54/2

Corduene region of NW Persia Roman dependency 31 BC, 33

Corfinium C Italy Roman Empire 270 BC, 30/3; Roman Empire 31 BC, 32

Corfu (*mod.* Kerkyra, *a/s* Kerkira, *anc.* Corcyra) island of W Greece 122/3; Venetian possession 1210, 146/3

Coria SW Spain Christian conquest by end 11C, 82/1

Corinth (*Lat.* Corinthus, *mod.* Korinthos) C Greece Greek mother-city 9C-6C BC, 14/1,2; Persian Wars 490-480 BC, 18/3; Athenian Empire 431 BC, 22/1; Corinthian League 337 BC, 22/3; Second Macedonian War 202 BC, 30/2; Roman Empire 146 BC, 30/3; 55 BC, 34/3

Cork (*Ir.* Corcaigh) S Ireland 60-; secured by England by 1172, 83/3

Corone (*a/s* Korone, *anc.* Asine) SW Greece Venetian possession 1190-1270, 86/4, 90/1

Corsica (*Fr.* Corse) island of W Mediterranean conquered by Rome 238 BC, 30/1; taken by Vandals c 460, 50/1; Byzantine Empire 554, 54/2; conquered by Lombards c. 725, 58/3; part of Republic of Genoa 1721, 138/2

Corsica et Sardinia Roman province of W Mediterranean AD 180, 38/3

Cortona N Italy Etruscan city 600 BC, 14/3; controlled by Rome 380 BC, 22/2

Corunna (*Sp.* La Coruña, *n/s* A Coruña) NW Spain 60-

Cottbus (*Lus.* Chóśebuz) E Germany in German Confederation 1815, 154/1,3

Courland (*Ger.* Kurland, *Latv.* Kurzeme) region of S Latvia Polish fief 1561, 119/2; within Poland 1683, 129; Treaty of Brest-Litovsk 1918, 174/1

Cracow (*Pol.* Kraków, *Ger.* Krakau) S Poland 69-; inherited by Władysław 1138, 83/2; to Habsburgs 1772, 146/2; occupied by Germany 1939, 178/1

Cracow, Republic of S Poland 1815, 155/3; independent 1815-47, to Austria 1847, 158/1

Cracowia (*a/c* Little Poland) region of S Poland inherited by Władysław 1138, 83/2

Crecy N France Hundred Years' War, 102/2

Creta (*mod.* Kriti, *Eng.* Crete) Greek city 375 BC, 22/2; Roman province AD 180, 38/3

Crete (*a/c* Candia, *Gr.* Kriti) island of E Mediterranean peopled by Dorians 800 BC, 10/4; Persian Wars 490-480 BC, 18/3; conquered by Rome 67 BC, 30/3; Byzantine Empire 527, 54/2; Venetian possession 1360, 98/2; to Egypt 1824-40, 159/3; to Greece 1913, 170/2; occupied by Germany 1941, 182/3

Crimea, Khanate of 1466-1721, 105-137; 1700, 135/2

Crimean Tartars WW2 migration 1944-45, 186/1

Crna Gora (Montenegro)

Croatia (*Cr.* Hrvatska, *Hung.* Horvátország) in Avar Empire 590-630, 58/2; independent from c.8000, 66/2; Kingdom of Louis the German 843, 66/3; in Hungary 1382, 98/1; occupied by Ottomans by 1538, 118/1; autonomous within Hungary 18-19C, 138/1, 162/2; Habsburg territory 1699-1789, 142/1; lost by Habsburgs 1809, 154/2; civil administration 1873, 166/3; occupied by Italy and Germany 1941, 182/3; puppet state 1941, 183/1; independence 1991, 191/2; Serbian Krajina 1992, 191/2

Croatia-Slavonia autonomous within Hungary 1914, 174/5

Croats emigration 1946, 186/1

Crocotus Campus C Greece subdued by Macedonia 336 BC, 22/3

Croton S Italy Greek colony 9C-6C BC, 14/1; Syracusan rule 375 BC, 22/2; Roman Empire 264 BC, 30/1

Cuenca C Spain Christian conquest by end 11C, 82/1

Cujavia (*Pol.* Kujawy) region of NW Poland 1223, 85

Cumae S Italy Etruscan control c. 530 BC, 14/3; Greek city 375 BC, 22/2; Roman colony 300 BC, 26/2

Cumania region of C Romania to Hungary early 13C, 86/3

Cumans early people of S Russia and Balkans 1180, 81

Curia (*mod.* Chur) E Switzerland Roman Empire AD 180, 36

Curonians people of Latvia 1223, 85

Cydonia (*mod.* Chania, *a/s* Khania, *a/c* Canea) W Crete Minoan city c.1500 BC, 10/2; Persian Wars 490-480 BC, 18/3

Cyme W Anatolia Ionian revolt against Persians 5C BC, 19/2; Athenian Empire 431 BC, 22/1

Cynoscephalae C Greece Second Macedonian War 202 BC, 30/2

Cyprus (*Gr.* Kypros, *Turk.* Kibris, *Fr.* Chypre) Phoenician colonisation 9C BC, 14/2; in Ptolemaic Empire 270-121 BC, 25, 29; Roman Empire, 31 BC, 33; Roman province AD 180, 38/3; Byzantine Empire 527, 54/2; kingdom 1270-1430, 89-101

Cyrenaica Roman province of N Libya AD 180, 38/3

Cythera (*mod.* Kithira, *a/s* Kythera, *It.* Cerigo) island of S Greece Persian Wars 490-480 BC, 18/3

Cythnos (*mod.* Kythnos, *f/s* Kithnos) island of S Aegean Second Macedonian War 202 BC, 30/2

Cyzicus NW Anatolia Greek colony 9C-6C BC, 14/1; Ionian revolt against Persians 5C BC, 19/2; Athenian Empire 431 BC, 22/1; Greek city 202 BC, 30/2

Czechoslovakia 1920-5, 173, 174/5; dismembered by Germany 1938-39, 178/2; population movements 1945-47, 186/1; secession of Slovakia and formation of Czech Republic 1993, 190/1

Czechs Slav people of C Europe 9C, 66/2; emigration 1945-47, 186/1

Czerkasy (*mod.* Cherkasy, *Russ.* Cherkassy) C Ukraine in Poland 1569, 119/3

Czernowitz (Cernăuţi)

Czerwién SE Poland to Kievan Rus 981, 70/1,3

Częstochowa (*Ger.* Tschenstochau) SW Poland to Prussia 1793, 146/2; occupied by Germany 1939, 178/1

Dacia ancient region of SE Europe Kingdom of Burebista 80-44 BC, 34/1; Roman province AD 180, 38/3; Roman diocese 324-337, 42/3; abandoned by Rome 215-271, 46/1

Dacians people of SE Europe 121 BC, 29

Daghestan region of N Caucasus 1530, 113; 1683, 129

Dagö (*mod.* Hiiumaa) island of W Estonia to Sweden 1561, 118/3

Dalmatia (*anc.* Illyricum, *Cr.* Dalmacija, *Fr.* Dalmatie, *Ger.* Dalmatien, *It.* Dalmazia) region of E Adriatic added to Roman Empire 229-168 BC, 30/3; Roman province AD 180, 38/3; abandoned by Rome by 3C, 46/1; to Hungary 1358, 98/1; in Venetian Republic 1797, 146/3; lost by Habsburgs 1805, 154/2; province

of Austria-Hungary 1849-68, 162/2; Austrian Crownlands 166/3; annexed by Italy 1941, 182/3, 183/1

Damascus (mod. Dimashq, a/c Ash Sham, Fr. Damas) SW Syria Seleucid Empire 301 BC, 26/1

Danelaw extent in 886, 70/2

Danzig (Pol. Gdańsk) NW Poland 89-101; 145-181

Danzig, Republic of 1807-10, 150/2-4; in Prussia 1807, 155/3; independent from Prussia 1807-14, 158/1; free city 1921, 174/4

Daugavpils (Dünaburg)

Dauphiné region of SE France Hundred Years' War, 102/2; added to Royal Domain by 1530, 114/3

Debrecen (f/s Debreczen) E Hungary 69-

Dedeagach (mod. Alexandroupoli) NE Greece occupied by Bulgaria 1913, 170/3; occupied by Bulgaria 1941, 182/3

Deira region of NE England Anglo-Saxon by end 6C, 54/3

Delos (mod. Dilos, a/s Dhilos) S Aegean Athenian Empire 431 BC, 22/1

Delphi (mod. Delfoi, a/s Dhelfoi) C Greece Persian Wars 490-480 BC, 18/3; Athenian Empire 431 BC, 22/1; Corinthian League 337 BC, 22/3

Demetrias (mod. Volos) E Greece Second Macedonian War 202 BC, 30/2; Roman Empire 100 BC, 30/3; 55 BC, 34/3

Denmark Anglo-Saxon settlement 350-450, 46/2; Viking state c.1000, 66/B; expansion 950-1223 87/1; loss of Schleswig-Holstein 1865, 162/3; European Union 1993, 190/3

Deols, County of C France fief of Duchy of Aquitaine 1030, 74/3

Dertosa (mod. Tortosa) NE Spain Roman Empire 55 BC, 34/3

Deutsch-Altenburg (Carnuntum)

Deva (mod. Chester) C England Roman Empire AD 80, 39/2

Dhilos (Delos)

Dhodhekanisos (Dodecanese)

Dhu'l-Qadr (Dulkadir)

Diadora (Iadena)

Dijon (anc. Dibio) E France 48-; in Frankish Kingdom 534, 54/1; Frankish Empire 843, 66/3; Hundred Years' War, 102/2

Dilos (Delos)

Dioscurias (mod. Sokhumi, Russ. Sukhumi) W Georgia Greek colony 9C-6C BC, 14/2; in Persian Empire 480, 17; in Alexander's Empire 323, 21

Diospolis Magna (Thebes)

Divodurum (Metz)

Djerba S Tunisia Viking rule 1135-60, 66/D

Dnepropetrovsk, Dnipropetrovs'k (Ekaterinoslav)

Dobruja (a/s Dobrudja) region of Romania/Bulgaria south gained by Bulgaria 1940, 182/2

Doclea S Montenegro Roman Empire 100 BC, 30/3; 55 BC, 34/3

Dodecanese (Gr. Dodekanisos, f/s Dhodhekanisos) islands of SE Aegean occupied by Italy 1912, 170/2; 1942, 182/3, 183/1

Doornijk (Tournai)

Dorians people of S Greece 800 BC, 10/4

Doris region of C Greece peopled by Dorians 800 BC, 10/4

Dortmund NW Germany Allied occupation 1920-5, 175/2; British occupation 1945, 186/2

Dorylaeum (mod. Eskişehir) W Turkey Roman Empire 55 BC, 34/3

Dovena town of Great Moravia 830, 66/2

Drač (Durazzo)

Drenthe district of N Netherlands independent 1581, 123/1

Dresden E Germany 80-; enters Confederation of the Rhine 1807, 151/2; in German Confederation 1815, 154/1,3; Russian occupation 1945, 186/2

Dublin (Ir. Baile Átha Cliath) E Ireland 50-; secured by England by 1172, 83/3

Dublin, Kingdom of E Ireland Viking state 916-980, 66/A

Dubrovnik (anc. Ragusium, mod. Ragusa) S Croatia occupied by Italy 1941, 182/3, 183/1; 1993, 191/2

Duisburg NW Germany Allied occupation 1923-5, 175/2

Duklja district of W Bulgaria 986, 70/4

Dulkadir (a/s Dhu'l-Qadr) Turkoman principality of E Anatolia 1382-1493, 97-109

Dünaburg (Russ. Dvinsk, Latv. Daugavpils, Pol. Dyneburg) SE Latvia 89-113; 1772, 146/2; 1942, 181

Dunkirk (Fr. Dunkerque) NE France added to France 1662, 131/1

Durazzo (anc. Epidamnus, later Dyrrachium, mod. Durrës) C Albania 1360, 98/1

Durham N England added to Wessex by 939, 71/2; 124-

Durocortorum (Rheims)

Durostorum (mod. Silistra, f/s Silistria) NE Bulgaria Roman Empire AD 80, 37

Durovernum (med. Lat. Cantuaria, mod. Canterbury, Fr. Cantorbéry) SE England Roman Empire AD 43, 39/2

Durrës (Durazzo)

Düsseldorf NW Germany Allied occupation 1923-5, 175/2; British occupation 1945, 186/2

Dvinsk (Dünaburg)

Dyfed principality of S Wales 600, 58/4; 796, 62/2; vassal of Wessex 70/2; Welsh unification 800-1057, 74/2

Dyneburg (Ger. Dünaburg, Latv. Daugavpils, Russ. Divinsk) SE Latvia in Poland 1572-1721, 117-137

Dyrrachium (It. Durazzo, mod. Durrës) C Albania Roman Empire 219 BC, 30/3; 55 BC, 34/3; in Bulgaria 986, 70/4

East Angles people of E England Kentish domination 600, 58/4

East Anglia region of E England Anglo-Saxon state by end 6C, 54/3; added to Mercia by 796, 62/3; added to Wessex by 924, 71/2

Eastern Rumelia region of S Bulgaria to Bulgaria 1885, 166/2

East Frankish Kingdom (mod. West Germany) 870-880, 66/4

East Franks people of W Germany 565, 52

East Friesland (Ger. Ostfriesland) region of NW Germany county 1648, 126/2; added to Prussia 1744, 142/1

East Germany (a/c German Democratic Republic) joined Federal Republic 1990, 190/1

East Prussia (Ger. Ostpreussen) Baltic region of Russia/Poland Polish fief from 1466, 118/3; secular duchy of Prussia from 1525, 119/2; in Prussia 1640, 135/1; 1720, 143/1; plebiscite 1920, 174/4

Eburacum (a/s Eboracum, mod. York) N England Roman Empire AD 78, 39/2; abandoned by Rome c 400, 46/1; Anglo-Saxon settlement 350-450, 46/2

Ecbatana (mod. Hamadan) W Iran Seleucid Empire 301 BC, 26/1

Edinburgh S Scotland 68-; added to Wessex by 939, 71/2

Edirne (Adrianople)

Eflâk (Wallachia)

Eger (mod. Cheb) W Bohemia acquired by Luxemburgs 1315, 102/4

Egripo (Euboea)

Egypt (Lat. Aegyptus, Ar. Misr) ancient Empire, 10/1; Assyrian conquest, 668-627 BC, 10/3; Roman province AD 180, 38/3

Eichstätt C Germany Bishopric 1648, 126/2; 1660, 122/3

Eion NE Greece Athenian Empire 431 BC, 22/1

Eire (f/c Irish Free State, n/c Republic of Ireland) 1940, 176; 1942, 180

Ekaterinoslav (Russ. Dnepropetrovsk, Ukr. Dnipropetrovs'k) S Ukraine 141-

Elaea W Anatolia in Pergamum 202 BC, 30/2

Elam country of S Mesopotamia to Assyrian Empire 668-627, 10/3

Elba island of W Italy annexed by France 1803, 146/4

Elbląg (Ger. Elbing) N Poland to Prussia 1772, 146/2

Elea (a/c Velia) S Italy Greek city-state 6C BC, 14/3; 375 BC, 22/2

Elis region of W Greece 900-800 BC, 10/4; Persian Wars 490-480 BC, 18/3; Second Macedonian War 202 BC, 30/2

Ellipi country of C Mesopotamia to Assyrian Empire 668-627, 10/3

Elmet Celtic state of N England 600, 58/4

Elsass (Alsace)

Elsass-Lothringen (Alsace-Lorraine)

Emerita Augusta (Ar. Maridah, mod. Mérida) SW Spain Roman Empire 180, 36; Visigothic rule 476, 50/3

Emona (mod. Ljubljana) C Slovenia Ostrogothic rule 508, 50/2

Emporiae (a/s Emporium, Gr. Emporion, mod. Ampurias) NE Spain Greek colony 9C-6C BC, 14/1; in Massilia 121 BC, 30/1

Enez (Aenus)

England Anglo-Saxon states 6C, 54/3; the Heptarchy 600, 58/4; supremacy of Mercia 625-796,62/2; Danelaw 917-54, 66/A; 899-1018, 70/2; Norman Conquest 78/2; Angevin Empire 1154-80, 83/3; Hundred Years' War 14-15C, 102/2

Enos (Aenus)

Ephesus (a/s Ephesos) W Anatolia Ionian city 800 BC, 10/4; Persian Wars 490-480 BC, 18/3; Athenian Empire 431 BC, 22/1; Kingdom of Lysimachus 301 BC, 26/1; Ptolemaic Empire 202 BC, 30/3; Roman Empire 100 BC, 30/2

Epidamnus (later Dyrrachium, mod. Durrës, It. Durazzo, SCr. Drač) C Albania Greek colony 9C-6C BC, 14/1; Greek city 275 BC, 26/3

Epirus (Gr. Epiros) region of Greece/Albania Persian Wars 490-480 BC, 18/3; Molossian Kingdom 334 BC, 22/3; Pyrrhus's Empire 295-275 BC, 26/3; Second Macedonian War 202 BC, 30/2; Roman province AD 180, 38/3; Ottoman conquest by 1500, 107/2

Epirus, Despotate of Albania/Greece successor state to Byzantine Empire 1190-1212, 86/4; Byzantine vassal from 1262, 90/1

Erdely (Transylvania)

Ereğli (Heraclea Pontica, Perinthus)

Eretna Turcoman principality of E Anatolia 1382, 97

Eretria E Greece Greek mother-city 9C-6C BC, 14/1,2; Persian Wars 490-480 BC, 18/3

Erfurt C Germany joins Confederation of the Rhine 1807, 150/2

Erivan (mod. Yerevan) C Armenia 93-169

Ermeland (n/s Ermland) district of N Poland acquired by Prussia 1656-7, 135/1; 1772, 143, 3

Érsekújvár (Ger. Neuhäusel, mod. Nové Zámky) Slovakia added to Ottoman Empire 1664, 130/3

Erythrae W Anatolia Ionian revolt against Persians 5C BC, 19/2

Eschental S Switzerland added to Swiss Confederation 1403-22, 110/2

Eschental district of N Italy in Swiss Confederation 1512-15, 126/1

Eski Cuma (Târgovişte)

Eskişehir (Dorylaeum)

Esseg (Eszék)

Essen NW Germany Allied occupation 1923-5, 175/2; British occupation 1945, 186/2

Essex region of E England Anglo-Saxon state 530, 54/3; dependency of Kent 600, 58/4; added to Mercia by 796, 62/2

Estonia to Denmark 1219, 87/1; to Sweden 1561, 119/2; added to Sweden 1582-1600, 130/2; independence 1918, 174/1; annexed by USSR 1940, 178/3; occupied by Germany 1942, 182/4; independence 1991, 190/1

Estonians WW2 migration 1944-45, 186/1

Eszék (mod. Osijek, Ger. Esseg) N Croatia to Croatia-Slavonia 1873, 166/3; Treaty of Trianon 1920, 175/5

Etruria, Kingdom of C Italy new name for Tuscany 1801, 146/4

Etruscan City States N Italy 550 BC, 12; 480 BC, 16; 323 BC, 20

Etruscans early people of N Italy 900 BC, 8; 6C-4C BC, 14/3

Euboea (Gr. Evvoia, It. Negroponte, med. Egripo, Euripos) island of E Greece peopled by Ionians 800 BC, 10/4; Persian Wars 490-480 BC, 18/3; Athenian Empire 431 BC, 22/1; Corinthian League 337 BC, 22/3; Macedonian dependency 202 BC, 30/2; Venetian possession 1190-1270, 86/4, 90/1

Eupen E Belgium to Belgium by plebiscite 1920, 174/3, 175/2

Euripos (Euboea)

Evvoia (Euboea)

Exeter (anc. Isca Domnoniorum) SW England 128-

Faeroe Islands (Dan. Faerøerne, Faer. Fóroyar) Norwegian rule 13-14C, 88; Danish from 15C, 112-

Faesulae (mod. Fiesole) N Italy Etruscan city 600 BC, 14/3

Falerio C Italy Roman Empire 270 BC, 30/3; Roman Empire 55 BC, 34/3

Fehérvár (mod. Székesfehérvár, Ger. Stuhlweissenburg) W Hungary national king crowned 1526, 118/1

Felicitas Julia (earlier Olisipo, Ar. Al Ushbunah, mod. Lisboa, Eng. Lisbon) W Portugal Roman Empire 55 BC, 34/3; Kingdom of Sueves 431, 46/3

Felsina (later Bononia, mod. Bologna) N Italy Etruscan city 600 BC, 14/3

Feodosia (Theodosia)

Fermo (Firmum)

Ferrara (anc. Forum Alieni) N Italy acquired by Papal States 757, 62/3; 278, 90/3; under the Este 1336, 95/3

Ferrara, Duchy of N Italy Treaty of Lodi 1454, 106/4; Venetian possession 1490, 110/1; independence from Papal States by 1559, 114/2

Fiesole (Faesulae)

Filibe (Philippopolis)

Finland part of Sweden 1523-1683, 130/2; independence 1918, 174/1; Karelian territory regained from USSR 1941, 182/4; proposed entry into European Union 1993, 190/3; 1993, 190/3

Finnic peoples NE Europe 565, 53

Finno-Ugrians early people of W Russia 9-

Finns migration 1944, 186/1

Firenze (Florence)

Firmum (a/c Firmum Picenum, mod. Fermo) C Italy Roman colony 300 BC, 26/2

Fiume (Cr. Rijeka) W Croatia acquired by Yugoslavia 1947, 187/4

Flanders (Fr. Flandres, Dut. Vlaanderen) region of Belgium/France Hundred Years' War, 102/2; Burgundian control 1404, 106/1; 1648, 123/1; added to France 1684, 131/1; lost by France 1697, 134/3; southwest occupied by Italy 1940 and 1942, 183/1

Flanders, County of NE France fief of French Crown 1030, 74/3

Flensburg (Dan. Flensborg) NW Germany plebiscite 1920, 174/3

Florence (anc. Florentia, mod. Firenze) C Italy taken by Lombards 590, 58/3; Frankish rule 774-814, 62/1; Frankish empire 843, 66/3; 1336, 95/3; added to French Empire 1809, 150/3

Florence, Republic of C Italy Treaty of Lodi 1454, 106/4; 1499-1559, 114/2

Florentia (mod. Firenze, Eng. Florence) Ostrogothic rule 508, 50/2; Byzantine Empire 554, 54/2

Foix region of S France outside Royal Domain in 1530, 114/3

Fokis (Phocis)

Forum Alieni (Ferrara)

Forum Julii (mod. Cividale del Friuli) NE Italy taken by Lombards 590, 58/3

Fosdinovo N Italy 1714-21, 138/2

France Greek colonisation in south 9C-6C BC, 14/1; Empire of Postumus 259-274, 43/1; abandoned by Rome by 3C, 46/1; occupied by Teutonic peoples by 475, 46/3; feudal fragmentation 987-1030, 74/3; William the Conqueror 1035-92, 78/2; Angevin Empire 1154-80, 83/3; growth of the Royal Domain to 1223, 86/2; Hundred Years' War 14-15C, 102/2; growth of Royal Domain to 1530, 114/3; expansion under Louis XIV 131/1; territorial losses after 1685, 134/3; revolutionary conquests 1789-97, 146/1; 1814-15, 154/4; alliances 1894-1904, 170/1; southwest occupied by Italy 1940 and 1942, 183/1; European Union 1993, 190/3

Franche-Comté (Ger. Freigrafschaft Burgund) region of SE France Habsburg possession 1520, 114/2; Holy Roman Empire 1648, 126/2; added to France 1678/9, 131/1

Franconia region of C Germany 565, 55/4

Franconia, Duchy of C Germany Hohenstaufen land 1179, 84/4

Frankfurt (a/c Frankfurt am Main, Eng. Frankfort, Fr. Francfort) W Germany 58-; American occupation 1945, 186/2

Frankish Empire (later called Carolingian Empire) France/Germany to 511, 51/4; partition 561, 55/4; growth to 814, 62/1; partition 843, 66/3; partition 870 and 880, 66/4; southern frontier in Spain 814, 74/1

Frankish Kingdom(s) NE France 476, 50/3; SW France taken from Visigoths 507, 50/1; France and Germany 511, 51/4; expansion to 561, 54/1

111/3; Jagiellonian inheritance of
Charles V 1526, 114/1; 1510-70, 118/1;
1648, 126/2; Habsburg possessions
1606-83, 130/3; Thököly's Principality
130/3; Habsburg reorganisation 18C,
138/3; Habsburg territory 1699-1789,
142/2; Treaty of Trianon 1920, 174/5
Huns people of E Europe 446, 46/1
Hvar (Pharus)
Hwicce people of W England Kentish
domination 600, 58/4; Mercian rule 796,
62/2
Hydruntum (Otranto)
Iadera (earlier Diadora, mod. Zadar,
It. Zara) W Croatia Byzantine Empire 554,
54/2; Byzantine Empire 870, 66/2
Iaşi (Jassy)
Icaria (n/s Ikaria) island of S Aegean
conquered by Persians 480 BC, 18/3
Iceland EFTA 1993, 190/3
Iceland Norwegian rule 13-14C, 88;
Danish from 15C, 112-; independent
1944, 184
Iconium (mod. Konya, f/s Konia) C Turkey
Roman Empire 55 BC, 34/3; Byzantine
Empire 527, 54/2. See also Rum
Ighranatah (Granada)
Île-de-France region of N France added
to Royal Domain by 1154, 114/3
Ilipa S Spain Roman Empire 181 BC, 30/1
Il-Khan Empire Mongol khanate of
Persia/Anatolia 1270-1328, 89, 91
Illiberis (Granada)
Illyria region of E Adriatic added to
Roman empire 33 BC, 30/3
Illyrian Provinces E Adriatic in French
Empire 1812, 149
Illyrians early people of the Adriatic 9-
Illyricum (mod. Dalmatia) Roman
province assigned to Caesar 55 BC, 34/3;
Roman diocese and praefectura 324-
337, 42/3
Imbros (mod. Imroz) island of NW Turkey
conquered by Persians 480 BC, 18/3;
Macedonian dependency 202 BC, 30/2
Ingria (a/c Ingermanland, Finn. Inkeri)
region of NW Russia added to Sweden
1583-95, 130/2
Ingushetia autonomous regon of
S Russia 1993, 190/1
Innsbruck W Austria 77-
Inoz (Aenus)
Ioannina (f/c Janina) NW Greece
occupied by Italy 1941, 182/3, 183/1
Iol (a/c Caesarea, mod. Cherchel)
N Algeria Roman Empire 31 BC, 32
Iolchus (a/s Iolchos) NE Greece
Mycenaean city c.1300 BC, 10/2
Ionian Islands W Greece British 1861,
157; to Greece 1863, 158/3
Ionians people of E Greece and
W Anatolia 800 BC, 10/4
Ipsus W Anatolia Seleucid Empire
301 BC, 26/1
Ireland Viking conquests 10C, 66/A;
1092, 78/2; Papal grant to England 1155,
83/3; European Union 1993, 190/3
Ireland, Republic of (a/c Irish Republic,
f/c Eire, earlier Irish Free State) 1993, 188
Isca Domnoniorum (mod. Exeter)
SW England Roman Empire AD 80, 39/2;
roman territory c 350 46/2
Ishbiliyah (mod. Seville) S Spain
Muslim conquest 732, 56; Muslim rule
64-84
Iskenderun (Alexandria)
Islamic Empire northern boundaries in
Spain and France c.740, 74/1
Ismail SW Ukraine to Moldavia 1856, 159/3
Isoudun, County of C France fief of
Duchy of Aquitaine 1030, 74/3
Issus in Persian Empire 480, 17; in
Alexander's Empire 323, 21
Istanbul (Constantinople)
Istria (Cr. Istra) region of NW Croatia
in Venetian Republic 1797, 146/3;
acquired by Yugoslavia 1947, 187/4
Istrus E Romania Greek colony
9C-6C BC, 14/2; in Persian Empire 480
BC, 18/1; Greek city taken by Burebista
c.45 BC, 34/1
Isurium (mod. Aldborough) N England
Roman Empire AD 80, 39/2
Italia Roman diocese of Italy 284-305,
42/2; Roman praefectura of Italy and N
Africa 324-337, 42/3
Italia Annonaria district of N Italy
Roman Empire 324-337, 42/3

Italians migration 1945-48, 186/1
Italy Greek colonisation 9C-6C BC, 14/1;
Etruscan expansion 6C-4C BC, 14/3;
Roman conquest 300-270 BC, 26/2;
Pyrrhus's Empire 295-275 BC, 26/3;
abandoned by Rome by 3C, 46/1;
Byzantine Empire 554, 54/2; Kingdom of
the Lombards 590-732, 58/3; Frankish
Empire 774-814, 62/1; Viking conquests
in south 1038-90, 66/D; Norman and
Byzantine conquest 1030-1156, 79/1;
under the Scaligers 1336, 95/3; Visconti
power in north 98/3; Treaty of Lodi 1454,
106/4; 1499-1559, 114/2; 1714-21, 138/2;
revolutionary republics 1797, 146/4; for-
mation of Kingdom 1861, 158/2;
alliances 1902-9, 170/1; expansion 1939-
42, 183/1; European Union 1993, 190/3
Italy, Kingdom of 870, 66/4; Holy
Roman Empire 1179, 82/4
Iyaslavl early principality of W Russia
1270-1328, 89,93
Izmir (Smyrna)
Izmit (Nicomedia)
Jajca (Cr. Jajce) N Bosnia lost to
Hungary 1463-4 110/1
Jämtland (Jemtland)
Janina (Gr. Ioannina, Turk. Yanya) NW
Greece 65-; in Bulgaria 986, 70/4;
Ottoman Empire 1464, 107/2; to Greece
1913, 170/2
Jarosław (Ger. Jaroslau) S Poland
to Habsburgs 1772, 146/2
Jassy (Rom. Iaşi) NE Romania 93-
Jbaïl (Byblos)
Jemtland (n/s Jämtland) region of W
Sweden added to Sweden 1658, 130/2
Jena C Germany in German
Confederation 1815, 154/3
Jerusalem (anc. Hierosolyma,
Rom. Aelia Capitolina, Heb. Yerushalayim,
Ar. Al Quds) C Israel Seleucid Empire
301 BC, 26/1; Byzantine Empire 527, 54/2
Jever district of N Germany ceded to
Russia 1806, 150/1
Jubail, Jubayl (Byblos)
Jülich, County of NW Germany
Bavarian territory 18C, 138/3
Jülich, Duchy of NW Germany
Holy Roman Empire 1648, 126/2
Kadesh Syria battle of, 1286 BC, 10/1
Kaffa (anc. Theodosia, It. Caffa)
Byzantine Empire 1003, 69
Kaisaria (Caesarea)
Käkisalmi (Kexholm)
Kaliningrad (Königsberg)
Kalisz (Ger. Kalisch) W Poland to Prussia
1793, 146/2; occupied by Germany 1939,
178/1
Kamieniec Podolski (Ukr. Kam'yanets'-
Podil's'kyy, Russ. Kamenets-Podil'skiy) W
Ukraine to Russia 1793, 146/2
Kammin E Germany Bishopric 1660, 122/3
Kara-Koyunlu Turcoman principality of
E Anatolia 1430-1466, 101, 105
Karaman Turcoman principality of
W Anatolia 1328-1430, 93-101
Karasi region of NW Anatolia 1328, 93
Karelia (f/s Carelia, Finn. Karjala,
Ger. Karelien) region of Finland/Russia
partly regained by Finland 1941, 182/4
Karelians migration 1944, 186/1
Karistos (Carystos)
Karkamiş (Carchemish)
Karlovac NW Croatia 1993, 191/2
Karlovy Vary (Ger. Karlsbad, f/s Carlsbad)
W Bohemia annexed to Germany 1938,
178/2
Kärnten (Carinthia)
Karpathos (Carpathos)
Kassa (Slvk. Košice, Ger. Kaschau,
mod. Košice) C Slovakia 89-; to
Czechoslovakia 1920, 175/5
Kaunas (Ger. Kauen, Pol. Kowno,
Russ. Kovno) E Lithuania 1430, 103/3;
occupied by USSR 1940, 178/3
Kaupang (a/c Skiringssal) S Norway
Viking town 814, 61; c.1000, 66/B
Kavalla (a/s Kavala) NE Greece occupied
by Bulgaria 1912, 170/2; annexed to
Bulgaria 1941, 182/3
Kayseri (Caesarea)
Kazakhstan independence 1991, 190/1
Kazan C Russia 1683, 129
Kazan, Khanate of E Russia 1466-1530,
105-113
Kea (Ceos)

Kefallinia (Cephalonia)
Kefe (med. Caffa) Crimea Ottoman
Empire 1493, 109
Kent region of SE England Anglo-Saxon
state 530, 54/3; the Heptarchy 600, 58/4;
added to Mercia by 796, 62/2
Kerch (anc. Panticapaeum) S Ukraine
occupied by Germany 1941, 182/4
Kerkira (Corcyra)
Kexholm (Finn. Käkisalmi, mod. Priozersk)
NW Russia added to Sweden 130/2
Khalkidiki (Chalcidice)
Khalkis (Chalcis)
Khania (mod. Chania, a/s Cydonia, a/c
Canea) W Crete 1300 BC, 10/2
Kharkov (Ukr. Kharkiv) NE Ukraine
123-; captured by Germans 1941, 182/4
Khazar Kingdom S Russia 732, 57;
frontiers to 967, 70/1
Khios (Chios)
Kibyra (Cibyra)
Kiev (Russ. Kiyev, Ukr. Kyyiv) C Ukraine
65-; 814, 61; in Kievan Rus 800, 70/1; in
Lithuania 1444, 111/3; in Poland 1569,
118/3; in Hetmanate 1667, 135/2
Kiev, Principality of W Russia
1095-1328, 77-93
Kievan Rus early state of W Russia
908, 65
Kievan Russ development 800-1031,
70/1
Kishinev (Rom. Chişinâu) C Moldova 149-
Kithira (Kythira)
Kithnos (Cythnos)
Kiyev (Kiev)
Klagenfurt (Virunum)
Klaipéda (Memel)
Klausenburg (Kolozsvár)
Kleve (Cleves)
Knidos (Cnidus)
Knin S Croatia held by Serbs 1993, 191/2
Knossos (Lat. Cnossus) C Crete Minoan
site c.1500 BC, 10/2
Koblenz (Coblenz)
Kolberg (Pol. Kołobrzeg) N Poland
to Prussia 1663, 135/1
Köln (Cologne)
Kołobrzeg (Ger. Kolberg) N Poland
in Poland 10C, 70/3; lost by Poland 74/4
Kolozsvár (Ger. Klausenburg, mod. Cluj-
Napoca, Rom. Cluj-Napoca, f/c Cluj) NW
Romania 77-; to Romania 1920, 175/5
Komárno (Hung. Komárom, Ger. Komorn)
S Slovakia annexed by Hungary 1939,
178/2
Konia (Iconium)
Königgrätz (Cz. Hradec Králové)
NE Bohemia 1871, 161
Königsberg (mod. Kaliningrad) W Russia
S Baltic 89-; in Prussia, 155/3
Konstanz (Constance)
Konya (Iconium)
Koper (Capodistria)
Korinthos (Corinth)
Korone (Corone)
Koroška (Carinthia)
Košice (Hung. Kassa, Ger. Kaschau) E
Slovakia annexed by Hungary 1939, 178/2
Kosovo region of SW Serbia First Balkan
War 1912, 170/2; added to Albania 1941,
182/3; Albanian minority 1993, 191/2
Kosovo Polje S Serbia 107/2
Kostroma early principality of W Russia
1270-1328, 89, 93
Kotor (Cattaro)
Kovno, Kowno (Kaunas)
Kragujevac C Serbia 1993, 191/2
Krain (Carniola)
Krajina Serb-held territory of Croatia
1994, 191/2
Krakau, Kraków (Cracow)
Kranj (Carniola)
Kremenets early principality of W Russia
1270-1328, 89, 95
Krevo (Bel. Kreva) NW Belarus in
Lithuania 1430, 103/3; Union of Lublin
1569, 118/3
Kristiania (Oslo)
Kriti (Crete)
Kronstadt (Brassó)
Kruševac C Serbia 1993, 191/2
Kujawy (Cujavia)
Kumanovo N Macedonia 1993, 191/2
Kurland (Courland)

Kursk W Russia 77-; captured by
Germans 1941, 182/4
Kurzeme (Courland)
Küstenland district of W Croatia province
of Austria-Hungary 1849-68, 162/2
Kuybyshev (Samara)
Kythera, Kythira (Cythera)
Kythnos (Cythnos)
Kyyiv (Kiev)
Laconia region of S Greece peopled by
Dorian 800 BC, 10/4; Second
Macedonian War 202 BC, 30/2
La Coruña (Corunna)
Lade (Hladir)
Ladoga (mod. Novaya Ladoga)
NW Russia in Kievan Rus 800, 70/1
La Marche, County of C France fief of
Duchy of Aquitaine 1030, 74/3
Lampsacus (mod. Lâpseki) NW Turkey
Greek colony 9C-6C BC, 14/1; Ionian
revolt against Persians 5C BC, 19/2
Landau W Germany lost by France
1815, 154/4
Landsberg, Margravate of N Germany
Wettin land 1179, 82/4
Languedoc region of S France added to
Royal Domain by 1530, 114/3
Lapland region of N Scandinavia added
to Sweden 130/2
Lapps people of N Scandinavia 1180, 81
Lâpseki (Lampsacus)
Lapurdum (Bayonne)
Larissa N Greece Athenian Empire
431 BC, 22/1; in Bulgaria 986, 70/4
Latin Empire 1190-1212, 86/4; decline
1212-70, 90/1
Latium (It. Lazio) region of C Italy
Roman control 380 BC, 14/3; controlled
by Rome 380 BC, 22/2
Latvia (Ger. Lettland) annexed by
USSR 1940, 178/3; occupied by
Germany 1942, 182/4; independence
1991, 190/1
Latvians WW2 migration 1944-45, 186/1
Lauenburg district of N Germany
North German Confederation 1867, 162/3
Lauriacum N Austria Roman Empire
AD 180, 36; in Frankish Kingdom 732,
58/2
Lausanne W Switzerland joined Swiss
Confederation 1536, 126/1
Lausitz (Lusatia)
Lazica country of W Caucasus 526-732,
49, 59; 732, 57; 814, 61; 908, 65
Lazio (Latium)
Łęczyca (Ger. Lentschütz,
Russ. Lenchitsa) C Poland inherited by
Władisław 1138, 83/2
Lefkada (Leucas)
Leicester (Ratae)
Leinster province of Ireland 1092, 78/2
Leipzig E Germany 69-; enters
Confederation of the Rhine 1807, 150/2;
in German Confederation 1815, 154/1,3;
Russian occupation 1945, 186/2
Lemberg (Pol. Lwów, Russ. L'vov,
Ukr. L'viv) W Ukraine 77-
Lemnos (Gr. Limnos) island of N Aegean
conquered by Persians 480 BC, 18/3;
Macedonian dependency 202 BC, 30/2;
Venetian possession 1210, 146/3
Lemovices (Limoges)
Lenchitsa, Lentschütz (Łęczyca)
Leningrad (St Petersburg)
Leon, Kingdom of NW Spain to Navarre
1034-5, 74/1; separated from Castille
1157, 82/1
Lérida (Cat. Lleida) NE Spain Christian
conquest by end 11C, 82/1
Lérida, Kingdom of NE Spain 1086, 79/3
Lesbos (a/c Mytilene, mod. Lesvos)
island of N Aegean Second Macedonian
War 202 BC, 30/2
Lesina (Pharus)
Lesser Armenia region of SE Anatolia
1223-1328, 85-93
Lettland (Latvia)
Leucas (mod. Lefkada, f/s Levkas,
It. Santa Maura) island of W Greece
Persian Wars 490-480 BC, 18/3;
Pyrrhus's Empire 295-275 BC, 26/3;
Second Macedonian War 202 BC, 30/2
Lichtenberg district of East Berlin
1945-90, 186/3
Liechtenstein 153-
Liège (Dut. Luik, Ger. Lüttich) E Belgium
annexed to France 1792-3, 146/1; 159/4

Messene (*mod.* Messini) SW Greece Second Macedonian War 202 BC, 30/2

Messenia region of SW Greece peopled by Dorians 800 BC, 10/4; Second Macedonian War 202 BC, 30/2

Messina (*anc.* Messana) E Sicily 69-; Byzantine possession 1036-43, 79/1

Messinia region of SW Greece Persian Wars 490-480 BC, 18/3

Metapontum S Italy Greek city 375 BC, 22/2; Pyrrhus's Empire 295-275 BC, 26/3; ally of Rome by 270 BC, 26/2

Methone NE Greece Athenian Empire 431 BC, 22/1; subdued by Macedonia 336 BC, 22/3

Methone, Methonia (Modon)

Metz (*anc.* Divodurum) E France 68-; controlled by France Frankish kingdom 507, 51/4; Frankish Empire 843, 66/3; 1648, 131/1

Middle Angles people of C England Kentish domination 600, 58/4; Mercian rule 796, 62/2

Mikligard (Constantinople)

Milan (*anc.* Mediolanum, *It.* Milano) NW Italy in Kingdom of Lombards 732, 57, 58/3; Frankish rule 774-814, 62/1; Frankish empire 843, 66/3

Milan, Duchy of N Italy under the Visconti 1336-90, 95/3; 98/3; to Habsburgs 1535, 114/1,2; 1714-21, 138/2; 1748, 142/2; lost by Habsburgs 1797, 154/2

Miletus (*a/s* Miletos) SW Anatolia Mycenaean city c.1300 BC, 10/2; Ionian revolt against Persians 5C BC, 19/2; Athenian Empire 431 BC, 22/1; Kingdom of Lysimachus 301 BC, 26/1

Military Frontier territory bordering Ottoman Empire in the Balkans 1700-1851, 142/3; dissolution 1873, 166/3

Milos (Melos)

Minden NW Germany to Prussia 1648, 135/1; 1720, 142/1

Minorca (*Sp.* Menorca) island of the Balearics British control 1699-1789, 132, 140

Minsk C Belarus 73-; in Lithuania 1562, 118/3; to Russia 1793, 146/2

Mistra district of S Greece Venetian possession 1360, 98/2

Mitannian Empire ancient kingdom of Middle East, 10/1

Mitilini (Mytilene)

Modena, Duchy of N Italy under the Este 1336, 95/3; Treaty of Lodi 1454, 106/4; independence from Papal States 1527, 114/2; 1714-21, 138/2; to Kingdom of Italy 1861, 158/2

Modon (*mod.* Methonia, *a/s* Methone) SW Greece Venetian possession 1212, 86/4; Venetian possession 1390, 98/2

Moesiae Roman diocese of Greece/Serbia 284-305, 42/2

Moesia Inferior Roman province of N Bulgaria AD 180, 38/3

Moesia Superior Roman province of Serbia AD 180, 38/3

Mogilev (*mod.* Mahilyow) E Belarus in Lithuania 1562, 118/3

Mohács S Hungary 1526, 118/1

Moldavia (*Rom.* Moldova, *Turk.* Boğdan) region of NE Romania Hungarian vassal state 1372, 98/1; Ottoman vassal from 1456, 107/2; Hungarian fief 1475-85, 110/1; vassal of Poland-Lithuania from end 15C, 111/3; Ottoman vassal 1815-29, 155/2; 159/3

Moldova (*a/c* Moldavia) independence 1991, 190/1

Molotov (Perm)

Monaco S France Treaty of Lodi 1454, 106/4; 153-

Montbéliard E France annexed by France 1793, 154/4

Montenegrins migration 1945-47, 186/1

Montenegro (*Serb.* Crna Gora) state of E Adriatic Ottoman vassal from end 15C, 107/2; in Ottoman Empire 1806-10, 150/1-4; autonomous 1815, 155/2; 1860, 158/3; 1868, 162/2; lost by Ottoman Empire 1878, 166/2,3; Balkan League 1912, 170/1; First and Second Balkan Wars 1912-13, 170/2,3; Italian rule from 1941, 182/3, 183/1; in 'rump' Yugoslavia 1993, 191/2

Montferrat, Margravate of N Italy Treaty of Lodi 1454, 106/4; to Savoy 1529, 114/2

Montpellier S France 1180, 82/1; Aragonese by 1349 and 1365-82, 94/2

Mons Belgium captured by French 1572, 176

Moravia (*Cz.* Morava, *Ger.* Mähren) to Poland 1003, 74/4; land of Bohemian Crown 1250, 91/2; acquired by Luxemburgs 1310, 102/4; to Hungary 1477-9, 110/1; 1660, 122/2; Habsburg territory 1699-1789, 142/2; province of Austria-Hungary 1849-68, 162/2; annexed by Germany 1939, 178/2. *See also* Great Moravia

Moray region of N Scotland 908, 64

Morea (*a/c* Peloponnese) region of S Greece Ottoman conquest by 1464, 107/2

Morgannwg principality of S Wales vassal of Wessex 70/2; Welsh unification 800-1057, 74/2

Morocco French by 1861, 156

Morocco (*Fr.* Maroc, *Sp.* Marruecos, *Ar.* Al Maghrib) French from 1912-56, 168-184; independence 1956, 188

Mörs NW Germany 1648, 123/1; added to Prussia 1702, 135/1

Mosapurc E Austria Frankish rule 774-814, 62/1; in Principality of Pribina 870, 66/2

Moscow (*Russ.* Moskva) W Russia 85-

Moscow, Great Principality of W Russia 1300-1466, 106/3

Mostar S Bosnia 89-; held by Croats 1993, 191/2

Mukačevo (*Ukr.* Mukacheve, *Russ.* Mukachevo, *Hung.* Munkács) W Ukraine annexed to Hungary 1939, 178/2

Mulhouse (*Ger.* Mülhausen) E France in Swiss Confederation 151, 126/1

Munich (*Ger.* München) S Germany 68-; American occupation 1945, 186/2

Munkács (Mukačevo)

Munster province of SW Ireland 1092, 78/2

Münster NW Germany 105-; Bishopric 1660, 122/3, 126/2

Murcia (Mursiyah)

Murcia, Kingdom of SE Spain 1086, 79/3

Murmansk N Russia 173-

Murom early principality of W Russia 1270-1382, 89-97

Murom-Ryazan early principality of W Russia 1180-1223, 81, 85

Mursiyah (*mod.* Murcia) SE Spain Muslim rule 1180, 82/1

Murviedro (Saguntum)

Muscovy early state of W Russia 1270-1430, 89-101, partly held by Lithuania before 1430, 103/3; growth to 1466, 106/3

Muslims minority within Bosnia and Serbia 1993, 191/2

Mycenae S Greece c.1300 BC, 10/2

Mykalayiv (Olbia)

Myriocephalum C Anatolia in Rum 1180, 81

Mytilene (*n/s* Mitilini) NW Aegean Aeolian city 800 BC, 10/4; Ionian revolt against Persians 5C BC, 19/2. *See also* Lesbos

Nafplio (Nauplia)

Nagorno-Karabakh disputed territory of W Azerbaijan 1993, 190/1

Nagyvárad (*a/c* Várad, *mod.* Oradea) NW Romania to Romania 1920, 175/5

Naissus (*later* Nissa, *mod.* Niš, *Eng.* Nish) SE Serbia Roman Empire AD 180, 37; Byzantine Empire 527, 54/2

Namur (*Dut.* Namen) SE Belgium 1648, 123/1; 159/4

Nancy E France lost to France 1697, 134/3

Nantes (*anc.* Condivincum, *Bret.* Naoned) NW France conquered by Clovis by 497, 51/4; West Frankish Kingdom 880, 66/4; Hundred Years' War, 102/2

Naples (*anc.* Neapolis, *It.* Napoli) S Italy 48-; Ostrogothic rule 508, 50/2; Byzantine Empire 554, 54/2; Byzantine Empire 732, 58/3; Viking rule 11-12C, 66/D; conquered by Normans 1130, 79/1

Naples and Sicily C Italy Habsburg kingdom 18C, 138/2

Naples and Sicily, Kingdom of renamed Parthenopean Republic, then Kingdom of Naples 1799, 146/4

Naples, Kingdom of S Italy conquered by Aragon 1435, 94/2; in personal union with Hungary 1348-51, 98/1; Treaty of Lodi 1454, 106/4; Spanish inheritance of Charles V 1516, 114/1; north to France 1550, 114/2; under Habsburgs 1714-35, 142/2; 1806-10, 150/1-4

Narbo (*a/c* Narbo Martius, *mod.* Narbonne) SW France Roman Empire 121 BC, 30/1; 58 BC, 34/2; Visigothic rule 476, 50/1,3

Narnia (*mod.* Narni) C Italy Roman colony 300 BC, 26/2

Narona S Dalmatia Roman Empire 177 BC, 30/3; 55 BC, 34/3

Narva E Estonia to Sweden 1581-3, 119/2

Narvik (*f/c* Victoriahavn) N Norway 169-

Nassau, Duchy of W Germany North German Confederation 1867, 162/3

Nassau, Principality of W Germany Holy Roman Empire 1648, 126/2

Nauplia (*mod.* Nafplio, *f/s* Navplion) S Greece to Duchy of Athens 1190-1270, 86/4, 90/1

Navahrudak (Novogorodok)

Navarre, Kingdom of N Spain 718-1030, 74/1; 1328, 94/1; Spanish inheritance of Charles V 1516, 114/1

Navplion (Nauplia)

Naxos E Sicily Syracusan rule 375 BC, 22/2

Naxos island of S Aegean conquered by Persians 480 BC, 18/3; Athenian Empire 431 BC, 22/1; Second Macedonian War 202 BC, 30/2

Naxos, Duchy of S Aegean Venetian possession 1190-1270, 86/4, 90/1; 1500, 107/2

Neapolis (*mod.* Napoli, *Eng.* Naples) S Italy Greek colony 9C-6C BC, 14/1; Etruscan control c 530 BC, 14/3; Greek city 375 BC, 22/2; ally of Rome by 270 BC, 26/2; Roman Empire 270 BC, 30/3; 55 BC, 34/3; abandoned by Rome by 3C, 46/1

Negropont (*mod.* Evvoia, *Eng.* Euboea) island of E Greece Ottoman conquest by 1464, 107/2

Nemetocenna (*a/c* Nemetacum, *mod.* Arras) NE France conquered by Rome 57 BC, 34/2

Nepos, Land of E Adriatic 476, 50/3

Netherlands Burgundian inheritance of Charles V 1477, 114/1; 1566-1648, 123/1; 1683, 128; annexed to France 1789-91, 146/1; in French Empire 1810, 150/4; European Union 1993, 190/3

Netherlands, Austrian 1721, 135/1; lost by Habsburgs 1797, 154/2

Netherlands, Spanish Holy Roman Empire 1648, 126/2; 683, 128

Neuchâtel canton of NW Switzerland added to Swiss Confederation 1401-6, 110/2; added to Prussia 1707, 135/1

Neuchâtel, Republic of W Switzerland 1806-10, 150/1-4

Neuhäusel (Érsekújvár)

Neukölln district of West Berlin 1945-90, 186/3

Neusandez (Nowy Sącz)

Neusatz (Újvidék)

Neustria NW France partition of the Frankish Kingdom 561, 55/4

Nevers (*anc.* Noviodunum) C France Hundred Years' War, 102/2

Nevers, County of C France fief of French Crown 1030, 74/3

Newcastle (*a/c* Newcastle upon Tyne) NE England 136-

New East Prussia C Poland to Prussia 1795, 146/2

New Sech S Ukraine 1667, 135/2

New Silesia SW Poland to Prussia 1795, 146/2

Nicaea (*mod.* Nice, *It.* Nizza) S France Greek colony 9C-6C BC, 14/1

Nicaea, Empire of W Anatolia Greek successor state to Byzantine Empire 1212, 86/4

Nice (*anc.* Nicaea, *It.* Nizza) S France under the Ostrogoths 526, 48, 50/3; Visigothic rule 477-500, 50/1; in Frankish Kingdom 534, 54/1, 56; to France 1860, 158/2

Nicomedia (*mod.* Izmit) NW Anatolia Roman Empire 55 BC, 34/3; added to Empire of Nicaea 1261, 90/1

Nicopolis W Greece Roman Empire 148 BC, 30/3

Nicopolis (*mod.* Nikopol, *Turk.* Niğbolu) N Bulgaria Roman Empire 55 BC, 34/3; Avar rule 590-680, 58/2; Ottoman Empire 1402, 90/2

Nicosia (*Gr.* Lefkosia, *Turk.* Lefkoşa) Cyprus 73-

Niğbolu (Nicopolis)

Nijmegen (Noviomagus)

Nikolayev (Olbia)

Nikopol (Nicopolis)

Nimrud N Mesopotamia Assyrian Empire 934 BC, 10/3

Nimwegen (Noviomagus)

Nineveh N Mesopotamia Assyrian Empire 934 BC, 10/3

Niš E Serbia 185-

Nish (*anc.* Naissus, *Serb.* Niš) SE Serbia 59-181

Nissa (*anc.* Naissus, *mod.* Niš, *a/s* Nish) E Serbia in Bulgaria 986, 70/4

Nitrava town of Great Moravia 830, 66/2

Nizhniy Novgorod (*f/c* Gor'kiy 1932-90) W Russia 105-; in Muscovy 1466, 106/3

Nizza (*mod.* Nice, *anc.* Nicaea) S France Aragonese dependency to 1258, 94/2

Noricum Roman province of Austria AD 180, 38/3

Normandy (*Fr.* Normandie) region of N France Viking conquest 911, 66/A; added to Royal Domain by 1223, 86/2, 114/3; Hundred Years' War, 102/2

Normandy, County of C France fief of French Crown 1030, 74/3

Normany, Duchy of William the Conqueror 1066, 78/2; Angevin Empire 1154-80, 83/3

North German Confederation 1867, 162/3

Northumbria region of NE England the Heptarchy 600, 58/4; 796, 62/2

Norway Viking state c.1000, 66/B; Danish rule 1028-35, 87/1; central part of country added to Sweden 1658-60, 130/2; EFTA 1993, 190/3

Novae N Bulgaria Ostrogothic rule 474-488, 50/2

Novellara N Italy 1714-21, 138/2

Novempopulana (*a/c* Gascony) region of SW France added to Frankish Kingdom 531-2, 54/1

Nové Zámky (Érsekújvár)

Novgorod early principality of W Russia 1095-1466, 77-105; partly held by Lithuania before 1430, 103/3; annexed by Muscovy 1478, 106/3

Novgorod (*anc.* Holmgard) NW Russia 105-; captured by Germans 1941, 182/4

Novgorod-Seversk early principality of W Russia 1180-1328, 81-93

Novgorod-Severski (*mod.* Novhorod-Sivers'kyy) N Ukraine Lithuanian by 1377, 103/3

Novibazar, Sanjak of district of S Serbia lost by Ottoman Empire 1878, 166/2; divided between Serbia and Montenegro 1913, 170/2

Noviodunum (*later* Augusta Suessionum, *mod.* Soissons) NE France conquered by Rome 57 BC, 34/2

Noviodunum (Nevers)

Noviomagus (*mod.* Nijmegen, *Ger.* Nimwegen) S Netherlands Roman Empire 31 BC, 32

Noviomagus (*a/c* Noviomagus Reginorum, *mod.* Chichester) S England Roman Empire AD 43, 39/2

Noviomagus (Spires)

Novi Pazar S Serbia 1993, 191/2

Novi Sad (Újvidék)

Novogrudok (*mod.* Navahrudak, *Pol.* Nowogródek) NW Belarus Lithuanian by 1263, 103/3

Nowy Sącz (*Ger.* Neusandez) S Poland to Habsburgs 1772, 146/2

Numidia region of N Africa Carthaginian control 149 BC, 30/1; Roman province 55 BC, 34/3

Nuremberg (*Ger.* Nürnberg) S Germany 76-; American occupation 1945, 186/2/1

Nystad (*Finn.* Uusikaupunki) W Finland 1721, 137

Oberpfalz (Upper Palatinate)

Oberschlesien (Upper Silesia)

Ödenburg (Sopron)

Odessa (*n/s* Odesa) SW Ukraine 145-; occupied by Romania 1941, 182/2

Odessus (*mod.* Varna) E Bulgaria Greek colony 9C-6C BC, 14/2; in Persian Empire 480 BC, 18/1; Greek city taken by Burebista c. 45 BC, 34/1; Byzantine Empire 527, 54/2

Odoacer, Kingdom of C Europe 476, 50/3

Oea (Tripoli)

Oescus N Bulgaria Roman Empire AD 180, 37; Ostrogothic rule 474-488, 50/2

Potsdam E Germany Russian occupation 1945, 186/2

Powys Celtic state of C Wales 600, 58/4; 796, 62/2; vassal of Wessex 70/2; Welsh unification 1057, 74/2; partly held by Normans 1086, 78/2

Požarevac (Passarowitz)

Pozzuoli (Puteoli)

Poznań (Ger. Posen) W Poland 69-; in Bohemia c.950, 70/3; inherited by Mieszko 1138, 83/2; to Prussia 1793, 146/2; 1815, 158/1; annexed by Germany 1939, 178/3

Pozsony (Ger. Pressburg, mod. Bratislava) SW Slovakia 69-; Habsburg king crowned 1527, 118/1; to Czechoslovakia 1920, 175/5

Praeneste (mod. Palestrina) C Italy ally of Rome 300 BC, 26/2

Prague (Cz. Praha, Ger. Prag) C Bohemia 69-; in German Confederation 1815, 154/1,3; annexed to Germany 1939, 178/1,3

Pressburg (Pozsony)

Preussen (Prussia)

Pribina, Principality of Hungary 830-870, 66/2,3

Priene SW Anatolia Ionian city 800 BC, 10/4

Priozersk (Kexholm)

Priština S Serbia Albanian minority 1993, 191/2

Privernum (mod. Priverno) Roman control 380 BC, 14/3

Provence (anc. Provincia) region of S France in Frankish Kingdom by 537, 54/1; Catalan-Aragonese fief 1180, 82/1; Aragonese dependency to 1258, 94/2; added to Royal Domain by 1530, 114/3

Provincia (mod. Provence) region of S France held by Visigoths 477-500, 50/1; taken by Ostrogoths 493, 50/2

Prusa (mod. Bursa) NW Anatolia Roman Empire 29 BC, 30/3

Prussia (Ger. Preussen, Pol. Prusy) rise of Brandenburg Prussia 1640-1720, 135/1; growth under Frederick the Great 142/1; 1806-10, 150/1-4; losses and gains 1806-15, 154/3; boundaries at 1861, 157; 1866, 162/3; in German Empire 1871, 166/1

Prussia, Duchy of 1530, 113

Prussians people of S Baltic 1180, 81

Przemyśl SE Poland to Kievan Rus 981, 70/1,3; under intermittent Hungarian control 1208-34, 86/3; to Habsburgs 1772, 146/2

Pskov early state of W Russia early town 908, 65; partly held by Lithuania before 1430, 103/3; annexed by Muscovy 1510, 106/3

Pskov W Russia 65-; captured by Germans 1941, 182/4

Pteria (Boğazköy)

Ptolemaic Empire Egypt and E Mediterranean 270 BC, 25; 301 BC, 26/1; 202 BC, 30/2

Ptolemais E Libya Byzantine Empire 527, 54/2

Ptolemy, Kingdom of Alexander's Empire 323, 22/4

Pula (Pola)

Punic Wars 264-146 BC, 30/1

Puteoli (mod. Pozzuoli) C Italy Roman Empire 55 BC, 34/3

Pylos (Lat. Pylus, mod. Pilos) S W Greece Second Macedonian War 202 BC, 30/2

Pyxus (a/c Buxentum) S Italy Greek city-state 6C BC, 14/3

Qadis (anc. Gades, mod. Cádiz) S Spain Muslim rule 814, 60-84

Quinque Basilicae SE Hungary East Frankish dependency 870, 66/2

Qurtubah (mod. Córdoba) S Spain Muslim conquest 732, 56; Muslim rule 814, 60-84

Radasbona (Castra Regina)

Raetia (a/s Rhaetia) Roman province of Switzerland AD 180, 38/3

Ragusa (anc. Ragusium, mod. Dubrovnik) S Croatia in Bulgaria 986, 70/4

Ragusa, Republic of E Adriatic Hungarian vassal 1358, 98/1; 1360, 98/2; 1683, 128; occupied by Russia 1806, 150/1; added to French Empire 1809, 150/3

Ramazan Turcoman principality of E Anatolia 1382-1466, 97-105

Rashka district of E Bulgaria 986, 70/4

Ratae (mod. Leicester) C England Roman Empire AD 43, 39/2

Ratisbon (anc. Castra Regina, Celt. Radasbona, Eng. Ratisbon, Ger. Regensburg) S Germany in Frankish Kingdom 561, 54/1; Bishopric 1660, 122/3

Ratisbon SW Netherlands 1648, 123/1

Rauracian Republic France/Switzerland annexed to France 1792-3, 146/1

Ravenna N Italy Byzantine Empire 554, 54/2; added to Papal States by 1278, 90/3; Ostrogothic rule 508, 50/2; Byzantine Empire 732, 58/3; added to Venetian Republic 1454, 106/4

Ravensberg, County of NW Germany in Prussia 1640, 135/1

Ravensburg N Germany in Prussia 1720, 142/1

Reged Celtic state of S Scotland 600, 58/4

Regensburg (Ratisbon)

Reggio di Calabria (Rhegium)

Reims (Rheims)

Reinickendorf district of West Berlin 1945-90, 186/3

Repton C England Mercian rule 625, 62/2

Rethel N France Burgundian control 1404, 106/1

Reval (Est. Tallinn, Russ. Revel) N Estonia 85-; to Sweden 1561, 119/2

Rhaetia (a/s Raetia, mod. Switzerland) in Frankish Kingdom by 537, 54/1

Rhegium (mod. Reggio di Calabria) S Italy Greek colony 9C-6C BC, 14/1; Syracusan rule 375 BC, 22/2

Rheims (Fr. Reims, anc. Durocortorum) N France Frankish kingdoms 526, 48-64; Hundred Years' War, 102/2

Rhineland (Ger. Rheinland) region of W Germany Allied occupation 1918 and demilitarized zone 1919, 175/2; re-occupied by Germany 1936, 178/1

Rhoedestus (Rodosto)

Rhodes (mod. Rodos, f/s Rodhos, It. Rodi, anc. Rhodus) island of E Mediterranean Athenian Empire 431 BC, 22/1; Corinthian League 337 BC, 22/3; 31 BC, 30/3; Roman dependency 31 BC, 33; added to Empire of Nicaea 1235-6, 90/1; Knights of St John 1390, 98/2

Ribagorza district of N Spain 1030, 74/1

Ribemont NE France West Frankish Kingdom 880, 66/4

Riga (Latv. Rīga) C Latvia 85-; independent 1561-81, 119/2; annexed by USSR 1940, 178/3; occupied by Germany 1941, 182/4

Rijeka (It. Fiume) W Croatia 1993, 191/2

Rimini (Ariminum)

Ripuarian Frankish Kingdom N France 476, 50/3

Rodez, County of S France fief of Duchy of Aquitaine 1030, 74/3

Rodhos, Rodi, Rodos (Rhodes)

Rodosto (mod. Tekirdağ, anc. Bisanthe, later Rhoedestus) NW Turkey Venetian possession 1212, 86/4; added to Empire of Nicaea 1225-36, 90/1

Romagna region of N Italy 1503, 114/2

Roman Empire Punic Wars 264-146 BC, 30/1; expansion in Balkans 270-31 BC, 30/3; under the Triumvirates 55 BC, 34/3; expansion 31 BC-AD 185, 38/1, 39/2; administrative divisions AD 180, 38/3; Postumus's secession 259-274, 43/1; reorganisation by Diocletian 284-305, 42/2; under Constantine 324-337, 42/3; losses 180-450, 46/1; Barbarian penetration of Western Empire 395-475, 46/3

Romania state of Latin Empire bordering the Sea of Marmara in Avar Empire 590-680, 58/2; direct Imperial rule 1212, 86/4

Romania autonomous 1868, 163/2; 1878, 166/2,3; Triple Alliance 170/1; 1920-5, 173, 175/5; territorial gains and losses 1940-41, 182/2

Romanians minority within Serbia 1993, 191/2

Roman Republic name for Papal States 1798-1800, 146/4

Rome (anc. Roma, It. Roma) C Italy Byzantine Empire 732, 58/3; Papal States 756, 90/3; 1178, 90/3; added to French Empire 1809, 150/3

Roskilde E Denmark Viking town c.1000, 66/B; 68-

Rostov (Russ. Rostov-na-Donu) S Russia 141-; captured by Germans 1942, 182/4

Rostov, Principality of W Russia 1223-1466, 85-105; annexed by Muscovy 1474, 106/3

Rostov-Suzdal early principality of W Russia 1095, 77

Rotomagus (med. Rodomun, mod. Rouen) N France Roman Empire 31 BC, 32

Rotterdam SW Netherlands 80-; 1648, 123/1

Rottweil S Germany in Swiss Confederation 1519-1632, 126/1

Rouad (Aradus)

Rouen (anc. Rotomagus, med. Rodomum) N France Frankish kingdoms 526, 48-64; Viking rule 911, 66/1A; Hundred Years' War, 102/2

Roussillon district of S France Aragonese possession 1382, 94/2

Ruad (Aradus)

Ruhr region of W Germany British occupation 1945, 186/2

Rum (a/c Iconium) region of Anatolia 1095-1270, 77-89

Rumelia region of S Bulgaria Ottoman conquest by 1389, 107/2

Ruppin district of E Germany control by Luxemburgs 1395, 102/4

Ruschuk (mod. Ruse) N Bulgaria 77-

Rusellae (Grosseto)

Russia Kievan Rus 908, 65; Viking states 9-10C, 66/C; alliances 1894-1909, 171/1

Russian Federation after break-up of USSR 1993, 190/1

Russians migration 1946-50, 186/1

Ruthenia (a/c Subcarpathian Ruthenia, Transcarpathia) region of W Ukraine annexed to Hungary 1939, 178/2

Ruthenia, Grand Duchy of W Ukraine 1658, 135/2

Ryazan, Principality of W Russia 1270-1493, 89-109; partly held by Lithuania before 1430, 103/3; annexed by Muscovy 1521, 106/3

Saar (Ger. Saarland, Fr. Sarre) region of W Germany plebiscite 1935, 174/3

Saarbrücken (Fr. Sarrebruck) W Germany lost by France 1815, 154/4; plebiscite 1935, 174/3

Saaremaa (Ösel)

Šabac (Szabács)

Sabaria district of NW Spain Visigothic rule 565, 54/2; added to Visigothic Kingdom 6C, 58/1

Sabaria (a/s Savaria) W Hungary Ostrogothic rule 508, 50/2

Sachsen (Saxony)

Saguntum (mod. Sagunto, f/c Murviedro) E Spain Roman Empire 197 BC, 30/1

Sahipata Turcoman principality of W Anatolia 1328, 93

St Alban's (Verulamium)

Saintonge, County of W France fief of Duchy of Aquitaine 1030, 74/3

St Petersburg (Russ. Sankt-Peterburg, f/c Leningrad 1924-91, earlier Petrograd 1914-24) NW Russia 137-

Salamanca (anc. Salmantica, Ar. Salmantiqah) W Spain 72

Salamis E Cyprus Greek city-state, 550 BC, 13; in Persian Empire 480, 17; in Alexander's Empire 323, 21; Roman Empire 55 BC, 34/3

Salamis S Greece 480 BC, 18/1

Salduba NE Spain Roman Empire 55 BC, 34/3

Salerno (anc. Salernum) S Italy Viking rule 11-12C, 66/D

Salerno, Principality of S Italy conquered by Normans by 1090, 79/1

Salernum (mod. Salerno) S Italy taken by Lombards c.645, 58/3

Salian Frankish Kingdom N France 476, 50/3

Salmantica (mod. Salamanca) N Spain Roman Empire 55 BC, 34/3; Visigothic rule 476, 50/3

Salonae (mod. Solin, Ital. Salona) S Croatia Roman Empire 168 BC, 30/3; 31 BC, 32; abandoned by Rome by 3C, 46/1; Avar rule 630, 58/2

Salonica (a/s Salonika, Gr. Thessaloniki, Turk. Selanik) NW Greece 49-; Byzantine Empire 527, 54/2; Ottoman Empire 1389, 107/2; by Greece 1913, 170/2

Salonica, Kingdom of N Greece state of Latin Empire 1212, 86/4

Rostov etc.

Saluzzo, Margravate of N Italy Treaty of Lodi 1454, 106/4; added to France 1548, 114/2

Salzburg NW Austria 56-; Frankish rule 774-814, 62/1; East Frankish Empire 870, 66/4; Archbishopric 1660, 122/3, 126/2; in Bavaria 955, 138/3; joins Confederation of the Rhine 1809, 150/3; province of Austria-Hungary 1849-68, 162/2; American occupation 1945, 186/2

Samara (f/c Kuybyshev 1935-91) C Russia 121-

Samaria Palestine Assyrian Empire, 721 BC, 10/3

Samarobriva (mod. Amiens) NE France conquered by Rome 57 BC, 34/2

Samos island of E Aegean Athenian Empire 431 BC, 22/1; independence 1832, 159/3

Samothrace (mod. Samothraki) island of N Aegean conquered by Persians 480 BC, 18/3; Macedonian dependency 202 BC, 30/2

Samsun (Amisus)

Sancerre, County of N France fief of French Crown 1030, 74/3

Sandomierz (Russ. Sandomir) SE Poland inherited by Henryk 1138, 83/2

Sandomiria region of SE Poland inherited by Henryk 1138, 83/2

Sankt Gallen E Switzerland added to Swiss Confederation 1451, 110/2; 1486, 126/1

San Stefano (mod. Yeşilköy) NW Turkey Treaty 1878, 166/2

Santa Maura (Gr. Lefkada, form. Levkas, anc. Leucas, Leucadia) island of W Greece Venetian possession 1210, 146/3

Santander N Spain in Asturias 718, 74/1

Santarém (anc. Scalabis, later Praesidium Julium) C Portugal Christian conquest by end 11C, 82/1

Santorini (Thera)

Saragossa (anc. Caesaraugusta, Ar. Saraqustah, Sp. Zaragoza) NE Spain 68-

Saragossa, Kingdom of NE Spain 1086, 79/3

Sarai S Russia 1223-1493, 85-109

Sarajevo (Turk. Bosna-Saray, a/s Bosna Serai, f/c Vrhbosna) C Bosnia 85-; Ottoman Empire 1464, 107/2; 1993, 191/2

Saraqustah (mod. Zaragoza, Eng. Saragossa) N Spain Muslim conquest 732, 56; Emirate of Cordova 814, 60; 908, 64

Saratov C Russia 121-

Sardes (a/s Sardis) W Anatolia Kingdom of Lysimachus 301 BC, 26/1; Roman Empire 29 BC, 30/3

Sardica (Serdica)

Sardinia (It. Sardegna) island of W Mediterranean conquered by Rome 238 BC, 30/1; taken by Vandals c 460, 50/1; Byzantine Empire 554, 54/2; conquered by Aragon 1322-1420, 94/2; Treaty of Lodi 1454, 106/4; under Habsburgs 1714-20, 138/2, 142/2

Sardinia, Kingdom of Spanish inheritance of Charles V, 1516, 114/1; under Habsburgs 1714-38 and 1748, 142/2; to Kingdom of Italy 1861, 158/2

Sarkel S Russia town of Khazar Empire 732, 57; 814, 61; 908, 65; to Kievan Rus by 800, 70/1

Sarmizegethusa (a/c Ulpia Traiana, mod. Sarmizegetusa, Hung. Várhely) W Romania in Kingdom of Burebista 80 BC, 34/1

Sarre (Saar)

Sarrebruck (Saarbrücken)

Saruhan (a/s Sarukhan) region of W Anatolia 1360, 98/2

Saruhan Turcoman principality of W Anatolia 1328-82, 93, 97

Sasanian Empire (Persian Empire)

Savaria (a/s Savaria) NW Hungary Roman Empire AD 180, 37

Savoy (Fr. Savoie, It. Savoia) region of France/Italy 1683, 128; within Kingdom of Sardinia 1714-21, 138/2; annexed to France 1792, 146/1; lost by France 1815, 154/4; to France 1860, 158/2

Savoy, Duchy of occupied by France 1536-59, 114/2

Saxons people of NW Germany 561, 54/1

Saxony (Ger. Sachsen) added to Frankish Empire 772/804, 62/1; additions

1600-1815, 154/1; in German Confederation 1815, 154/3; 1861, 156

Saxony, Duchy of N Germany Guelph land 1179 82/4

Saxony, Electorate of Holy Roman Empire 1648, 126/2; 17C, 154/1

Saxony, Kingdom of C Germany North German Confederation 1867, 162/3; in German Empire 1871, 166/1

Sayn NW Germany in Prussia 1741-83, 142/1

Scania (Sw. Skåne) region of S Sweden added to Sweden 1658, 130/2

Schaffhausen N Switzerland added to Swiss Confederation 1486, 110/2; 1486, 126/1

Schaumberg-Lippe, Principality of North German Confederation 1867, 162/3; in German Empire 1871, 166/1

Schlesien (Silesia)

Schleswig (Dan. Slesvig) region of N Germany lost by Denmark to Prussia 1865, 162/3; North German Confederation 1867, 162/3; plebiscite in North Schleswig 1920, 174/3

Schleswig-Holstein-Gottorp, Duchy of N Germany 1683, 128

Schöneberg district of West Berlin 1945-90, 186/3

Schönefeld airport for Russian sector of Berlin 1945 186/3

Schröttersburg (Płock)

Schwiebus (Pol. Świebodzin) W Poland acquired by Prussia 1685-95, 135/1

Schwyz canton of E Switzerland added to Swiss Confederation 1291, 110/1

Scio (Chios)

Scotland south given up by Rome c. 185, 46/1; 1092, 78/2; territory lost to England 1157, 83/3

Scupi (Serb. Skoplje, mod. Skopje) C Macedonia in Bulgaria 986, 70/4

Scyros (a/s Scyrus, n/s Skyros, f/s Skiros) island of C Aegean conquered by Persians 480 BC, 18/3

Scythians ancient people of S Russia 13-

Sebastopol (anc. Chersonesus, Russ. Sevastopol') S Crimea 141-

Sebtum (mod. Ceuta) NW Africa Visigothic rule 618, 58/1

Segestica (Siscia)

Segna (Zengg)

Seisyllwg principality of SW Wales Celtic state of S Wales 796, 62/2; vassal of Wessex 70/2; Welsh unification 800-1057, 74/2

Selanik (Salonica)

Seleuceia (a/s Seleucia, a/c Seleucia Pieria) SE Turkey Seleucid Empire 301 BC, 26/1

Seleuceia (a/s Seleucia) S Mesopotamia Seleucid Empire 301 BC, 26/1

Seleucid Empire Persia/Mesopotamia 301 BC, 26/1; western boundary at 202 BC, 30/2

Seleucus, Kingdom of Alexander's Empire 323 BC, 22/4

Seljuk Empire 1095, 77

Senj (Zengg)

Sens (Agedincum)

Septem Provinciae Roman diocese of S France 324-337, 42/3

Septimania region of S France added to Frankish Empire 759, 62/1; 1030, 74/1

Serb Empire 1355, 98/2

Serbia 908, 65; state of Chaslav 931-950, 70/4; north annexed by Hungary 1229, 86/3; Hungarian vassals in north 1358-65, 98/1; Ottoman conquest by 1464, 107/2; north under Habsburgs 1718-39, 142/2; north returned to Ottomans 1739, 142/3; 1861, 157; 1817 and 1833, 158/3; autonomous 1868, 163/2; Treaty of San Stefano 1878, 166/2; Balkan League 1912, 170/1; First and Second Balkan Wars 1912-13, 170/2,3; German occupation 1941, 182/2, 183/1; basis of 'rump' Yugoslavia 1992, 191/2; minorities 1993, 191/2

Serbs migration 1945-47, 186/1

Serbs, Croats and Slovenes, Kingdom of (later Yugoslavia) 1920-5, 173, 174/5

Serdica (a/s Sardica, Gr. Triaditsa, Bulg. Sredets, mod. Sofia) W Bulgaria Roman Empire 180, 37

Sestus NW Turkey Greek colony 9C-6C BC, 14/1; Ionian revolt against

Persians 5C BC, 19/2; Athenian Empire 431 BC, 22/1

Sevastopol' (Sebastopol)

Seville (anc. Hispalis, Ar. Ishbiliyah, Sp. Sevilla) S Spain 88-

Seville, Kingdom of SW Iberia 1086, 79/3

Sexi S Spain Phoenician colony 9C-6C BC, 14/1

Sharqat (Ashur)

Sibir, Khanate of (a/c Khanate of Siberia) E Russia 1466-1530, 105-113

Sicily (It. Sicilia) island of S Italy Dionysius I of Syracuse 375 BC, 22/2; Pyrrhus's Empire 295-275 BC, 26/3; Greek cities 275 BC, 26/3; conquered by Rome 241 BC, 30/1,3; Byzantine Empire 535, 54/2; Viking kingdom 1038-90, 66/D; conquered by Normans by 1090, 79/1; conquered by Aragon 1282, 94/2; held by Savoy 1714-20, 138/2; under Habsburgs 1720-35, 142/2

Sicily, Kingdom of acquisitions in Epirus 13C, 90/1; Spanish inheritance of Charles V 1516, 114/1; 1799, 146/4

Sicyon C Greece Persian Wars 490-480 BC, 18/3

Side S Anatolia Roman Empire 55 BC, 34/3

Siebenbürgen (Transylvania)

Siena, Republic of Holy Roman Empire 1336, 95/3; under the Visconti 1390, 98/3; Treaty of Lodi 1454, 106/4; added to Florence 1557, 114/2

Silchester (Calleva)

Silesia (Ger. Schlesien, Pol. Śląsk, Cz. Slezsko) region of SW Poland inherited by Władisław 1138, 83/2; Luxemburg power 1327-68, 102/4; to Hungary 1477-9, 110/1; lost by Habsburgs to Prussia 1742, 142/1,2; 1815, 154/2; province of Austria-Hungary 1849-68, 162/2

Silistra, Silistria (Durostorum)

Singidunum Avar rule 590-732, 58/2

Sinope (mod. Sinop) N Turkey Greek colony 9C-6C BC, 14/2; Greek city 301 BC, 26/1; in Empire of Pontus 121 BC, 34/4, Roman Empire 55 BC, 34/3

Sion (Ger. Sitten) W Switzerland 1486, 126/1; added to Swiss Confederation 1417, 110/2

Siracusa (Syracuse)

Sirmium (mod. Sremska Mitrovica) N Serbia Roman Empire 284-337, 42/2,3; Ostrogothic rule 508, 50/2; Avar rule 590-732, 58/2; in Bulgaria 986, 70/4

Sisak C Croatia 1993, 191/2

Siscia (a/c Segestica, mod. Sisak, Ger. Sissek, Hung. Sziszek) N Croatia Roman Empire 31 BC, 32

Sitten (Sion)

Skåne (Scania)

Skiringssal (Kaupang)

Skiros (Scyros)

Skoplje (Mac. Skopje, Turk. Üsküb, anc. Scupi) C Macedonia annexed by Bulgaria 1941, 182/3; 1993, 191/2

Skyros (Scyros)

Śląsk (Silesia)

Slavonia (Cr. Slavonija, Hung. Szlávónia) region of N Croatia autonomy within Hungary 18C, 138/1; within Military Frontier 142/3; autonomous within Hungary 1868, 162/2; civil administration 1873, 166/3

Slavs people of E Europe 13-

Slesvig (Schleswig)

Slezsko (Silesia)

Slovakia south to Hungary 1938, 178/2; independent 1939, 178/3

Slovaks migration 1946-47, 186/1

Slovenes Slav people of C Europe 9C, 66/2

Slovenia western part annexed by Italy 1941, 182/3, 183/1; independence 1991, 191/2

Sluys (n/s Sluis, Fr. L'Écluse) SW Netherlands Hundred Years' War, 102/2

Smolensk W Russia 69-; in Kievan Rus 800, 70/1; in Lithuania 1444, 111/3; captured by Germans 1941, 184/4

Smolensk, Principality of W Russia 1095-1382, 77-97

Smyrna (mod. Izmir) W Anatolia Ionian city 800 BC, 10/4; Roman Empire 55 BC, 34/3; Byzantine Empire 527, 54/2; 1390, 98/2; Ottoman Empire 1464, 107/2

Só district of S Hungary 14C, 98/1,2

Sobrarbe district of N Spain 1030, 74/1

Sofia (anc. Serdica, a/s Sardica, Gr. Triaditsa, f/c Sredets) C Bulgaria 93-

Soissons (anc. Noviodunum, later Augusta Suessionum) NE France Frankish kingdom 481, 51/4

Sokhumi (Dioscurias)

Solferino N Italy to Sardinia 1859, 158/2

Solin (Salonae)

Solothurn canton of N Switzerland added to Swiss Confederation 1464, 110/2; 1486, 126/1

Sophene region of SE Anatolia Roman dependency 31 BC, 33

Sopron (Ger. Ödenburg) to Hungary after plebiscite 1921, 174/3,5

South Ossetia disputed territory of N Georgia 1993, 190/1

South Prussia W Poland to Prussia 1793, 146/2

Sovetsk (Tilsit)

Soviet Union (USSR)

Sozopol (Apollonia)

Spain Greek colonisation 9C-6C BC, 14/1; conquered by Rome 181 BC, 30/1; Roman Empire 270 BC, 30/1; Empire of Postumus AD 259, 43/1; abandoned by Rome by 3C, 46/1; occupied by Teutonic peoples by 475, 48/3; south to Byzantine Empire 554, 54/1; Visigothic Kingdom 565-732, 58/1; Muslim conquest 732, 56; Church states of Northern Spain 718-1030, 74/1; successor states of the Caliphate of Cordova 1086, 79/3; Reconquista 1085-1180, 82/1; Reconquista after 1180, 94/1; Spanish inheritance of Charles V 1516, 114/1; European Union 1993, 190/3

Spalato (anc. Spalatum, mod. Split) SW Croatia Venetian possession 1003-1328, 69-93; to Hungary 1179, 86/3; in Hungary 1382, 97; Venetian 1430-1789, 101-141; in French Empire 1812, 149; in Illyrian Kingdom 1815, 155; Austrian Empire 1861-1914, 157-169; annexed by Italy 1941, 182/3, 183/1

Spalatum (mod. Split, It. Spalato) W Croatia Byzantine Empire 870, 66/2

Spandau district of West Berlin 1945-90, 186/3

Spanish March region of NE Spain added to Frankish Empire 759, 62/1

Spanish Morocco 1912-1956, 168-184; joined independent Morocco 1956, 188

Sparta (mod. Sparti) S Greece 8C BC, 10/4; city-state 550 BC, 13; Persian Wars 490-480 BC, 18/3; Athenian Empire 431 BC, 22/1; independent Greek city 301 BC, 26/1; Roman Empire 100 BC, 30/3; Roman Empire 55 BC, 34/3

Speyer (Spires)

Spina N Italy Etruscan control c. 550-400 BC, 14/3

Spires (Ger. Speyer, Fr. Spire, anc. Noviomagus, Civitas Nemetum, Augusta Nemetum) W Germany Bishopric 1618, 122/3, 126/2; lost by France 1697, 134/3

Spiš, Spisz (Zips)

Split (anc. Spalatum, It. Spalato) SW Croatia 1993, 191/2

Spoletum (mod. Spoleto) C Italy Roman colony 300 BC, 26/2

Spoleto (anc. Spoletium) C Italy taken by Lombards 590, 58/3; added to Papal State by 1219, 90/3

Spoleto, Duchy of C Italy Frankish rule 774-814, 62/1; partly conquered by Normans 1144, 79/1

Sredets (Serdica)

Sremska Mitrovica (Sirmium)

Stagirus (a/s Stagira) NE Greece Athenian Empire 431 BC, 22/1; subdued by Macedonia 336 BC, 22/3

Štajersko (Styria)

Stalin (Brassó, Varna)

Stalingrad (f/c Tsaritsyn, n/c Volgograd) S Russia limit of German advance 1942, 182/4

Staraya Ladoga (Aldeigjuborg)

Starodub early principality of W Russia 1270-1328, 89, 93

Stato dei Presidi W Italy to Spain 1557-9, 114/2; 1683, 128; 1714-21, 138/2; under Habsburgs 1714-35, 142/2; to Tuscany 1800, 146/4

Stębark (Tannenberg)

Steglitz district of West Berlin 1945-90, 186/3

Steiermark (Styria)

Steinamanger (mod. Szombathely) E Hungary Frankish rule 774-814, 62/1

Stettin (Pol. Szczecin) NW Poland in Germany 1223, 84-120; to Sweden 1648, 125-133; to Prussia 1720, 135/1; 1807, 154/3

Stobi (mod. Gradsko) C Macedonia Roman Empire 148 BC, 30/3; 55 BC, 34/3

Stockholm E Sweden 93-

Strasbourg (anc. Argentorate, Ger. Strassburg) E France 68-; conquered by Franks by 507, 51/4

Strassburg in Frankish Kingdom 511, 54/1; Bishopric 1660, 122/3; Bishopric 1648, 126/2; occupied by France 1681, 131/1

Strathclyde Celtic state of S Scotland 600, 58/4; 796, 62/2

Streanaeshalach (mod. Whitby) NE England in Northumbria 796, 62/2

Stuhlweissenburg (Fehérvár)

Stuttgart W Germany 69-; American occupation 1945, 186/2

Styria (Ger. Steiermark, Slvn. Štajersko) region of SE Austria Hungarian control 1254-60, then acquired by Bohemia 1260, 90/1; Habsburg possession 1282, 102/1; 1477, 114/1; to Hungary from 1485, 110/1; 1660, 122/2; province of Austria-Hungary 1849-68, 162/2

Styria, Duchy of SE Austria Guelph land 1179, 82/4; Holy Roman Empire 1648, 126/2

Subcarpathian Ruthenia (Ruthenia)

Subotica (Szabadka)

Suceava (Ger. Suczawa) N Romania 108-

Sudetenland region of W Czechoslovakia lost to Germany 1938, 178,1,2

Sueves, Kingdom of the Portugal/ W Spain 43/1, 46/3; added to Visigothic Kingdom 586, 58/1

Sukhumi (Dioscurias)

Sundgau district of SW Germany Habsburg possession 1282, 102/1

Sur (Tyre)

Sussex region of SE England Anglo-Saxon state 530, 54/3; dependency of Kent 600, 58/4; added to Mercia by 796, 62/2

Suzdal N Russia 69-

Suzdal-Nizhegorod early principality of W Russia 1270-1382, 89-97

Svizhden early principality of W Russia 1270-1328, 89, 93

Swabia, Duchy of S Germany Hohenstaufen land 1179, 82/4

Sweden Viking state c.1000, 66/B; Danish rule in south c.950, 87/1; expansion 1523-1683, 130/2; EFTA 1993, 190/3

Swedish Pomerania 1721, 135/1

Świebodzin (Schwiebus)

Swiss Confederation growth 1291-1486, 110/2; additions from Italy 1512-24, 114/2; to 1648, 126/1; renamed Helvetian Republic 1798, 146/4

Switzerland EFTA 1993, 190/3

Sword Brothers, Order of the N Baltic 1223, 83

Syagrius, Land of N France 476, 50/3

Sybaris S Italy Greek colony 9C-6C BC, 14/1

Syracuse (Lat. Syracusae, mod. Siracusa) E Sicily Greek colony 9C-6C BC, 14/1; Dionysius I 390-375 BC, 22/2; Greek city 275 BC, 26/3; Roman Empire 241 BC, 30/1,3; Roman Empire 55 BC, 34/3; abandoned by Rome by 3C, 46/1

Syria (Ar. Suriyah, Fr. Syrie) Roman province assigned to Crasus 55 BC, 35/3; Roman province of Palestine AD 180, 38/3

Szabács (Srb. Šabac) lost to Hungary 1471-6, 110/1

Szabadka (now Subotica) N Serbia occupied by Hungary 1941, 182/3

Szczecin (Ger. Stettin) NW Poland in Poland 929-82, 70/3; lost by Poland, 74/4

Szeged (f/s Szegedin) S Hungary 69-

Székesfehérvár (Fehérvár)

Szendrö N Serbia lost by Hungary 1459, 110/1

Sziszek (mod. Sisak, Ger. Sissek) NW Croatia to Croatia-Slavonia 1882, 166/3

Szlávónia (Slavonia)

Szombathely (Steinamanger)

Uri canton of S Switzerland added to Swiss Confederation 1291, 110/2

Üsküb (anc. Scupi, Serb. Skoplje, mod. Skopje) N Macedonia in Ottoman Empire 1430-1885, 101-165

Uskudama (Adrianople)

USSR (a/c Soviet Union) German invasion 1942, 182/4; dissolution 1991, 190/1

Ústí nam Labem (Ger. Aussig) NW Bohemia annexed by Germany 1938, 178/2

Utica N Africa Phoenician colony 9C-6C BC, 14/1

Utrecht C Netherlands Union of Utrecht 1579, 123/1

Utrecht, Bishopric of E Netherlands added to Burgundy 1467-77, 106/1

Uusikaupunki (Nystad)

Vác (Ger. Waitzen) N Hungary added to Ottoman Empire 1620, 130/3

Valachia (Wallachia)

Valais canton of S Switzerland added to Swiss Confederation 1417, 110/2

Valais, Republic of E France added to French Empire 1810, 150/4

Valencia (anc. Valentia, Ar. Balansiyah) E Spain 68-; Christian conquest by end 11C, 82/1

Valencia, Kingdom of E Spain 1086, 79/3; acquired by Aragon 1233-1304, 94/2

Valentia (Ar. Balansiyah, mod. Valencia) E Spain Roman Empire 55 BC, 34/3; Empire of Postumus 259-74, 43/1; abandoned by Rome by 3C, 46/1; Visigothic rule 476, 50/1,3

Valois, County of NE France fief of French Crown 1030, 74/3

Valona (Avlona)

Valmy NE France 1797, 144

Valtellina district of N Italy in Swiss Confederation 1512-24, 126/1

Vandals, Kingdom of the N Africa 431, 46/3; 419-555, 50/1

Várad (a/c Nágyvárad, Ger. Grosswardein, mod. Oradea) NW Romania Treaty 1538, 118/1; added to Ottoman Empire 1664, 130/3

Varaždin N Croatia 1993 191/2

Várhely (Sarmizegethusa)

Varna (f/c Stalin 1949-56, anc. Odessus) E Bulgaria 64-; Byzantine Empire 1190, 86/4

Vaud (Ger. Waadt) canton of W Switzerland joins Swiss Confederation 1536, 126/1

Veii N Italy Eruscan city 600 BC, 14/3

Velestinon (Pherae)

Velia (Elea)

Veligrad town of Great Moravia 830, 66/2

Veliki Ustyug early principality of W Russia 1270-1382, 89-97

Velsuna (Volsinii)

Velzna (Volsinii)

Venaissin district of S France 1797, 146/3; annexed by France 1791, 154/4

Vendôme, County of N France fief of French Crown 1030, 74/3

Venecia (mod. Venezia, Eng. Venice) N Italy Byzantine Empire 554, 54/2

Venetia region of NE Italy lost by Austria to Italy 1866, 162/2

Venetian Republic (a/c Republic of Venice) NE Italy E Adriatic and Aegean 1336, 95/3; 1390, 98/3; expansion 1360-1454, 106/4; 1499-1559, 114/2; 1683, 128; in Bavaria 955, 138/3; 1714-21, 138/2; 1797, 146/3; lost by Habsburgs 154/2

Venice (It. Venezia, Ger. Venedig, Fr. Venise) NE Italy Byzantine Empire 732, 58/3; 61-; lost by Habsburgs 154/2

Venosa (Venusia)

Venta Belgarum (mod. Winchester) S England Roman Empire AD 43, 39/2

Venta Icenorum (mod. Caistor St Edmunds) E England Roman Empire AD 43, 39/2

Venusia (mod. Venosa) Roman colony 300 BC, 26/2

Verdun (anc. Verodunum) NE France Frankish Empire 843, 66/3

Vermandois, County of NE France fief of French Crown 1030, 74/3

Verodunum (Verdun)

Verona N Italy Roman Empire 55 BC, 34/3; abandoned by Rome by 3C, 46/1;

Ostrogothic rule 508, 50/2; Byzantine Empire 554, 54/2; taken by Lombards 590, 58/3; Frankish rule 774-814, 62/1; under the Scaligers 1336, 95/3; in Venetian Republic 1721, 138/2

Verroia (Berrhoea)

Verulamium (mod. St Alban's) S England Roman Empire AD 43, 39/2

Vesontio (mod. Besançon) E France conquered by Rome 58 BC, 34/2

Vetulonia C Italy N Italy Eruscan city 600 BC, 14/3, ally of Rome by 270 BC, 26/2

Vexin, County of N France fief of French Crown 1030, 74/3

Victoriahavn (Narvik)

Vienna (anc. Vindobona, Ger. Wien, Hung. Bécs, Turk. Beç) E Austria 69-; to Hungary from 1485, 110/1; Allied occupation 1945, 186/2

Vienna (mod. Vienne) SE France Roman Empire 58 BC, 34/2

Viennensis Roman diocese of S France 284-305, 42/2

Vikings conquests 800-1200, 66/A-D

Villafranca N Italy 1861, 158/2

Vilna (Pol. Wilno, mod. Vilnius) SE Lithuania to Poland 1922, 174/4

Vilna Strip district of NE Poland annexed by Lithuania 1939, 178/3; annexed by USSR 1940, 178/3

Vilnius (Ger. Wilna, Pol. Wilno, Russ. Vilna) SE Lithuania 85-

Vindobona (mod. Wien, Eng. Vienna, Fr. Vienne) E Austria Roman Empire AD 10, 38/1

Vinnitsa (Pol. Winnica, Ukr. Vinnytsya) C Ukraine 85-

Viroconium (mod. Wroxeter) W England Roman Empire AD 80, 39/2; Roman territory 350, 46/2

Virunum (mod. Klagenfurt, Slvn. Celovec) SE Austria Roman Empire AD 180, 36; Ostrogothic rule 508, 50/2

Vis (Lissa)

Visigoths, Kingdom of the SW France and Spain 431, 46/3; 419-555, 50/1,3

Vitebsk (Bel. Vitsyebsk, Pol. Witebsk) N Belarus 69-

Viterbo C Italy acquired by Papal States 787, 62/3; 1219, 90/3

Vitez C Bosnia 1993, 191/2

Vitsyebsk (Vitebsk)

Vlaanderen (Flanders)

Vlachs people of SE Europe 732, 57

Vladimir (mod. Volodymyr-Volyns'kyy, Pol. Włodzimierz) W Ukraine Lithuanian by 1377, 103/3

Vladimir early principality of W Russia 1270-1328, 89-93

Vladimir-Suzdal-Smolensk early principality of W Russia 1223, 85

Vlorë (Avlona)

Voiotia (Boeotia)

Vojvodina (f/s Voivodina, Hung. Bácska, Ger. Wojwodina) district of N Serbia in Hungary 1868, 162/2; Hungarian minority 1993, 191/2

Volaterrae (mod. Volterra) C Italy Etruscan city, 600 BC, 14/3; Roman colony 300 BC, 26/2

Volci C Italy Roman colony 300 BC, 26/2

Volga Bulgaria early state of C Russia 814, 61; 908, 65

Volgograd (Stalingrad)

Volhynia (Pol. Wolyń, Russ. Volyn) region of NW Ukraine to Russia 1793-5, 146/2

Volhynia early principality of W Russia 1180, 81

Volodymyr-Volyns'kyy (Vladimir)

Volos (Demetrias)

Volsinii (Etr. Velzna, mod. Bolsena) C Italy controlled by Rome 380 BC, 22/2; Roman colony 300 BC, 26/2

Volsinii (a/c Velsuna, later Urbs Vetus, mod. Orvieto) N Italy Eruscan city 600 BC, 14/3

Volterra (Volaterrae)

Volubilis C Morocco Roman Empire AD 180, 36

Volyn (Volhynia)

Vorarlberg district of W Austria province of Austria-Hungary 1849-68, 162/2

Voronezh W Russia captured by Germans 1942, 182/4

Vorpommern (West Pomerania)

Vrhbosna (Sarajevo)

Vukovar E Croatia held by Serbs 1993, 191/2

Vulci N Italy Etruscan city 600 BC, 14/3; controlled by Rome 380 BC, 22/2

Vyazma W Russia Lithuanian by 1430, 103/3

Waadt (Vaud)

Waitzen (Vác)

Waldeck, Principality of N Germany Holy Roman Empire 1648, 126/2; North German Confederation 1867, 162/3; in German Empire 1871, 166/1

Wales principalities as vassals of Wessex 70/2; unification 800-1057, 74/2; Norman conquest 1062-86, 78/2

Wallachia (Rom. Valachia, Turk. Eflâk) region of SE Romania Hungarian vassal 1365, 98/1; Ottoman vassal from end 14C, 107/2; Hungarian fief at times from 1477-90, 110/1; Ottoman control from 1526, 118/1; occupied by Russia 1806, 150/1; Ottoman vassal 1815, 155/2, 159/3

Warsaw (Pol. Warszawa, Ger. Warschau) C Poland 77-; to Prussia 1793-5, 146/2; occupied by Germany 1939, 178/1,3

Warsaw, Grand Duchy of created 1807, 151/2; union with Saxony 1807, 154/1

Washshukanni N Mesopotamia ancient Mitannian city 10/1

Wattasids Muslim dynasty of Morocco 1493, 109

Wedding district of West Berlin 1945-90, 186/3

Weissensee district of East Berlin 1945-90, 186/3

Wessex kingdom of S England Anglo-Saxon sate 530, 54/2; dependency of Kent 600, 58/4; Mercian dependency from 777, 62/2; 899-1018, 70/2

West Frankish Kingdom (mod. France) 870-880, 66/4

West Galicia region of SW Poland to Habsburgs 1795, 146/2

West Pomerania (Ger. Vorpommern) District of N Germany added to Sweden 1648-79, 130/2

West Prussia (Ger. Westpreussen) region of NE Germany added to Prussia 1772, 143/1; to Prussia 1772, 146/2

West Wales Celtic state of SW England 600, 58/4; Mercian dependency from 777, 62/2

Whitby (Streanaeshalach)

White Russia (a/c Belorussia, n/c Belarus) occupied by Germany 1942, 182/4

Wien (Vienna)

Wiener Neustadt (Bécsújhely)

Wiesbaden W Germany Allied occupation 1918-30, 175/2

Wifflisburg (Aventicum)

Wilmersdorf district of West Berlin 1945-90, 186/3

Wilno (Lith. Vilnius, Russ. Vilna) E Lithuania to Russia 1795, 146/2

Winchester (anc. Venta Belgarum) S England Mercian rule 777, 62/2

Winnica (mod. Vinnytsia, Russ. Vinnitsa) W Ukraine in Grand Duchy of Ruthenia 1658, 135/2; to Russia 1793, 146/2

Witebsk (n/s Vitsyebsk, Russ. Vitebsk) E Belarus to Russia 1772, 146/2

Włodzimierz (Vladimir)

Wohlau, Principality of E Germany Holy Roman Empire 1648, 126/2

Wojwodina (Vojvodina)

Wolyń (Volhynia)

Worms C Germany Archbishopric 1660, 122/3

Wrocław (Ger. Breslau, Hung. Boroszló) SW Poland inherited by Władysław 1138, 83/2

Wroxeter (Viroconium)

Württemberg, Duchy of S Germany Holy Roman Empire 1648, 126/2

Württemberg, Kingdom of acquired by Habsburgs 1477, 114/1; in German Confederation 1815, 156; 1861, 156; 1866, 162/3; in German Empire 1871, 166/1

Würzburg C Germany conquered by Franks by 497, 51/4; Bishopric 1660, 122/3; Bishopric 1648, 126/2

Yanya (Janina)

Yaroslavl W Russia in Muscovy 1466, 106/2

Yaroslavl early principality of W Russia 1270-1466, 89-105

Yerevan (f/s Erivan) C Armenia 173-

Yeşilköy (San Stefano)

York (anc. Eburacum, a/s Eboracum) N England in Northumbria 796, 62/2

York, Kingdom of N England added to Wessex 924-939, 71/2

Yugoslavia Kingdom of Serbs, Croats and Slovenes 1920-5, 173, 174/5; Axis occupation 1941-42, 182/3; population movement 1945-48, 186/1; breakup 1991, 191/2

Yuriev early principality of W Russia 1270-1328, 89, 93

Zacynthus (Gr. Zakynthos, n/s Zakinthos, It. Zante) Persian Wars 490-480 BC, 18/3; Second Macedonian War 202 BC, 30/2

Zadar (anc. Diadora, a/c Iadera, It. Zara) W Croatia 1993, 191/2

Zágráb (mod. Zagreb, Ger. Agram) N Croatia 69-; to Croatia-Slavonia 1873, 166/3

Zagreb (Hung. Zágráb) N Croatia 173-; 1993, 191/2

Zakinthos, Zakynthos (Zacynthus)

Zakro Crete Minoan site c.1500 BC, 10/2

Zama SW Tunisia Roman Empire 146 BC, 30/1

Zancle, Zankle (Messana)

Zante (Gr. Zakynthos, a/s Zakinthos, anc. Zacynthus) island of W Greece Venetian possession 1210, 146/3

Zaporogia region of S Ukraine Cossacks 1667-1775, 135/2

Zaporogian Cossacks people of S Russia 1683, 129

Zara (mod. Zadar, anc. Diadora, a/c Iadera) W Croatia to Hungary 1179, 86/3; Venetian city 1003-1789, 69-141; in Hungary 1382, 97; French Empire 1812, 149; Illyrian Kingdom 1815, 155; Austrian Empire 1861-1914, 157-69; to Yugoslavia 1925, 173; annexed by Italy 1941, 182/3, 183/1; acquired by Yugoslavia 1947, 187/4

Zaragossa (Saragossa)

Zayyanids Muslim dynasty of NW Africa 1270-1530, 88-112

Zeeland district of W Netherlands to Burgundy 1433, 106/4; Union of Utrecht 1579, 123/1

Zehlendorf district of West Berlin 1945-90, 186/3

Zela (mod. Zile) N Turkey in Empire of Pontus 121 BC, 34/4

Zengg (mod. Senj, It. Segna) NW Croatia to Croatia-Slavonia 1882, 166/3

Zeta district of E Adriatic temporary Aragonese fief mid-15C, 94/2

Zeugma N Syria Roman Empire 55 BC, 34/3

Zhitomir (Pol. Żytomierz, mod. Zhytomyr) W Ukraine Lithuanian by 1377, 103/3

Zile (Zela)

Zips (Slvk. Spiš, Pol. Spisz, Hung. Szepes) district of Slovakia/Poland to Hungary 1769-70, 146/2

Zug canton of C Switzerland added to Swiss Confederation 1291, 110/2

Zurich (Ger. Zürich) NE Switzerland 56-; added to Swiss Confederation 1415, 110/2; 1486, 126/1

Zutphen C Netherlands Union of Utrecht 1579, 123/1

Żytomierz (mod. Zhytomyr, Russ. Zhitomir) W Ukraine in Poland 1569, 118/3; in Grand Duchy of Ruthenia 1658, 135/2; to Russia 1793, 146/2